Firewalking and Religious Healing

PRINCETON MODERN GREEK STUDIES

*This series is sponsored by
the Princeton University Committee on
Hellenic Studies under the auspices of
the Stanley J. Seeger Fund*

Loring M. Danforth

FIREWALKING AND RELIGIOUS HEALING

The Anastenaria of Greece and the American Firewalking Movement

PRINCETON UNIVERSITY PRESS

Published by Princeton University Press, 41 William Street,
Princeton, New Jersey 08540
In the United Kingdom: Princeton University Press, Oxford

Library of Congress Cataloging-in-Publication Data

Danforth, Loring M., 1949–
Firewalking and religious healing : the Anastenaria of Greece and the
American firewalking movement / Loring M. Danforth.
p.   cm. — (Princeton modern Greek studies)
Bibliography: p.   Includes index.
ISBN 0-691-09454-3 — ISBN 0-691-02853-2 (pbk.)
1. Fire walking—Greece. 2. Fire walking—United States.
3. Spiritual healing—Greece. 4. Spiritual healing—United States.
5. Greece—Religious life and customs. 6. United States—Religious life
and customs. I. Title. II. Series.
BL980.G8D36 1989   306.4'61—dc20   89-31581

This book has been composed in Linotron Caslon

Clothbound editions of Princeton University Press books are printed on
acid-free paper, and binding materials are chosen for strength and
durability. Paperbacks, although satisfactory for personal collections, are
not usually suitable for library rebinding

Printed in the United States of America by Princeton University Press,
Princeton, New Jersey

Designed by Laury A. Egan

TO PEGGY

When you walk through fire you
    shall not be burned,
and the flame shall not consume
    you.

(Isaiah 43:2)

Contents

List of Illustrations

Preface

I WOULD LIKE to thank here the many people who have contributed so much to this study.

For years I have been fascinated by Greek culture (both ancient and modern) as well as by intense religious experiences such as spirit possession. These two interests first intersected when I read the *Bacchae* of Euripides with Anne Lebeck. Her teaching was a rare gift I was truly fortunate to have received.

I visited the village of Ayia Eleni in Greek Macedonia to see the Anastenaria in May 1973 and again in May 1975 while I was living in Athens. During this time my life was enriched by many people associated with Athens College, where I lived and taught. I especially valued the good friendship of the families of Xenophon and Sophia Tenezakis and Yannis and Olga Lappas.

From September 1975 through September 1976 I carried out fieldwork on the Anastenaria in Ayia Eleni. Then I spent almost two months visiting the other communities in northern Greece where the Anastenaria is performed. This research was supported by grants from the National Science Foundation (SOC 74-23895) and the Wenner-Gren Foundation for Anthropological Research (#3089).

My early work on the Anastenaria was carried out while I was a graduate student in the Department of Anthropology at Princeton University. Vincent Crapanzano and Hildred Geertz served as my principal dissertation advisers and offered me much useful advice.

In May 1981 I was able to see the Anastenaria again during three weeks of fieldwork in Ayia Eleni carried out in conjunction with a course I was teaching at Bates College entitled Modern Greek Culture and Language in Greece. Another trip to Ayia Eleni in May 1986 was supported by Bates College through a Roger C. Schmutz Faculty Research Grant. Katharine Butterworth became a good friend and a valuable link to Greek culture during these years, when I was unable to be in Greece for long periods of time.

Ken Cadigan generously invited me to observe—and participate in—two firewalking workshops he led in central Maine in December 1985 and January 1986. The people who attended the first of these workshops (whose names I have changed) kindly shared their experiences with me and helped me better to understand a world of which I am almost a part.

The first draft of this book was written at the National Humanities Center in Research Triangle Park, North Carolina, during the year 1986/1987 while I was on a sabbatical leave from Bates College. My year there was made possible by a fellowship grant from the Mellon Foundation. The National Humanities Center is truly an ideal place to write a book, and I am grateful for the opportunity to have worked in the stimulating yet peaceful environment the center provides.

Anna Caraveli, Jane Cowan, Vincent Crapanzano, Dimitri Gondicas, Michael Herzfeld, and George Marcus have been kind enough to read an earlier version of this manuscript and offer many valuable comments and suggestions. Maggie Blades of the National Humanities Center and Claire Schmoll of Bates College carefully typed the various drafts of this book, while Gail Ullman and Cathy Thatcher of Princeton University Press guided it smoothly toward final publication.

Kostilides throughout Greek Macedonia and the people of Ayia Eleni in particular demonstrated great patience, trust, and good will by sharing their lives with me and by talking with me so openly about the Anastenaria. I have tried to express through this book the gratitude I feel for their hospitality and friendship as well as the respect and admiration I have for the Anastenaria as a form of religious healing and as a vital celebration of community in a rapidly changing world.

Because the names of the villages and towns where the Anastenaria is publicly performed are well-known in Greece, the use of pseudonyms would have served no purpose. I have, however, changed the names of two villages where Kostilides involved with the Anastenaria expressed a desire to avoid publicity. Similarly I have not used pseudonyms for the leaders of the Anastenarides since they are public figures whose names have appeared in both popular and scholarly articles on the Anastenaria. By using pseudonyms for all other Anastenarides and by changing some details of their lives I have sought to protect their personal anonymity. This anonymity, however, is not absolute, and I ask readers of this book to act responsibly with the portrait of the Anastenaria presented here. The people of Ayia Eleni deserve no less.

Finally I would like to dedicate this book to my wife, Peggy Rotundo. Both in Greece and in the United States she has always been a source of perceptive advice and steady support. For this I thank her deeply.

Firewalking and Religious Healing

Introduction

IN THE POSTMODERN WORLD of the late twentieth century it has become increasingly difficult to sustain the notion that even the most "exotic" people anthropologists write about—from the Trobriand Islanders to the Yanomamo—live in totally alien, isolated, and self-contained cultures. Our world has grown smaller; its societies and cultures, unique and diverse though they are, are now woven together in a complex web of interconnections and mutual influences that forms a thoroughly interdependent "world system." In response to the many serious challenges posed by such a world, anthropology today, like other disciplines in the humanities and the social sciences, is experiencing what George Marcus and Michael Fischer (1986:7) have called "a crisis of representation."[1]

Much of the recent ethnographic writing that has appeared during this "experimental moment" (Marcus and Fischer 1986) has been shadowed by a loss of confidence in the legitimacy of widely accepted theories and paradigms as well as by a sense of uncertainty concerning the possibility of adequately representing other cultures within the well-established but, until recently at least, relatively unexamined genre conventions of realist ethnography. As a result many ethnographers have become increasingly self-conscious about how they construct the texts they write; they have begun to experiment with new narrative forms and new ethnographic genres.

Of all the dilemmas now facing ethnographers perhaps none is more challenging than that of defining an authorial voice at a time when a multiplicity of other voices are clamoring to be heard. How can ethnographers establish an authoritative presence within a text when one of their explicit goals—in both a literary and a political sense—is the dispersal of ethnographic authority?[2] How, in other words, can they let

[1] On postmodernism in general see Lyotard (1984) and Jameson (1983 and 1984); on the concept of a "world system" see Wallerstein (1974). Clifford (1988), Fischer (1986), and Tyler (1986) discuss postmodernism in the context of anthropology more specifically.

[2] See Clifford (1983).

other voices speak in the texts they write? How can the ethnographic *monographs* of their offices and libraries remain most faithful to the ethnographic *dialogues* of the field?

Fortunately some tentative answers to these difficult questions are beginning to emerge in the growing number of experimental ethnographies that have appeared over the past ten years. Many of these works, written in a variety of voices, genres, and styles, have suceeded in portraying the richness of other cultures in a way that preserves all the ambiguities of the fieldwork encounter in the ethnographic text. They have achieved an uneasy but creative balance between two types of rhetoric—"that which attempts to close off an account neatly with a satisfying self-contained explanation . . . and that which leaves the world observed as open-ended, ambiguous, and in flux" (Marcus and Cushman 1982:45). The best of these works have also achieved a similar balance between an understanding of the self and an understanding of the other by integrating into one text interpretation of other cultures and reflection on the processes of ethnographic fieldwork and writing that lead to this interpretation. In this way these experimental ethnographies have brought us one step closer to realizing the elusive goal of letting the people who read them hear more clearly the voices of the people who speak through them.[3]

In writing this book I have been greatly influenced by many of these recent trends in ethnographic writing. I too have experimented; but I have done so, I hope, without loosing sight of the more traditional concern of interpretive anthropology: the analysis of specific cultural forms as "socially established structures of meaning" embodied in systems of symbols (Geertz 1973a:12).

The primary aim of this book is to offer an interpretation of the Anastenaria, a northern Greek ritual involving firewalking and spirit possession which is performed by a group of refugees from eastern Thrace, known as Kostilides, who settled in Greek Macedonia in the early 1920s.[4] The ritual cycle of the Anastenaria in the village of Ayia

---

[3] For valuable critiques of recent developments in ethnographic writing see Clifford and Marcus (1986), Geertz (1988), and Marcus and Cushman (1982). Particularly interesting examples of experimental ethnographic writing include Crapanzano (1980), Dumont (1978), Dwyer (1982), Favret-Saada (1980), Jackson (1986), Price (1983), and Rabinow (1977).

[4] In Greek "Anastenaria" is a plural noun. I use it in the singular in English, however, to refer to a single ritual complex seen as an integrated whole. Participants in the rite

Eleni, where the largest group of Kostilides settled, reaches its climax on May 21, the day the Orthodox Church celebrates the festival of Saints Constantine and Helen. The Anastenarides believe that Saint Constantine has the power both to cause and to heal a wide variety of illnesses. They also believe that it is Saint Constantine who possesses them when they dance and protects them from getting burned when they perform their spectacular acts of firewalking.

Drawing on recent work in medical and psychiatric anthropology as well as more established anthropological approaches to the study of religion, I present an interpretive approach to the study of religious healing. I argue that illnesses and their symptoms may be understood as somatic symbols that express the social and psychological problems that people encounter in their daily lives. Spirit possession is a particularly powerful religious idiom or language that enables people to articulate and often resolve these problems by redefining their relationship with the possessing spirit so that they acquire the supernatural power they need in order to be healed. Ritual therapy is, therefore, a process of transformation and empowerment through which people are metaphorically moved from a state of illness to a state of health.

Central to the Anastenaria is the figure of Saint Constantine, who in Greek Orthodox tradition is considered to be the founder of the Byzantine Empire and the defender and savior of the Christian religion. During the celebrations of the Anastenaria the dance of the possessed Anastenarides, which is an expression of their relationship to Saint Constantine, is transformed from a dance of suffering to a dance of joy. Because the majority of Anastenarides are women, an analysis of the Anastenaria reveals a great deal about the role of women in rural Greece. By participating in the Anastenaria women, who occupy a particularly marginal position in the community of Kostilides, are able to act as men and in that way gain an increased sense of power and control over their lives without actually challenging the legitimacy of an offi-

---

generally are known as "Anastenarides." The masculine singular is "Anastenaris," the feminine singular "Anastenarissa," the feminine plural "Anastenarisses." Kostilides are "people from Kosti," a village in eastern Thrace. The masculine singular is "Kostilis," the feminine singular "Kostilou." Alternatively a Kostilis may be referred to as a "Kotsianos," a term that is also derived (by metathesis) from "Kosti." In the transliteration of Greek words and phrases in the text I have been guided by a desire to approximate modern pronunciation. The names of authors cited in the bibliography, however, are given in more conventional transcription.

cial ideology of male dominance. The conflict-laden family relationships that may often be responsible for the illnesses that lead people to become involved with the Anastenaria are symbolically expressed and resolved in the songs that are sung when the Anastenarides dance. Metaphors of emergence, release, and opening up are also an important part of the therapeutic process of the Anastenaria, as is fire, a powerful symbol of passage, purification, and transformation.

In addition to analyzing the Anastenaria as a system of religious healing, I also examine the Anastenaria as a symbolic expression of the collective identity of the Kostilides. The Anastenaria is both a celebration of community and a celebration of the past. Through it Kostilides scattered throughout Greek Macedonia are able to maintain their extensive kinship networks and keep alive the past they share by preserving the memory of their lost homeland in eastern Thrace.

The Anastenaria, however, is by no means a static, "traditional" ritual on the verge of being destroyed by the broad currents of social and cultural change that have swept through Greece in the past few decades. It has maintained its vitality in spite of the often strained relationships between the Anastenarides and officials of the Orthodox Church and in spite of the severe conflict that has recently arisen between the sacred power of the Anastenarides and the secular power of local political leaders. Economic development, tourism, and the mass media have also had a significant impact on the Anastenaria. In addition, a new generation of Anastenarides has emerged—a generation that includes alienated university students, bohemian artists and intellectuals, and members of the upwardly mobile and increasingly urbanized middle class. In the face of all these changes the Anastenaria has demonstrated the capacity to acquire new meanings and appeal to a younger generation of Greeks by celebrating new communities and new pasts in a way that is at once traditional and modern.

A more conventional interpretive ethnography of the Anastenaria would end here, but in the postmodern world in which contemporary anthropologists work it is necessary to do more. We must move "from a simple interest in the description of cultural others to a more balanced purpose of cultural critique which plays off other cultural realities against our own in order to gain a more adequate knowledge of them all" (Marcus and Fischer 1986:x). In this book I have tried to meet the challenge of presenting an informative account of another culture while at the same time offering a critique of our own through a juxtaposition of the Anastenaria and the American Firewalking movement, one of the more spectacular developments in that vast collection of belief systems, social causes, and healing practices known as the New Age movement, which has spread rapidly across the United States in the 1970s and 1980s.

People who participate in the American Firewalking movement, like people who become involved in other forms of New Age healing or any of the alternative religious movements that have flourished in the United States since the 1960s, are concerned with self-realization and personal growth. They hope that by walking on fire at an evening seminar or workshop they will be able to heal their relationships with other people, overcome their fears, and find more meaning in their lives.

Somewhat surprisingly perhaps, the American Firewalking movement and the Anastenaria exhibit many remarkable similarities. Both are concerned with moving people from a negative state of illness to a positive state of health through a persuasive rhetoric of empowerment and transformation. In addition, they both make use of a complex set of metaphors involving fire, release from confinement, and removal of obstacles. As might be expected, however, given the very different cultural contexts in which they exist, the American Firewalking movement and the Anastenaria exhibit an equal number of striking differences. They draw on very different conceptions of the individual and of society, and they adopt very different attitudes toward science. Finally, the psychological idiom of the American Firewalking movement contrasts sharply with the religious and somatic idioms of the Anastenaria.

By presenting an analysis of two therapeutic systems that are paradoxically so similar and yet so different, I have tried to achieve "a distinctly anthropological cultural critique" by using "the juxtaposition of cases (derived from ethnography's built-in Janus-faced perspective) to generate critical questions from one society to probe the other" (Marcus and Fischer 1986:117). It is my hope that the two ethnographic analyses presented here are sufficiently attentive to both detail and context to stand on their own *and* that the juxtaposition of the two will offer new and revealing insights into both Greek and American cultures that would otherwise remain unexplored.

Ethnographic accounts that make use of this technique of "defamiliarization by cross-cultural juxtaposition" (Marcus and Fischer

1986:138) frequently present a series of incongruous images that have the jarring effect of making the exotic worlds of cultural others appear more familiar, while simultaneously making the familiar world of the anthropologist appear more exotic. In the end this at times almost surrealistic juxtaposition of different cultures calls into question the anthropological endeavor itself.[5] It invites us in a provocative and occasionally unsettling way to subject ourselves and our own discipline to the same critical gaze we so often cast only on others.

With these goals in mind I have tried to construct a "mixed-genre text" (Marcus 1986:188) in which I move back and forth among several narrative voices. At times I adopt the fairly traditional authoritative voice of the interpretive anthropologist concerned with the tasks of ethnographic description and analysis. At times I adopt the less authoritative voice of the literary journalist seeking to evoke the worlds of the Anastenaria and the American Firewalking movement more directly and powerfully than is possible in standard ethnographies. Finally I occasionally adopt the more private voice of an individual engaged in a personal quest for meaning through the practice of anthropology.

In this book I have taken the risk of introducing myself into the text as a first person presence in order to expose rather than conceal the self in its encounter with the other. Only in this way are self and other rendered equally vulnerable. Only in this way is the cultural reality of the anthropologist, not just that of the ethnographic subject, placed in jeopardy.[6] In this way I also hope to raise the question of how the personal experiences of the anthropologist facilitate or hinder specific insights into other cultures.

My goal at all times has been to integrate a reflexive understanding of the self and the interpretive process with a more traditionally ethnographic understanding of the other in a single text. Therefore, while I have inserted myself as a character into the text, somewhat paradoxically perhaps, I have also tried to mute or marginalize my voice in order to give the Anastenarides of northern Greece and participants in the American Firewalking movement an increased narrative presence in the text as well. I have tried to let them speak for themselves as much as possible in long narrative passages that convey something of the vividness and color of their worlds.

---

[5] The relationship between ethnography and surrealism has been explored in detail by Clifford (1981).

[6] On vulnerability in anthropology see Dwyer (1982).

In these narrative passages I have sought to avoid portraying "abstract a-historical 'others' " who are "inscribed in bounded, independent cultures" (Clifford 1983:119). Instead I have made use of detailed biographical portraits to achieve more concrete characterizations of particular individuals. I have also presented extended accounts of dramatic incidents in a way that emphasizes the fact that these events are interpreted quite differently by the very people who participate in them. Thus instead of presenting an authoritative and totally consistent portrait of the Anastenaria and the American Firewalking movement I have stressed the contradictions, the ambiguities, and the uncertainties that are inherent in these worlds. This results occasionally in humor, irony, and the undermining of one interpretation, one voice, by another.

At certain points these narratives are interrupted by passages that are separated from the rest of the text and set in italic type. These passages are an even more direct expression of the voices of the people who took part in the many complex ethnographic encounters from which this book has emerged. They consist of stories, dreams, newspaper articles, publicity brochures, and advertising posters, and they form a kind of ethnographic collage that complicates even further the narrative structure of the text.

It is my hope that this book will contribute to the opening up of the possibilities inherent in ethnographic writing. I realize all too well that any attempt to achieve the goal of dispersed authority in ethnographic writing by granting others an increased narrative presence runs many risks—risks of inconsistency, fragmentation, and disorientation. These risks must be taken, however, if we hope to present more faithful, more honest accounts of the actual experience of ethnographic fieldwork. I am confident that the risks of constructing such open-ended texts are more than offset by the challenging opportunities they offer readers to become actively involved in the ongoing process of cultural interpretation.

I

The Festival of
Saints Constantine
and Helen

✤

"LIGHT THE FIRE! LIGHT THE FIRE!"

OLD YORGAKIS YAVASIS stood in front of the icons of Saints Constantine and Helen and crossed himself three times. He lit a small incense burner, made the sign of the cross with it in front of the icons, and placed it on a large trunk underneath the icon shelf. As the thick, sweet-smelling smoke clouded up around him, Yavasis placed a hand on each of the two icons and stood motionless. Suddenly all the gold coins and jewelry, all the silver votive offerings and little bells, that hung from the icons began to jingle and rattle quietly.

Yavasis carried the censer around the room. As he passed, people waved some smoke toward their faces with their hands and crossed themselves. Yavasis returned to the icon shelf and put the censer down.

"Good evening," he said. "Welcome. And may you all be helped. May everyone who has served Saint Constantine by coming tonight receive a gift. The Saints don't want big gifts; they only want service and devotion. If you believe, they will give you gifts."

People had come to Yavasis' house in the village of Ayia Eleni on the eve of May 21, 1976, to see the Anastenaria. Some had come out of curiosity, to enjoy the spectacle. Others had come out of hope, to

look for a miracle. Still others, including the Anastenarides themselves, their relatives, and many of their fellow Kostilides, had come
to the *konaki*, the shrine of the Anastenarides, to serve Saint Constantine. After lighting a candle, crossing themselves, and kissing the icons
of Saints Constantine and Helen, they greeted the others present with
a warm embrace or a more formal kiss on the back of the hand. Then
they sat down on one of the low benches that lined the walls of the
room.

The powerful presence of Saints Constantine and Helen gazing
down from the richly decorated icon shelf seemed to dominate the konaki. Each icon depicted the two Saints dressed in purple and blue
robes standing on either side of a silver crucifix. The halos of the
Saints, like the edges and handles of the icons, were plated with silver.
Draped over the icons hung large red kerchiefs known as *simadia*, and
on the icon shelf nearby lay icon covers made of purple, pink, and
white satin. The flames of the two olive-oil lamps suspended above the
icons were reflected off the many small metal plaques hanging from the
icon covers, the simadia, and the other embroidery that decorated the
icon shelf. These votive offerings depicting hands, legs, eyes, breasts,
kidneys, children, soldiers, and wedding crowns were moving testimony to the ability of Saints Constantine and Helen to perform miracles.

By early evening the konaki was hot and crowded. Yavasis, dressed
as usual in his coarsely woven black suit and his worn gray flannel shirt,
went over to a table that stood near the icon shelf and put out some
candles that were burning low. Two simadia tied together at the corners
hung from around his neck. As he sat down under the icon shelf,
Maria Kondou, a fifty-year-old woman from a nearby city, began to
tremble. Her legs were shaking rapidly; she was pounding her knees
with her fists. After a few minutes the trembling stopped and Maria
crossed herself. Next to her sat Kiriakoula, her sister, crying.

People in the konaki talked about Kosti, their old village in eastern
Thrace, about old Anastenarides who had died, and about new Anastenarides who were just "coming out" and starting to dance. They
talked about their families and the other villages where the Anastenaria
was being celebrated.

A few minutes later Maria began to tremble again; her feet were
bouncing violently up and down. Then she stood up and danced over
to the icon shelf. Her heavy footsteps could be heard clearly as she

The icon shelf in the konaki at Yavasis' house (Photograph by Loring M. Danforth)

shuffled across the rough wooden floor. She stared at the icons and danced in place, her head rocking back and forth, her arms moving out and up toward the icons as if she were beckoning them to come to her. Finally she crossed herself, stopped dancing, and greeted the icons.

A little after seven o'clock, at a slight nod from Yavasis, a man sitting opposite the icon shelf began tuning a Thracian *lira*, a small three-stringed wooden instrument played with a bow. As the high, tight, droning sound of the lira became louder and more regular, people grew quiet, their faces sad. The atmosphere in the konaki was one of tense expectation. The lira player began a long, slow, seemingly rhythmless tune. When he started to sing a plaintive song about a young Greek woman who was kidnapped by an old Turk, some people began to cry. One woman suddenly clapped loudly three times, jumped to her feet, and began to dance. Another woman began writhing and twisting in her seat. Yavasis sat down next to her and gave her a simadi. She kissed his hand, stood up, and joined the dance.

At this point the lira player began a faster, more rhythmic tune. He was soon joined by a man playing a large drum. An old widow dressed in black, holding an icon cover with both hands high over her head, danced in front of the musicians and with strong powerful steps set a rhythm for them to follow. Musicians and dancers began to sing loudly and intensely—verses about a child seized by a wolf, about young Constantine riding off to war, about a man searching in vain for his lost son.

Maria danced up to the icon shelf. Yavasis crossed himself, reached up, and took one of the icons off the shelf. He kissed it and handed it to her. After crossing herself Maria kissed Yavasis' hand in return and danced off cradling the icon gently in her arms. A heavy woman with a round face and tightly braided hair was dancing with her hands out, palms to the floor, making sweeping circular gestures. Then Mihalis Kitsos, a small man who had spent several years working in a factory in Germany, approached the icon stand. He crossed himself and took several deep breaths, then he reached out and shook the icon that remained on the shelf. He raised it up a few inches, shook it again, and put it back, as if it were too heavy for him to hold. Finally he lifted it from the shelf and held it high in the air. His neck seemed to tighten and swell. His head fell back and he gazed up at the icon. Then he danced across the room holding it with both hands in front of his face.

An old Anastenarissa dances alone in front of the musicians (Photograph by John Demos/Apeiron)

With a proud smile he danced slowly around the room holding the icon out for all those present to greet.

After about twenty minutes the Anastenarides stopped dancing one by one. They crossed themselves and gave their icons and simadia to Yavasis, who returned them to the icon shelf. Maria continued to dance for a few minutes after the music stopped, but soon she took her seat on the bench next to Yavasis under the icons. During the ten or fifteen minute break that followed most people remained in the konaki talking quietly. Some men went out into the hall or onto the small balcony overlooking Yavasis' yard for a cigarette. Soon the sound of the lira drew people back into the konaki, and the dancing resumed.

By nine o'clock the konaki was even more crowded. Yavasis began calling people up to the icon shelf. As they gathered in front of him, he handed out the censer, a tall white candle, the two icons, the simadia, and the icon covers. With much hand kissing and some dancing a procession slowly formed. To the accompaniment of the lira and the drum the procession of Anastenarides made its way through the streets of Ayia Eleni. In many doorways women stood with lit censers and candles in their hands, marking the passage of Saints Constantine and Helen and the Anastenarides.

The procession stopped at the *ayiasma*, a small building at the edge of the village that consisted of little more than a door opening on a damp, dark stairway that led down to a well. Yavasis entered the ayiasma and went down to the well. With the procession of Anastenarides arrayed up the steps behind him Yavasis drew a bucket of water and made the sign of the cross over it with each of the two icons. After pouring the bucket of water back into the well he ordered everyone back outside and filled the bucket again.

Emerging from the ayiasma Yavasis hurled the bucket of water over the heads of the twenty or thirty people who crowded around him. He did this three more times. Then he brought up another bucket of holy water so people could drink from it, sprinkle their heads, or fill small bottles they had brought for just this purpose. When the blessing of the waters was completed, the procession returned to the konaki by a different route, moving in a circle counterclockwise or "always to the right."

After several more hours of dancing Yavasis announced that the evening's work was finished, but he reminded everyone to gather again early the next morning because there was still much work left to be done. Then he thanked everyone for their service to the Saints and expressed the hope that they receive some benefit from it in return. People filed by the icon shelf and greeted the icons before saying good night to Yavasis and the other Anastenarides. At eleven o'clock a simple meal of bread, olives, and cheese was served to the ten people who planned to spend the night at the konaki.

Maria was the first person to light a candle and greet the icons the next morning. She asked Yavasis if the large white candle she had brought could lead the procession. He said yes.

People slowly gathered: Anastenarides, other Kostilides, and a bus load of women from Thessaloniki. At ten o'clock Yavasis lit the incense burner. The music started and several women began to dance. One by one Yavasis handed out the icons and the simadia to the appropriate people. He wrapped some money and a piece of rope in a simadi and gave it to Panayotis Vlastos, the son of an old Anastenarissa who could no longer dance. Just then Thodoros Yannas, a tired looking man from Mesopotamo with a lined face and a thin mustache, came bursting into the room, clapping, shouting, and dancing wildly. Yavasis held out a simadi as Thodoros danced back and forth in front of him. Yavasis angrily shouted, "Come on! We have work to do." Thodoros stopped dancing, crossed himself, and took the simadi from Yavasis' hand.

As the procession of Anastenarides approached the house of one of the two village shepherds, an Anastenarissa began to dance and hiss. A black lamb stood alone in the fenced-in area beside the house. Three times Panayotis passed first the censer and then the simadi over the lamb's head. Then he tied the rope and a bright red ribbon around the lamb's neck and gave the shepherd the money from the simadi.

The lamb, stopping occasionally by the side of the road to graze, led the procession back to the ayiasma. Despite the presence of several policemen trying to keep order, people crowded closely around the large hole being dug nearby. When the lamb had been wrestled to the ground, Panayotis held its head over the edge of the hole. Several Anastenarides began to dance, driving back the crowd with waves of their arms.

Just then Keti, an artist from Athens dressed in blue jeans and a brightly colored blouse, started to cry and tremble. For the past few years she had been coming to Ayia Eleni for the festival of Saints Constantine and Helen, but she had never danced before. As Yavasis put a simadi over her shoulder, Keti began to sob more loudly and strike her chest with her hand. Then she danced a few halting steps. Yavasis held her and cried. Yannis Zoras, wearing a gray three-piece suit and an old embroidered apron, untied the red ribbon, dropped it into the hole, and cut the lamb's throat. The bright red blood stained the brown earth of the freshly dug hole.

When the Anastenarides arrived back at the konaki, Keti went up to the icon shelf and leaned her head on one of the icons of Saints Constantine and Helen. She took a few deep breaths and kissed the icons. An old Anastenarissa grabbed her by the shoulders and shook her saying, "Don't be afraid! It's a hard road, but it's a road of health and joy." Another Anastenarissa called out to her, "Let yourself go! It's nothing. It's power; it's peace."

After lunch and a short rest the Anastenarides gathered again. A constant stream of people passed through the konaki all afternoon, lighting candles, greeting the icons, and watching with a mixture of curiosity and awe the dance of the Anastenarides. Toward evening the dancing grew more intense. As the music started once again, Thodoros, who had been sitting near the door with his head in his hands, suddenly leapt up and went hurtling across the room. He landed on his side underneath the icon shelf and rolled over on his back. Several Anastenarisses immediately began to clap and dance. Yavasis placed a simadi on his chest and returned to the icon shelf, where he continued decorating the icons with roses and sprigs of basil. Two Anastenarisses dragged Thodoros to his feet. Another Anastenarissa danced up to him and shook his arm in time to the music. Thodoros immediately regained consciousness shouting "Ah! Ah! Ah!" and danced off. Several minutes later he was dancing strongly with one of the icons of Saints Constantine and Helen in his hands.

Another young man, a distant relative of Thodoros', was dancing now, bent low at the waist with his arms and head hanging down loosely. A middle-aged Anastenarissa sat with her arms clasped over her head rocking back and forth. With a clap and a wave she danced over to Keti, stamped several times loudly in front of her, and danced off. Another man stood at the side of the room blinking frequently and swaying to the music. He kissed Mihalis' hand as Mihalis danced by. An old Anastenarissa encouraged him to leave the room, but he refused. He just stood there crying and wiping his eyes.

Suddenly one of the Anastenarides shouted, "Light the fire! Light the fire!" Yavasis lit a candle from one of the oil lamps above the icon

A second lamb, offered to Saint Constantine in fulfillment of a vow, is wrestled to the ground (Photograph by John Demos/Apeiron)

shelf and gave it to the man who had led the procession the evening before. He walked quickly from the konaki to an open area near the ayiasma where several thousand people had gathered. The crowd formed a large circle about forty yards across, in the center of which stood a huge cone-shaped pile of logs over six feet high.

As it grew dark, the pile of logs slowly collapsed into a large mound of flaming pieces of wood and glowing red coals. The Anastenarides, who had been dancing in the konaki all afternoon, were notified when the fire was ready. At the sound of the lira and the drum the men tending the fire began to spread out the coals with long poles until they formed a large oval bed about three yards wide, eight yards long, and an inch or so deep.

A wave of excitement swept through the crowd as the procession of Anastenarides burst into the open area around the fire. For a few minutes twenty Anastenarides holding icons, simadia, and icon covers danced barefoot around the fire. Suddenly an Anastenarissa in a blue dress, holding an icon high over her head, ran across the fire. Cries of disbelief and amazement rose from the crowd. Other Anastenarides entered the fire, running and dancing back and forth across the bed of coals, stirring up showers of sparks and glowing embers. Thodoros scooped up some coals in one hand, squeezed them in his fist, and scattered them in the air. Mihalis took ten or twelve defiant dance steps across the coals, pounding down forcefully with his feet. One Anastenarissa knelt at the edge of the fire and slapped at the coals with her hands shouting, "May it turn to ashes!"

Yavasis stood with Keti, who was dancing hesitantly at the edge of the fire—now toward the fire, now back. Several times he led her away from the fire and guided her around the outside of the bed of coals. Keti was new, and her road wasn't open yet, so Yavasis had to make sure she didn't get confused and go into the fire by mistake. If she did, she might get burned.

When most of the coals had turned gray and the fire was almost out, the Anastenarides gathered around Yavasis at the edge of the fire. They danced hand in hand circling the coals in a counterclockwise direction with Yavasis, Keti, and Maria alternating in the lead. Twenty or thirty minutes after they began the Anastenarides left the site of the fire and returned to the konaki. The crowd surged forward pushing through the rope barriers and closing in around the fire. Some people commented on how hot the coals still were. One man went into the fire with his shoes on and patted the coals gingerly with his hands. A woman yelled angrily, "Take off your shoes and try that, why don't you!"

Back at the konaki a victory celebration was taking place. The Anastenarides, the soldiers of Saint Constantine, had defeated the fire. Maria's husband was there, and several of Keti's friends from Athens were hovering around her. As the Anastenarides wiped the ashes and soot off their feet, they exchanged comments about how hot the fire had been, how well Maria had danced, and how many people the Saint had gathered together.

With the help of other village women Yavasis' wife served a meal of lamb, rice, and wild greens to everyone present. At the end of the meal they sang a long song about Turkish bandits, burned villages, a plundered church, and the slaughter of a young man in the arms of his new wife. As Yavasis lit the censer to conclude the meal, an Anastenarissa began to clap and rock back and forth on her feet. The Anastenarides danced again. Toward midnight the day's celebrations drew to a close.

✣

The first year I was afraid I'd get burned. Even now, every year when I approach the fire, I'm afraid. As Mihalis I'm afraid, but as an Anastenaris I'm not. When I go into the fire, someone else is leading me—the Saint. As Mihalis I may say stupid things, but on those *days, as an Anastenaris, I don't. It's the Saint who's talking.*

When I start to dance in the fire, my spirit changes. Bodily Mihalis goes into the fire, but spiritually the Saint does. Even I *wonder why I'm not in control of myself then. Before I go into the fire, I have my own mind. I'm afraid of the fire, and I think "How can I go in? I'll get burned." Then, when I get to the fire, Mihalis changes. I go in as if I weren't Mihalis. When I see the fire, I calm down; I don't feel any fear. If I were still Mihalis and felt fear, I'd cross myself, give the icon to Yavasis, and kiss his hand.*

When I'm on the fire, the spirit guides me, and the power. On the fire I don't exist as Mihalis anymore, but I know what's happening around me; I hear what people say. When I'm on the fire, I feel the warmth, but I don't feel any pain. It's as if I had tender feet and was walking barefoot on gravel for the first time. After leaving the fire I feel satisfaction because I've done my duty; I've done the will of the Saint. He says "You're mine. Do my will!" If I do my own will and not the Saint's, then I'll be punished. I only have power from the Saint on those days. The Saint wants his miracles, so he has to choose people to perform them. I don't know why he chose me. The Saint gets all the credit for the miracle, not the Anastenarides.

If the Saint calls you, if you have an open road, then you don't feel the fire as if it were your enemy. You feel it as if it were your husband or your wife. You feel love for the fire; you have courage. What you see isn't a mountain; it's nothing. That way you go in freely. But if you go in of your own will, then you have fear and doubt. It seems like an enemy, like a mountain. If your courage is from the Saint, you really want to go into the fire. The power comes from outside. You're a different person.

✣

MIHALIS KITSOS: LIKE LEAVES IN THE WIND

When Mihalis was two years old, his mother died. Vasiliki, a young cousin, kept house for Mihalis' father until he remarried a few years later. Mihalis' father was a quiet man, and in order to avoid arguments with his wife, he let her favor the two children she had by her first marriage. After all, when a father is out in the fields all day, a stepmother can lie and say that *his* child has been misbehaving. He has to believe her. What else can he do?

When Mihalis was discharged from the army, his parents moved to Thessaloniki from Limnohori, the small village where he had been born. His parents didn't help him financially at all. The income from the fields that belonged to his real mother went to help his stepmother's children. They had all received some kind of education or training and now worked at good jobs in Thessaloniki.

While he was engaged, Mihalis argued with his father about visiting his fiancée in Ayia Eleni for the festival of Saints Constantine and Helen. His father refused to let him go. When Mihalis insisted, his father told him not to come home again, so Mihalis just stayed in Ayia Eleni. His stepmother persuaded his father not to go to his wedding. She said he was no relative of hers.

Among the Kostilides only a poor man like Mihalis becomes a *sogambros* and moves in with his wife's parents. Usually a man brings his wife to live with him in his parents' house or in a house they build next door. People say that a sogambros is henpecked—that he's like a bride, only worse, because he's a man. He can't do anything on his own. His wife is in charge. He can't even have sex with her when he wants to. Everything's the opposite of the way it should be.

For the first few years of his marriage Mihalis and his wife lived in an old mud brick house that belonged to his father-in-law. Mihalis had no money of his own and for a year was completely dependent on his father-in-law. Then for several years he and his wife lived modestly off the income they earned from the small plot of land Mihalis' wife had received as part of her dowry. Mihalis earned some additional money by selling snacks to the men building irrigation canals nearby.

When their first son was born, Mihalis did not want to name him Yorgos after his own father as was the custom; he wanted to name him Thanasis after his father-in-law, Thanasis Petrakis. But Mihalis' wife insisted they follow the usual practice and name him Yorgos after Mihalis' father, so Yorgos it was. Mihalis' father danced at the baptism of his other grandchildren, but he didn't even come to the baptism of Mihalis' children.

Mihalis saw the Anastenarides dance for the first time in May of 1967, while he was visiting his fiancée in Ayia Eleni. At that time he made fun of them; he thought they were all crazy. But later when they went into the fire, he broke down and cried. He didn't feel well, so he went home. That night he saw an icon with a big "K" on it. The icon said, "If you need me, you'll find me in Langadas." When he woke up the next day, he warned his wife not to joke about the Anastenarides. She was surprised and said, "But just yesterday you were making fun of them yourself."

On the third day of the festival Mihalis began hitting his head against the wall and tearing his hair. His mother-in-law called Yavasis and the other Anastenarides. When they asked Mihalis what the matter was, he told them all he had suffered and all he had dreamed. Yavasis lit some incense, placed a simadi on Mihalis' shoulder, and told him to incense the family icons. Mihalis felt better. The Anastenarides had taken a weight off his shoulders.

For the next few years, particularly on important religious holidays, Mihalis felt upset and out of sorts. The doctors at the clinics he went to said it was some kind of nervous disorder, but people in Ayia Eleni said it was a sign he would soon be called by Saint Constantine. In 1969 he began urinating uncontrollably. It only happened on important saints' days. Kidney specialists in Thessaloniki couldn't find anything wrong with him. An old Anastenarissa told Mihalis' wife, "If he's suffering from the Saint, he'll be all right, but if it's a disease, then he'll have it forever."

In 1970, three years after his marriage, Mihalis went to work as a *gastarbeiter* in a factory in Germany. His wife joined him there, but she didn't like the climate, and she worried constantly about her children who were living with her parents in Ayia Eleni. After a year or so she returned to Greece. In May 1971 Mihalis found himself alone and depressed. He was sick; he had to find a way to get a leave of absence from his job so he could go back to Ayia Eleni for the festival. That's when Saint Constantine gave him his instructions. He told Mihalis to tell his foreman that he'd just received a letter from his wife in Greece: she had fallen and was in the hospital. Mihalis was given three weeks off without pay.

After spending the first day of the festival in Ayia Eleni Mihalis went to Thessaloniki to see his father. On the second day of the festival he went to Langadas, where he danced and went into the fire for the first time. He returned to Ayia Eleni for the third day of the festival, but in the evening, instead of going to the konaki to serve the Saint, he went to a restaurant for dinner. He ate and drank for two hours with his wife and his cousin Vasiliki. Then all of a sudden he felt cold and began to tremble. Vasiliki was upset too. They went home immediately.

Mihalis lit some incense and they calmed down. They both knew they had made a mistake. Later that night, when Vasiliki couldn't fall asleep, she went into the room where Mihalis and his wife were sleeping and said she was afraid; she wanted to sleep with Mihalis. Mihalis' wife laughed and said all right, so Mihalis slept with Vasiliki. She had been like a mother to him because she had taken care of him when he was a boy. The next morning Mihalis wouldn't eat anything; he just lay in bed all day. They called an Anastenarissa who lived next door. She picked Mihalis up and shook him by the shoulders, shouting, "Where were you? Why weren't you at the konaki? You didn't finish your job!"

By 1975 Mihalis had saved enough money to build a house on a lot at the edge of the village, so he left Germany and returned to Ayia Eleni for good. From then on he participated regularly in the Anastenaria. Most people liked Mihalis, but the men in the village didn't take him seriously. They often teased him about how short he was or about the time he hurt himself carrying a bale of clover. Children took more liberties with him than they did with other men. Mihalis seemed more comfortable telling jokes and showing off in front of a group of women at the konaki than he did speaking at a meeting of the village agricultural cooperative. As one of Mihalis' neighbors said, "If he weren't an Anastenaris, he'd be one rung lower on the ladder."

When Mihalis lifted the icon of Saints Constantine and Helen off the icon shelf by himself in 1976, many people were shocked. Some said it was a serious mistake; he had done it on his own, he had insulted Yavasis, and he would suffer. Others thought it was perfectly all right for Mihalis to pick up the icon by himself; he was a man and he obviously had an open road to do it. Still others thought it was all right because the icon he picked up had been brought to Ayia Eleni from Kosti by the great-grandmother of Mihalis' wife. Mihalis himself would not explain the significance of what he'd done. "Only the leader can take the icon down," he said. "But I did take it down myself."

Mihalis complained that sometimes Yavasis gave the icons to women when he should really give them to men. The women were always arguing over who should hold the icons. If Yavasis didn't give them the icons, they'd get angry, and they might stop dancing, so Yavasis gave them the icons even though he shouldn't. He knew Mihalis would never get angry.

Yavasis in turn criticized Mihalis for promising to help with certain jobs—like cleaning the ayiasma—and then not keeping his word. "When he was coming out, Mihalis said that he wanted to take charge, that he wanted to be first. I told him to go ahead, but when the time for the festival came, he went to Langadas. When he came back to Ayia Eleni, he was crying and pounding his head against the wall. His wife's whole family came to me. They were upset, but I said to them, 'Did I make him cry? No. The Saint struck him down.'

"Mihalis is first with his lips but not with his heart. He's like the leaves. As long as the wind blows, they move; but when the wind stops, then the leaves stop too."

✤

A long time ago, they say, back in Kosti, a man named Stefanos became an Anastenaris. He'd been working with his father cutting wood in the mountains. They'd stay out for two or three weeks, come back to town for just a day or two, and then go back out again.

One year they came home on Holy Thursday, just before Easter. Stefanos went into his house and didn't come out until January. The whole time he just sat in front of the fireplace sifting the coals in his hands. The Saints put him there. He played with the fire as if it were a toy.

Whenever his mother lit a fire to bake bread or to cook a meal, he'd scoop up the coals with his hands until he put the fire out. His mother would cry and beg him to leave the fire alone. She needed to bake bread so her family could eat. But everytime she lit the fire, he'd put it out again.

He was afraid to go out of the house, even to go to the bathroom. He had to have his mother near him all the time. Sometimes he just sat there in a daze; other times he was wild. We were afraid to go near him. All those months he just sat there in the hearth playing with the fire.

Then in January, on the morning of the festival of Saint Thanasis, he told his mother to get out his good clothes. He put them on and went to see one of the old Anastenarisses, the mother-in-law of old Hristakena. He told her all the things he had seen and heard.

Every year after that he danced in the konaki but never in the fire. He just stood at the edge of the fire and put out the coals with his hands.

✛

"THE ICON MUST GO WHERE IT BELONGS"

Early in the morning of May 22, 1976, Yavasis, Maria, her sister Kiriakoula, and a well-respected Anastenarissa from Mavrolefki, Eleni Grigoriou, were sitting in the konaki. Kiriakoula was telling Yavasis that when Maria was at home in the city she worried about everything and was always sick. When she came to the konaki she was much happier; she was a different person.

"What's going on?" Kiriakoula asked Yavasis. "If you know anything, tell us."

Ignoring Kiriakoula's question Yavasis asked Maria about her house. Where were the doors? What could you see out the windows? Kiriakoula asked him if perhaps they should move the family icon. Yavasis said he didn't know anything.

Maria told Yavasis that she hadn't slept well lately and that she often felt a trembling and a tightness in her heart, the way she did when she was about to dance. Yavasis wanted to know more about her house. Where was the icon? Where did the sun come in? Where did she like to sit?

When Maria had answered all of Yavasis' questions, Eleni suddenly shouted, "Ah! Ah! Ah!" and waved her arms violently. Then she crossed herself and sat in silence. Yavasis motioned to Eleni to come sit next to him. He put his left arm on her shoulder and took her right hand in his. They sat there silently staring off into space. Yavasis grimaced several times as if in pain. His face grew red, and he began to cry.

Maria talked quietly about her family icon. It was very old. It had originally been in her parents' house, but Maria had recently brought it to the apartment where she and her husband lived.

"It must leave! It must leave! It must go where it belongs!" Eleni shouted angrily.

Maria began talking again.

"I'm ready to do anything you say, anything the Saint wants. If you want to come to my house to see if anything is wrong . . ."

"What does the icon look like?" interrupted Yavasis.

"It's old and dark," replied Maria. "You can't really make out what's on it."

"You will paint it! You will paint it!" cried Eleni.

Maria repeated her willingness to do whatever she had to, if only she could regain her health. Yavasis took Maria's hand and Eleni's and held them tightly in his lap. In a tender, comforting tone of voice Yavasis told Maria that she should first put the icon in a bright sunny place so it could look out the window.

"In its place! In its place!" shouted Eleni, pounding the table violently.

Yavasis continued quietly, checking every so often with Eleni for confirmation.

"After you've put the icon in a sunny place, wait. See if you feel any better. If not, take the icon to an icon painter. Tell him to paint it over exactly as it is. Tell him not to add or subtract anything. The icon must wear the same clothes."

He asked Kiriakoula if she would be willing to help her sister and contribute to the cost of repainting the icon. She assured Yavasis that she believed and that she would do whatever was necessary. Eleni asked Maria if her husband believed and whether he would have any objections. Maria said he would agree to anything they said.

"After you've had it repainted, take it to the Church of the Cross," instructed Yavasis. "Ask the priest to bless it and leave it there for forty days. Then bring it home and put it in its new place. Wait and see how you feel. If anything else needs to be done, it will be revealed. You may have to take it back to your parents' house. But remember, wherever the icon is, it should be on a shelf. It's a guest in your house. It should have a place to sit down; it should never be hung from the wall."

Maria was worried about what the people who were renting her parents' house would say if she had to keep the icon there. She didn't want to impose on them, but she would ask their permission. She would even offer to bring oil for the lamp that hung above the icon.

Yavasis and Eleni told her not to worry. Everything would be fine. In this way she would find her health.

MARIA KONDOU: THE DOCTORS AND THE SAINTS MADE HER WELL

Maria's father used to light the fire in Kosti. He died before World War II, and Maria's mother, who served a meal to the Anastenarides in Kosti, never remarried. Before her death she went to Ayia Eleni every year for the Anastenaria. She believed in the Anastenaria a great deal, and she always told Maria to believe. It was a good thing. Maria remembered going to Ayia Eleni with her mother as a child and seeing the fire, but in the ten or twelve years since her mother's death she had only attended the festival once or twice.

When she went in May 1975, she only intended to help Yavasis' wife. She had no idea she would dance, but when she saw the other women take off their shoes and go into the fire, some power just came to her and she began dancing. She went into the fire, too, without knowing what happened. At first she didn't even know the dance steps, but by the third day she was dancing really well, just like an old Anastenarissa. Before that, she said, she'd been a mess.

"The icon was tormenting me. I beat my legs with my fists so hard that afterward they were black and blue. Everyone was watching me because I was suffering more than anyone else. I was like Christ. I was suffering even while I danced. Afterward I was exhausted."

When her legs first started to tremble, Yavasis came over to her and asked her if her husband would give her permission to dance. Without his permission Yavasis couldn't give her a simadi or let her dance. Eleni went and called her husband on the phone. When he came to Ayia

Eleni the next day, Yavasis told him his wife had started on a good road and asked him if he would let her go freely. He said yes.

On the third night of the festival Maria slept in the room across the hall from the icons, but she couldn't fall asleep. She heard the bells on the icons ringing, so she went in and lay down right underneath them, but she couldn't fall asleep there either. She kept hearing footsteps on the icon shelf. The next morning Yavasis told her that the Saints were pacing back and forth because they were upset. They were getting ready to leave; the next day they would have to separate.

Some people in Ayia Eleni couldn't understand how a person like Maria had become an Anastenarissa. She'd been married twice, and there were rumors about her fighting in public and running around with wealthy men.

"How could such a woman become a holy saint and walk on fire?" one woman wondered aloud. "I touch a hot stove and get burned, and she walks in fire up to her knees. How could the Saint forgive her? When people see a woman like that in the fire, they don't believe any-more."

According to some villagers now that Maria had grown old and couldn't play around anymore, she'd decided to improve her reputation by becoming an Anastenarissa. She *pretended* to cry and suffer to get attention—to show people she'd repented—but she didn't fool any-body. At least one villager, however, disagreed. "Even if she's done some bad things in her life, she repented and went into the fire. At that moment she believed, and so the Saint protected her."

The day after the festival of Saints Constantine and Helen in May 1976 Maria seemed enthusiastic, confident, and proud of her perfor-mance. She commented on how big the fire had been and on how many people had been watching. She thought she'd danced better than the other women who clapped and shouted a lot. She'd even heard that a rose from one of the icons had fallen into the fire and hadn't been burned.

Ten days later Yavasis visited Maria in her apartment in the city. Sitting in Maria's kitchen, a small, dark room cluttered with embroi-dery and knickknacks, they talked about Maria's icon stand, an inex-pensive wooden frame with a glass door that hung on the wall above her refrigerator. In it stood the icon of the Virgin Mary that Maria had brought from her parents' house, as well as a small cardboard icon of Saint Katerina and an even smaller plastic one of Saint George. Yavasis told her to move her icon into the reception room where there was more space and where it was cleaner. Then late one night she should incense the icon, and it would reveal what else it wanted to be done.

"You should make a shelf for the icon," he said. "And don't go putting lots of little icons and crosses on it. They can cause trouble. You buy a cross. Several years later you see another one you like, and you buy it too. You shut the first one up in a drawer, lock it, and forget about it. Then you start to suffer, and you don't know why."

A few months later Maria talked about the problems she'd been having recently. She spoke slowly and flatly. Her legs trembled slightly, and she chewed candy because her mouth was always dry. Her favorite nephew, Kiriakoula's son, died in December 1975. Her first anxiety attack occurred twenty days later. She said it was from her nerves. She got confused easily; she spoke nonsense and couldn't concentrate. Sometimes she saw her dead brother and her dead mother in the hallway and thought they were coming toward her. She jumped out of bed at odd times and bit the sheets. She felt hot and sweaty.

"One day while I was visiting Kiriakoula's daughter-in-law, I was overcome with anxiety—the same anxiety I feel when I dance. All I could think about was going home and lighting my lamp. I went home and lit it, and then I danced. My husband tried to stop me because he thought I'd get more upset, but I just pushed him away. After I danced for a while, I came to and I lit some incense. I felt better then; I calmed down. My worries passed with the help of Saint Constantine.

"I get upset sitting at home alone so much. These apartments are like cages. I'd rather live in a single family house like my parents', where I could have a garden and take care of flowers, but my husband wants to stay here. I really enjoy going to the konaki, though. Yavasis takes my worries away. I love to sit and listen to him tell stories about Kosti, the icons, and how things were done in the old days.

"When I'm at the konaki I'm really a different person. I don't even take my pills. I tell my husband I do, so he won't get mad. He thinks I'm sick, so he sends me to doctors. He says I have to take my pills or I'll get worse, but Yavasis tells me not to. I don't feel any better when I take them; I still feel the anxiety, the tightness in my chest. I take the pills so I won't fight with my husband. What else can I do? I'm a woman; I can't take on my husband. I'm lucky he lets me go to the konaki and dance. If he didn't, I'd get much worse.

"I think I'm suffering from the Anastenaria. If the anxiety I feel is from the Saint, then I'll feel it whether I take the pills or not. The Saint is making me suffer for some mistake I made. Maybe I have to repaint the icon; maybe I have to take it back to my parents' house. But their house is far away, and the woman who lives there isn't from Kosti. She might be scared; she might not want to take care of the icon."

Maria's husband felt sorry for his wife because she suffered so much. He never watched her when she danced. If he did, he would see her suffer and he'd want to take her home. He said that her nerves were "strained" and that with the tragedy of her nephew's death she had suffered a nervous breakdown.

"The icon has nothing to do with her problems," he said, "but worrying about it might make her condition worse. She's going to a neurologist now; she's in a doctor's care. For three days he gave her some different pills, and she got worse; she was upset all day. Now she takes tranquilizers so she can sleep."

In 1981 Maria still had not had her icon repainted. It would have cost a lot of money, she said. Besides, it was basically in good condition. There were no worm holes in it, no rot; it was just dark and faded and a little warped. When Yavasis told her to move it out of her kitchen, she did. She moved it to her reception room, but she just didn't feel comfortable with it there, so she moved it back to the kitchen. She made that decision all by herself. She sits in the kitchen a lot and feels warm inside when she looks up at it and sees the lamp burning above it.

"After my nephew died, I was really sick," Maria concluded. "It was my nerves. I'm better now, I suppose. Sometimes I still get upset and take my pills, but not as often as before. I went to the doctors *and* the Saints. Even the doctors say 'First God, then us.' "

✛

Have you heard the story about Stella Nikolaou? When she was a little girl, she fell in love with her elementary school teacher, but he didn't pay any attention to her. That was when she began to act strangely.

Once the teacher gave the children little icons to take home. Stella buried hers in the ground near her house. Then she went around telling people to dig there. When they found the icon, she said it was a miracle. Some people said she was going to become an Anastenarissa; other people said she was crazy. Every day she'd go to the little chapel near the ayiasma and sweep the floor and light the lamps. She'd go up to people and shout, "You don't believe in Saint Constantine. You must believe! You must believe!" Sometimes she would even go to the church and bang on the doors, demanding to get in so she could dance with the icons.

A few years later she tried to burn down her house. She said it had to be destroyed because Saint Constantine wanted a chapel built there. Her family called the Anastenarides and she calmed down, but she did it again a few days later. Then she fell in love with Kostas Lazaridis, the lira player, but he ignored her too. Then she really went crazy. She set fire to his barn and even tried to stab him with a knife. At the trial the doctor said she was a psychopath, so they sent her to a clinic in Thessaloniki.

When I was serving in the army there in 1956 I went to see her. She recognized me and talked normally, but she had a big beard. She spent three years in the clinic. When she got out, her father didn't want to bring her home. She's married now and lives in Thessaloniki, but her family has nothing to do with her. They never even talk about her.

✣

"MAY SAINT CONSTANTINE GIVE YOU LEGS, LITTLE GIRL!"

Later in the morning of May 22, 1976, Yavasis, Maria, Kiriakoula, and Eleni were joined by other Anastenarides and fellow villagers. After a short period of dancing Yavasis lined people up and distributed the icons and simadia. Yavasis' wife greeted the procession by kissing the icons, the simadia, and the hands of the Anastenarides who carried them. She offered everyone a sip of ouzo and a handful of raisins and roasted chickpeas and wished them "a good road." Yavasis greeted the procession himself and gave a few coins to a thirty-five-year-old man named Nikos, who had just arrived that morning from Thessaloniki with his mother. He would be the "treasurer" for the day.

The Anastenarides left the konaki and began their circuit of the village led by a tall, well-dressed man in a three-piece suit holding a censer and a long white candle. He was followed by Nikos and a woman in black each carrying a bright red simadi, Mihalis and Thodoros each carrying an icon of Saints Constantine and Helen decorated with red and white roses, and then Eleni, Maria, and Keti who held simadia and icon covers. A short distance behind them came the musicians, curious spectators, and a group of women carrying plastic bags to collect the offerings the people of Ayia Eleni would give to Saint Constantine.

On this the second day of the celebration the procession of Anastenarides would visit almost half of the roughly two hundred houses in the village. Every year their route was the same—"always to the right." The Anastenarides were usually met in front of each house by a woman holding an incense burner and a candle. They entered the house, passed through all the rooms, and then stopped in the room where the family icons were kept. There the members of the family greeted the procession. Their offerings of coins, raisins and chickpeas, fruit, or other sweets were met with wishes that the Saints help them in whatever way they desired.

At a few houses where the Anastenarides were not welcome the procession was met with drawn curtains and a closed door. At several houses the Anastenarides and their followers stopped to rest. On two occasions they were served meals consisting of boiled potatoes or beans, olives, bread, and cheese. In addition, the Anastenarides danced at four or five houses that had large icon shelves where the icons and simadia carried by the Anastenarides could also rest.

At the house of old Hristakena, a frail old Anastenarissa who had been bedridden for many years, Yavasis took the censer into the small room where she lay. He told her that the icons would be there soon; then he called the musicians in and signaled them to begin to play. Yavasis placed the censer in her hand and helped her make the sign of the cross. He put his arm around her, held her, and rocked her back and forth in time to the music. They cried. An Anastenarissa danced into the room, kissed old Hristakena's hand, and danced for a moment in front of her.

At this point Nikos began to cry; his hands were shaking badly. Yavasis told him not to be afraid. Another Anastenarissa shouted, "No tears! Don't worry! Your time hasn't come yet, but you'll be all right." When the Anastenarides stopped dancing, they formed a procession again and filed through old Hristakena's room so she could greet the icons. Then they made their way down the stairs and out the door into the bright sunlight.

Toward late afternoon the Anastenarides returned to the konaki, having completed their work for the day. For three or four hours people sat there relaxing and talking casually. Nikos told a story he'd heard from his grandfather about an icon that had been found buried in the ground back in Kosti. He stuttered occasionally and sometimes slurred

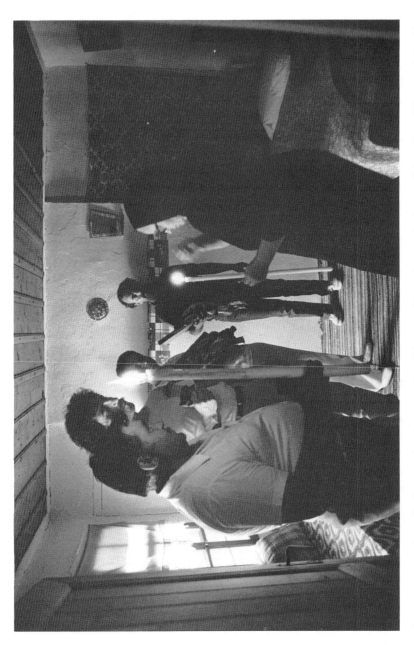

A woman crosses herself before greeting the procession of Anastenarides as it tours the houses of the village (Photograph by John Demos/Apeiron)

his words together. He talked about how his mother had become an Anastenarissa. She used to faint when she was out in the fields working. People said it was from the Saint, but Nikos' father thought she should see a doctor. He didn't want her running around with the Anastenarides. Once he even threatened her with a knife to keep her from dancing at the konaki.

Then Nikos told his own story. A few years ago he'd gone to Australia to work. After three months he got sick. He had trouble with his feet so he couldn't walk, and his stomach hurt. He wrote his mother and told her that he was sick, that she'd been right, he shouldn't have left home. His mother suffered a great deal because he was so far away she couldn't take care of him. But Saint Constantine protected him. One night he saw the Saint looking down at him from a sign above the entrance to a movie theater. Sometimes he saw strange, horrible shapes that the Saint assumed to frighten people. After ten months in a hospital in Australia he returned to Greece. If he hadn't been a Kostilis and if Saint Constantine hadn't protected him, he might never have come home safely. His stomach was still bothering him, though. That's why he was taking pills.

Saint Constantine helped Nikos in other ways as well. Nikos had smoked for a long time in spite of his parents' repeated requests that he quit. Then after the festival of Saint Athanasios the previous January, whenever he lit up a cigarette, he heard a voice in tears begging him not to smoke. It was the old man, the grandfather, Saint Constantine; so Nikos stopped smoking right away.

Someone mentioned the icons of Saints Constantine and Helen that had been taken from the Anastenarides of Mavrolefki by the Bishop of Drama. The Anastenarides in Mavrolefki couldn't celebrate, and people everywhere were suffering because Saint Constantine was in jail. Nikos' mother said that one night about a month ago Nikos woke up everyone in his apartment building in Thessaloniki with his shouts. He was running up and down the stairs crying, "Saint Constantine is king of the world. He's in enemy hands. The grandfather wants to come out." People thought Nikos was crazy. They didn't know anything about the Anastenaria, so they wanted to call the police. Fortunately a man from Nikos' village who lived next door convinced them not to.

Nikos asked Yavasis why *they* were responsible for the icon being in jail. Yavasis didn't answer.

"I hope it gets out soon," said Nikos, "so we can find some peace."

About nine o'clock the musicians entered the konaki. Soon the Anastenarides were dancing again. An old Anastenarissa began dancing in her seat. She sat on the floor bouncing up and down with her legs outstretched in front of her while her arms made the usual dance gestures. Yavasis and Eleni helped her to her feet and guided her over to the icon shelf. A moment later she was dancing across the room holding a simadi. Nikos was sitting out in the hall with his head in his hands crying. The dancing continued until midnight with only one or two pauses. As people prepared to leave, Yavasis reminded them that the next day was the most difficult of all. They had to complete the circuit of the village and perform another firewalk before their work was finally done.

It was almost noon by the time the procession of Anastenarides set off from the konaki the next day. As they came out of a house a few doors down the street, Yavasis' wife called to them to stop. A severely crippled young woman with badly misshapen legs approached the procession from the direction of the konaki. She walked with crutches and the support of both her parents. Yavasis was almost in tears as he helped her greet the icons and the simadia. Several people called out to her, "May Saint Constantine give you legs, little girl!" While the procession of Anastenarides continued down the street, Yavasis helped the young woman back to the konaki.

After sitting together under the icon shelf for a few minutes, Yavasis put a red icon cover on her legs and a simadi on each of her shoulders. He lit the incense burner and made the sign of the cross with it over her legs. Then he passed the censer around her head three times. He was crying.

With a sprig of basil Yavasis made a cross over the censer. After dipping the basil in a glass of holy water he sprinkled it on the young woman's forehead, shoulders, and legs. Then he gave her some holy water to drink, put the sprig of basil in her hand, and incensed again.

In a soft, gentle voice Yavasis called on Christ and the Virgin Mary to help this poor little girl. He told her to kiss the red icon cover and then get up and walk around the room. He helped her up and held her as she hobbled awkwardly around the empty room. She was much taller than Yavasis.

When they sat down again, Yavasis took her hand.

"What joy we'll have when you get well! What joy when you get well! Have you had an operation? No? That's all right. God and Saint Constantine will help you. Don't be afraid." Yavasis held out his hand for her to kiss. He sighed and went to blow out some candles.

Once more Yavasis helped her up, and they struggled around the room. Then Yavasis began to sing to her. It was a song about young Constantine setting off to war, but Yavasis sang it softly and sweetly as if it were a lullaby.

Yavasis adjusted her feet so they were together in front of her. Bending down he hugged her legs and rocked them in time to the music. She looked away, as if she were bored or embarrassed. Yavasis continued singing:

Κι η κόρη που ντον αγαπά δεξιά μεριά ντου στέκει.
Κρατεί κερί και φέγγει ντον, ποτήρι και κερνά ντον.

And the girl who loves him stands to his right.
She holds a candle to light his way, a glass to offer him a drink.

For a third time Yavasis helped her to her feet. Now the young woman was crying. Nothing had changed. She still couldn't walk.

Yavasis' wife brought in a glass of water. She squeezed in some lemon juice, added a spoonful of honey, and offered the glass to the young woman with a loving, happy laugh. The young woman's family entered the room, and her little brother came and sat next to her. Yavasis smiled when he learned the boy's name was Kostas and told him to light a candle for his sister. Then Yavasis stood up and addressed her parents: "May all the Saints take your pain away. May they give your daughter legs so she can walk. May all the Saints help you and make her well."

After Yavasis helped the young woman out to her parents' car, he kissed her cheek and held out his hand for her to kiss in turn. As they drove off, Yavasis' wife called out after them, "May Saints Constantine and Helen help you."

The sound of the drum and the lira could be heard faintly in the distance. Yavasis sat in front of his house for a few minutes before rejoining the procession of Anastenarides on the far side of the village.

LORING DANFORTH:
THE ANTHROPOLOGIST WHO DIDN'T BELIEVE

All this time I had been watching from a distance, sitting on a chair by the door outside of the room where Yavasis and the young woman were waiting for a miracle. I was writing in a notebook on my lap. I was crying. I felt awkward, embarrassed, and out of place. How could I just sit there and take notes? What right did I have to be there anyway? I was angry at myself for not having left. But most of all I felt guilty. I felt guilty because I didn't believe in miracles. I felt guilty because I just didn't believe Saint Constantine had the power to make her walk.

At the same time I found myself hoping that the miracle I didn't believe in would actually happen. I wanted the incense and the holy water and the songs about young Constantine to work, but I was afraid that my presence had interfered somehow. I was afraid that a miracle might have happened if only I hadn't been there. I had distracted them. I had made them self-conscious. I didn't believe.

For several days I wondered whether Yavasis had really believed that a miracle would happen or whether he'd simply wanted to comfort the young woman and her parents. When I finally found the courage to ask him, he said that he hadn't been trying to cure her. He didn't have any power. He was just doing his job as he'd learned it from those who'd come before him: he kept his house open and the candles lit. If the young woman was suffering from the Saint, she would get well from the Saint when her time came. He was just doing his job—not for himself but for the whole world.

To me Yavasis, more than anyone else, was the embodiment of Saint Constantine. He was a small, almost fragile-looking man over eighty years old, with a firm grip and a deep, penetrating gaze. He had power over me because I wanted to know everything he knew. I was possessed by him, in a way, just as the Anastenarides were possessed by Saint Constantine, because he had the religious power that I found so mysterious and so attractive.

I was particularly fascinated with this power given how weak and

Yavasis dances with the power of Saint Constantine (Photograph by Loring M. Danforth)

helpless I often felt during my stay in Ayia Eleni. I felt I had to maintain a smiling, passive persona at all times. I thought I had to become a virtual nonperson, someone who accepted everything, someone who never got angry. I found it especially difficult to assert myself when dealing with the blustery intimidation of village men or the solid presence of village women, who were all too ready to assume a maternal role toward me by giving me advice or serving me food.

I soon realized, however, that if I wanted to do my work I would have to become more assertive. Most of the people in Ayia Eleni did not want to talk about the Anastenaria, about family conflict, or about mental illness. They were embarrassed; they were afraid of Saint Constantine. My questions were often met with long silences or with sudden changes in the topic of conversation. I was furious when I found out that a man I had talked to for a long time hadn't told me that his own wife was an Anastenarissa, and again when a man told me he didn't know a particular song that several people had heard him sing. At times like that I wanted to show people I hadn't been fooled, but I said nothing.

I was aware, too, that I spent most of my time with women and old people at the konaki, in church, in kitchens and backyards. I spent as little time as possible in the male world of the coffeehouse and the village square. After all, I was interested in "women's things"—religion, illness, and family life—not "male" topics like agriculture, economics, or politics. As village men enjoyed pointing out, I couldn't carry a heavy bale of hay on my shoulder, and the only callus I had on my hands was from writing.

In time, Saint Constantine and the power he represented became very real to me. Once when I accidently crossed in front of the procession of Anastenarides while taking photographs, Yavasis shouted angrily at me, "You know you shouldn't cut the Saint's road!" For several days I worried about my mistake; I felt guilty; I wondered if anything bad would happen to me. Anastenarides told me that I'd cried at the konaki because Saint Constantine loved me and that I would keep coming back to Ayia Eleni because I had gotten "tangled up" in the Anastenaria. They said the Saint would help me pass my examinations because I had honored him so faithfully with my presence at his festivals.

When a young man from Athens tried repeatedly to prevent a friend of mine from taking photographs in the konaki, I wrote in my notes: "I was really angry at him. I felt a kind of rage that's hard to control.

It would have been nice to shout 'Ah! Ah! Ah!' and have him do the will of the Saint."

✥

Later that summer I dreamt that I was sitting on a bed with my wife Peggy, who had recently returned to the United States, and my father, who had visited us in Ayia Eleni several months earlier.

Dimaressa, an old Anastenarissa who lived next door and who served a meal to the Anastenarides on Saint Pandeleimon's day, sat next to us. She asked us when we wanted to serve our meal to the Anastenarides. My father said, "On Saint Constantine's day." My wife said, "On the day of the Transformation of the Savior." Then, as the bed we were sitting on heaved up and down, I shouted out in a deep thunderous voice, "On Saint Pandeleimon's day!"

Dimaressa accepted my answer and described what we should do to prepare for the meal. She told us what food we should buy and just how we should cook it. I was worried; I wanted to make sure we did everything properly.

✥

"Anyone can build an icon shelf, but who will come and sit on it?"

Five years later, on the morning of May 23, 1981, the third day of the festival of Saints Constantine and Helen, the procession of Anastenarides entered the house of Sotiria Fotiadi. Mihalis Kitsos, the new leader of the Anastenarides, set the icons and the simadia down on a clean white cloth that had been spread out carefully on the floor next to a wall of the reception room. To the right in the corner of the room hung a small icon stand. Mihalis sat on a stool on one side of the icons; Yavasis sat on the other. The crowded room grew quiet when Evripidis Petrakis, the brother of Mihalis' father-in-law, asked loudly, "Do you know why we've stopped here?"

"No," replied Mihalis.

"This is why," said Evripidis. "Because Sotiria has something to say to us."

"We've stopped here," echoed Mihalis, "so Sotiria can tell us what's going on. If anyone knows anything, speak up."

"I've been sick for a long time," Sotiria began. "Every night I light my lamp and my censer. I incense my icon and the lamp; then I incense the wall. I hear a voice. It says to me, 'Why do you incense the bare wall? That's enough!' Then I say, 'Why do you just tell this to *me*? Why don't you tell all the Anastenarides? Give them a sign! Clear words!' "

Keti, who had been crying softly, put her hands over her mouth and screamed in a high, shrill voice, "Ah! Oh! Ah! Oh!"

"Speak clearly!" said Sotiria. But Keti continued to cry and tremble.

"What's in your mouth?" Evripidis called out.

Keti stood up and went over to the empty wall. She pounded it with her fist and shouted, "Make it! Make it!"

"I know I should build an icon shelf. But where should I put it?" said Sotiria, as if talking to herself. "I have to be careful. I don't want to make a mistake. I want to get better; I don't want to get worse. How high should it be? How long? This big or this big? Maybe it should be big enough for all the Saints to sit together. What kind of wood should it be made of? Does anyone else know anything?"

Keti was still crying and trembling. Yavasis told her to calm down. Then he turned to Sotiria.

"Do you know who spoke to you?"

"It was Saint Constantine," she replied. "He said, 'Why are you always incensing the wall? Why?' Then I told him, 'I'm willing to do whatever you want, whatever you tell me.' "

Evripidis told Sotiria's husband to go and stand beside her. After motioning to Mihalis to light the censer, Sotiria incensed all through the house. When she returned, she said, "My heart is heavy. Here I go again, incensing the bare wall. Show me what to do!"

Keti was still sobbing. Yavasis hushed her. Then Mihalis incensed through the house.

"He showed me a shelf from here to here," said Sotiria, indicating a long shelf that would go around the corner of the room, like the shelf at the konaki.

"No! No! No!" shouted Eleni Grigoriou abruptly, with a forceful wave of her arm. She crossed herself.

"I'll do it any way you want. The Saint said, 'I will sit on the throne you build for me. That's where I'll stay.' "

"The topic is open for discussion in front of everyone," said Mihalis. "We made a good beginning. Maybe it's not time for the final decision to be made yet."

Censer in hand, an Anastenarissa dances in front of her family icons and the icons of the Anastenarides on the shelf below (Photograph by John Demos/Apeiron)

Thodoros leapt to his feet dancing and clapping. He shouted, "Yes! Yes! Yes! No! No! No!"

Mihalis continued calmly and quietly, "We need to be very careful. We mustn't hurry."

Evripidis turned to Sotiria, "Yavasis asked you who you saw."

"Saint Constantine."

"But last year on the third night of the festival you danced with the simadi of Saint Pandeleimon. Was he the one who spoke to you?"

"No! It was Saint Constantine."

Eleni clapped loudly several times and shouted: "Yes! Yes! Yes!"

"I want my health," said Sotiria. "I don't want trouble. I don't want to wallow in the mud."

"You should invite Mihalis and a few other Anastenarides to your house some evening and talk things over," advised Yavasis. "How many times did you see him? How many times did Saint Constantine speak to you?"

"Many times. He told me many times to get the wood for the shelf, but my road was closed."

"Who will make the shelf?" asked Yavasis.

"First we have to decide what shape it will be," said Sotiria.

"In a few days call some of these people to your house," Yavasis suggested again. "Find out just what to do and just how to do it—to avoid any mistakes. We shouldn't do anything on our own. Anyone can build an icon shelf, but who will come and sit on it? We know that Saint Constantine wants to be here—you have his simadi. But he may want to be by himself, or he may want a big shelf with room for everyone. We have to prepare our food well before we cook it."

"In a few days buy some ouzo and some raisins and chickpeas. Then some Saturday evening invite five or six of these people to your house. Anyone who knows anything will speak. Whatever it is will come out into the open. If we make decisions on our own, we'll get worse instead of better. The meal you serve is a long road. If you start it, you can never give it up. And if you do give it up, *they* will make you start again. These things take a lot of work; they take a long time. To make a cart you need to get the wheels and choose the oxen first. Then you can build the cart."

"I don't have to finish it right away," agreed Sotiria.

After a long pause Yavasis asked Sotiria another, more difficult question.

"Why did you close your door to the icon all those years? I gave you a simadi. Did I give it to you so you could shut your door?"

"I didn't do it on my own," Sotiria protested vehemently.

"Poor Olga," said Yavasis with tears in his eyes. "When she was a young girl, she suffered naked and all alone."

Olga, a cousin of Sotiria's husband, was standing in the doorway glaring angrily at Sotiria. She nodded her head in agreement and clapped loudly. Olga had suffered from the icon of Saint Pandeleimon, which had belonged to her grandfather back in Kosti, the grandfather of Sotiria's husband. Olga became an Anastenarissa and danced in the fire for several years before she got married, but now her husband refused to let her dance. She was still suffering from the Saint.

Evripidis began to sob. He picked up an icon of Saints Constantine and Helen and shook it. Two other Anastenarisses began to clap and hiss.

"Olga was wandering around like a wild buffalo," Yavasis continued. "In the middle of the night she would run out into the fields in her slip with her father chasing after her. No one could calm her down. How many times did we call the Anastenarides together to find out why she suffered?"

Yavasis was still crying. Olga clapped again.

"The father made a mistake, and the daughter suffered," shouted Eleni.

Sotiria called her husband's mother and sister into the room for support. Her husband's sister said that everyone in the village hated her family.

"They said I was crazy. They shut me out," cried Sotiria.

"No," said Yavasis. "*You* shut *them* out."

"I shut myself in. I was dizzy and confused. I was suffering."

People tried to quiet her, but she insisted. "They said I was crazy. They said that I locked my door and went out into the fields, that I set cornstalks on fire and danced on them."

Mihalis stopped her. Enough. Enough had been said. It was time to move on. There was much work left to be done.

As the procession formed, Sotiria began to dance. She greeted the icons with waving, clapping, and hissing. When Mihalis pointed out that Yavasis had left the house without being offered any raisins and chickpeas, Sotiria ran out to the yard to give him some. At the door Sotiria and Olga kissed each other's hands without exchanging a word.

After the procession had set off down the street toward the next house, Sotiria complained to an old Anastenarissa from Mesopotamo: "Things like that should be discussed in private. They humiliated me; they left me a nervous wreck. No one supported me."

A few people tried to comfort her, telling her not to worry and assuring her that everything would be all right. But Sotiria continued to wander around the house nervously, crying and trembling with anger.

SOTIRIA FOTIADI:
THE LAST HOLE ON THE CLARINET

In 1976 Sotiria and her husband were quiet, lonely people, isolated from the mainstream of village life. Sotiria rarely visited her neighbors to crochet and talk, and her husband practically never went to the coffeehouse in the evening to sit with the other village men. Some people said he was a little "backward," that he couldn't really carry on a good conversation. The lives of Sotiria and her husband were dominated, it seemed, by one tragic fact. They had no children.

Sotiria's involvement with the Anastenaria had been a long and turbulent one. She came to Ayia Eleni as a new bride in January 1960. By May she was suffering. She was depressed; she felt weak and dizzy, but the doctors couldn't find anything wrong with her.

"On May 21 I went to the square to see the Anastenaria. When the women passed by in front of me, I prayed to Saint Constantine for help. Just then I felt a breeze. A voice said to me, 'Don't worry! Everything will be fine.' My mother-in-law called Yavasis. He said that I was suffering from the Saint and that my time would come. He used to bring me incense and holy water. I'd feel better during the day, but then at night I'd feel sick again. I'd see dreams. I'd tell them to my mother-in-law, and then she'd go tell them to Yavasis. He said I should come to the konaki."

The following May Sotiria was not well either, so she went to the konaki with her mother-in-law and her husband. She lit a candle and sat down. After listening to the music for a while and watching the women dance, she heard a voice that said, "Get up!" She didn't know how she began to dance, but she did. The next day she went back to the konaki to serve the Saint. This time she really wanted to dance. Yavasis gave her a simadi of Saint Pandeleimon, but she was still afraid of the fire. Yavasis told her not to be afraid, just to do her job every year.

"When I dance, I hear a voice that tells me 'Walk! Go forward! I am right behind you.' Sometimes I see him too—like a soldier all dressed up with his uniform and his sword. His power comes to me. Your own spirit leaves and goes to the Saint; your mind, all your attention, is focused on him, waiting for his voice. He tells you where to go, how many times to cross the fire, and just where to stop. The Saint has control over you then. If you're in charge yourself, you'll get burned."

During the early years of her marriage Sotiria's relationship with her parents-in-law was difficult.

"Everything I suffered I suffered at their hands. The whole time we lived with them my father-in-law was in charge of the cash box; my husband and I had nothing. We worked hard so we could eventually build a house of our own and be independent. I had so much work to do then I didn't have time to think about how difficult my life was. As a new bride I made all the beds, I cleaned, and I cooked. I even baked bread for the dogs. But I didn't complain. I just tried to keep my parents-in-law happy. A few years later we were ready to move into our own house, but they didn't want us to leave because they knew they'd have more work to do themselves. We finally did in 1964. They tried to get us to stay with them a few more years, but I'd ask my mother-in-law, 'How much longer will we be held hostage working for others?'

"Once my mother-in-law noticed that the only dress I owned was old and worn and had short sleeves, so she said to me, 'Let's buy you a long-sleeved dress for winter.' We went outside to buy some cloth from a salesman who was passing by. Just then my husband's sister saw us. She told my mother-in-law not to buy it for me, so she didn't. I was so upset I went back to my room and cried. When I stopped crying, I came out and didn't say a word. A daughter-in-law has to lie low. The only thing you can do is keep everything inside, even though that can upset you and make you sick.

"I felt better when I became an Anastenarissa, but I was never really healthy until 1973. That's when the Saint helped me get well; he ordered me to stop going to the konaki. I didn't leave on my own; the power of the Saint told me to. Since then I've been all right. The Saint ordered me to stay home, keep my door closed, and not let the Anastenarides into my house. If I started to go to the konaki on my own when I heard the music, the Saint's voice came to me and said, 'Stay at home!' So now I don't go anywhere."

Sotiria claimed that the other Anastenarisses never accepted her out of envy. They envied her because so many people came to her for help, to see if she "knew" anything; because she was the best, she was the king. Sometimes Sotiria was afraid to go to the konaki. When she went there, the other women would "weigh her down with devils." Instead of greeting her they would curse her. But the Saint told her to be patient and not to say anything, so she just sat there all huddled up like a ball of yarn, praying quietly to Saint Constantine, saying to herself, "These women will kill me." Another Anastenarissa would see her crying, come up to her, and in an angry tone of voice say, "Why are you crying? What's the matter? Are you crazy?" Sotiria went to the konaki for her health, but when she came home, she felt even worse. "They treated me as if I were the last hole on the clarinet," she said. "I didn't have any place to go. I was afraid to go outside. The countryside was full of bears.

"The first year I danced I went into the fire. From then on the Saint ordered me to dance around the fire with my shoes on. The other Anastenarisses in the circle would shout 'Foreigners get out!' If they'd helped me, I would have become an Anastenarissa without suffering. The Saint wanted me, but the other Anastenarisses didn't. The Saint said 'They don't want you, but I do.'

"Once Yavasis wanted to give me an icon, but old Vlastessa signaled him not to. The other women didn't let him call me when someone was sick. What could he do? Women are stronger and more clever than men. They get the best of a man, and he gives in. The other Anastenarisses go there for glory; I go for my health. But they're all Kostilides, and I'm not. They're all one race so they stick together.

"When we were all eating together at the konaki, they'd send me out of the room; they couldn't stand to see me there. I was happy in the room with the icons because the Saint was near me. There were times when I just wanted to leave, but the Saint made me stay, so I had to stay. He said 'Stay with me or else they'll drive you crazy like they did Stella Nikolaou.' "

Sotiria called the Anastenarides "evil people." She said they wouldn't let her have a child.

Many people in Ayia Eleni claimed that Sotiria had never been a

real Anastenarissa. She wasn't from Kosti, and she never went into the
fire; she just danced around the edges. Sometimes she fainted when the
Anastenarides were setting out for the fire. She was afraid. Some people
said that she just *tried* to be an Anastenarissa or that she went to the
konaki to serve Saint Constantine in the hope that she would have a
child with the Saint's help. But she still had no child, so now she didn't
go to the konaki at all. She didn't even let the icons in her house.

Other people said that Sotiria had been mistreated by the Anastenarides. They never gave her a simadi. There were rumors that one
Anastenarissa had threatened to grab Sotiria and pull her into the fire
so she'd get burned and that another Anastenarissa had actually hit her
on the head with an icon and knocked her down. The Anastenarides
excluded her just because she wasn't a Kostilou; but that wasn't fair.
The Saint doesn't discriminate; only people do. Besides, her husband
was a Kostilis. One woman said that Sotiria was afraid to go into the
fire because the Anastenarides didn't support her. They didn't show her
any respect, so she got mad and left.

Nearly everyone, however, even those who admitted that she'd been
mistreated by the Anastenarides, thought Sotiria had been wrong to
shut her doors to the icons. That was a sin, and she should be punished
for it. She was being punished for it.

Sotiria maintained that she had a clear conscience. She loved the
Saint, and his power was always with her. The Saint was in her house
all the time because she had him in her heart. She wasn't closing out
the Saint, just the people who held the icons. She believed in the icons
and the Saint. What's more, his power came into her house whenever
she did. That was even better than having the icons come into her
house.

By 1981, however, much had changed. When the Anastenarides
gathered in Sotiria's house to discuss the question of whether she should
build an icon shelf, Mihalis Kitsos had become leader of the Anastenarides, and the women who had been most opposed to Sotiria's participation in the rite had themselves withdrawn. Now Sotiria danced powerfully in the konaki and entered the fire regularly, while her husband
proudly carried the simadi of Saint Pandeleimon when the Anastenarides processed through the village.

Sotiria was not at all pleased with the inconclusive results of the gathering of the Anastenarides at her house. The word for her to build the
icon shelf should have come from the leader of the Anastenarides, not

Keti. No one else had confirmed what Keti had said, so Sotiria would have to gather the Anastenarides again. The Saint had shown Sotiria what to do; now he had to show the others.

According to Sotiria the Anastenarisses who were against her had started a rumor that one year on May 21 she'd set some cornstalks on fire all by herself out in the fields and danced on them there. That was a lie. She wasn't crazy like the old man in Kosti who just sat in the fireplace and played with the coals. Yavasis was trying to blame her for Olga's suffering, but that was ridiculous; Sotiria wasn't even living in Ayia Eleni when Olga got sick.

Another Anastenarissa said that Keti was confused and didn't know what she was saying. She was new, she was a foreigner, and on top of that she was a woman. Her words were *not* to be trusted. Sotiria had wanted to build an icon shelf for a long time. She wanted to move up a rung on the ladder; she wanted "to put down roots" and be a part of the rite forever.

"It doesn't matter what Sotiria wants," this Anastenarissa concluded. "It's what the icons want that counts."

II

The Interpretation of
Religious Healing

✠

THE ANASTENARIA is concerned with healing in the broadest sense. It is both a religious ritual and a form of psychotherapy. Any attempt to understand the Anastenaria as a system of religious healing must therefore integrate approaches from medical anthropology with those from the anthropological study of religion. It must bring together the concerns of transcultural psychiatry and those of symbolic anthropology. Such a synthesis, which constitutes an interpretive or hermeneutic approach to the study of ritual therapy, provides the theoretical framework for this study of the Anastenaria.

AN INTERPRETIVE APPROACH
TO MEDICAL ANTHROPOLOGY

The tradition of interpretive anthropology has adopted a fundamentally semiotic approach to the study of culture. According to Clifford Geertz (1973a:3-30) "culture consists of socially established structures of meaning" embodied in systems of symbols. It is through these structures of meaning, these "webs of significance," that we order our experience and make sense of the world. Human behavior is above all symbolic or meaningful behavior; the task of interpretive anthropology is to make more accessible the imaginative universes in which other people live.[1]

Interpretive anthropologists have devoted much attention to the analysis of religion as a symbolic system that plays an important role in the construction and maintenance of people's meaningful worlds. In his article "Religion as a Cultural System" (1973b:87-125) Geertz argues that the power of religious symbols lies in their ability to transform experience by constructing a sacred reality upon which the realities of everyday life are grounded. This sacred reality must be maintained in the face of what Geertz (1973b:112) has called "the discordant revelations of secular experience," which include threats posed by the existence of evil, death, illness, and suffering. Religion generally, and religious rituals concerned with healing in particular, attempt to deal with the problem of human suffering by placing it in meaningful contexts in which it can be expressed, understood, and either eased or endured.

The recent adoption of an interpretive approach by medical anthropologists has led to the development of a "meaning-centered" medical anthropology (Good and Good, 1981 and 1982). This shift away from a narrow biomedical perspective, which has characterized much work in medical anthropology, has important implications for the way sickness and healing are understood. In an interpretive approach to medical anthropology medicine is seen as a cultural system that can only be understood holistically in the context of other social and cultural systems.

According to Arthur Kleinman (1980, 1986) health care systems construct their own clinical reality just as religious systems construct their own sacred reality.[2] The clinical reality of a particular culture provides the members of that culture with explanatory models with which to make sense of sickness and healing. Proponents of an interpretive approach to medical anthropology view sickness as meaningful human experience and not simply as an exclusive result of biological pathology. Similarly, they view healing as an interpretive process that involves "the construction of culturally specific illness realities" as well

[1] Important works in interpretive anthropology include Basso and Selby (1976), Crick (1976), Douglas (1975), Geertz (1973a, 1983), Parkin (1982), and Rabinow and Sullivan (1979).

[2] On the social construction of reality in general see Berger and Luckmann (1967).

as "therapeutic efforts to transform those realities" (Good and Good 1981:174).

The most challenging task facing a truly holistic and interpretive medical anthropology is to deal satisfactorily with the dialectical relationship that exists between culture and biology, between the "meaningful and the somatic aspects of sickness and healing" (Good and Good 1981:174). Healing, like becoming sick, is at once a cultural, social, psychological, and physiological process. In all cultures powerful sets of symbols mediate between the sociocultural world, on the one hand, and psychophysiological states, on the other. Meaning, in other words, ties together social relationships, emotional states, and physiological conditions.

It is precisely the symbolically constructed interrelationships between these different domains that are crucial for the understanding of sickness and healing. In order to do full justice to the complexity and power of the healing process an interpretive medical anthropology must focus on the precise mechanisms by which "symbolic reality, either directly or via its effects on psychological reality, connects the social environment with physiological processes" (Kleinman 1980:42).

An analysis that remains sensitive to the dialectical relationship between body and society must distinguish between disease, "a malfunctioning of biological and/or psychological processes," and illness, "the psychosocial experience and meaning of perceived disease" (Kleinman 1980:72). Disease, the concern of biomedicine, involves physiological pathology, regardless of whether it is culturally recognized or not, while illness involves the interpretation members of a particular culture place on a variety of undesirable states (including, but not limited to, disease). Sickness is a more general term referring to situations that involve illness and/or disease. A similar distinction must be made between the process of curing, which deals with disease as a natural condition, and the process of healing, which deals with illness as a cultural condition (Young 1982:264-265).

Illness, therefore, is a culturally constructed response to disease, misfortune, or other form of suffering. As Kleinman suggests, it may be difficult to distinguish between illness and disease, especially in cases of minor or chronic psychiatric disorders, where illness may occur in the absence of disease as a result of emotional problems or interpersonal crises (Kleinman 1980:74). Whether it is associated with a particular disease or not, an illness is a symbol that expresses in a culturally patterned form a wide range of meanings including fear, stress, tragedy, conflict, and alienation.

Just as illness is equated with disease in a biomedical model, so the symptoms associated with an illness are considered to have exclusively biological referents. They are treated simply as the manifestation of pathological bodily processes. In an interpretive approach, however, symptoms, like illnesses, are understood to be somatic symbols that have meaning for the sick person. Using the body as a symbolic vehicle, symptoms express the psychological and social problems associated with the experience of being ill.

In his discussion of the "symbolic bridge" that links body and society in this way Kleinman focuses much attention on the process of somatization. Traditionally somatization has been associated with complaints of physical symptoms that cannot be attributed to any organic pathology. For Kleinman, however, somatization is defined as "the expression of personal and social distress in a language of bodily complaints and through a pathway of medical help-seeking" (1986:x). Somatization is thus a key process in the dialectical relationship between the biophysical domain, on the one hand, and the sociocultural domain, on the other.

Kleinman (1986:51-67) makes it clear that somatization is not always pathological and should not necessarily be equated with psychiatric disorder. It is an idiom for coping with psychological and social problems and is the predominant method for expressing "difficulties in living" in many parts of the world. Somatization is particularly common in societies where mental illness is heavily stigmatized, where it is improper to discuss personal or family difficulties with outsiders, and where no form of psychotherapy is available. In such situations, because of a lack of any acceptable psychological or social idiom for the expression of distress, somatization occurs, and distress is expressed in a more acceptable somatic idiom.

Somatization, therefore, is often an adaptive, culturally constituted coping mechanism that provides a legitimate medium through which people can communicate what would otherwise be unsanctioned personal or social distress. When such distress is encountered, it is articulated through the medium of the body. Illnesses, their symptoms, even pain itself, can thus be seen as powerful symbols that express through the body something about the social situation and the psychological condition of people who are ill.

RELIGIOUS HEALING

The realization that sickness involves both illness and disease and that illness is essentially semantic or meaningful in nature obviously has important implications for the understanding of the therapeutic process. The treatment of sickness must not be reductionistically equated with the curing of disease, as important as that may be in many situations. The treatment of sickness also involves the healing of illness, and that is an inherently interpretive or hermeneutic process.

The diagnosis of an illness involves the construction of a cultural interpretation with which to make sense of the disease, the stress, or the troubled relationships that prompted medical help-seeking in the first place. In this way chaotic and frightening experiences of pain and suffering are made more concrete, more comprehensible, and therefore more manageable by being identified with a specific illness. The therapeutic process is, therefore, fundamentally metaphoric. Metaphor, according to James Fernandez, involves "a strategic predication upon an inchoate pronoun [or subject] which makes a movement and leads to a performance." Through metaphor people are able to articulate and communicate a variety of inchoate experiences "by appealing to a range of more easily observable and concrete events in other domains of their lives" (Fernandez 1971:43 and 58).[3]

One domain in which vaguely defined psychological and social problems can be metaphorically expressed is the somatic. In cases involving somatization physical symptoms can be understood as bodily metaphors for emotional stress or social tension. Somatization, therefore, is an integral part of the therapeutic process itself. It does what all therapeutic systems must initially do; it provides people with a set of metaphors, a symbolic language or idiom, with which to make sense of and begin to deal with the difficulties they encounter in their daily lives.

Another domain in which a wide variety of social, psychological, and physiological ills can be metaphorically expressed is the sacred. Sacred symbols play an important part in systems of religious healing that are often sought out by the same people who are likely to express distress somatically: powerless people suffering from chronic or minor psychiatric disorders in cultures where a psychological or social idiom

[3] See also Fernandez (1974 and 1977). Herzfeld (1986) has made excellent use of this approach to metaphor in his analysis of the treatment of the "evil eye" in Greece.

for the expression of distress is not available. It must be emphasized, however, that systems of religious healing provide a vehicle for the interpretation of virtually any experience of suffering or misfortune, including those not defined as illness. Religious healing involves the construction of a sacred reality, which is at the same time a clinical reality, for the healing of illness.

Systems of religious healing enable people to deal with the problems they face (whether they have been somatized or not) in a sacred idiom. A religious interpretation is imposed on their experience, and a process of translation is begun from an unarticulated psychosocial idiom (or from a somatic idiom) into a sacred idiom. A new set of religious metaphors is invoked to communicate feelings of distress, suffering, and hopelessness that had previously remained inchoate or had been expressed somatically. Illness experiences, which are already cultural constructions of disease, are reformulated and expressed anew in the language of the sacred. In cases of somatization, symptoms—already metaphors themselves—become second-order metaphors when they are translated into a religious idiom.

There are therefore important similarities between somatization and religious healing. Both involve the construction of a powerful set of metaphors, which are in different domains it is true, but which are structurally parallel nonetheless. Kleinman (1986:173) points out that somatization involves "interpretive schemata for making sense of life problems," "rhetorical devices" for controlling social relationships and empowering the sick person, as well as "symbolic forms" that express important cultural themes. This is an equally apt description of religious healing. Both processes enable people to do the same thing—to make sense of suffering and misfortune and to deal with them in a way that minimizes the guilt, the responsibility, and the attendant stigma that are so often associated with a psychological or social idiom. Religious healing actually locates the cause of people's problems in a sacred domain that is a metaphor for, but external to, their person and their social world.

Much of the power of systems of religious healing lies in the ability of the sacred symbols they employ to serve as both models *of* and models *for* a sick person's social, psychological, and physiological condition (Geertz 1973b:93). Sacred symbols are models *of* a sick person's condition insofar as they reflect or express that condition. More important for the understanding of religious healing, however, is the fact that these sacred symbols also serve as models *for* a sick person's condition. They have the power to change the course of a person's illness by influencing his symptoms and even altering his behavior.

The goal of religious healing, therefore, is to reformulate people's interpretation of their own condition so that they are ritually moved from a state of illness to a state of health. In the process of religious healing sick people are initially presented with a set of sacred symbols that constitute a model *of* their present condition. Then the symbolic system is restructured or transformed in such a way that they are presented with a new model—a model *for* their future condition that is the opposite of their previous condition. A model *of* illness is transformed into a model *for* health. As Kleinman (1980:365) has shown, "the switch in models and metaphors is from negatively valued, anxiety-laden ones to positively valued, adaptive ones." These new models and metaphors for health are often associated with the resolution of psychological and social conflict, a sense of power, and a rise in social status.

In an article entitled "The Rhetoric of Transformation in Ritual Healing," T. J. Csordas (1983) argues persuasively that the key to the therapeutic effectiveness of systems of religious healing is precisely this ability to reorganize or restructure the conceptual worlds of people who are ill. This is accomplished through the "cultural rhetoric at work in the discourse of healing." This rhetoric "brings about a transformation of the phenomenological conditions under which the patients exist and experience suffering or distress." As patients come to inhabit the new sacred reality that is constructed for them, they are healed, "not in the sense of being restored to the state in which they existed prior to the onset of illness, but in the sense of being rhetorically 'moved' into a state dissimilar from both the pre-illness and illness reality" (Csordas 1983:346). This movement takes place simultaneously in many domains: the cultural, the social, the psychological, the physiological. The relevance of Fernandez' definition of metaphor as a strategic predication that makes a movement and leads to a performance is clear. Religious healing involves ritual performances that move people metaphorically from illness to health. It is in the power of these healing metaphors that the therapeutic efficacy of religious healing lies.

An early formulation of this approach to religious healing was Claude Lévi-Strauss's important essay "The Effectiveness of Symbols" (1967). Here Lévi-Strauss argues that ritual systems of psychotherapy provide people who are ill with a symbolic language through which unexpressed psychological and social states can be articulated. This makes it possible for them "to undergo in an ordered and intelligible form a real experience that would otherwise be chaotic and inexpressible" (193). Lévi-Strauss refers to this symbolic language that enables people to restructure their experience as "a social myth" that people receive from the outside and that does not correspond to their former personal state (195). Through the manipulation of sacred symbols, people's social, psychological, and even physiological condition is transformed so as to conform with the social myth. For Lévi-Strauss, then, "it is the effectiveness of symbols which guarantees the harmonious parallel development of myth and action." The transformation brought about by religious healing consists of "a structural reorganization" that induces the patient "to live out a myth" whose structure is analogous to that of the state of health that is so eagerly sought (196-197).

The therapeutic efficacy of religious healing must therefore be evaluated at all analytical levels. Cultural healing in the broadest sense consists of the "provision of personal and social meaning for the experience of illness" (Kleinman 1978:87). At this level healing is successful if it is able to identify people's suffering with a particular illness and prescribe a course of therapy. By giving people's suffering new meaning in this way religious healing is able to bring about a change in people's attitudes toward themselves, their suffering, and their entire social world. People can be healed even if their disease is not cured or their symptoms alleviated. Healing in this sense is comparable to a conversion experience. Through the construction of adaptive models and the use of powerful cultural symbols religious healing is often able to transform what might otherwise be defined as deviant or pathological behavior into socially acceptable or even highly valued behavior.

At the psychological and social levels religious healing often proves effective by virtue of its ability to address directly the psychosocial problems that constitute an illness. Healing rituals may reduce the stress, conflict, and tension generated by various social or political institutions or by disturbances in people's relationships with others in a variety of ways. They may, for example, provide group support to people who are isolated or alienated from others. As these people are incorporated into new social groups, they receive attention, comfort, and sympathy, which may be of therapeutic benefit. In addition, as people are healed, they assume a new social status that is often higher than the one they previously enjoyed. This change in self-image and social identity often gives people a position of increased respect and prestige within the community. All these changes may in turn bring about a realignment or restructuring of important social relations. A crucial aspect, then, of the therapeutic effectiveness of systems of religious healing is their ability to resolve both the psychological and the social conflicts associated with illness and bring about the integration of people's personalities and their integration into society as well.[4]

Religious healing may also operate at a physiological level as well. As Daniel Moerman (1979) has demonstrated, healing metaphors and other symbolic components of medical treatment are able to influence people's physiological states in important ways. While the understanding of religious healing has long been hindered by the Cartesian distinction between mind and body that has so dominated Western thought generally and Western medicine in particular, Moerman draws on recent research in the field of neurophysiology to argue convincingly that there are specific pathways through which physiological and psychological states are linked and that "these pathways are the stage on which metaphoric concepts of performance . . . influence biological processes" (62).

Spirit Possession

Rituals involving trance and possession are found in societies throughout the world and often play an important part in systems of religious healing. In many cases it is the experience of entering a trance state and being possessed that constitutes the crucial step in constructing a new clinical and sacred reality for people and in transforming their condition from one of sickness to one of health.[5]

---

[4] Studies of religious healing that explore these issues further are Crapanzano (1973), Frank (1961), Kapferer (1979), Kiev (1972), McGuire (1982), Nichter (1981a and b), and Obeyesekere (1981). For valuable review articles that cover the fields of religious healing, the anthropology of sickness, and non-Western medical systems see Bourguignon (1976a), Young (1982), and Worsley (1982), respectively.

[5] Bourguignon (1968, 1973, and 1976a) presents a cross-cultural and comparative approach to the study of trance and possession. The authors of the essays in *Case Studies in Spirit Possession* adopt what I find to be a more valuable interpretive approach to the subject (Crapanzano and Garrison 1977). See also Freed and Freed (1964), Lewis (1971), Mischel and Mischel (1958), Peters (1982), and Prince (1968).

The distinction between trance and possession is an important one and parallels the distinction between disease and illness discussed above. Trance refers to a particular physiological or psychological condition, while possession refers to a belief system, explanatory theory, or cultural interpretation placed upon various conditions that may or may not include trance states.

Trance states are altered states of consciousness that can be induced psychologically, physiologically, or pharmacologically. They involve dissociation (removal or separation from the world of everyday reality) as well as changes or discontinuities "in consciousness, awareness, personality, or other aspects of psychological functioning" (Bourguignon 1976b:8), and they are recognized subjectively by the person in trance or objectively by an observer as representing a significant deviation from the person's usual condition during alert waking consciousness.

The definition of possession I find most useful is "any state or condition, particularly any altered state of consciousness, indigenously interpreted in terms of the influence of an alien spirit."[6] A person who is possessed is changed, often dramatically, as a result of the influence of the possessing spirit. This change is generally experienced as coercive, as involving external control and a loss of individual autonomy. The specific form this influence may take is suggested by the various metaphors that are used for possession experiences. The spirit may strike, ride, invade, inhabit, or marry the possessed person. What is most relevant for a discussion of the relationship between spirit possession and religious healing, however, is that the possessing spirit is often believed to be responsible both for making people ill and for making them well.

The set of beliefs and practices associated with spirit possession in any given culture constitutes a spirit idiom or language that provides people with a means for self-articulation and a vehicle for making statements to others about themselves and their experiences. The spirits that possess people—whether they be gods, demons, saints, or ancestors—are the most important component of any spirit idiom. Spirits are the dominant symbols (Turner 1967), the organizing metaphors (Fernandez 1971) through which people interpret their world, and as such they

---

[6] I have slightly broadened Vincent Crapanzano's (1977:7) definition of possession to include states or conditions other than altered states of consciousness in order to incorporate nontrance phenomena such as illness into the definition of possession.

refer to many different kinds of experiences. At the social level spirits
may represent significant others in the lives of the possessed; they may
also stand for important community values or for the entire community
itself. At the psychological level spirits may stand for a variety of feelings, desires, and behavorial attributes. They may serve as role
models, or as a kind of external superego. Finally, at the physiological
level spirits may be held responsible for pain, symptoms of illness, and
other physical problems.

The relationships between people and the spirits who possess them
are thus metaphors for people's social, psychological, and physiological
conditions. A positive relationship with a spirit is generally an expression of harmonious and well-ordered social relationships, an integrated
personality, and physical health, while a negative relationship is conversely an expression of social and psychological conflict, alienation,
and illness. Spirits are, therefore, polysemic symbols that integrate or
synthesize in a religious idiom social, psychological, and physical experiences. In this way they serve as the "symbolic bridge" that unites
the different aspects of human experience and plays a crucial role in the
process of religious healing.

It is important to emphasize that the idiom of spirit possession is a
cultural idiom through which idiosyncratic individual experience is expressed in a belief system that is shared by others. As Crapanzano
(1977:10, 12) points out, "spirit possession is an unquestioned given"
in the world of the believer; the spirits themselves are "consensually
validated and ritually confirmed existents exterior to the individual."
For this reason spirit possession does not in and of itself constitute deviance or pathology. Similarly the possessed cannot simply be given a
psychiatric diagnosis and labeled hysterical, neurotic, psychotic, or
schizophrenic (Crapanzano 1977:13-14). In fact, people who are seriously disturbed are generally *not* able to express or resolve their idiosyncratic problems through the cultural symbols provided by the idiom
of spirit possession, and they often fail to become fully accepted members of the ritual group. For the majority of people who *are* able to
participate fully in these rituals spirit possession is an adaptive response
through which they are able to resolve social and psychological problems in a widely accepted, and sometimes well-respected, cultural
idiom.

By participating in possession rituals people enter into relationships
with spirit others and through these relationships dramatize in a public

context the problem or conflict they are experiencing. Because spirits are part of the culturally constructed reality of the possessed, the ritual performances that enact the conflicts of the possessed often have significant effects on the social relationships, the psychological condition, and even the physical health of the possessed. Spirits, then, are powerful symbolic representations of important aspects of the reality of the possessed that can reorder disturbed social relations, reintegrate fragmented personalities, and heal illnesses from which the possessed suffer.

When an illness, misfortune, or other form of suffering is attributed to a spiritual being, a diagnosis is made that employs a spiritual idiom to interpret the negatively defined condition. In this way the locus of the problem is situated outside the individual, and responsibility is attributed to an external spiritual agent. Any feelings of guilt that the possessed may harbor are thus alleviated, a process that may in itself be of therapeutic benefit.

The use of a spirit idiom to interpret illness or suffering also renders an inchoate experience more specific and concrete. The spirit idiom structures or defines a problematic experience by establishing a set of metaphors between a sacred or cosmological reality, on the one hand, and a psychosocial or physical reality, on the other. In the case of illnesses involving somatization, a diagnosis of spirit possession involves a second-order interpretation. Psychosocial problems that were initially "translated" and expressed metaphorically in a somatic idiom are "translated" again and expressed in a spirit idiom. The three idioms are structurally parallel; they are homologous or isomorphic expressions in different cultural domains of a negatively defined condition. The possession experience parallels the psychosocial aspects of the illness experience, whether they were somatized or not. Socially sanctioned trance behavior interpreted as spirit possession takes the place of stigmatized or deviant behavior interpreted as illness.

The diagnostic process, then, is fundamentally interpretive. Symptoms of illness are given new meaning; they become signs of possession. This process may be therapeutically effective not only because it gives concrete form to previous inchoate experience and removes responsibility for suffering but also because it expresses the problems people face in a spirit idiom that provides specific procedures for resolving the problems believed to have been caused by the spirits involved.

The establishment of a metaphoric relationship between people's relationship to a possessing spirit, on the one hand, and their psychosocial or physical condition, on the other, does not in and of itself constitute healing. People are still in a negatively defined condition requiring some kind of action or intervention to move them toward a more positive state. If the possessing spirit is essentially evil, the therapeutic process usually involves exorcism. In cases where the possessing spirit is essentially moral, however, the goal of therapy is the conversion of the spirit from a malevolent to a benevolent being. The spirit who punished the possessed by causing illness or suffering must be transformed into a spirit who forgives the possessed, supports them, and restores them to a state of health.

The development of a positive relationship with a possessing spirit generally requires a long process of learning to be possessed. Often the new relationship the possessed enjoy with a spirit is a permanent one; it may even lead to a new profession or career. The development of a new relationship with a spirit other is usually the crucial step in bringing about the significant changes in people's social, psychological, and even physiological realities that constitute healing. The idiom of spirit possession, as Crapanzano (1977:19) suggests, "provides a powerful rhetorical strategy for the definition of self and world . . . a strategy whose motivation lies outside human control but requires human redress."

As people "learn to be possessed" (Crapanzano 1977:15) and become regular participants in possession rituals, changes also take place in the nature of their possession behavior. Early in the course of therapy people's behavior when possessed bears remarkable similarities to symptoms of illness; possession is defined negatively as a form of suffering or punishment caused by the spirit. As the relationship between the possessed and the spirit is transformed, the nature of the possession behavior often changes dramatically. It occurs more regularly, at more appropriate times, and involves more patterned, socially acceptable behavior. These changes are attributed to the new relationship the possessed enjoy with the spirit, a relationship in which the possessed are forgiven, blessed, or somehow supported by the spirit. The crucial element in this new relationship is the access the possessed gain to the positive supernatural power of the possessing spirit.

People who are healed through spirit possession in this way become identified with a spirit who embodies precisely the qualities that the possessed lack and seek to acquire. The possessed are powerless, isolated, and ill; the spirit represents power, the community, and health. By entering into a positive relationship with the spirit, the possessed are able to become the people they are not. The possessed are provided with a symbolic language that contrasts their present state of illness with an ideal state of health. The process of healing consists of movement from their present condition toward the ideal condition personified by the spirit (Kleinman 1980:368). This movement, which is the essence of the restructuring and transforming process of healing, is brought about by the organizing concept of the possessing spirit.

The establishment of a positive, permanent relationship with a spirit other, the goal of systems of religious healing involving trance and possession like the Anastenaria, may often bring about far-reaching changes in the social, psychological, and even physical condition of the possessed. As the relationship of the possessed to the spirit is transformed from a negative to a positive one, so the relationship between the possessed and everything the spirit stands for is similarly transformed. This process involves an identification with important cultural values and ideals that can restructure the social relationships of the possessed and reorganize their personalities. Thus the possessing spirit is an effective vehicle for both psychological and social transformation. As Moerman (1979) and Kleinman (1980) have shown, such transformations often bring about positive physiological changes as well. Developing a positive relationship with a spirit other is therefore a powerful metaphor for the healing of illness.

III

The Anastenaria

✢

THE RITUAL CYCLE OF
THE ANASTENARIA OF AYIA ELENI

THE VILLAGE of Ayia Eleni is located fifteen kilometers south of Serres, an important commercial center in the eastern part of Greek Macedonia with approximately forty thousand inhabitants. The Strymonas River flows nearby on its eighty-kilometer journey from the Bulgarian border to the Aegean Sea. It is the water of the Strymonas distributed through an elaborate irrigation network that is largely responsible for the high standard of living that the people of Ayia Eleni and the other villages of the Serres basin have come to enjoy.

In 1976 Ayia Eleni had a population of just over seven hundred people. They were farmers who grew sugar beets, clover, wheat, and tomatoes in the flat, fertile fields surrounding the village. Most men in the village owned tractors; a few had combines, baling machines, and huge, expensive new machines for harvesting sugar beets as well. Villagers also raised cows both for milk and for slaughter to supplement the income they earned from their fields.

Most of the houses in Ayia Eleni were old two-story brick buildings or more recently built, single-story cinder block structures. They were surrounded by elaborate fences that enclosed carefully maintained courtyards and gardens. A few of the poorer villagers still lived in old two-room mud-brick houses. Facing each other across one village square stood two coffeehouses, which also sold basic foodstuffs and supplies. Around the other square were clustered a restaurant, an elementary school, and a building that housed the offices of the secretary and the president of the village. A short distance away stood the village church—dedicated to the memory of Saints Constantine and Helen.

Ayia Eleni is composed of several different groups of people each living in a separate neighborhood. In 1976 the Kostilides, who arrived in Ayia Eleni in the 1920s as refugees from Kosti in eastern Thrace, made up about half the population of the village. They constituted by far the wealthiest and most politically powerful group in the village and were referred to by other people there as "Thracians," or simply as "refugees." The next largest group in the village, comprising almost a third of the population, consisted of people who had worked as serfs on the large Turkish estates that had existed in the area before the Turks left Macedonia early in the twentieth century. Adults were bilingual in Greek and Macedonian, while young people spoke only Greek, since the speaking of Macedonian has for a long time been actively discouraged by the Greek government. These people referred to themselves formally as "indigenous Macedonians," or more casually as "natives" or "locals" (*dopii*). Other villagers, however, often referred to them in a derogatory manner as "blacks" or "gypsies" on the grounds that many of them were somewhat dark-skinned. The Macedonians were the poorest and least powerful of the social groups in the village.[1] The rest of the population of Ayia Eleni consisted of a small group of refugees from what is now Turkish Thrace and several families from the Peleponnesos in southern Greece.

Ayia Eleni is known throughout Greece as one of the two places where the Anastenarides perform their spectacular firewalk at the festival of Saints Constantine and Helen on May 21.[2] Every year at this

---

[1] The existence of Macedonians in Greece is officially denied on the grounds that it might serve Bulgaria's unfulfilled irredentist claims to Greek Macedonia or lead to the formation of an independent Macedonian state. In formal discourse Macedonians are generally referred to as "Slavophone Hellenes." On the "Macedonian question" see Dakin (1966), Kofos (1964), and Zotiades (1954). In the Serres basin there are many villages of indigenous Macedonians, as well as several villages of sedentary Romany-speaking Gypsies.

[2] The name "Anastenaris" is usually thought to be derived from the word *anastenazo*, to sigh. It is said to refer to the cries and shouts of the possessed Anastenarides. The Anastenarides themselves, however, use the word *tsirizo*, to scream or shriek, to describe their utterances. It is more likely that the term "Anastenaris" is derived from *asthenis* (*astenis*, *astenaris*), a sick person, preceded by the pleonastic privative *an-*. The name *Asthenaria* is

time newspaper headlines read "Barefoot Anastenarides Dance on Fire Again," film clips of the firewalk appear on national television, and several thousand people travel to Ayia Eleni to witness the celebration of the Anastenaria. For the rest of the year Ayia Eleni receives little special attention from the outside world. The Anastenarides, however, are active year-round on important religious holidays and whenever someone who is suffering needs their help.

The ritual cycle of the Anastenaria of Ayia Eleni, which is closely tied to the ecclesiastical calendar of the Orthodox Church, begins on October 26, the festival of Saint Dimitrios and the traditional beginning of the new agricultural year.[3] In the past the leader of the Anastenarides, the president of the village, and several other men associated with the Anastenaria went from house to house collecting contributions for the purchase of a lamb to be sacrificed the following May. By 1975 the officers of the Folklore Society of Ayia Eleni, an organization founded in 1971 to preserve and promote the Anastenaria, had assumed this job.

On New Year's Eve, the eve of the festival of Saint Vasilios, the Anastenarides gather in the konaki.[4] In 1976 after Yavasis blessed the ayiasma, which had been cleaned the last Sunday in December, the Anastenarides returned to Yavasis' house for the cutting of the traditional Saint Basil's cake. Then the Anastenarides were possessed by Saint Constantine and danced.

The second most important festival of the ritual cycle of the Anastenaria begins on the eve of January 18, the festival of Saint Athanasios. After blessing the ayiasma again, the Anastenarides dance in the konaki. In 1976 at a signal from Yavasis, burning pieces of wood and coals were pulled from a small metal stove onto the floor of the konaki, which had been covered by a layer of hardened mud to protect the old

---

recorded from the thirteenth century as a contemptuous reference to the "sickly" appearance of a group of Vlachs and Bulgarians who were "possessed by demons" (Giorgakas 1945–46).

[3] The ecclesiastical calendar of the Orthodox Church is described by Ware (1963:304–310), the yearly ritual cycle in rural Greece by Megas (1963).

[4] The term konaki is derived from the Turkish *konak*, mansion or government house, and was used by Greeks living under Ottoman rule to refer to the building that housed the local administrative authorities. These authorities were referred to as the *dodekada*, or group of twelve, a term that is still sometimes used to refer to the Anastenarides collectively as a council of elders.

wooden floor. The Anastenarides then put out the fire by dancing on it with their bare feet. Over the next two days the Anastenarides visited all the houses of the village; they danced and entered the fire the next two evenings as well. On the third night of the festival a meal was served to the small group of villagers who had gathered at the konaki.

On the first Sunday after the festival of Saint Athanasios, Yavasis and several other men made a down payment on the lamb that was to be sacrificed on May 21. Yavasis incensed over the lamb and made the sign of the cross above its head with a simadi. In this way he "marked" (*simadepse*) the lamb as belonging to Saint Constantine. This lamb had to be black and male, and unlike other newborn lambs it was not weaned from its mother until it was taken to be sacrificed by the Anastenarides the following May.

On the eve of Clean Monday, the first day of Lent in the Orthodox Church, the Anastenarides gather at the konaki, where the younger Anastenarides kiss the hands of the older Anastenarides, asking their forgiveness and being forgiven in turn. In the same way on this evening young people throughout Greece traditionally ask the forgiveness of their parents, godparents, and other elders (Megas 1963:69).

Preparations for the festival of Saints Constantine and Helen begin early in May. The ayiasma is cleaned on May 2, the day the Orthodox Church celebrates the deposition of the relics of Saint Athanasios. In 1976, about a week before May 21 the Anastenarisses and other women involved with the Anastenaria came to the konaki to wash the simadia, which are often called "the clothes of the grandfather" (*ta rouha tou papou*), that is, the clothes of Saint Constantine. While the simadia were drying, a light meal was served to the ten or twelve women present.

After the festival of Saints Constantine and Helen the Anastenarides gathered again on the evening of July 27, 1976, the festival of Saint Pandeleimon, when an old Anastenarissa, a relative of the owner of the icon of Saint Pandeleimon, served a meal. During the first week in August the simadia were washed for a second time. Then on August 6, the festival of the Transfiguration of the Savior, another meal was served to the Anastenarides by a descendant of the man in whose house the icon of the Transfiguration of the Savior had originally been found. Afterward another meal was served at the konaki.

The final event in the yearly cycle of the Anastenaria is the festival of the Dormition of the Mother of God, which takes place on August

15. On this day in 1976 Anastenarides and Kostilides from Ayia Eleni and other villages, about fifty people in all, gathered at a small church in a neighborhood on the outskirts of Serres where a small group of Kostilides had settled in the 1920s. It was here that the icon of the Virgin Mary was kept. After the celebration of the liturgy a meal was served in a room adjoining the church. That evening at Yavasis' house in Ayia Eleni another meal was served, bringing to a close the yearly ritual cycle of the Anastenaria.

In 1976 there were about fifteen hundred Kostilides living in Greek Macedonia and approximately a hundred Anastenarides, over two-thirds of whom were women. Twenty-five Anastenarides (eighteen women and seven men) participated in the festival of Saints Constantine and Helen held in Ayia Eleni that year. In Ayia Eleni itself nine women and two men were generally considered to be Anastenarides because they regularly danced and walked on fire while possessed by Saint Constantine. Four very old women who had danced and performed the firewalk in the past were also considered Anastenarides. In addition there were four other villagers who had at one time been considered Anastenarides but who had withdrawn from the rite and were no longer considered Anastenarides by most Kostilides. Of these nineteen people, sixteen were Kostilides; the other three were women who were not Kostilides but who had married Kostilides.

Like Ayia Eleni, Langadas is known throughout Greece for the firewalking ritual of the Anastenarides. Langadas is a town of seven thousand people with several hotels and small factories located about twenty kilometers from Thessaloniki, the largest and most important city in northern Greece. The Anastenarides of Langadas enter the fire on all three nights of the festival of Saints Constantine and Helen, and on the morning of May 21 they sacrifice a young bull instead of a lamb. In Langadas there are two icons of Saints Constantine and Helen that were both brought from Kosti.

The Anastenaria has also been celebrated publicly, but intermittently and on a much smaller scale, in three other villages in Greek Macedonia: Mavrolefki, Meliki, and a village I call Limnohori. The Kostilides of Mavrolefki, near Drama, have two icons of Saints Constantine and Helen, one of which is said to be the oldest of all the icons of the Anastenarides; the other was made in the 1950s. The Kostilides of Meliki, near Verria, have one relatively new icon of Saints Constantine and Helen, while the Kostilides of Limnohori have two icons that they brought with them from Kosti, one of Saints Constantine and Helen and one of Saint Pandeleimon, the patron saint of healing.

In addition, a village I call Mesopotamo has a small community of Kostilides that has never publicly celebrated the Anastenaria because they fear the ridicule of their fellow villagers who are not Kostilides as well as the persecution of church authorities. The Kostilides of Mesopotamo have an icon of the Transfiguration of the Savior that they brought with them when they fled their homes in eastern Thrace. The Anastenarides of all these villages often gather privately, and if there is no celebration of the Anastenaria in their own village, they attend the festival of Saints Constantine and Helen in Ayia Eleni or Langadas.

An increasing number of Kostilides have recently been moving to Thessaloniki—as part of the general process of rural-urban migration that has been taking place in Greece over the past few decades. In 1977 the Anastenaria was celebrated there for the first time in the working-class neighborhood of Meteora. The celebration was organized by several Kostilides who were not on good terms with the Anastenarides of Langadas or Ayia Eleni. In 1986 the firewalk was still being performed in Thessaloniki by fifteen Anastenarides with the support of local government officials.[5]

RELIGIOUS CONTEXT:
SAINTS, ICONS, AND SUPERNATURAL POWER

Although the Anastenaria has repeatedly been denounced by officials of the Orthodox Church as a sacrilegious survival of pre-Christian idolatrous rites, the Anastenarides consider themselves Orthodox Christians and maintain that their participation in the Anastenaria is com-

[5] The earliest accounts of the Anastenaria are those of Slavejkoff (written in 1866 and summarized by Megas in 1961) and Hourmouziadis (written in 1873 and reprinted in 1961). Other valuable descriptions of the rite can be found in Kakouri (1963 and 1965), Megas (1961), Romaios (1944–45), and the series of articles by Papachristodoulou and others that appeared in the *Arhion tou Thrakikou Laografikou ke Glossikou Thisavrou* between 1934 and 1961. For more information on the Anastenaria of Ayia Eleni see Danforth (1978, 1979, and 1983). On the Anastenaria of Langadas see Christodoulou (1978), Makrakis (1982), and Mihail-Dede (1972–73 and 1978). Films on the Anastenaria have been made by Hadjipandazis (1972) and Haramis and Kakouri (1969).

pletely consistent with their Orthodox faith.[6] What is more, the Anastenaria as a symbolic system is firmly grounded in the religious beliefs and ritual practices of the Orthodox Church.

In the traditional world view of the Orthodox Christians of rural Greece nothing happens in the world that is not the will of God. A person who does God's will should be rewarded accordingly, while any misfortune that befalls a person who does not may be interpreted as divine punishment or retribution. Exceptions to this ideal (the suffering of a good person, for example) are explained by saying that God punishes those he loves or that God punishes innocent people to test their faith.

Both God and the saints of the Orthodox Church are identified with the spiritual power or *dinami* that is the source of all that is good in the world. The power of God and the saints to do good is closely related to the concept of "grace" (*hari*). A common expression in praise of a saint is "Great [is] his grace" (*Megali i hari tou*). In fact, Kostilides often referred to both the saints and their icons as "*hares*" (the plural of *hari*), as in the wish "May all the *hares* help you." One woman explained this usage by pointing out that it was the saints who "grace us with (*mas harizoun*) life and healing."

Another manifestation of the power of God in the Orthodox world view is the Holy Spirit (*To Ayio Pnevma*), a spiritual force through which God communicates with saints and with human beings, who each in turn have their own spirit, or *pnevma*, which is given by God. The pnevma, usually identified with the mind or the faculty of reason, is thought to control a person's behavior. People in Ayia Eleni often said that God and the saints communicated with their pnevma through visions and dreams.

The power of God and the saints, however, is also accessible to human beings in a variety of material forms. Of these, icons are by far the most important. The prominence of icons (painted wooden representations of God, Christ, the Virgin Mary, and the saints) is perhaps the most distinctive feature of Orthodox worship. These icons are a primary point of contact between the divine or spiritual realm and the

---

[6] The position of the Orthodox Church with regard to the Anastenaria is presented in the *Thriskeftiki ke Ithiki Egkiklopedia*, vol. 3:634–637.

human; they are material objects in which supernatural power and grace reside.

Although the power of a saint is present in all of his icons, some of these icons possess more of this power than others. As a result there are many miracle-working icons in Greece believed to possess a variety of supernatural abilities, one of the most dramatic of which is the ability to heal illness. People suffering from illnesses or other misfortunes, especially women, often make pilgrimages to churches, monasteries, or shrines where miracle-working icons are located in order to gain access to the supernatural power they possess.

These activities are part of a more general attempt to secure the beneficial effects of the supernatural power of God by establishing a personal relationship of mutual obligation with a particular saint. The saints of the Orthodox Church are spiritual beings who serve as intermediaries between human beings and God, and it is to them that people appeal when they find themselves in difficult circumstances. A vow or offering made to a saint is generally motivated by the belief that such a gift will induce, if not oblige, the saint to reciprocate by granting the favor (*hari*) a person seeks.[7]

Faith or belief (*pisti*) is one of the most important components of a person's relationship to a saint. Belief in a saint, belief in his power to do good and perform miracles, is a prerequisite for obtaining his help. Specific actions that testify to a person's faith are also considered to be a necessary part of establishing a mutually beneficial relationship with a saint. As Kostilides often said, "Faith is invisible. Faith without works is dead." In Greece religious observances that demonstrate faith are primarily the responsibility of women and include not only making pilgrimages, fulfilling vows, and mourning the dead but also caring for the family icons that are found in virtually all houses in rural Greece. Proper care of these icons, which are often valuable family heirlooms, involves cleaning and incensing them as well as lighting the olive-oil lamps that hang above them.[8]

The icons of Saints Constantine and Helen that the Anastenarides

---

[7] As Campbell (1964:341–346) points out, relationships between human beings and saints are very similar to social systems of patronage. Herzfeld (1985 and 1987) discusses the importance of reciprocity in Greek culture generally.

[8] For more on family icons see Friedl (1962:41), Hirschon (1981:83 and 1983:117), Pavlides and Hesser (1986), and Rushton (1983).

An icon of Saints Constantine and Helen draped with simadia and votive offerings (Photograph by Loring M. Danforth)

hold while they dance are believed to possess supernatural power and the ability to perform miracles. They consist of a linen cloth (*pani*) glued to a rectangular wooden board and covered with a thin layer of plaster on which the representations of the Saints are painted. If the surface of an icon becomes worn, or if an icon is damaged, it must be repainted. Several times when this has happened the Anastenarides have instructed an icon painter to remove the old cloth from the damaged icon, replace it with a new one, and then repaint the icon. Later the old cloth may be placed on a new piece of wood and painted to create a second icon. In this way the icons of the Anastenarides have increased in number since the arrival of the Kostilides in Greek Macedonia. In such cases both icons are "old" and are said to possess the supernatural power of Saints Constantine and Helen because they both contain some of the physical substance of the original icon. This is significant because the older an icon is the more power it is said to possess.

According to the Anastenarides each icon, as a particular manifestation of Saint Constantine, has a will of its own and can demand to be moved or repainted. In order to make its wishes known an icon can cause someone to suffer, often the person responsible for the icon's care. When the will of the icon is done, the person's suffering comes to an end.

The sense of reciprocal exchange and mutual obligation that generally characterizes relationships between saints and human beings in Greece is also central to the Anastenaria. People honor Saint Constantine with their faith and their actions; in return he helps them by bestowing on them the beneficial effects of his supernatural power. The two most important ways to demonstrate one's faith in Saint Constantine are to offer a vow to the Saint or to visit the konaki in one of the communities of Kostilides.

In addition to the usual vows offered to saints throughout Greece, certain vows are unique to the Anastenaria. People seeking the help of Saint Constantine may offer a lamb to be sacrificed to the Saint on May 21, or they may offer to serve a meal to the Anastenarides at the May and the January festivals. They may also offer to "serve the Saint" in some other way by attending the festivals of the Anastenarides and offering assistance of some kind (tending the fire or participating in the procession through the village, for example). People who fail to fulfill the vows they have made to the Saint may suffer as a result, for a vow is a debt or an obligation they owe the Saint, and, as Anastenarides often say, "the Saint wants his vow."

Anyone who serves Saint Constantine or offers him a gift is wished "May it be to your benefit! May it help you!" (*Voithia sas!*). This wish expresses the hope that the person who served Saint Constantine will be helped by the Saint in return. In this way Saint Constantine and those who believe in him are linked in a positive relationship of mutual reciprocity. The more people there are who believe in the Saint, the more miracles he will perform; and the more miracles he performs, the more people will believe in him. The inverse of this is also true, however. Anyone who displeases Saint Constantine by expressing a lack of faith in his power will be punished. This type of negative relationship can be transformed into a positive one, punishment can be transformed into help, if a person repents, seeks forgiveness, and begins to believe in and serve the Saint.

The idea that saints are able to help people as a result of the supernatural power they possess is a common one in Greece. The Anastenarides, however, say that just as the saints acquire power from God, so the Anastenarides acquire power from Saint Constantine. This power comes to them when they are possessed by the Saint and dance. It is this power that enables them to walk on fire, to "know" things other people do not know, and to diagnose the cause of other people's suffering, illness, and misfortune. Just as the saints mediate the relationship between God and human beings, rendering the supernatural power of God more accessible to people, so the Anastenarides mediate the relationship between the saints and human beings, rendering this supernatural power even more accessible. [9]

The Anastenaria, then, can be seen as an elaborate system of exchange between Saint Constantine, on the one hand, and human beings, particularly the Kostilides and the people of Ayia Eleni, on the other. During the processions of the Anastenaria people give money and offerings of raisins and chickpeas to Saint Constantine through the Anastenarides. At the conclusion of the festivals the Anastenarides, acting on behalf of the Saint, distribute the raisins and chickpeas to all those present in the konaki. In the same way the people of Ayia Eleni give money to Saint Constantine for the purchase of a lamb to be sacrificed on May 21. After the sacrifice a small piece of meat is given to each family in the village. By virtue of their association with Saint Constantine these offerings are said to partake of his supernatural power and be "good" for the people who receive them. [10]

[9] One Anastenaris, for example, told Mihail-Dede (1972–73:82): "As human beings we men can't go directly to God. . . . The Saints are representatives of God, and the Anastenarides are representatives of the Saints."

[10] I have encountered a similar attitude toward the taking of communion throughout Greece. A person who has just received communion is also wished "*Voithia sas!*"

MEDICAL CONTEXT: DOCTORS,
NERVES, AND "SUFFERING FROM THE SAINT"

In rural Greece sickness is generally considered to be an indication of weakness and vulnerability. The social stigma attached to any serious illness, especially any form of mental illness, may even make it difficult for a person with a family history of such illness to marry well. It is not surprising, therefore, that a family often goes to great lengths to prevent other people from learning the exact nature of any serious illness afflicting one of its members.[11]

Since 1949 and the conclusion of the Greek Civil War, which followed World War II, Greek villagers have gradually gained more ready access to the biomedical health care system. By the mid 1970s physicians trained at Greek medical schools were being assigned by the Greek government to serve even remote rural areas, while specialists of all kinds, state hospitals, and private clinics could be found in most cities. As a result, the importance of traditional therapeutic systems declined, and the range of illnesses they were called upon to treat became increasingly restricted. Biomedical science, however, was certainly not the only socially sanctioned therapeutic system available to the people of rural Greece. Villagers who fell ill still made use of alternative therapeutic systems by consulting traditional healers or by visiting shrines and churches known for their ability to bring about miraculous cures.

Factors that influence the choice of a therapist in any specific illness episode include the nature of the symptoms, the suspected cause of the illness, and the accessibility and cost of the therapy. When a person's symptoms clearly point to a particular illness with a definite cause, a certain type of therapy is often indicated, but if the symptoms are more vague, then several different kinds of therapists may be consulted. For example, a headache may be caused by the evil eye, tight nerves, bad blood, or fever. Each etiology suggests a different therapy: spells to ward off the evil eye, tranquilizers to relax the nerves, cupping to remove the bad blood, or aspirin to reduce the fever. If the therapy indicated by the first diagnostic hunch proves ineffective, a new diagnosis is made and the appropriate therapy initiated. When a particular ther-

---

[11] See Blum and Blum (1965:63), du Boulay (1974:91), Herzfeld (1981a), and Safilios-Rothschild (1968:101).

apy finally does prove effective, the diagnosis is confirmed, and the illness is healed. In any given instance, therefore, the cause of an illness is only known for certain after it has been healed. Even then, when people recover after resorting to several different therapeutic systems, they are often unable or unwilling to attribute their return to health to any one source. They want to avoid offending any therapeutic agency, whether it be a saint, an aunt's secret spell, or a new antibiotic prescribed by a specialist.

Illnesses with naturalistic explanations constitute an important category in the system of medical knowledge that prevails in rural Greece. These illnesses are called "bodily" (*somatikes*) or "physical" (*fisioloyikes*) illnesses and are said to involve some malfunction or infirmity of the human organism, conceived of in mechanistic terms. Just as tractors break down when something goes wrong with their engine, so people become sick if their *organismos* is weakened or damaged. Illnesses of this sort are the proper concern of a physician or a traditional healer (*praktikos*), both of whom are skilled in the use of various techniques and substances that can restore a malfunctioning organismos to its former state of health.

There are also many illnesses that people do not attribute to naturalistic causes and that cannot be healed with the drugs of a physician or the herbal teas or compresses of a praktikos. These illnesses fall into two general categories, those whose treatment involves spells or magic, on the one hand, and those whose treatment is more explicitly religious in nature and is sanctioned by the Orthodox Church, on the other. Perhaps the most important illness in the former category is the "evil eye," which is held responsible for a wide range of physical symptoms and other misfortunes and which is treated by various divinatory practices and spells invoking the healing power of Christ and the Virgin Mary.[12] Mediums and sorcerers may also be consulted, particularly if an illness or problem is attributed to a personal enemy or to a rejected lover.

In other cases people are said to be suffering from illnesses caused by God or the devil. If God is believed to have sent an illness in order to punish or test a person, or if the devil has possessed someone, doctors and drugs are thought to be useless; religious healing offers the only

[12] Herzfeld (1981a, 1984a, and 1986) has made an important contribution, both ethnographic and theoretical, to the study of the "evil eye."

hope. People in this situation, as well as people suffering from serious illnesses that have not responded to other forms of treatment, often go on pilgrimages, make offerings and pray to miracle-working icons, drink holy water, buy amulets, and receive the blessings of priests and monks. In short, they take advantage of all the means at the disposal of the Orthodox Church in their efforts to regain their health.

If in the end all forms of therapy prove ineffective and a person dies, the consensus is generally that it was the will of God. The following couplet vividly captures the ineffectiveness of various therapeutic systems in the face of the inevitability of death.

> Στου Χάρου τις λαβωματιές βοτάνια δε χωράνε,
> Ούτε γιατροί γιατρεύουνε, ούτε Άγιοι βοηθάνε.

In the wounds of Haros herbs have no place,
Doctors do not heal, even Saints cannot help.

Within the general category of illnesses with naturalistic explanations the illness commonly referred to as *nevrika* (from *nevra* meaning "nerves") is particularly interesting. Nevrika is said to involve a weakness or malfunctioning of the nervous system, which is understood as a network of nerves spreading throughout the body and controlling bodily movements and sensations. In relatively mild cases common symptoms of nevrika include headache, chest pain, rapid heartbeat, trembling, dizzy spells, fatigue, loss of appetite, inability to sleep, and lack of interest in work.

In more serious cases, however, symptoms of nevrika include temporary or partial paralysis, hallucinations, incoherent speech, or any unusual or uncontrolled behavior regarded as deviant. A person exhibiting such behavior is said to have experienced a "nervous attack" (*nevriki krisi*) or to have suffered a "nervous breakdown" (*nevrikos klonismos*). Other terms are also used to describe these more serious cases of nevrika: a person is suffering "psychologically" (*psiholoyika*) or "in the head" (*sto mialo*). In extreme cases a person is said to be "psychopathic" (*psihopathis*) or more colloquially "to have gone crazy" (*trelathike*).

Serious cases of nevrika thus occupy an ambiguous position with regard to the important distinction usually drawn between "physical" or "bodily" illnesses, on the one hand, and "psychological" illnesses, on the other. This ambiguity is also expressed in the various terms used to refer to the institutions where people suffering from serious cases of nevrika are placed. They are called neurological clinics, psychiatric clinics, or again, more colloquially, "madhouses" (*trelokomia*). This ambiguity is even replicated in the official title of the medical specialist who would be consulted in such cases—"neurologist-psychiatrist."[13]

It is clear, however, that significantly less social stigma is attached to a diagnosis of nevrika than to a diagnosis of psychological or psychiatric illness. People use the terms nevrika, neurologist, and neurological clinic euphemistically when talking about someone for whom they feel compassion or sympathy, someone they are related to or want to protect. Conversely they use terms suggesting a psychological or psychiatric disorder (and, in more extreme cases, terms suggesting craziness) when talking about someone with whom they feel little solidarity.

Kostilides, like villagers throughout Greece, recognize the close relationship between people's health and their emotional state. I was often told that the main cause of nevrika was worry, anxiety, distress, or depression, a range of emotions most frequently designated as *stenohoria*. The word *stenohoria*, which literally means "narrowness" or "lack of space," suggests the close association between images of confinement, on the one hand, and negative emotions and the illnesses these emotions are believed to cause, on the other. People who have a "closed" character or personality, people who are quiet, shy, and introverted, are said to be more likely to suffer from nevrika because they "collect" or "swallow" their emotions.

In the past Greek villagers suffering from headaches and dizzy spells, who couldn't eat, sleep, or work, consulted general practitioners only to be told that there was nothing "medically" or "physically" wrong with them. After consulting several doctors without seeing any improvement in their condition, they decided that "they were not for a doctor" and turned for help to one of the other therapeutic systems available to them. By the early 1960s, however, facilities for out-patient psychotherapy and specialists in the field of "neurology-psychiatry" had become more accessible to the people of rural Greece (Blum and Blum 1965:105 and Safilios-Rothschild 1968:111). At this time people who were not satisfied with the treatment they received from general practitioners were referred to one of these new specialists who told them that they were suffering from nevrika. Patients of these neu-

---

[13] By 1986 neurology and psychiatry had become separate fields of specialization in Greek medical schools.

rologist-psychiatrists, the vast majority of whom were women, were comforted and given assurances that their reaction to stress was quite normal. Then they were given a prescription for valium or some other tranquilizer.[14]

In addition to the illness categories, etiological theories, and therapeutic alternatives found generally throughout rural Greece, the Anastenaria provides the Kostilides of Greek Macedonia with another very powerful set of beliefs and practices with which to deal with a wide range of illness experiences. Whenever an illness or misfortune of any kind is thought to be caused by Saint Constantine, the people involved are said to be "suffering from those things" (i.e., the Anastenaria) or "suffering from the Saint." Kostilides believe that people who are suffering from the Saint cannot be healed by a physician because there is nothing wrong with their *organismos* for the physician to treat. In fact, Kostilides often say that a person who is suffering from the Saint is not "sick" (*arostos*) or has no "disease" (*asthenia*). Alternatively they may say that such a person "is sick without having a disease" (*ine arostos horis na ehi asthenia*), using a phrase that reveals a category distinction similar to that made by Kleinman between an illness and a disease.

In eastern Thrace prior to 1914, when biomedical treatment was virtually unavailable to Kostilides, the Anastenarides were consulted in practically all cases of illness and misfortune. "The Saints were our doctors then," people said. After the arrival of the Kostilides in Greek Macedonia as biomedical care became more available and more effective, the range of illnesses attributed to Saint Constantine and treated by the Anastenarides was gradually restricted to illnesses physicians found difficult to treat, such as mental disorders and illnesses associated with general life problems. In such cases Kostilides continued to recognize the Anastenaria as the only effective therapeutic system available. With easier access to neurologist-psychiatrists and psychiatric clinics, alternate diagnoses (particularly nevrika) became very com-

[14] Nevrika, like neurasthenia as described by Kleinman (1982 and 1986) in the contexts of contemporary China and turn-of-the-century America and Western Europe, is a form of somatization often associated with depression and other disorders that serves as a coping mechanism in many societies throughout the world where mental illness is highly stigmatized and forms of psychotherapy are unavailable. See Dunk (1985) for a discussion of nevra in the Greek community of Montreal.

mon, and biomedicine encroached even further on the therapeutic domain of the Anastenaria.

The diagnosis that a person is suffering from the Anastenaria is preferable to other diagnoses because of the stigma associated with mental illness, the tendency to mistrust doctors, and the great reluctance of people to be removed from their family and home in order to be hospitalized. This diagnosis is also preferable because strictly speaking "there is nothing wrong" with people who are suffering from the Saint; they are not "sick" at all. Therefore, their prognosis is excellent. If they simply heed the recommendations of the Anastenarides and obey the will of Saint Constantine, they will recover. When people do not recover, either they failed to carry out the instructions of the Anastenarides properly or the diagnosis was incorrect in the first place. In the case of long, complex, and eventually fatal illnesses that were initially diagnosed as caused by Saint Constantine, Kostilides say that the person suffered from the Anastenaria and was cured but then developed cancer or diabetes and died.

This does not mean that the diagnosis that someone is suffering from the Saint is desirable or even completely free from social stigma. The status of being an Anastenaris is definitely an ambivalent one. Although Anastenarides do enjoy a high degree of prestige and respect in the eyes of those who believe in the Anastenaria, nevertheless, even within the community of believers the Anastenaria is also associated with feelings of embarrassment and fear. Discussion of the rite is guarded: the Anastenaria is referred to as "those things," the Anastenarides as "those people," and the konaki as "that place."

Most Kostilides would prefer not to become involved with the Anastenaria. Even Anastenarides themselves would prefer that their children not participate in the rite. They acknowledge, however, that the matter is not in their hands; it is in the hands of Saint Constantine. Kostilides also recognize that many of the Anastenarides are not "serious" or "stable" people, and they know that no one becomes an Anastenarissa unless she has problems.

The stigma associated with becoming an Anastenaris is even greater in the wider community where many people do not believe in the rite. The Anastenarides are often accused by outsiders of being drunk, crazy, or involved in illicit sexual activities.[15] Many people dismiss out

[15] These accusations are grounded in the real behavioral similarities that exist between

of hand the claim that the Anastenarides are protected by Saint Constantine, arguing that the firewalk is performed in conjunction with the devil, that it involves some form of "black magic," or that it is just a trick requiring careful timing, confidence, and calloused feet.

There are certain symptoms that strongly suggest that a person is suffering from the Anastenaria. These include any unusual behavior involving fire; any obsessive or deviant behavior of a religious nature (such as persistent dreams or visions involving Saint Constantine or repeated visits to the konaki or the village church); as well as periods of unconsciousness, paralysis, uncontrolled urination, or other involuntary or unacceptable behavior. In addition, any of the symptoms associated with nevrika may also indicate that a person is suffering from the Saint. This overlap between the symptoms of nevrika and "suffering from the Saint" occasionally leads to conflict over which diagnosis is the correct one.

Nevrika is the more likely diagnosis if precipitating factors such as poverty, family problems, or the death of a close relative can be identified. If no such factors are present, or if treatment by a neurologist-psychiatrist proves ineffective, then the Anastenarides will probably be consulted. The diagnosis that a person is suffering from the Saint is strengthened if the person is a relative of an Anastenaris or a descendant of a person who originally found an icon of the Anastenarides. It is also strengthened if the person is known to have ridiculed the Anastenaria or insulted Saint Constantine in some way, or if the onset of the person's illness coincided with a ritual gathering of the Anastenarides.

In all these cases Saint Constantine is considered to be the primary cause of the person's suffering and the Anastenaria the only effective mode of therapy. It is the people who are suffering in this way who often become Anastenarides as they are healed. In cases involving physical illnesses or accidents, however, Saint Constantine is believed to be a secondary or indirect cause of people's suffering. Then other modes of therapy are employed concurrently with the Anastenaria.

A woman who suspects that her suffering is associated with the

---

being drunk, being crazy, and being sexually excited, on the one hand, and being possessed by Saint Constantine, on the other. All four of these conditions involve the loss of self-control in the face of some powerful force: alcohol, "craziness," sexual excitement, or Saint Constantine. On occasion the specific force responsible for certain behavior is sharply contested. Consider, for example, the ambiguity inherent in the description of a possessed Anastenaris as being "drunk . . . not from alcohol, from the Saint."

Anastenaria generally invites the Anastenarides to gather at her house
or at the konaki. If an Anastenarissa "knows" something, that is, if she
receives "enlightenment" from Saint Constantine, she dances briefly
and "shouts" some message to the woman who is ill. The possessed
Anastenarissa usually directs the sick woman to correct some ritual fault
or mistake (*sfalma*) that the sick woman has committed and that she
may or may not be aware of. For example, a woman may have deliberately insulted the Anastenaria, or unbeknownst to her, her grandmother may have made a vow to Saint Constantine that she was unable
to fulfill.

A sick woman who repents and promises to correct whatever sfalma
she has committed will be forgiven by the Saint and will be healed. If
no specific sfalma is identified, the woman may be told she is suffering
simply because Saint Constantine wants her to be his "servant" and
participate in the Anastenaria by performing some specific task. She
must then "offer" or "dedicate" herself to the Saint in order to regain
her health. People who do not recover after carrying out the will of the
Saint may assemble the Anastenarides again and seek another diagnosis
of the cause of their suffering. On occasion the Anastenarides say they
know nothing and suggest that the sick person is "not for the Anastenaria but for the doctors."

Any time during this diagnostic and therapeutic process people who
are ill may be "called" or "seized" by Saint Constantine, begin to
dance, and become Anastenarides. Crying, trembling, or fainting at a
ritual gathering of the Anastenarides is an indication that people are in
the process of becoming Anastenarides. At this point the leader of the
Anastenarides "marks" (*simadevi*) people by placing a simadi around
their neck or over their shoulders. The majority of Anastenarides begin
to dance when their own suffering is diagnosed as caused by Saint Constantine. There are some Anastenarides, however, who just suddenly
begin to dance in the konaki or simply run out of the crowd into the
fire. If people reject the diagnosis of the Anastenarides, refuse to carry
out their instructions, or resist the "call" of the Saint, then Saint Constantine will continue to make them suffer. Unlike someone who is
suffering from the Saint and has tried to comply with his will, such
people are held responsible for their suffering. While they did not
choose to be ill, they did choose to disobey the Saint.

Just as Saint Constantine has the power to cause people who have
committed a sfalma to fall ill, so he has the power to heal their illness

if they repent, correct their sfalma, and submit to his will by promising to believe in the Anastenaria and serve him faithfully. As the Anastenarides say, "Saint Constantine causes you pain, but then he heals it." The Saint is pleased when people acknowledge their sfalma and promise to correct it; he is pleased by a multitude of offerings and by a successful, well-attended festival. In turn he rewards people by giving them the power to dance and walk through fire without being burned, but above all he rewards them by healing their illnesses and restoring them to a state of health.

IV

*From Illness and
Suffering to Health
and Joy*

⁘

"THEN I DANCED WITH THE POWER OF THE SAINT AND WAS HEALED"

IN THE ANASTENARIA religious healing is brought about by the transformation of a person's relationship with Saint Constantine from a negative one involving illness and suffering to a positive one involving health and joy, a transformation that takes place when a person becomes an Anastenaris and acquires the supernatural power of the Saint. A person's relationship with Saint Constantine can, therefore, be seen as a powerful metaphor for the person's social, psychological, and physiological condition. The Anastenaria provides people who are in a weak, vulnerable, or subordinate position with a spirit idiom that they can use to gain power over their lives and transform both themselves and their social world in a positive way.

The Anastenaria also provides people with a somatic idiom—dance—which is structurally parallel to this spirit idiom. Through dance possessed Anastenarides are able to express their social, psychological, and physiological condition and resolve the conflicts and tensions they face in their everyday lives. This dance is an alternative to the somatic idiom provided by the symptoms of illnesses such as nevrika; it is also a powerful expression of an Anastenarissa's relationship to Saint Constantine. As her relationship to the Saint changes, so does the nature of her dance. When Saint Constantine is punishing an Anastenarissa, she is ill, and she suffers when she dances. When she transforms her relationship to the Saint, she is healed, and she dances with power and joy. Thus the figure of Saint Constantine and the dance of the possessed Anastenarides are two of the most powerful symbolic forms in the therapeutic system of the Anastenaria.

Saint Constantine is identified with Constantine the Great, the first Roman Emperor to profess Christianity and the person largely responsible for the development of the Roman Empire into a Christian state. As a claimant to the throne, Constantine invaded Italy in 312. According to Eusebius, Constantine's victory over his rival Maxentius at the battle of the Milvian Bridge was preceded by a vision in which Constantine saw a cross of light in the sky bearing the inscription "In this sign conquer!"

In 324 Constantine became sole ruler of the Roman Empire and later dedicated Constantinople, formerly Byzantium, as the Empire's new eastern capital. Constantine was baptized shortly before his death in 337, having been an effective military leader and a supporter of Christianity throughout his reign. In later Greek Orthodox tradition Constantine is regarded as the founder of the Byzantine Empire and the defender and savior of the Christian religion. Helen, his mother, who has also been canonized by the Orthodox Church, is credited with the discovery of the True Cross during a pilgrimage to the Holy Land.[1]

In the context of the Anastenaria the figures of Constantine and Helen take on additional significance. Constantine's military victory, his miraculous vision, and his conversion to Christianity serve as models for the possession of the Anastenarides and their miraculous victories over illness and fire. Similarly Helen's discovery of the True Cross is a model for the Anastenarides' discovery of their own icons long ago in eastern Thrace.

The importance of Saints Constantine and Helen for the Anastenarides is apparent in the many stories Kostilides tell about the origin of the firewalk. According to one account, a long time ago the church of Saints Constantine and Helen in Kosti caught fire. As the church

---

[1] For more on the life of Constantine see Barnes (1984).

burned, cries were heard from among the flames; the icons were calling out to be saved. Some people ran into the burning church to rescue them, and neither the icons nor the people who saved them were burned. The Anastenarides commemorate this miracle every year on May 21 by walking through fire themselves.

Whenever people told me this account of the origin of the Anastenaria, they pointed out some specific historical association of the event with Saint Constantine himself. One Kostilis, for example, said that the church that burned down had been built by Saint Constantine. Another said that the church caught fire in the destruction that followed Saint Constantine's defeat of the Turks. A third said, "It was the soldiers of Saint Constantine who entered the fire and saved the icons. That's why the Anastenarides go into the fire today; they are the soldiers of the Saint."

According to another story, the firewalk of the Anastenarides celebrates a miraculous act of firewalking performed by Constantine himself when the city of Constantinople fell to the Turks in 1453.

> Helen and her son Constantine found the True Cross in Jerusalem and brought it back to Constantinople. They had it in the palace when the Turks were laying siege to the city. The Turks lit a huge fire all around the city walls. Constantine climbed up onto the walls and saw the flames; then he returned to the palace and brought out the True Cross. Holding the True Cross in his hands he stepped into the fire. Wherever he walked, he put the fire out, so he left behind a path where there weren't any flames. That way all the Christians left the city, and no one was burned.

Just as Constantine and the True Cross helped the Christians escape the besieged city of Constantinople and saved them from destruction by fire and death at the hands of the Turks, so the supernatural power of Saint Constantine and the icons of the Anastenarides protect people from fire and heal their illnesses.

Another account of the origin of the Anastenaria establishes a link between the miraculous vision of Constantine, the firewalk of the Anastenarides, and the town of Kosti.

> Saint Constantine was a general; originally he was an unbeliever, but his mother Saint Helen was a very religious woman. One day Constantine was fighting his enemies, the infidels, in

Thrace near Kosti. He defeated them, and they fled. To block his pursuit his enemies lit a huge fire and burned down the forest. This was the fire that destroyed all the old villages around Kosti. Constantine stopped in front of the fire. What could he do? But then in the sky he saw the words "In this sign conquer!" That meant he could pass through the fire unharmed. It happened on May 21.

Here Saint Constantine's vision is interpreted as granting him and his followers the ability to walk through fire safely. Saint Constantine's victory over fire is associated with his victory over his enemies. Similarly the Anastenarides' victory over fire symbolizes their victory over illness and other misfortunes. What is significant in all these narratives is that the origin of the Anastenaria is situated in the wider context of Greek history. In this way the local traditions of the Kostilides are linked with the historical traditions of the Byzantine Empire and the Orthodox Church.

Saint Constantine has meaning for Kostilides on a more personal level as well. Anastenarides often told me about dreams they had in which Saint Constantine appeared to them as an army officer, a policeman, or a doctor. He is a male figure of power and authority who is loved and respected but who is feared as well. I often heard him referred to as "the master" or "the boss" (*afendiko*) and as "the head of the family" (*nikokiris*).

The Anastenarides sometimes referred to themselves as "the children of Saint Constantine," as in the following verses, which were occasionally sung by possessed Anastenarides as they danced.

Του Κωσταντίνου τα παιδιά δεξιά συγκεντρωμένα,
Κι ο Κωσταντίνος τα ρωτά, σιγά τα ομιλάει:
"Πάρτε, παιδιά μ', το λίβανο και το σταυρό σας κάντε."

The children of Constantine all gathered together on his right.
Constantine questions them; he speaks to them softly.
"Take the incense, my children, and make the sign of the cross."

Several Anastenarides told me that they felt at times like Saint Constantine was a father to them. In fact, the term most commonly used to refer to Saint Constantine is *papous*, meaning grandfather, ancestor, or old man. One Kostilis told me that a *papous* was simply an "old father" (*palios pateras*). The plural, *papoudes*, is also used to refer to all the icons of the Anastenarides and to all the saints more generally.[2]

For female Anastenarides Saint Constantine is also a symbolic representation of a husband. When a woman becomes an Anastenarissa and each time she dances, she is symbolically married to the Saint. The conceptualization of the relationship between possessing spirit and possessed worshiper as one of marriage is quite common and is found in rituals involving trance and possession throughout the world. The sexually suggestive nature of possession dances and the orgasmic nature of the pleasure and release they provide have also been widely noted.[3]

In the case of the Anastenaria this relationship of marriage is expressed most clearly through the exchange of simadia. These large red kerchiefs, many of which were brought with the icons of the Anastenarides from Kosti, were originally given as offerings to Saint Constantine and are kept with the icons in the konaki. They are said to possess the supernatural power of the Saint and to be effective in healing illnesses that are attributed to him. A person who is suffering from the Saint may be given a simadi to keep for forty days. Similarly when an Anastenarissa is possessed by Saint Constantine for the first time, a simadi is placed on her shoulder or around her neck to indicate that she has been "offered" to the Saint and that she now "belongs" to him. From then on every time she dances, she is given a simadi to hold for the duration of her dance. In the context of the Anastenaria, then, these simadia symbolize the relationship between Saint Constantine and the possessed Anastenarides.

In eastern Thrace these same red kerchiefs were exchanged by the bride and groom at engagement ceremonies. In this context, as in the Anastenaria, these kerchiefs were referred to as simadia (marks or signs) or as *amanetia* (tokens or pledges). They symbolized the relationship that was being established between husband and wife. On formal occasions men wore these simadia at their waist folded over a purple cummerbund. The secular use of kerchiefs to wrap things up or tie them together makes them particularly appropriate symbols for the union or bond that is established between two people involved in a ceremonial exchange (Kaloyeropoulou 1973:216).

[2] Friedl (1962:78) reports that the people of Vasilika referred affectionately to God as "the grandfather above" (*o papous apano*).

[3] See Bourguignon (1976b:22), Crapanzano (1973:146), Kennedy (1967:192), Lewis (1971:59–64), and Obeyesekere (1981:33 and 40).

The simadia around her neck are "signs" that a new Anastenarissa has been "offered" to the Saint (Photograph by Loring M. Danforth)

I occasionally heard joking references to the similarities between the "marking" of the new Anastenarissa and the "marking" of the lamb to be sacrificed to Saint Constantine. In addition, the proud beauty of the lamb was compared to that of a bride on her wedding day. This complex series of images links the young bride, the sacrificial lamb, and the new Anastenarissa. When a woman becomes an Anastenarissa, she is offered to the Saint like the lamb; she is symbolically married to him as well.

The relationship between an Anastenarissa and Saint Constantine can therefore be seen as a metaphor involving a kind of transference, in which the Saint comes to stand for important men in the Anastenarissa's life. Saint Constantine also serves as a vehicle for articulating important aspects of an individual's psychological condition. He can be seen as the counterpart, in a spirit idiom, of what would be called the superego or the conscience in a psychological idiom. Groping for the right words to explain why Mihalis Kitsos had returned suddenly from Serres to complete an important job associated with the Anastenaria, a woman told me, "It was his conscience. His conscience made him come back." Just then another woman interrupted, saying: "No! No! Tell him it was the Saint that made him do it." On another occasion a woman who felt she had suffered because she and her husband had failed to fulfill a vow to sacrifice a lamb told me: "When we finally did sacrifice the lamb, a weight left me. I was released from that obligation; my conscience was lightened."[4]

The Anastenaria, then, provides people with a framework for interpreting and dealing with guilt and other emotions in a socially acceptable manner. Saint Constantine is a powerful symbol that stands for many aspects of the psychological and social reality of the Kostilides. He embodies important cultural ideals and in many ways serves as a role model for the Kostilides. It is the figure of Saint Constantine that structures the trance experience of the Anastenarides, and it is by transforming their relationship to him that people are moved from a state of illness and suffering to a state of health and joy.

---

[4] On the hypocognition of guilt and the interpretation of it as illness or spirit possession see Levy (1984:219) and Obeyesekere (1981:70). On the relationship between "conscience" and "custom" or "sense of social responsibility" in Greece see Herzfeld (1980a:346–347 and 1985:239–240 and 287).

THE DANCE of the possessed Anastenarides, which is an expression at the somatic level of the relationship they have with Saint Constantine, plays an important part in structuring their trance experience. Just as the long-term goal of the therapeutic process of the Anastenaria, which is realized over the course of the entire career of an Anastenaris, is the transformation of illness into health, so the short-term goal of the ritual, which is realized over the course of one dance session, is the transformation of a negative trance experience into a positive one. What began as a dance expressing anxiety and tension becomes a dance that expresses the acquisition of supernatural power.

When Anastenarides dance, people say that Saint Constantine has "seized" or "called" them. Initially the trance experiences of many Anastenarides are extremely difficult. They say that Saint Constantine is punishing or torturing them; they report feelings of dizziness and tightness in their chest and throat. As one Anastenaris told me, "At that time anxiety (*stenohoria*) grips me; a trembling seizes me. Something threatens me." When Anastenarides are possessed in this way, they say they feel conflict; they are upset; they are having troubles. They beat themselves, and they break down. In such cases the dance of the Anastenarides consists of wild, violent, and spasmodic movements. If an Anastenarissa writhes or twists in her seat, for example, people say that she is "dancing sitting down" (*horevi kathisti*).

Occasionally Saint Constantine is said to strike or slap an Anastenaris. Yavasis told me that when Thodoros Yannas collapsed on the floor of the konaki on May 21, 1976, the Saint had struck him down because he'd stayed home to work in his fields the previous evening instead of coming to the konaki to do the work of the Saint. Yavasis compared what happened to Thodoros with what happened to Peter when he denied Christ three times:

> The Bible says that when Peter heard the cock crow, he "wept bitterly." That's the slap. It's the emotion, the distress, that Peter felt. That can make you dizzy or sick; it can keep you from sleeping. At that moment you understand your mistake and you repent. That's what happened to Judas, too. He betrayed Christ and then hung himself.

When an Anastenarissa is experiencing a difficult trance, other Anastenarides try to ease her suffering by helping her achieve a transition to a more satisfying trance experience. Gradually she begins to dance more comfortably, standing upright and moving her feet in regular dance steps. The crucial point in this transformation occurs when the dancing Anastenarissa is given an icon or simadi of Saints Constantine and Helen, which she holds for the remainder of the dance. It is at this point that the Anastenarissa most dramatically receives the supernatural power of Saint Constantine, which is responsible for the transformation of a dance of anxiety and suffering into a dance of power and joy. In the words of one Anastenarissa, "It is impossible for you to understand how much an Anastenarissa suffers until she takes the icon in her hands. Then she dances satisfied and pleased" (Kavakopoulos 1956:283). This is the point at which an Anastenaris is truly said to be "dancing with the power of the Saint."[5]

The dance of the Anastenarides is a uniquely sacred version of the traditional Thracian folk dance known as the kerchief dance (*mandilatos horos*). Throughout rural Greece dancing plays an important part in the celebrations that accompany joyful occasions such as baptisms, weddings, and village festivals. Several women in Ayia Eleni told me how eagerly they looked forward to the relatively infrequent occasions when they had the opportunity to dance. They described the feelings of excitement and enthusiasm that dance music aroused in them, as well as the release of tension that they experienced when they danced.

In contrast to these somewhat obvious associations of dance with feelings of joy, happiness, and catharsis, images of dance and dancing were also used by Kostilides to express conditions characterized by nervous tension, suffering, punishment, and unpleasant but obligatory activity. A man who was high-strung and irritable was said to be "dancing because of his nerves." Similarly, the shaking and trembling that may occur during periods of intense stress or anxiety were often referred to as dancing. A woman who argued frequently with her mother-in-law said, "After really bitter arguments with her I'd go and lie down, but my body would be shaking and trembling like a fish. It was as if my body were dancing." When a young child was slapped or struck by one of his parents as a form of discipline, he danced—that is, he jumped about, twisting and turning, trying to escape from his parent's grasp.

---

[5] This is also the point at which Crapanzano's (1977:19) insight that spirit possession involves the transformation of a negative metaphor into a positive metonym is most apt. The possessed—ill, powerless, and often female—become what they were not—healthy, powerful, and male.

The child's dance, usually referred to as "the dance of the rod" (*o horos tou ksilou*), is a response to the punishment of the parent, just as the early portion of the dance of the Anastenarides is a response to the punishment of Saint Constantine.

The verb "to dance" (*horevo*), when used transitively, may mean "to control" or "to manipulate." A strong-willed wife who dominated her weak and ineffectual husband was said to "dance him any way she pleased," that is, "she had him at her beck and call." In the same way Saint Constantine has complete control over the Anastenarides when he orders them to dance.

Kostilides also referred to the performance of an unpleasant but obligatory task as dancing. The proverb "if you join the dance, you will dance" implies that if you become involved with a certain group of people, then you must carry out the activity the group is engaged in. The phrase "I did it and I danced" was used by Kostilides to mean "I did it, and I paid the penalty," "I did it, and I suffered the consequences." It refers to something a person did that should not have been done. A woman's son, for example, became ill shortly after she stopped serving a meal to the Anastenarides at the festival of Saints Constantine and Helen. When her son had recovered and when she had begun serving the meal again, she referred to her decision to stop the meal by saying, "I did it, and I danced."

These examples suggest the ambivalent nature of dance in rural Greek culture. This ambivalence is the very quality by which the dance of the Anastenarides is able to transform one complex set of emotions into its opposite. Each time an Anastenaris is possessed, a dance expressive of anxiety and suffering is transformed into a dance expressive of joy and access to supernatural power. This transformation is brought about by the structuring process that the dance imposes on the intense emotional and physical outbursts that constitute negative trance experiences. At festivals of the Anastenarides wild, clumsy, and often violent behavior is structured according to rhythmic and kinesic patterns and is transformed into a dance of beauty and grace.

This transformation, which takes place over the course of a single dance and which reaches its climax when the Anastenarides take an icon or simadi of Saints Constantine and Helen into their hands, is structurally parallel to the transformation from a state of illness to a state of health that takes place over the course of the entire career of an Anastenaris. After their initial trance experiences, which are usually un-

Suffering from the Saint (Photograph by Loring M. Danforth)

pleasant, people who are becoming Anastenarides gradually begin to enter trance more easily and dance more freely; they learn to be possessed. The point at which a woman dances powerfully and well for the first time is the point at which people say she becomes an Anastenarissa. This is also the point at which she is likely to situate the healing of the illness that led to her involvement with the Anastenaria in the first place, saying: "Then I danced with the power of the Saint and was healed." Later she will be given a simadi by the leader of the Anastenarides to keep at home on her family icon shelf. This simadi symbolizes the fact that she has entered into a permanent relationship with Saint Constantine.

As long as an Anastenarissa continues to fulfill her ritual obligations to the Saint by participating regularly in the ritual gatherings of the Anastenarides, she will remain healthy. By believing in Saint Constantine and serving him with her actions she receives from him help and supernatural power. In this way what was originally an undesired calling or affliction is transformed into a highly valued vocation (Peters 1982:40). Just as the dance of a possessed Anastenaris is transformed from an expression of suffering to an expression of joy, so illness is transformed into health when a person becomes an Anastenaris and dances with the power of the Saint.[6]

POWER AND GENDER IN THE ANASTENARIA

The essential feature of the ritual therapy of the Anastenarides is the establishment of a proper relationship with Saint Constantine and the acquisition from him of supernatural power. The dance of the possessed Anastenarides is a symbolic language that actually creates the concrete, bodily experience of this power. Participation in the Anastenaria then *empowers* people. It enables them to restructure their problematic relationships with other people and in this way gain more control over their lives.[7]

---

[6] On the role of dance in systems of ritual therapy and on the anthropology of dance more generally see Hanna (1978, 1979), Royce (1977), and Spencer (1985).

[7] As McGuire has observed in her discussion of Pentecostal Catholics, systems of ritual therapy give people "an experience of being *empowered* to handle their world and to function in it more effectively" (1982:8; emphasis added).

This concept of empowerment is fundamental to an understanding of the therapeutic effectiveness of the Anastenaria. The people who become Anastenarides are generally speaking people who occupy a marginal or peripheral position in the community, people who occupy a subordinate position in their most important social relationships. More specifically, it is people from poor and politically unimportant families, people who are outsiders to the community in some way, and above all women, who are the main participants in the Anastenaria, as well as the main beneficiaries of the therapy it provides.

Throughout the world women are found in precisely these positions. Their lives are often characterized by subordination, powerlessness, and alienation, and they often experience a high incidence of mental illness.[8] It is not surprising, then, that throughout the world women figure prominently in rituals involving spirit possession and religious healing like the Anastenaria. Lewis has observed that in many cases spirit possession as illness is an experience "virtually restricted to women" (1971:30). While I would not want to overemphasize the involvement of women in such rites, I agree with Lewis's general point that rituals involving spirit possession may serve as a vehicle of protest for the politically impotent and provide an opportunity for the socially marginal to assert their rights, influence others, and gain some sense of power and control in their lives without challenging the legitimacy of the social order.[9]

The participation of women in the Anastenaria must therefore be understood in the context of the position of women in rural Greece in general and in the village of Ayia Eleni in particular. In rural Greece, as in many other parts of the world, women do not enjoy the prestige and the authority that men are accorded.[10] This leads to an asymmetrical relationship in the cultural evaluation of the sexes in which women are clearly subordinate to men (Rosaldo and Lamphere 1974:17). The vast majority of prestigious public roles that exist in rural Greek society

[8] See Carmen, Russo, and Miller (1981) and Kleinman (1982:123).

[9] On the involvement of women in spirit possession cults see also Broch (1985), Freed and Freed (1964), Lewis (1966 and 1971), Messing (1959), and Prince (1974).

[10] Dubisch (1986) and Macrakis and Allen (1983) contain important recent work on the position of women in Greek society. For earlier material see Campbell (1964:31–35, 263–304), du Boulay (1974:100–141), Friedl (1967), and Hirschon (1978, 1981). See Denich (1974) for the position of women in Balkan societies and Michaelson and Goldschmidt (1971) for women's roles in peasant societies generally.

are not available to women. Women are also denied access to many public places that are open to men and must show deference to men on public occasions. In short, men exercise culturally legitimated authority over women.

The marginal position of women in rural Greece is indicated by the fact that "feminine roles are organized around a single element, that is to say, the presence or the lack of a man. . . . Thus, socially as well as symbolically, a man is the vital validating factor of a woman's life" (du Boulay 1974:121). A woman's identity and her position in society are largely defined in terms of the men to whom she is related. Hirschon (1978:74) reports that even in an urban setting women are said to belong to the "weaker sex" and are thought to be "always inferior." While pointing out the complementarity of male and female roles, Hirschon also notes "the inequality of their status relationship," pointing specifically to the unchallenged notion of male superiority and the husband's position of authority over his wife.

The same authors who acknowledge the existence of a gender-based hierarchy in which women are subordinate to men are nevertheless quick to point out how misleading an exclusive focus on this official ideology can be. By contrasting "the appearances of prestige" with the "realities of power" (Friedl 1967), or by referring to the "myth of male dominance" (Rogers 1975:729), these authors point out the necessity of carefully examining the complex and varied systems through which gender roles are defined. Rogers (1985:66), for example, states that women "are not, in fact, as powerless as an exclusive focus on patterns of public deference to men would seem to indicate." The important interpretive task, then, is to go beyond an overly narrow study of formal political authority and investigate the specific ways women use the considerable power they do enjoy to influence or manage the men in their lives.

Among the Kostilides of Ayia Eleni the position of women is perhaps more marginal than it is in other areas of Greece because of the particular importance Kostilides place on agnatic kinship and because in communities of Kostilides residence after marriage is traditionally virilocal. As is generally true throughout Greece kinship among the Kostilides is reckoned bilaterally. There is, however, a definite emphasis placed on kinship in the male line, an emphasis that is most clearly expressed in the definition Kostilides give to the term *soi*, which in many other parts of Greece refers to a bilateral kindred.

As conceptualized by the Kostilides soi can best be translated (following Herzfeld 1985:52) as "patrigroup." Members of a soi share a common surname and are said to "have the same blood." Given the traditional preference for virilocal residence, the adult male members of a soi also live together in a block of houses or a neighborhood associated with that soi. One Kostilis told me, "We are related to people through the father and the mother, but we are soi with people only through the father." Other Kostilides attempted to explain this by saying, "The man is the soi," or "Blood is transmitted by the father."

The men and women of Ayia Eleni attributed the subordination of women to men to the fact that women are both physically and emotionally weaker than men. They said that women are unable to do the work men do and that they are more sensitive and less able to control their emotions than men. One man from Ayia Eleni told me that a woman's husband is her God and that "just as God protects man, so a husband protects his wife."

Women I talked with also stressed the confinement that is such a pervasive feature of the lives they lead. They described themselves as "shut in," "restricted," and "restrained." Their lives are focused on the private or domestic sphere, as opposed to the public sphere, which is associated primarily with male activities. A man, unlike a woman, can go out in the evening to relax and forget his troubles by drinking and talking with his friends. The confinement which women experience is said to contribute to the harmful buildup of anxiety and tension that is held responsible for nevrika, an illness known to afflict women far more frequently than men.

In public situations only the man of the family may properly play an active role. It is essential that the family, the social unit with respect to which public and private are defined, is represented to the outside world as a united whole—united, that is, *behind* the man of the family. Women who insist on playing the dominant public role in the family are sharply criticized because they bring humiliation and embarrassment upon themselves, their husbands, and their entire families.

Situations in which a family maintains the public appearance of male authority, while in private a wife is actually more assertive than her husband, are treated very differently. If a woman defers to her husband in public but is the moving force in the family in private, neither the husband, the wife, nor the family as a whole is exposed to criticism. Judging from my own observations and the comments of many Kostilides, both men and women, this is often the case. One woman from Ayia Eleni mentioned several families in which "the husband goes in front, but the wife gives the orders."

In androcentric communities like those of the Kostilides women are clearly subordinate to men and experience a variety of psychological and social conflicts that are often dealt with through involvement in spirit possession rituals like the Anastenaria. Through these rituals women seek to address the discrepancies that characterize the relationship between an official ideology of male dominance and a social reality in which women actually exercise a significant degree of power. Spirit possession, then, provides a context for the resolution of conflict often associated with gender roles and gender identity.

Through participation in the Anastenaria women have opportunities for the exercise of power that are not available to them in most secular contexts. In the Anastenaria, as in the case of other religious activities such as pilgrimages to shrines, attendance at church, and the performance of death rituals, women are able to assume influential public roles in a socially acceptable manner. Caraveli (1986:178) has shown how mourning constitutes a "sphere of aesthetic, religious, and social interaction" in which women "undergo emotional catharsis, and reinforce their individual identity and group membership." This statement applies equally well to the Anastenaria. In addition, participation in the Anastenaria, like the performance of death rituals, offers women opportunities for developing friendships with other women and experiencing a sense of female solidarity.

In an analysis of women's friendships in rural Greece Kennedy (1986:130,135) refers to the "transformative quality" of these relationships as well as the "psychologically empowering" effect they have on the women who enter into them. Kennedy argues that "women's friendships are both a powerful coping mechanism and a unique expression of special energies that are not adapted to the dominant culture" (127). While the Anastenaria provides women with a religious context in which to develop close friendships, it also provides them with a unique opportunity to act as males, in public, and with an authority that would ordinarily be restricted to men. In the Anastenaria women are able to act as men because they have acquired the supernatural power of Saint Constantine.

Although the ritual gatherings of the Anastenarides at the konaki and the firewalk itself are very public events, women by virtue of their status as Anastenarisses are deferred to by all those present who are not Anastenarides, including men. On one occasion, for example, a young Anastenarissa entered the konaki, greeted the icons of Saints Constantine and Helen, and then looked around for a seat. At that point an elderly man stood up, kissed her hand, and offered her his seat. Deference that would regularly be shown by a woman toward a man was here shown by a man toward a woman.

The dancing of the possessed Anastenarides also illustrates the fact that Anastenarisses are able to engage in what would on other occasions be considered male behavior. In the context of the Anastenaria the kerchief dance is performed individually rather than in a line as it is on other occasions such as baptisms and weddings. Several elderly Kostilides told me that in the past only men ever danced individually. The one exception to this was the dance of the possessed Anastenarisses, who were able to dance as men because they were dancing "with the power of the Saint."

Although women have more recently begun to dance individually at village festivals, baptisms, and weddings, the dancing of a possessed Anastenarissa involves flamboyant, demonstrative, even flirtatious behavior that is considered more appropriate for men. This dancing may become so intense that the Anastenarissa collapses exhausted and sweating profusely into the arms of other Anastenarides. This dance style contrasts sharply with the downcast gazes and modest steps of the line dances traditionally performed by women throughout rural Greece. As such it constitutes a public performance more characteristic of men than of women.

By far the most spectacular public performance in the ritual cycle of the Anastenaria is the firewalk itself. Most years it is attended by television crews, university professors, high government officials, and other visiting dignitaries. At the conclusion of the firewalk individual Anastenarisses are often interviewed by newspaper or television reporters while their husbands stand awkwardly in the background. Many of these uneducated village women enjoy the publicity and attention they receive as a result of their participation in the Anastenaria. In this way the Anastenaria clearly provides women with a unique opportunity to assume prestigious public roles that are normally available only to men. Women who become Anastenarisses are able to acquire greater power and higher status than they ever could if their activities remained restricted to the private sphere of home and family.

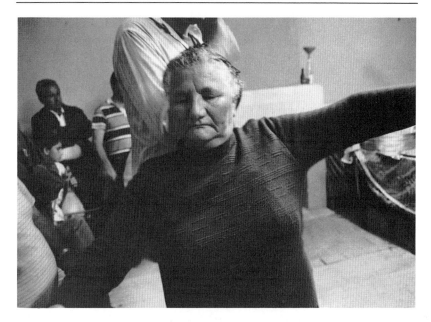

An Anastenarissa on the verge of collapse (Photograph by John Demos/Apeiron)

What distinguishes Anastenarisses from other women is the fact that they are possessed by a male saint. This enables them to become what they are not. Anastenarisses become symbolically male and gain substantial power because their words and deeds are endowed with the culturally legitimated and legitimating authority of Saint Constantine. For example, at a public meeting in the konaki an elderly Anastenarissa interrupted a man who was discussing some past conflict in an inappropriate manner by shouting, "No! No! No!" The next day I asked her if she had been angry at the man. No, she said, she hadn't been angry; she hadn't spoken on her own. The words had come to her from Saint Constantine. They weren't an expression of her anger—if they had been, she would have controlled herself. As a woman she couldn't say anything at a meeting like that. It was the Saint's anger, and the Saint's anger cannot be controlled.

Participation in the Anastenaria is not, however, restricted exclusively to women. Men who are poor and who do not enjoy much status or prestige within the community also become involved with the Anastenaria. Being possessed by Saint Constantine, or actually becoming the leader of the Anastenarides, provides an opportunity for such men to enjoy a degree of public status and prestige that they are not usually accorded. Nevertheless, as a religious ritual the Anastenaria still belongs to the world of women.

Of the relatively few male Anastenarides who danced in Ayia Eleni in 1976 several were *sogambri*, that is, men who married uxorilocally, in spite of the strong preference shown by Kostilides for virilocal residence. At marriage a man traditionally moved into a house built for him and his wife by his father adjacent to his father's house. If a man's father could not afford to build him a house, then he and his wife would live with his parents until a house could be built. The youngest son usually remained in his father's house, which he ultimately inherited after his parents' death.

A man would only become a sogambros and marry into the household of his wife if he were from a poor family that could not provide him with a house of his own. As Friedl (1962:65) and du Boulay (1974:126) have observed, and as Kostilides have caustically confirmed, there is a definite social stigma attached to being a sogambros.[11] On several occasions I heard a sogambros compared to a *nifi* (a bride, daughter-in-law, or brother's wife; the female counterpart of a gambros). For example, a woman once said to her husband's brother, a man who had married as a sogambros into another village, "You're a sogambros and I'm a nifi. We're both outsiders (*kseni*)." Another woman teased a sogambros by saying: "You're a nifi like me."

The social status of a sogambros is structurally parallel to that of a nifi. Both are marginal or peripheral outsiders whose only social status is derived from their spouse's family. A sogambros is forced into a position of subordination to his parents-in-law, a position more frequently occupied by women. By becoming an Anastenaris, a sogambros, or any other poor, politically powerless man, gains access to the supernatural power of Saint Constantine and comes to enjoy a new sense of respect and prestige.

In spite of the fact that the Anastenaria enhances the power of the otherwise fairly marginal and powerless people who become involved with it, the dominant ideology of the Anastenaria is not one of empowerment but somewhat paradoxically one of submission. Anastenarides

[11] The term sogambros refers literally to a *gambros* who is living "inside" or "within" (*[e]so*) his wife's household. A gambros is a groom, son-in-law, sister's husband, or, more generally, a man who has married a member of a person's family or other social group.

only acquire the power of Saint Constantine if they submit to his will. When the Saint "seizes" or "calls" people, they must "obey." Anastenarides are the "slaves" of the Saint, and their behavior must conform to public expectations of what the will of the Saint is. Only in this way will their words and deeds be accepted as a legitimate expression of his will; only then will their status as Anastenarides be fully acknowledged. If Anastenarides are accused of acting on their own, doing what they want rather than what the Saint wants, their status as Anastenarides will be denied, and they will be deprived of the power that status conveys.

The Anastenaria does empower people. It provides them with access to the supernatural power of Saint Constantine, which enables them to participate in the dramatic public performance of the firewalk, to speak forcefully in public meetings dealing with ritual matters, and to restructure their important social relationships to their advantage. According to the Anastenarides themselves, however, the power they enjoy is not their own; it comes from Saint Constantine. The culturally legitimate authority with which they act is that of the Saint. It is only under his aegis that they exercise their power. Paradoxically, then, the Anastenarides gain power only through submission.[12]

The Anastenaria, while allowing fairly powerless people to achieve a high degree of status and prestige, nevertheless replicates the structural principles of the wider society of which it is a part. Female power, as real and as important as it is, is ultimately subordinate to male authority as expressed through the will of Saint Constantine. Commenting on the position of women in rural Greece generally du Boulay (1986:167) says that "whatever the stature of woman in this society, and it is undeniably great, it is achieved always on the condition that she remain loyal to her husband and obedient to the spiritual principle embodied in him." Saint Constantine is, among other things, the personification of this spiritual principle of male authority.

SONGS OF LOSS AND SEPARATION

The songs associated with the Anastenaria deal with various social and psychological conflicts that play an important part in the lives of the

---

[12] Csordas (1983:353) notes a similar paradox when he observes that the rhetorical message of the laying on of hands among Catholic Pentecostals is one of "submission to divine Authority as well as reception of divine Power." See also Bourguignon (1976b:40).

Kostilides. They evoke the pain and anxiety associated with loss and separation as well as the anger and frustration often generated by difficult family relationships. Kostilides associate these songs with the past and with their old homeland of Kosti in eastern Thrace, and they are deeply moved when they hear them sung at the festivals of the Anastenaria.

The songs that are sung during celebrations of the Anastenaria constitute what Lévi-Strauss (1967:195) has called "a social myth." They provide a symbolic language for the expression of the painful emotions associated with the problems that in many cases lead to people's initial involvement with the Anastenaria. In addition, some of these songs also present a solution to the problems they pose. In this way they serve both as models *of* negatively valued and anxiety laden situations associated with illness and as models *for* more positively valued situations associated with health. These songs depict the process of empowerment and transformation that participation in the Anastenaria brings about. In this way they depict the healing process itself. What is more, by listening to these songs, by singing them, and by identifying with the characters and situations they present, people are rhetorically moved from a position of weakness and suffering to a position of power and joy.

The songs of the Anastenaria are traditional folk songs that have been sung for hundreds of years in rural areas throughout the Greek world.[13] Whenever the Anastenarides gather in the konaki the first song they sing is "Pa se prasino livadi" (In a Green Meadow). It is an arhythmic "song of the table" performed by the lira player. While it is being sung, most people sit quietly, sadly, and listen; some people cry.

> Πα σε πράσινο λειβάδι
> Κάνταν τρία παλληκάρια
> Με σπαθιά και με δοξάρια.
> Την ημέρα τρων και πίνουν
> Και το βράδυ κάνουν βίγκλα.
> Κάνουν βίγκλα και βιγκλίζουν,

[13] Ioannou (1970), Petropoulos (1958, 1959), and Politis (1978) contain important collections of modern Greek folksongs. Beaton (1980) presents a valuable analysis of these songs from a literary point of view. On the songs of the Anastenaria more specifically see Megas (1961) and Mihail-Dede (1978). The texts of the songs presented here were recorded during fieldwork in Ayia Eleni; the translations are my own.

Και βιγκλίζουν τους διαβάτες
Να βρουν Τούρκο να σκοτώσουν
Και Ρωμιό να ξεσκλαβώσουν.
Πιάσαν ένα γέρον Τούρκο
Πό 'σερνε μια Ρωμιοπούλα.
"Καλημέρα παλληκάρια."
"Βρε καλώς τον γέρον Τούρκο.
Δε με λες, βρε γέρον Τούρκο,
Πού τη βρήκες τη Ρωμιέσσα;"
"Δώκα γρόσια και την πήρα,
Και φλουριά την αγοράσα."
"Βρε γελά σας, παλληκάρια.
Πε το σπίτι μου με πήρε.
Το παιδί μου μέσ' στην κούνια,
Το ψωμί μου μέσ' στο φούρνο.

In a green meadow
Sit three young men
With swords and bows.
By day they eat and drink,
And at night they stand guard.
They stand guard,
And they check the passers-by
To find a Turk to kill
Or a Greek to set free.
They captured an old Turk
Who had a young Greek woman with him.
"Good morning, young men."
"Welcome, old Turk.
Tell me, old Turk,
Where did you find that young Greek woman?"
"I paid piasters, and I took her;
I paid florins, and I bought her."
"He's lying to you, young men.
He took me from my home.
My child was in the cradle;
My bread was in the oven."

This song deals with the abduction of a young Greek woman by a Turk. The figure of the Turk, a non-Christian and the traditional enemy of the Greeks, is a powerful symbol of otherness, of all that is foreign and hostile. For a Greek woman abduction by a Turk would represent a frightening separation from her home, her family, and the entire community of Greek Christians. Several people I spoke with referred to this song as "a song of slavery" and added that it made them think of the four hundred years of Turkish rule during which Greece was part of the Ottoman Empire. Other Kostilides said the song reminded them of the past, their dead relatives, and their experience as refugees. When they listened to it, they felt grief, sorrow, and a longing for their lost homeland.

Loss and separation are clearly the dominant themes of this song. In spite of the intervention of the three Greek men, the young woman's desire to return to her home and family is not fulfilled. The conflict between this desire and her capture by the Turk is unresolved. The song, however, does leave open the possibility that she will be rescued. Her rescue would involve a transformation from a position of subordination to a wicked Turk, a *ksenos* (that is, an outsider, stranger, or foreigner), to a position of subordination to good fellow Greeks. In the rescue that is held out as a possibility, the subordination of women to men would be maintained but would be transformed from a negative to a positive experience.

More specifically I suggest that this song expresses the anxiety experienced by women at marriage in a society where postmarital residence is traditionally virilocal. Being abducted by a Turk may symbolize a woman's sudden and complete separation from her family of origin at marriage.[14] Initially a woman's husband is a ksenos to her, just as she is kseni in her family of marriage. With time, however, a transformation takes place. Just as the three Greek men will rescue the woman of the song from the Turk, so a woman's husband will become a figure of protection and solidarity as she transfers her loyalty from her family of origin to her family of marriage. One young woman describing her feelings at the time of her wedding several years earlier

---

[14] The emotional force of this separation is emphasized in the metaphors linking marriage and death that can be found in Greek funeral laments. See Alexiou (1974:120–122), Danforth (1982:74–90), and Herzfeld (1981b).

said, "You make yourself a kseni; you become alienated (*apoksenonese*). But now," she added sadly, "my parents' house feels as foreign (kseno) to me, as my husband's did when I first got married."

In the context of the symbolic structure of the Anastenaria the rescue of the young Greek woman from the Turk by the three Greek men represents the transformation in the relationship between a woman and Saint Constantine that takes place when she becomes an Anastenarissa, dances, and is healed. At this point Saint Constantine, who is symbolically identified with the husband of the Anastenarissa, is transformed from a figure who punishes and causes suffering into one who protects and heals. The association between Saint Constantine and the three Greek men in the song is sometimes made explicit. One Anastenarissa told me that the three Greek men were "soldiers of the Saint." According to another Kostilis they were three saints or three icons of the Anastenarides who "had the power to save the Christians, the whole world, from slavery" (Megas 1961:481). This song, then, expresses both the anxiety and the hope associated with a desired movement from a condition of confinement and alienation to a condition of freedom and belonging.

At ritual gatherings of the Anastenarides "Pa se prasino livadi" is often sung in its entirety. However, if an Anastenaris shows signs of being possessed or actually begins to dance, the lira player begins to play another song known as "Kato ston Ai Thodoro (Down at [the Church of] Saint Thodoros), which is sung to a much faster, more rhythmic tune known as "the tune of the dance" or "the tune of the fire." At this point the lira player is joined by the drummer. As other Anastenarides are possessed by Saint Constantine and begin to dance and sing, the rhythm quickens and grows stronger.[15]

Κάτω στον Άη Θόδωρο, στον Άγιο Παντελέημον,
Πανεγυρίτσι γίνοντου τ' Αγιού του Κωσταντίνου.
Το πανεγύρ' ήνταν πολύ κι ο κόσμος ήνταν λίγος.
Δώδεκα δίπλες ο χορός, δεκαοχτώ μπαλαίστρες.
Κι ο λύκος άρπαξε παιδί πε μέσ' απ' τη μπαλαίστρα.
Και το παιδί ήνταν μικρό, τη μάννα του φωνάζει:

---

[15] Frequently the lira player will begin "Kato ston Ai Thodoro" before he is finished with "Pa se prasino livadi" and sing verses from the two songs alternately in a suggestive, almost teasing, manner.

"Θυμάσαι που κοσκίνισες τη στάχτη αντίς αλεύρι
Και τσίριζες και φώναζες: 'Πάρτε καθάριο αλεύρι';
Θυμάσαι όταν σκότωσες το φίδι στην πεζούλα
Και τσίριζες και φώναζες: 'Πάρτε θαλάσσιο ψάρι';"

Down at the church of Saint Thodoros, at the church of Saint
    Pandeleimon,
A festival of Saint Constantine was taking place.
The festival was large, but the crowd was small.
There were twelve rows of dancers and eighteen wrestling arenas.[16]
A wolf seized a child from inside the wrestling arena.
The child was young and called out to his mother:
"Do you remember when you sifted ashes instead of flour
And shouted: 'Buy pure flour!'?
Do you remember when you killed the snake on the sill
And shouted: 'Buy fish from the sea!'?"[17]

This song, which is usually only sung through line six when it is
performed at the konaki of Ayia Eleni, also deals with the themes of
loss and separation. A young child, who in line 6 of some versions of
the song is identified as "young Kostandinos," is dramatically taken
away from his mother by a wolf. Comments by Kostilides and examination of versions of this song from other parts of Greece suggest that
the seizure of the child occurs in fulfillment of an oath uttered by the
mother that took the form "May a wolf devour my only child if I have
put ashes in the flour!" The mother is punished for the adulteration of
food by the loss of her son. Because the exchange of food in rural
Greece is such an important expression of the maintenance of proper
social relationships, the adulteration of food is a powerful symbol of
the complete negation of these relationships.

Several Kostilides told me that the wolf was sent by Saint Constantine to punish the mother for her sins. Others said that the wolf was
really Saint Constantine himself, who miraculously made off with the
child in fulfillment of the mother's oath, because an oath, like an offering to the Saint, is a promise that must be fulfilled. Saint Constantine

---

[16] Wrestling contests were traditional events at village festivals in many parts of Greece.
[17] For other versions of this song see Akadimia Athinon (1962:390–392) and Schortsanitis and Haritos (1959:536–537).

here seems to act as an agent of social control sternly enforcing the maintenance of proper moral standards.

Some Kostilides offered an interpretation of this song that bears even more directly on the Anastenaria. They said that the wrestling arena mentioned in the song was actually the site of the firewalk, which, in fact, is often referred to as the threshing floor (*aloni*), the place where wrestling contests traditionally take place in rural Greek folk songs. They also said that the image of the wolf seizing the child represented Saint Constantine as he possessed the child and made him dance on the fire. One Kostilis added that the Saint sent the wolf to punish the mother not only because she lied but also because she did not believe in the Anastenaria. This interpretation suggests that becoming an Anastenaris may be a form of punishment from Saint Constantine for some failure to maintain proper relationships with family members or other members of the community.

After "Kato ston Ai Thodoro" the music and the dancing continue. The lira player and some of the Anastenarides begin to sing the song known as "Mikrokostandinos" (Young Kostandinos).

Ο Κωσταντίνος ο μικρός, ο Μικροκωσταντίνος,
Μικρό ντον είχ' η μάννα ντου, μικρό ντ' αρραβωνιάζει,
Μικρό ντον ήρτε μήνυμα στο μπόλεμο να πάει.
Νύχτα σελλώνει τ' άλογο, νύχτα το καλιγώνει.
Βάν' ασημένια πέταλα, μαλαματένιες λόθρες.
Πήδηξε, καβαλλίκεψε σαν άξιο παλληκάρι.
Ώσπου να πει: "Έχετε γεια", σαράντα μίλια πάει.
Κι απάνω στα σαρανταδυό ψιλή φωνή ακούστη:
"Εσύ διαβαίνεις, Κωσταντή, κι εμένα πού μ' αφήνεις;"
"Πρώτα σ' αφήνω στο θεό κι ύστερα στους Άγιους,
Κι ύστερα κι όλο ύστερα στη 'στερινή μου μάννα."
"Τί να με κάνει ο θεός; Τί να με κάνουν οι Άγιοι;
Τί να με κάνει η μάννα σου χωρίς την αφεντιά σου;"
"Μάννα μου, ντη γκαλίτσα μου, μάννα μου, ντη γκαλή μου,
Γλυκό ντη δίνεις το πρωί, γλυκό το μεσημέρι,
Και το ηλιοβασίλεμα να στρώνεις να κοιμάται."
Μα 'κείν' η σκύλα η άνομη, οβρέσσας θυγατέρα,
Πα στο σκαμνί ντην έκατσε, κι αντρίκια ντην κουρεύει.
Μια γκούγκλα ντην εφόρεσε, ντη δίνει και ντουλιάγκα.
Ντη δίνει δέκα πρόβατα κι εκείνα ψωργιασμένα.

Ντη δίνει και τρία σκυλιά κι εκείνα λυσσασμένα.
Ντην παραγγέλνει στα γερά, γερά ντη συντυχαίνει:
"Θα πάεις 'πάνω στα βουνά τα αψηλοκορφάτα,
Που 'ναι τα κρύα τα νερά κι ο δροσερός ο ίσκιος.
Κι α δε ντα κάνεις εκατό, κι α δε ντα κάνεις χίλια,
Και τα σκυλιά 'βδομηνταδυό, στους κάμπους μην κατέβεις.
Σ' όλους τους πόρους πάνε ντα, σε όλους πότισέ ντα,
Και στο Γιορδάνη ποταμό μήν τύχει και τα πάεις,
Γιατ' έχει φίδια κι όχεντρες, θα ξέβουν να σε φάνε."
Παίρνει και πάει στα βουνά με δάκρυα φορτωμένη.
"Έλα Χριστέ και Παναγιά με το Μονογενή σου.
Εις το βουνό που βρίσκομαι να φτάσει η ευχή σου."
Γίνηκαν χίλια πρόβατα, χίλια και πεντακόσια,
Και τα σκυλιά 'βδομηνταδυό, στους κάμπους εκατέβη.
Σ' όλους τους πόρους πήγε ντα, σε όλους πότισέ ντα,
Και στο Γιορδάνη ποταμό πήγε και στάλισέ ντα.
Κι επέρασε κι ο Κωσταντής και τηνε χαιρετάει:
"Καλημερά σου, τσόμπανε." "Καλώς τον Κωσταντίνο."
"Τίνος είναι τα πρόβατα; Τίνος είναι τα γίδια;
Τίνος είναι και τα σκυλιά με το χρυσό γιορντάνι;"
"Του Κωσταντίνου του μικρού, του Μικροκωσταντίνου,
Μικρό ντον είχ' η μάννα ντου, μικρό ντ' αρραβωνιάζει,
Μικρό ντον ήρτε μήνυμα στο μπόλεμο να πάει."
Χτυπά το βάθιο ντου κλωτσιά, στη μάννα ντου πηγαίνει.
"Μάννα μ', πού 'ν' η γυναίκα μου, πού 'ναι κι η καλή μου;"
"Γυναίκα σου επέθανε εδώ και τρία χρόνια."
"Δείξε μου το μνήμα ντης να πάω να ντην κλάψω."
"Το μνήμα ντης χορτάριασε και γνωρισμό δεν έχει."
Από ντη μέσ' ντην άρπαξε, στο βάθιο ντου ντη βάζει.
Χτυπά το βάθιο ντου κλωτσιά, δυο κομμάτια γίνη.

Kostandinos the young, young Kostandinos,
His mother cared for him when he was young; he got engaged when
      he was young.
He was young when he was sent off to war.
At night he saddled his horse; at night he shod it.
He put on silver horseshoes and golden horseshoe nails.
He mounted his horse like a brave young man.
By the time he bid farewell, he'd gone forty miles.

When he'd gone forty-two miles, a shrill voice was heard:
"You're going away, Kostandis, but where are you leaving me?"
"I'm leaving you first in the care of God and then in the care of the
    Saints,
And last but not least I'm leaving you in the care of my mother."
"What will God do with me? What will the Saints do with me?
What will your mother do with me, while you're away?"
"Take care of my wife, mother! Take care of my wife!
Feed her sweets in the morning, feed her sweets at noon;
And in the evening make her bed so she can lie down and go to
    sleep."
But that wicked bitch! That daughter of a Jew!
She sat her on a stool and cut off her hair so she'd look like a man.
She put a shepherd's hat on her and gave her a shepherd's staff.
Then she gave her ten mangy sheep
And three rabid dogs.
She gave her strict orders; she spoke to her harshly:
"Go up into the mountains where the peaks are high,
The water is cold, and the shade is cool.
If the sheep don't multiply and number one hundred, if they don't
    multiply and number one thousand,
And if the dogs don't multiply and number seventy-two, then don't
    come back down to the plains.
Take them and water them at all the watering places,
But don't take them to the Jordan River
Because it has snakes and vipers that will come out and eat you."
She went up into the mountains loaded down with tears.
"Christ and All Holy Virgin Mary with your only begotten Son,
May your blessing reach me here, high in the mountains."
Soon there were one thousand sheep, one thousand five hundred.
There were seventy-two dogs, and she went down to the plains.
She took them and watered them at all the watering places.
She took them to the Jordan River, and there she rested them.
Then Kostandinos passed by and greeted her:
"Good morning, shepherd." "Welcome, Kostandinos."
"Whose sheep are these? Whose goats are these?
Whose dogs are these with the golden collars?"
"They belong to Kostandinos the young, to young Kostandinos.

His mother cared for him when he was young; he got engaged when
    he was young.
He was young when he was sent off to war."
He gave his horse a kick and went to find his mother.
"Where is my wife, mother? Where is my wife?"
"Your wife died three years ago."
"Show me her grave so I can go and mourn her death."
"Her grave is covered with weeds and cannot be found."
He seized her by the waist and put her on his horse.
He gave his horse a kick, and she became two pieces."[18]

The relationships between husband and wife, mother and son, and
mother-in-law and daughter-in-law play a central role in this song.
Where postmarital residence is traditionally virilocal, as it is among
the Kostilides, the mother-in-law, daughter-in-law, and son or husband
usually live in close contact with one another. In such cases this trian-
gular set of relationships plays a central role in everyday family life.

Throughout rural Greece the relationship between mother-in-law
and daughter-in-law is a difficult one.[19] As might be expected, conflict
between women in this difficult relationship often arises over the
proper performance of household jobs, over the raising of children,
and over the management of household finances. During the early years
of her son's marriage a woman is in a position of unquestioned authority over her daughter-in-law. As many Kostilides told me: "The
mother-in-law is in charge. The mother-in-law holds the reins." A
daughter-in-law is subordinate to her mother-in-law because she is the
younger of the two and because she is a newcomer to the house. If a
daughter-in-law does not obey her mother-in-law and conflict arises,
the daughter-in-law is inevitably held responsible.

Young married women I spoke with stressed the difficulties they
encountered in their relationships with their mothers-in-law. They
were not respected; they could show no initiative; and they could not
act independently. Several women spoke of the embarrassment and

---

[18] For other versions of this song see Beaton (1980:13–34).

[19] See Campbell (1964:78), Danforth (1983:217–218), Doumanis (1983:34), du Boulay (1974:18, 155 and 1986:147), and Rushton (1983:66). On the figure of the "evil
mother-in-law" in Greek folklore see Ioannou (1970:65–71 and 1975:175–178). For
comparable material in other cultures see Michaelson and Goldschmidt (1971:335–343),
Nichter (1981a:380), and Simić (1983:73).

shame they felt in front of their mothers-in-law. They were afraid that if their performance as housewives was found wanting, their mothers-in-law would gossip about them with other village women. One woman in this situation told me she felt like a prisoner in her own house.

To make matters worse, a daughter-in-law is a kseni in her family of marriage. She and her mother-in-law live together in the same household as mother and daughter do, but their relationship can never be that of mother and daughter. According to a well-known proverb: "A daughter-in-law can never become a daughter" (*I nifi kori de yinete*). The peripheral or marginal quality of the position of women in a village where residence after marriage is virilocal is also indicated by expressions such as: "A woman has no village" and "A daughter is just a guest."

The focus of the conflict between mother-in-law and daughter-in-law is most often the son or husband, for he has authority over both women by virtue of the fact that he is a man. Ideally a man should make sure that his mother treats his wife fairly and that his wife in turn takes care of his mother as she grows old. If a man must take sides, however, his sympathies must ultimately lie with his wife. Yet it is often very difficult for a man to discipline or even criticize his mother, especially during the first years of his marriage when his wife is in greatest need of his support. With both women trying to win the favor of the man through whom they are related, the balance of power in this conflict-laden relationship often depends on which woman is able to gain his support.

When a man fails to support his wife in her dealings with her mother-in-law, she finds herself in a very isolated and vulnerable position, and she may experience a great deal of tension and conflict in her relationships with members of her husband's family. A young woman in this position may become depressed, anxious, and unable to eat, sleep, or work. She may then be diagnosed as suffering from the Anastenaria, become an Anastenarissa herself, and regain her health.

Over time the balance of power in the relationship between mother-in-law and daughter-in-law shifts in favor of the daughter-in-law as a man's loyalty is gradually tranferred from his mother to his wife. The wife becomes more fully incorporated into her family of marriage when she becomes a mother and contributes children to her husband's soi. In addition, as the mother-in-law grows older and becomes less able to care for herself and her household, the daughter-in-law gains the upper hand. It is precisely this process that is the central theme of the "Mikrokostandinos" song.

All the Kostilides I spoke with identified the Kostandinos of this song with Saint Constantine. Invariably and emphatically they said that Mikrokostandinos was the Saint when he was young. In addition, most Anastenarides when discussing this song said that Saint Helen was the wife, not the mother, of Saint Constantine. Several people told me that Mikrokostandinos was Saint Constantine, the son of Saint Helen, and that the father of the Saint, the husband of Saint Helen, was Constantine the Great. For the Anastenarides, then, "Mikrokostandinos" is a song about Saint Constantine when he was young, his wife (usually identified with Saint Helen), and their conflict with Kostandinos' mother.[20]

The first few lines of this song suggest a concern for the individual life cycle and the problems of generational passage associated with it. Kostandinos' youth is emphasized, as is his dependence on his mother. His early engagement points to the impending break in his relationship with his mother, while his departure for war constitutes a crucial separation from his wife. The anxiety generated by this separation is indicated by the questions Kostandinos' wife asks after Kostandinos tries to comfort her by saying he will leave her in the care of God, the saints, and his "sweet mother." Kostandinos' wife is obviously worried about what will happen to her during her husband's absence because she has no security and no social identity other than that which she derives from her relationship with her husband.

In spite of his instructions to the contrary Kostandinos' mother treats her daughter-in-law in a most cruel fashion. By cutting her hair like a

---

[20] Roderick Beaton (1980:20) claims that with the exception of the name of the hero, none of the details of this song correspond to details of the Anastenaria: "The behavior of Kostantinos' mother in the song, and his treatment of her at the end, surely preclude any identification between her and Saint Helen. . . . As regards the equation of Kostantinos with the Christian saint, it seems to me that his final action in the song, that of murdering his mother, absolutely disqualifies him from this role." As the following analysis will show, Beaton has completely failed to understand this song and its relationship to the Anastenaria. On the identification of Mikrokostandinos with Saint Constantine see Mihail-Dede (1972–73:60). On the identification by the Anastenarides of Saint Helen with the wife of Saint Constantine see *Thriskeftiki ke Ithiki Egkiklopedia* (vol. 3: 636).

man's, dressing her like a shepherd, and sending her up to the mountains, Kostandinos' mother deprives her daughter-in-law of both her sexual and social identity. The daughter-in-law is no longer a woman, she is no longer Kostandinos' wife, and she is no longer a member of society. The opposition between mountains and plains, which figures prominently in this song, represents the opposition between the world of nature, on the one hand, and the social or cultural world, on the other. In some versions of this song the daughter-in-law is dressed like a monk, a figure that symbolizes a person who is outside of society and who will not leave any offspring. The rejection by Kostandinos' mother of her daughter-in-law is an egregious failure to maintain proper family ties.

The first eighteen verses of this song deal with the themes of loss, separation, and exclusion. This is the portion of the song that is regularly sung at gatherings of the Anastenarides in Ayia Eleni. In what follows the conflict between mother-in-law and daughter-in-law is dramatically resolved in favor of the daughter-in-law.

Kostandinos' wife is given a small number of mangy, rabid animals and told not to return from the mountains to the plains unless they multiply a hundred or a thousandfold. She is also told not to water the animals at the Jordan River because it has snakes and vipers that will come out and eat her. In another version of the song she is told that if she goes to the Jordan River she will find "snakes and vipers and pregnant wolves."

Kostandinos' wife goes off forlornly to the mountains where she prays for help to Christ and the Virgin Mary. Her prayers are answered when her flock multiplies a thousandfold, and she takes her animals down to the plains to the Jordan River where she meets her husband. Through divine intervention the animals of Kostandinos' wife are made healthy and fertile and multiply miraculously. It is this miracle of fertility that is responsible for the reentry of Kostandinos' wife into society and for her reunion with her husband.

The snakes, vipers, and pregnant wolves that lie in wait for Kostandinos' wife at the Jordan River are images of impregnation. It is almost as if Kostandinos' mother is warning her daughter-in-law that if she goes to the Jordan River she will become pregnant. In fact, young children in rural Greece are sometimes told that babies come from rivers, in much the same way that young children in the United States might be told that babies are brought by storks. Commenting on this portion of the song, one Anastenarissa said to me: "God protected Kostandinos' wife. Instead of finding snakes, she found her husband."

The reunion of Kostandinos and his wife represents the restoration of the proper relationship between husband and wife. That this restoration should be associated with images of fertility and reproduction is not surprising. Just as in the song the miracle of fertility and birth is a precondition for the return of Kostandinos' wife to the social world, so in everyday life it is a precondition for a woman's more complete incorporation into her husband's family.

Following this recognition scene Kostandinos returns home and asks his mother about his wife. His mother tells him that she has died. When Kostandinos asks where his wife's grave is, his mother replies that it is overgrown and cannot be found. This neglect of her daughter-in-law's grave is another example of the complete failure of Kostandinos' mother to fulfill her social obligations to her daughter-in-law. It serves to emphasize in a particularly dreadful way her total rejection of her daughter-in-law.[21] Kostandinos then punishes his mother for mistreating his wife by tying her to his horse and tearing her in half.

In the "Mikrokostandinos" song, then, the conflict between mother-in-law and daughter-in-law is resolved in favor of the daughter-in-law when she receives divine assistance and the support of her husband. Discussions with many young Anastenarisses suggest that they identify closely with the wife of Kostandinos. Thus the very conflict that has contributed to the illness of many Anastenarides is symbolically expressed and resolved in a song that is sung during their ritual gatherings.

In addition, both factors in the resolution of this conflict (divine assistance and the support of the husband Kostandinos) characterize the relationship between the possessed Anastenarides and Saint Constantine. In the context of ritual possession the source of the divine assistance that the Anastenarides receive is the Saint himself. It is from him that the Anastenarides receive the supernatural power that enables them to perform the firewalk unharmed. More importantly, however, it is through the beneficent power of Saint Constantine that their own illnesses are healed. The parallel between the plot of this song and the relationship that develops between the Anastenarides and Saint Con-

---

[21] For the importance of caring properly for the grave of a dead relative see Danforth (1982:117–127).

stantine is further emphasized by the fact that the Anastenarides, who often identify with the wife of Kostandinos in the song, are symbolically married to Saint Constantine when they become Anastenarides and each time they are possessed by him and dance.

During the course of the ritual therapy of the Anastenaria the conflict between a young woman and her mother-in-law is expressed and resolved at a symbolic level in the songs that accompany the dance of the possessed Anastenarides. As each young woman becomes an Anastenarissa and is healed, she receives divine assistance that consists of the supernatural support and protection of Saint Constantine, her spirit husband. A structurally parallel resolution of this same conflict, the very conflict that was at least partially responsible for her illness, takes place simultaneously at the social level as well. A woman's participation in the Anastenaria may actually restructure her family relationships in such a way as to resolve the conflicts present in her dealings with her mother-in-law. By becoming an Anastenarissa a woman gains the support of her husband, since he is forced to commit himself publicly to helping her regain her health.

A woman who is diagnosed as suffering from the Anastenaria is encouraged to attend the ritual gatherings of the Anastenarides in the konaki. If she begins to show signs of being possessed, she must become an Anastenarissa and dance in order to be healed. Because this is an extremely public act, a woman needs the permission of her husband in order to do so. If he grants his permission, she may dance in public, perform the firewalk, and be healed.

If a man refuses to give his wife permission to dance, she may writhe and twist in her seat. If she is not even allowed to go to the konaki, she may suffer at home. In either case her suffering may be interpreted as a form of punishment that Saint Constantine imposes on those who do not carry out his will. More importantly, though, if a woman is not allowed to dance, she may remain ill indefinitely.

There are many reasons why a man might not allow his wife to participate in the Anastenaria. He may not believe in the rite, or he may simply believe that her illness could be better treated by medical doctors. On the other hand, he may want to avoid the notoriety that surrounds a woman who becomes an Anastenarissa. If his wife continues to suffer, however, he may give in and allow her to dance. He must then attend a ritual gathering of the Anastenaria with his wife and formally give his permission for her to dance by saying: "May she be well, and may she dance" (*As yini kala, ky'as horepsi*). He must also be willing to contribute his time and money to whatever ritual activities and offerings the Saint may demand. In short, he must commit himself publicly to his wife's therapy and support her in her attempt to regain her health.

Thus a woman's participation in the Anastenaria may actually change the social relationships within her family of marriage. By changing her relationship with her husband, her participation in the rite changes the balance of power within her family in such a way as to resolve the conflict between her and her mother-in-law. Just as in the "Mikrokostandinos" song the wife of Kostandinos receives her husband's assistance, and just as the possessed Anastenarissa receives supernatural power from her spirit husband Saint Constantine, so a woman is able to enlist the support of her husband when she becomes involved with the Anastenaria. Through the symbolic resolution of conflict, together with a structurally parallel resolution of conflict at the social level, the Anastenaria often proves therapeutically effective in the treatment of a wide variety of illnesses.[22]

After singing the first part of the "Mikrokostandinos" song the lira player and some of the dancing Anastenarides often sing verses fifteen through seventeen of the following song generally known as "Daskala pou 'ne to pedi" (Teacher, Where Is My Child?).[23]

Ο Κωσταντίνος ο μικρός, ο Μικροκωσταντίνος,
Από μικρό στα γράμματα, μεγάλο στο σχολείο.
Τα σχόλασε ο δάσκαλος να παν να γεμάτισουν.
Βρίσκει τη μάννα τ' κι έπαιζε μ' έν' άξιο παλληκάρι.
"Έννοια σου, μάννα μ', έννοια σου, κι αν δεν το μαρτυρήσω.
Το βράδυ θά 'ρθει ο πατέρας μου και θα το 'μολογήσω."
"Τί είδες, βρε παλιόπαιδο, και τί θα μαρτυρήσεις;"

[22] This rather extended analysis of the "Mikrokostandinos" song and the relationships between mother-in-law, daughter-in-law, and son or husband unambiguously supports Wilson's refutation of Lewis's (1966 and 1971) view that spirit possession is an expression of some "war between the sexes." Wilson argues convincingly that spirit possession is often correlated "with social situations which regularly, though not necessarily, give rise to conflict, competition, tension, rivalry, or jealousy between members of the *same* sex rather than between members of opposite sexes" (1967:366; emphasis in the original).

[23] Although only a portion of this and the "Mikrokostandinos" song are actually sung at the Anastenaria of Ayia Eleni, many Kostilides are familiar with the complete plots of both songs.

Απ' τα μαλλιά τον άρπαξε, σαν πρόβατο το σφάζει.
Τον έπλυνε, τον αλάτισε, στο φούρνο τον πηγαίνει.
"Ψήσε, φούρναρη, το φαΐ, στ' αλάτι μην το βλέπεις."
Νά κι ο μπαμπάς του κι έρχεται απ' το έρημο κυνήγι.
"Γυναίκα, πού 'ναι το παιδί, πού 'ναι ο Κωσταντίνος;"
"Τον έλουσα, το χτένισα, και στο σχολειό τό 'στειλα."
Χτυπά το άλογο βιτσιά και στο σχολειό πηγαίνει.
"Δασκάλα, πού 'ναι το παιδί, πού 'ναι ο Κωσταντίνος;"
"Έχω τρεις μέρες να το δω και τρεις να το διαβάσω,
Κι αν δεν το δω και σήμερα το νου μου θε να χάσω."
Χτυπά το άλογο βιτσιά, πάλι στο σπίτι πάει.
"Γυναίκα, πού 'ναι το παιδί, πού 'ναι ο Κωσταντίνος;"
"Κάτσε να φας, κάτσε να πιεις, κι ο Κωσταντίνος θά 'ρθει."
Στρώνει τραπέζι ολόχρυσο με ασημένια πιάτα,
Και το φαΐ εμίλησε πε μέσ' από τα πιάτα:
"Αν είσαι λύκος φάγε με, σκύλος κατέλυσέ με.
Κι αν είσαι ο πατέρας μου, σκύψε και φίλησέ με."
Απ' τα μαλλιά την άρπαξε, στο μύλο την πηγαίνει.
"Άλεσε, μύλε, άλεσε ξανθές και μαυρομάτες,
Να βγάλω κόκκινο πίτερο να γράψω ένα γράμμα,
Για να το στείλω στο ντουνιά να τό 'χει ο κόσμος θάμα."

Kostandinos the young, young Kostandinos,
He learned to read and write when he was young; he went to school
  when he was older.
The teacher sent the children home for lunch,
And Kostandinos found his mother playing with a handsome young
  man.
"Watch out, mother! Watch out! I'll reveal what you have done.
In the evening my father will come home, and I'll tell him what I
  saw."
"What did you see, you little brat? And what will you tell him?"
She grabbed him by the hair and slaughtered him like a lamb.
She washed him, she salted him, and she took him to the oven.
"Baker, cook this food, but don't look at it too closely!"
And here is his father returning home from the lonely hunt.
"Wife, where is my child? Where is my Kostandinos?"
"I bathed him, I combed his hair, and I sent him to school."
He gave his horse a whipping and rode to the school.

"Teacher, where is my child? Where is my Kostandinos?"
"It's been three days since I saw him, three days since I gave him a
     lesson.
If I don't see him today, I'm going to lose my mind."
He gave his horse a whipping and rode back home again.
"Wife, where is my child? Where is my Kostandinos?"
"Sit down and eat! Sit down and drink! Kostandinos will come."
She prepared a feast with silver plates on a golden table,
And the food spoke right from the plates:
"If you're a wolf, eat me. If you're a dog, devour me.
But if you're my father, bend down and kiss me."
He grabbed her by the hair and took her to the mill.
"Grind, mill! Grind! Grind up women with blond hair and women
     with black eyes!
So I can have red bran to write a letter
To send to all mankind so the whole world will learn of the
     miracle."[24]

This song like "Mikrokostandinos" deals with the failure of women
to maintain proper social relationships with other members of their
family in the absence of men. While Kostandinos is away at school and
his father is out hunting, his mother commits adultery. When Kostandinos threatens to reveal her illicit affair to his father, she kills him. In
this way Kostandinos' mother completely rejects her ties to her husband, her son, and to her family of marriage in general.

Kostandinos' determination to tell his father about his mother's affair
demonstrates that his loyalty to his father takes precedence over his
loyalty to his mother. The great affection Kostandinos' father has for
his son is indicated by the immediate concern he shows for his son's
whereabouts when he returns home. The exchange between Kostandinos' father and his teacher in the only three lines of the song actually
sung by the Anastenarides of Ayia Eleni contains an expression of deep
anxiety over Kostandinos' disappearance. When Kostandinos' mother
cooks his body and serves it to his father to eat, she grossly perverts the
proper offering of food and totally denies her responsibilities as a wife
and mother.

A miracle then takes place in which Kostandinos speaks from among

[24] For other versions of this song see Akadimia Athinon (1962:368–371), Petropoulos
(1938–39:200), and Politis (1978:137–139).

the plates and reveals his mother's terrible deed. He contrasts the love that characterizes the father-son relationship with the evil, inhuman, and asocial qualities of a dog (the term used to describe the mother-in-law in the "Mikrokostandinos" song) and a wolf (the animal that stole the child in "Kato ston Ai Thodoro"). Finally Kostandinos' father kills his wife, grinds up her body at a mill, and writes a letter using her blood as ink so the whole world will learn of the miracle that has taken place. In other versions of the song the letter is explicitly written so that other women will learn the fate of Kostandinos' mother and not be tempted to commit the same heinous crimes.

At a festival of Saint Athanasios in Langadas I once heard this song sung in its entirety. As the Anastenarides sang the verses in which Kostandinos' mother cooks her son, an Anastenaris named Hristos shouted angrily, "She was a traitor! She cooked her son!" Later Hristos' wife, who was also an Anastenarissa, told me that Kostandinos' father had married a second time and that it was really Kostandinos' *stepmother* who had killed him, cooked him, and served him to his father. She added that she herself had been treated just as badly by *her* stepmother, who hadn't let her go to school, hadn't fed her well, and had beaten her frequently.

When I spoke with Hristos, I learned that his father had died when he was twelve years old. Then his mother, who was an Anastenarissa as well, remarried and had another son. After Hristos married he and his wife and their two sons lived with his mother and stepfather for thirteen years, but when Hristos' stepbrother married, Hristos' mother and stepfather forced Hristos and his family to move out of the main family house into two small run-down rooms in the back of the main house. Hristos' parents left their house and all their land to his stepbrother. This upset Hristos so much that he suffered a relapse of pneumonia and had to be admitted to a sanatorium. Hristos summed up the whole incident by saying, "My own mother threw me into the stable."

It is clear that "Daskala pou 'ne to pedi" speaks directly to the specific conflict-laden parent-child relationships that play an important part in the lives of Hristos, his wife, and many other Anastenarides, relationships that are particularly difficult when one parent has died and the other has remarried. Anastenarides who have experienced rejection or mistreatment at the hands of their parents or stepparents identify with Kostandinos, the son, whose horrible death at his mother's hands is avenged by divine intervention and the support of his father. When

they dance, the Anastenarides themselves are possessed by Saint Constantine, a father figure, from whom they acquire the supernatural
power with which they are able to walk on fire and be healed.

Constantine, the central figure in the songs of the Anastenaria and in
the entire ritual system, is a complex symbol with many biographical
reference points—father, husband, son, and self. Songs about him constitute a highly malleable symbolic idiom that is refracted through social experience and interpreted by individual Anastenarides in a variety
of ways. The songs of the Anastenaria, then, provide people with a
social myth with which to express and resolve the conflicts that are responsible at least in part for the illnesses that lead to their involvement
with the Anastenaria in the first place.

METAPHORS OF EMERGENCE

The Anastenaria, like all rituals of religious healing, transforms people
by moving them rhetorically from a negatively defined condition of
illness to a positively defined condition of health. Central to this rhetorical movement of transformation is an elaborate set of metaphors of
emergence, release, and opening up. During the therapeutic process
negative metaphors of obstruction and confinement are transformed
into positive metaphors of freedom and openness. By participating in
the Anastenaria a person emerges from a "closed" condition to an
"open" one.

As Hirschon (1978:76) has shown, the categories of "open" and
"closed" play an important part in Greek culture:

> In its ideal sense "opening" is an auspicious state; it is propi-
> tious and desired. "Closing" is associated with misfortune, it is
> unfavorable and, in its ideal sense, should be avoided. "Opening"
> is related to sets of positive notions regarding social life and soci-
> ability, while "closing" suggests an abhorred state of isolation and
> the absence of contact and association.

The symbolic categories of "open" and "closed" are central to any
discussion of the position of women in Greek society. Women's lives
are in many ways confined to the private domestic sphere of home and
family. The state of being "closed," which in Greek culture generally
is negative, is the proper or positive state for women. As Hirschon

(1978:80) points out, virtuous young women are described as being "of the house," while immoral women are "of the road." For women, exposure and openness involve the violation of social norms and the vulnerability that such violation entails.[25]

There is, however, a way out of this double bind, a way for women to achieve some degree of "openness" without damaging their reputation. By marrying and having children, particularly sons, women are able to achieve a positive, if limited, form of "openness." According to Hirschon (1978:71 and 78) people say that at marriage a woman "emerges" or "comes out" (*vyeni*) into society. This is the only way in which "a woman can play a full and acceptable role in adult social life." "Openness" for a woman, then, is positive only in the context of her family and her relationship to her husband. As Hirschon (86) concludes, women are, in the last analysis, "dependent on men to attain fully auspicious 'openness.'"

Metaphors of emergence and release also figure prominently in discussions of healing in rural Greece. The categories of "open" and "closed" are closely associated with states of health and illness respectively. Healing involves opening up that which was closed in order to let out or expel the harmful substance or emotion that was responsible for the illness. When someone has the chills, cupping is practiced in order to "pull out the cold." In more severe cases bloodletting is performed so that the "black," "dead," or "bad" blood will leave the body.

In the case of nevrika, an illness often said to be caused by excessive *stenohoria* (worry and anxiety, literally "narrowness" or "lack of space"), this set of images is central. People with "closed characters" and women who lead particularly confined lives are most likely to suffer from nevrika. One woman with nevrika said she felt "gripped" or "squeezed" by *stenohoria*. Another woman was said to have become ill with nevrika because her husband shut her up in the house while he was out running around with other women; he never took her out in the evenings to restaurants or nightclubs.

According to Greek villagers the proper way for people to deal with negative emotions like anxiety and anger is to get rid of them, to get them out of their systems. This indigenous theory of catharsis is explicitly applied to the expression of grief through the performance of

---

[25] See Herzfeld (1979:293) for further discussion of the relationship between exposure and violation.

funeral laments and other death rituals (Caraveli 1986:171–178 and Danforth 1982:146). The therapeutic value of such catharsis is also suggested by the fact that rural Greek women value their friendships with other women precisely because they provide opportunities for the release of anxiety (Kennedy 1986:133).

Given the close association between illness and closure, on the one hand, and health and openness, on the other, it is not surprising that metaphors of emergence, release, and opening up play an important part in the religious healing of the Anastenaria. Religious metaphors of emergence involving icons, ayiasmata, and the relationship between Anastenarides and Saint Constantine are structurally parallel to the somatic, psychological, and social metaphors of emergence that are central to an understanding of the position of women in Greece and the illness nevrika. The religious metaphors of the Anastenaria have the power to transform people's lives and move them from a "closed" state of illness to an "open" state of health.

Becoming an Anastenaris is itself a process of emergence. Strictly speaking a person does not "become" an Anastenaris, a person "comes out [as] an Anastenaris" (*vyeni Anastenaris*). When an Anastenarissa describes how she became involved with the Anastenaria, she frequently says "And then I came out, I danced, and I was healed" (*Ke tote vyika, horepsa, ke eyina kala*). She is referring to the point at which she danced in the konaki for the first time. This marks her emergence from a private, female world associated with illness into a public, male world associated with health.

Anastenarides say that when they dance freely and easily, they feel light, calm, and joyful. An image often used to describe this type of dance is that of "flying like a bird," a state associated in discussions of dream symbolism with freedom from sin and anxiety. One young woman described the difficult trance experiences she had before her husband finally gave her permission to dance this way: "When I started to dance, I suffered a great deal; it was as if there were chains on my feet. Then when my husband gave me permission to dance, my feet were untied. I was set free, and I danced."

The image of "an open road" also emphasizes the fact that becoming an Anastenarissa is a process of emerging from confinement. This image refers to the "course" or "path" a woman follows in the process of becoming an Anastenarissa and regaining her health. When an Anastenarissa is finally able to dance with the power of Saint Constantine, people say that the Saint "opened a road for her" (*tis anikse dromo*) or that the Anastenarissa "came out onto that road" (*vyike s'afto to dromo*). The same image is used in reference to the performance of any particular act associated with the Anastenaria. For example, an Anastenarissa may say, "I had a road to dance" or "My road was open to go to Mavrolefki." Having an "open road" to do something is the equivalent of having the power of Saint Constantine to do it.

If an Anastenarissa is unable to dance freely and easily—if she does not have "an open road"—it may be because "something is obstructing or blocking her [from dancing]" (*kati tin embodizi*). The cause of this obstruction is often some ritual fault, or *sfalma*, that has been committed, some mistake that has been made in the performance of some ritual duty. Frequently the ritual fault itself involves the improper confinement or obstruction of some sacred object. Conversely the correction of this fault consists of releasing the sacred object from confinement or removing whatever obstacle is blocking its way. This process clearly symbolizes the unleashing of the supernatural power of Saint Constantine and the cathartic release of becoming an Anastenaris that this power makes possible.

Such imagery occurs frequently in narrative material dealing with the origin of the Anastenaria and the discovery of the various icons and ayiasmata associated with the rite. Icons of Saints Constantine and Helen trapped in a burning church were rescued from the flames. Old icons that had been buried in the ground wanted to come out. The water of an ayiasma that was blocked up needed to be released.

Anastenarides continue to interpret suffering and illness as a result of the improper confinement of icons of Saints Constantine and Helen. In 1972, for example, two icons of Saints Constantine and Helen were taken from the konaki of Mavrolefki at the instructions of the local bishop and placed in the cathedral of Drama. In 1976 many Anastenarides argued that several Kostilides were suffering because these icons were "imprisoned," because "the grandfather wanted to come out." At about that time a young married man with two children had an accident near Mesopotamo. He was found lying on the ground near his donkey in a sheep pen in the hills outside the village. Most people thought he'd fallen and been kicked by his donkey; but the Anastenarides thought it had been the Saint, not the donkey, that had struck him. The doctors were puzzled because they hadn't found any bruises or broken bones. The Anastenarides said that the young man's feet were tied; that he didn't have a road. But everyone agreed on one thing. The young man couldn't walk; he lay paralyzed from the neck down in an orthopedic hospital in a nearby city.

Vaso, an Anastenarissa from Mesopotamo, described to me a dream she had had shortly after the accident. She was standing in front of a large cupboard with two doors. The mother of the paralyzed man shut the doors and locked them three times; she said that something smelled bad. Vaso told her that the bad smell came from the wounds of the icon that was shut up in the cupboard. Then Vaso saw the paralyzed man waving his arms back and forth as if the Saint had seized him. Vaso hugged him tightly and cried, "Get up! Get up! Get up!" But he replied, "I can't. I can't walk." Vaso told me that the cupboard was the cathedral of Drama and that the icon had been wounded when it was burned and thrown into a river a long time ago.

The damaged icon of Saints Constantine and Helen imprisoned in the cathedral of Drama clearly represents the paralyzed young man himself. The ritual faults that were believed to have caused his suffering were metaphors for his physical condition. In addition, the description of his symptoms bears a remarkable similarity to those of an Anastenaris who is unable to "come out" and dance. At both a religious and somatic level what is required for the young man to regain his health is a therapeutic and cathartic release from confinement.

The ritual faults, then, that are held responsible for suffering and illness involve powerful religious metaphors of improper confinement and obstruction, the same metaphors that are used to characterize suffering and illness at the social, psychological, and somatic levels as well. In the process of religious healing as it is accomplished by the Anastenaria these negative metaphors are transformed into positive metaphors of openness and freedom. The emergence of sacred symbols from confinement serves as a model for the structurally parallel movement of the Anastenarides from a state of weakness, isolation, and illness to a state of power, sociability, and health.

FIRE AND TRANSFORMATION

The climax of the festival of Saints Constantine and Helen occurs when the possessed Anastenarides enter the fire and dance back and forth over the glowing coals until they are extinguished. For the Anastenarides the firewalk is an act of faith, a miracle they perform every year that ritually confirms their belief in the existence and power of Saint Constantine. As the Anastenarides themselves say, the firewalk is a "trial by fire"; it demonstrates whether people enter the fire with the power of the Saint (in which case they will not be burned) or whether they enter of their own volition (in which case they will be burned). The firewalk is dramatic proof that the Anastenarides, and they alone, enjoy the supernatural power and protection of Saint Constantine.[26]

The significance of the firewalk in the ritual therapy of the Anastenaria must be understood in the context of the many symbolic associations of fire, flames, heat, and burning in Greek culture generally. Fire is first and foremost associated with danger and destruction. In conversations about the firewalk Kostilides repeatedly contrast the fact that the Anastenarides dance for a long time on a huge fire and are not burned with the obvious fact that most people are burned by even the slightest contact with a cigarette, hot pan, or metal stove.

The taken-for-granted, common-sense notion that fire burns, which is so powerfully shattered by the firewalk of the Anastenarides, receives expression in several well-known proverbs, wishes, and curses. "The three evils of the world," as the saying goes, are "fire, women, and the sea." The common wish for someone's well-being, "May God protect you from fire and water," also suggests the dangerous and destructive aspects of fire, as does the curse, "May fire burn you." The association of fire with hell, the terrors of the damned, and the destruction of the world at the Second Coming further emphasizes the negative connotations of fire. In addition, the phrase "I was burned" is often used metaphorically in Greek, as it is in English, to mean "something bad happened to me." At the firewalk, then, Saint Constantine protects the Anastenarides from a powerful force of danger and destruction.

Kostilides explicitly compare the Anastenarides performing the firewalk to soldiers fighting a battle. Both enter "the fire of battle," and both must display discipline and courage in a situation that is fraught with danger. More specifically, the Anastenarides are "soldiers of Saint

---

[26] On religious rituals involving firewalking and fire handling in other parts of the world see Armstrong (1970), Brewster (1977), Furley (1981), Hopkins (1913), Kane (1982), Katz (1982), Mead (1964:362–363), Obeyesekere (1978), and Thomas (1934).

With the protection of Saints Constantine and Helen Anastenarides—old and new—cross the fire unharmed (Photograph by John Demos/Apeiron)

Constantine." Their job is to "do battle against the fire," and they are victorious over it when they extinguish it completely by reducing the red-hot coals to a harmless bed of gray ash with nothing but their bare feet.

Fire also has another very different and very positive set of connotations which does not receive such explicit expression in discussions of the Anastenaria but which is significant nonetheless. Fire is associated with the hearth, the home, and the family; it conveys feelings of warmth, comfort, and pleasure. A dream involving fire may foretell either loss and misfortune or peace, family happiness, and good fortune (Pazinis n.d.:320).

In calendrical rites of passage throughout Greece fire is an important symbol of cleansing and purification. Passing over fire or simply coming in contact with it is associated with protection from all that is bad, evil, and dangerous, as well as with the acquisition of fertility and other blessings. On the eve of the festival of Saint John the Baptist (celebrated on June 24 at the time of the summer solstice), people traditionally jump over bonfires lit in the streets. In Ayia Eleni when people did this, they shouted "Come in good year, and go out bad year!" or "Out with Bad John, so that Good John may come in!" As one Kostilis put it: "We jump over the fire to burn all the bad things we've suffered." Megas (1963:135) reports that people in other parts of Greece shout "I leap over the fire so that sickness will not touch me" and that after the fire has gone out women may take some ashes home "for protective and divinatory purposes."[27]

The firewalk of the Anastenarides is a rite of cleansing and purification as well. Megas (1961:499, citing Arnaudoff 1917:57–59) reports that the fire lit by the Anastenarides was "for [good] health; it burned all sicknesses." The parallel between the fire of the Anastenarides and the fires of Saint John is also suggested by the fact that after the Anastenarides have completed the firewalk spectators often pick up embers from the fire to keep as charms or amulets. In both cases passing over fire represents a desired transition from bad to good, from a negative state of illness and misfortune to a positive state of health and good fortune. The firewalk of the Anastenarides, however, unlike the fires

[27] For further discussion of fire in rural Greek rites of passage see Blum and Blum (1970:104 and 139–140), Danforth (1982:42), Loukatos (1981:50–53), Politis (1920:86–88), and Romaios (1944–45:94–97).

of Saint John, is also miraculous proof that the Anastenarides possess
the supernatural power of Saint Constantine through which the transition is brought about.[28]

Another set of images involving fire, flames, and burning is used to
express the negative emotions of anxiety and grief. Kostilides often refer to a feeling of anxiety as a "flame" or "a burning sensation." An old
Anastenarissa trying to express how she felt before she began to dance
at the konaki said, "Anxiety was burning me up. I had flames inside
me." Another Anastenaris said that before he danced he felt all hot
inside; he wanted to dance and to perform the firewalk in order to "cool
off." Feelings of pain and grief caused by death are similarly described
in terms of fire, flames, and burning (Danforth 1982:107-108). After
a funeral in Ayia Eleni a woman explained the practice of stepping over
a tray of smouldering embers before entering the house of the deceased
by saying, "Just as the fire is extinguished, so may the grief and sorrow
[of the mourners] be extinguished."

Finally, in Greek again as in English, images of fire and heat are
associated with feelings of sexual excitement. A person who is sexually
aroused may be said to be "burning" or to be "on fire." Sexual intercourse, with the release of sexual tension it provides, is sometimes described as "putting out the fire," while in jokes and humorous songs a
vagina is compared to an oven or fireplace, a penis to a hot red pepper.
In similar contexts sexual arousal is compared to an illness that needs
to be healed, sexual intercourse to a "dance." The dance of the Anastenarides, possessed by their spirit husband Saint Constantine, is thus
linked through a complex set of imagery to the processes of sexual release, cooling off, and healing.

In his perceptive analysis of the symbolism of fire Bachelard
(1964:55) emphasizes what he calls the "essential ambiguity," the
"profound duality," of fire. As Bachelard points out, "the properties of
fire . . . appear to be charged with numerous contradictions" (102).
Fire is associated with vitality and destruction, good and evil, pleasure
and pain. However, fire is not only a symbol of utter ambivalence and

---

[28] The position of water in the symbolic structure of many Greek rituals is quite similar
to that of fire. Water is both destructive and life-giving. It is also a powerful symbol of
cleansing and purification, as is indicated by the central role ayiasmata play in the ritual
cycle of the Anastenaria. The most important blessing of the waters in Greece takes place
on January 6, Epiphany, the day Christ was baptized in the Jordon River by Saint John
the Baptist.

paradox; it is also a symbol of the power of transformation, the transformation from one of the extremes represented by fire to the other. In Bachelard's words, "through fire everything changes" (57).

Fire, therefore, is a central symbol in the therapeutic system of the Anastenaria because it represents two totally opposite states or conditions and the power to transform one of these into the other. Under most circumstances contact with fire results in burning and destruction. With the power of Saint Constantine, however, it results in purification and healing. Recall Mihalis Kitsos' eloquent description of his complex feelings toward the fire of the Anastenarides. As Mihalis he felt fear and doubt as he approached the fire, but with the power of Saint Constantine he felt courage, love, and hope. If he were acting on his own he would feel pain; he would be burned. But because he was doing the will of the Saint, he felt warmth, satisfaction, and power. For Mihalis Saint Constantine has the power to transform the fire from a mountain into an open road, from an enemy into a wife.

The fire the Anastenarides dance through is not the only symbol of ambivalence and transformation in the Anastenaria. The dance of the possessed Anastenarides is also both an expression of anxiety and a release from anxiety. It is both a symptom that a person is suffering from the Saint and a sign that he is in the process of being healed. Similarly, Saint Constantine himself both punishes and forgives; he causes suffering and brings joy. Above all he has the power to transform illness into health. This transformation is the essence of the therapeutic process of the Anastenaria.

V

History, Folklore, Politics, and Science

✛

Russia and Turkey were at war. That's when all the old villages around Kosti were destroyed: Tripori, Stavrohori, Kastania, Palioklisia. Turkish bandits were fighting the Tartars. They burned down the villages, and everyone fled. Later people came together in one place and founded Kosti. The first person to settle there was an old man named Kostis.

In the beginning he lived all alone with his family in a cave up in the mountains. As it turned out, his children were forced to marry each other; brothers married sisters. The church forbids this, but sometimes it happens by accident. Here it happened by necessity. After a while old Kostis came down from his cave in the mountains and built a hut. Then people who had fled during the fighting and scattered everywhere heard that old Kostis had started a village. They came back and lived there. That's how the village of Kosti was founded.

People would ask Kostis where their old villages had been, and he would take them out to look at the ruins. You could still see the burned out shells of some of the old churches. Those are the places where the icons were found. The Saint would make people suffer so they'd go out and dig them up. The icons wanted to come out.

✛

FROM KOSTI TO AYIA ELENI

Before the Balkan Wars of 1912 and 1913 the Anastenaria was performed in the northeastern part of what was then Turkish Thrace. Within this area, which is now split by the border between Bulgaria and Turkey, the Anastenaria was celebrated in about twenty villages inhabited by both Greeks and Bulgarians. The most important of these was Kosti, a Greek village situated in the low wooded mountains near the Black Sea coast. In 1914 Kosti had several thousand inhabitants who were primarily engaged in farming, lumbering, and raising animals.

The Anastenaria was a specialized form of the more general religious festivals that were held on important holidays in the religious calendar of the Orthodox Church. In Kosti the festival of Saints Constantine and Helen lasted eight days. Every evening the Anastenarides were possessed by Saint Constantine and danced in the fire to the music of a Thracian lira, bagpipe, and drum. A bull was sacrificed, and the meat was distributed to all the families in the village. The Anastenarides were also involved in many other activities as well: attending the festivals of neighboring villages, blessing new houses, warding off droughts and epidemics, and, above all, healing illnesses.

The three oldest icons of Saints Constantine and Helen were named Kotsianos, Triporinos, and Kastaniotis after the names of the villages of Kosti, Tripori, and Kastania where they had been found. When the Kostilides fled eastern Thrace in 1914, there were five icons of Saints Constantine and Helen as well as icons of Saint Pandeleimon, the Dormition of the Virgin, and the Transfiguration of the Savior, which all played an important part in the Anastenaria. In Kosti at one time these icons were kept in the village church and were taken from there to the konaki for the festivals of the Anastenaria. Priests participated in the celebrations by blessing the ayiasmata as well as the sacrificial bull. Later, however, local priests were instructed by their superiors not to participate in the rite, and the icons of the Anastenarides were taken to the konaki where they were kept throughout the year.

The Greeks of Kosti and the surrounding villages lived in relative security in the northeast corner of the Ottoman Empire until the beginning of the twentieth century, when harrassment by Bulgarian bandits became severe. Then for safekeeping the icons were given to descendants of the Anastenarides who had originally discovered them. In this way when the Kostilides were finally driven from their homes, they were able to take these icons with them and bring them safely to Greece so that the Anastenaria would continue.

With the outbreak of the Balkan Wars in 1912 the area around Kosti fell under Bulgarian control. When the Balkan Wars were over the following year and the boundary between Bulgaria and Turkey was drawn where it now stands, the northeastern portion of Turkish Thrace, including Kosti and the surrounding villages, was awarded permanently to Bulgaria. The Bulgarian bandits who entered Kosti at this time rounded up all the men of the village in the church and confiscated their money, their guns, and all their other valuables. Greek schools and churches were closed, Greek teachers and priests were expelled and replaced by Bulgarians, and the speaking of Greek was forbidden. When Bulgarian refugees who had been driven out of Turkish Thrace arrived in search of homes and land, the Greeks were finally forced to flee.

In July 1914 the people of Kosti walked ten kilometers to the port of Agathoupolis (the present-day Ahtopol), where they spent the summer living in tents on the shore. In the fall they boarded a Bulgarian steamship for the trip to Istanbul. There, with the help of the Greek Patriarch, a Persian steamship was found to transport them to Thessaloniki. During World War I most Kostilides lived in refugee camps on the outskirts of the city and survived by begging from the French and British soldiers stationed there. When Greece regained much of Turkish Thrace after the war, many Kostilides returned to eastern Thrace and settled as close as they could to their original homeland, which was now completely inaccessible to them because it lay on the other side of the border in Bulgaria. Two years later, with the disastrous conclusion of the Asia Minor campaign in 1922, Turkey regained control of eastern Thrace, and the Greek population was forced to flee once again. By 1924 the majority of Kostilides had settled in Ayia Eleni, Langadas, and several other villages in Greek Macedonia.

For over twenty years the Kostilides performed the Anastenaria in secret because they feared both the persecution of the Church of Greece and the hostility of the local population. Shortly before World War II the president of the Society for Psychic Research, Dr. Angelos Tanagras, who had known of the existence of the Anastenaria in Thrace, succeeded in locating the Kostilides in their new communities in

Macedonia. Tanagras, an Athenian physician, thought that when the Anastenarides entered a state of ecstasy, their bodies emitted some kind of "radioactivity" or "psychic energy" that formed "a fireproof shield" around their feet. The Anastenarides' great faith in Saint Constantine protected their feet from normal "physiochemical reactions" and made them invulnerable to fire. In Tanagras' opinion the Anastenaria definitely involved "the realm of the supernatural" and made "a mockery of our wise theories and scientific knowledge."

It was only with great difficulty that Tanagras persuaded the Kostilides to perform the Anastenaria in public. Persecution of the Anastenaria by the Orthodox Church proved to be a genuine threat. In 1947, when the Anastenarides of Ayia Eleni danced on fire in public for the first time, the president of the Holy Synod of the Church of Greece informed the Bishop of Serres that the Anastenaria was "an idolatrous survival of the orgiastic worship of Dionysos [that] must be abolished using all the spiritual means at the disposal of the Church." Four years later the Bishop of Thessaloniki expressed the opinion that the Anastenaria was "in complete opposition to the beliefs and forms of worship of the Christian Religion." The Church of Greece also accused the Anastenarides of sacrilegiously dancing with sacred icons, indulging in feasts during which "whole jars of wine are consumed" and "the orgies of Aphrodite are allowed." According to the Church, therefore, the Anastenarides' miraculous ability to walk on fire could not possibly come from God; it must come from Satan. This hostile attitude has troubled many Anastenarides. They maintain that their participation in the rite demonstrates their devotion to both God and the saints. "How can people say we're not Christians?" they protest. "We use candles, incense, and olive oil."

The Bishop of Serres eventually agreed to allow public performances of the Anastenaria in Ayia Eleni, but he imposed two conditions. First, all the money collected by the Anastenarides had to be given to the village church, and, second, the two icons of Saints Constantine and Helen had to be kept in the church throughout the year. They could only be taken to the konaki for the celebration of the Anastenaria.

In 1970 this uneasy standoff between the Anastenarides of Ayia Eleni and the Church of Greece came to an end. A week before the festival of Saints Constantine and Helen the Bishop of Serres called Yavasis and the president of Ayia Eleni to his office to inform them that they would not be allowed to take the icons out of the church that year. They could celebrate the Anastenaria and perform the firewalk but without the icons. Under these conditions, replied Yavasis, they could not perform the rite at all.

Several days later the Anastenarides and several respected village men gathered at Yavasis' house. Everyone except Yavasis thought the festival should take place anyway—without the icons. Finally, Yavasis agreed to celebrate it with just the simadia. The president of Ayia Eleni informed the bishop that they would not use the icons but warned him not to remove the icons from the village church.

When the Anastenarides arrived at the church on the morning of May 21, the icons of Saints Constantine and Helen were gone. The previous evening two priests accompanied by a policeman had removed them from the church by hiding them under their robes. When Yavasis discovered that the icons were missing, he immediately announced that there would be no festival that year.

Some people said that the bishop had hoped they would enter the fire without the icons. Then he'd have proof that the rite was not religious, and he'd never give the icons back. Other people said that the Anastenarides weren't afraid to go into the fire without the icons as long as they knew that the icons were safe in the village church. But when they learned that the icons had disappeared, they were afraid, because they get their courage from the icons.

The village president confronted the bishop, but he said he knew nothing. In a few weeks some priests brought the icons back to the church. The village president learned from the police that the icons had probably been taken to a monastery up in the mountains above Serres. Several months later the head of the village church committee showed the president a book he had found. It was a record of church property dating back to 1950, and it contained a reference to two icons of Saints Constantine and Helen that belonged to the Yavasis and the Petrakis families. The book bore the seal and the signature of the secretary of the Bishop of Serres.

A trial was held in Serres in the spring of 1971. The position of the Church was that these icons received both the veneration and the offerings of the public; therefore they belonged to the Church. Several village men who had been born in Kosti testified that the icons had been brought from Thrace by specific individuals and belonged to their descendants; therefore the icons were private property. This testimony together with the church record book proved decisive. The court ruled that the icons were in fact private property, and the icons were promptly returned to the village and placed in the konaki in Yavasis' house.

✣

Remember Papaspiros, the priest in Kosti? He wanted to stop the Anastenaria because he didn't believe. So one year he hid the icons in a cupboard under the icon stand in the church. When the Anastenarides went to the church to get the icons, they didn't find them in their place. They asked the priest, but he said he didn't know anything about it.

A little while later the priest and his wife went mad. The Saint punished them because they didn't believe. Soon the priest was wandering around the church making clucking noises—klou, klou, klou, klou—like a chicken. Then his wife, instead of holding her baby to her breast to nurse, held him to her anus. This lasted for a few months; then they called the Anastenarides. Those people knew where he'd hidden the icons. They asked him if he'd ever take them again, and he said no. "The Saint forgives you," they told him. "You'll be all right."

And so the priest and his wife calmed down.

✣

THE FOLKLORE SOCIETY OF AYIA ELENI

The Folklore Society of Ayia Eleni was founded in the spring of 1971 for the immediate purpose of helping the Anastenarides regain possession of their icons. It had an official constitution, membership dues, annual meetings, and elections held every other year for an executive committee that consisted of a president, a vice-president, a secretary, and a treasurer.

The founder and the first president of the Folklore Society was Tasos Reklos, a young medical student at the University of Thessaloniki, whose grandfather had been responsible for the financial affairs of the Anastenarides back in Kosti. According to Tasos the job of the Folklore Society was to assist the Anastenarides in their dealings with government officials and to help preserve the wealth of traditional Thracian folklore that linked the people of Ayia Eleni with their past. The Folklore Society would also protect the Anastenaria and help it develop into something the people of Ayia Eleni could be proud of.

The celebration of the festival of Saints Constantine and Helen in Ayia Eleni was becoming an increasingly expensive and complicated affair. With the growth of tourism in Greece and the national media attention that was being focused on the Anastenaria, ever greater crowds were coming to the village for the May festival. This caused a variety of problems that the newly created Folklore Society would deal with. Now that all ties between the Anastenarides and the Church had been severed with the confiscation of the icons, the Folklore Society would also assume responsibility for the financial affairs of the Anastenarides, which had been handled by the village church committee since the first public performance of the rite just after World War II.

In the first few years of its existence the Folklore Society succeeded in obtaining yearly grants from the prefecture of Serres, the Ministry of Northern Greece, the Ministry of Culture and Sciences, the Ministry of National Education and Religions, the National Lottery, and the National Tourist Organization. This money was used to erect a welcome sign at the entrance to the village, to build a road to the site of the firewalk, and to paint the ayiasma and the nearby chapel.

By 1976 the officers of the Folklore Society were responsible for many of the arrangements necessary for the successful performance of the festival of Saints Constantine and Helen. They bought the wood for the fire, roped off the area of the firewalk, rented chairs, sent invitations to local dignitaries, distributed fliers, and arranged for announcements of the firewalk on the radio. There was even talk of seeking additional funds for the construction of a public building near the site of the firewalk that would serve as a konaki and provide space for a small museum and an office for the Folklore Society as well.

All this money did more than inspire ambitious plans for the future; it provoked much conflict and bitterness within the village. At meetings of the Folklore Society men argued endlessly. Should tickets be sold at the firewalk? Should Anastenarides from other villages be reimbursed for their travel expenses when they came to Ayia Eleni to dance in May? Should musicians be paid for their services? Accusations and complaints were rampant: the officers had spent money improperly; they were in it just for the money and the glory; they quit when they found out it was just a lot of hard work.

The Kostilides of Ayia Eleni complained that the other villagers, the

Macedonians and the other Thracians, didn't support the Folklore Society; the other villagers were insulted because they had never been invited to enroll. The president of the Folklore Society didn't get along with the president of the village. Officers resigned, membership dwindled, and there was talk of disbanding.

The Anastenaria was not immune to all the conflict stirred up by the Folklore Society. People said the rite was becoming too commercialized. It wasn't religious anymore; it was just folklore.

The relationships between the officers of the Folklore Society and the Anastenarides were becoming increasingly strained. The original intention had been for the Folklore Society to be completely separate from the Anastenaria. The officers would listen to the Anastenarides and carry out their instructions; they would do whatever Yavasis told them to. But the officers of the Folklore Society were politically powerful men from wealthy village families, while most of the Anastenarides were women. The few male Anastenarides were poor men who were not involved in village politics. Therefore charges that the Folklore Society did not defer to the wishes of the Anastenarides and that it had simply taken over the rite were inevitable. Many people felt that the officers of the Folklore Society ignored the Anastenarides and just went ahead and did whatever they wanted.

Whenever this issue came up, people mentioned the decision to move the site of the firewalk from the village square to the open area near the ayiasma. The officers of the Folklore Society had made that decision without consulting the Anastenarides because they knew the Anastenarides would refuse to move. When Yavasis announced that there would be no firewalk at the new site, Tasos Reklos said he would take a simadi and lead the Anastenarides into the fire there himself. Asked if the Anastenarides had been consulted about a plan to build a cinder block wall around the site of the firewalk, an officer of the Folklore Society replied "Why should they be? They couldn't object to something that was good for the rite."

On several occasions the tension between the Anastenarides and the Folklore Society manifested itself in particularly dramatic form over the issue of precisely when on the evening of May 21 the Anastenarides would enter the fire. Officers of the Folklore Society and other village officials liked to tell the police and visiting dignitaries exactly when the firewalk would take place. If the prefect of Serres planned to arrive at nine o'clock, the firewalk shouldn't take place at eight-thirty. But whenever Yavasis was asked when the firewalk would begin, he'd simply shrug his shoulders and say "It's not up to me. The call for the fire comes from the Saint."

In 1976 the husbands of several Anastenarisses felt so strongly about what they saw as the interference of the Folklore Society in the affairs of the Anastenarides that they refused to let their wives dance. One man said that the husbands of the Anastenarisses should be on the executive committee of the Folklore Society. As things stood now, it was the rich men on the committee who got all the glory, while the Anastenarisses themselves, who did all the work, were ignored. Since the husbands were in charge of their wives, and since it was their wives who went into the fire, the committee should at least *consult* the husbands. One Anastenaris had an even simpler solution to the problem: the executive committee of the Folklore Society should be composed of Anastenarides. They would receive instructions directly from Saint Constantine and then just carry them out themselves.

Early in May 1976 the executive committee of the Folklore Society met with the prefect of Serres. He told them he wanted the rite to be performed in an impressive manner so that the crowds of visitors who came to see it would be pleased and would want to come back again. He was ready to provide money for major improvements, particularly for a new konaki that would be larger and safer than the present konaki on the second floor of Yavasis' old house. On their way back to Ayia Eleni after the meeting members of the committee talked about whether the Anastenarides would agree to celebrate the festival in a new konaki. They joked about the fact that the icons were ready to move.

A few days later the officers of the Folklore Society invited the Anastenarides to gather in the konaki. Present were Yavasis, Mihalis Kitsos, a few older Anastenarisses, the husbands of several Anastenarisses (some of whom were not present), and the officers of the Folklore Society. Directly under the icon shelf in the corner of the room sat the president of the Folklore Society, Tasos Reklos' uncle; Yavasis sat next to him. When the room grew quiet, Yavasis crossed himself three times and incensed the icon shelf and the rest of the room. Standing in front of the icons Yavasis welcomed everyone and encouraged them to express their opinions freely and clearly. As he spoke, an old Anastenarissa danced briefly in her seat.

The president of the Folklore Society said that the prefect wanted them to build a new konaki near the ayiasma, by the site of the firewalk.

He wanted to know if they could bring the icons to such a place and celebrate the festival there. Several people thought that would be fine.

"But who would take care of the icons while they were there?" asked an old Anastenarissa. "Who would clean the building? Who would feed all the people who gathered there? No one!"

Then Yavasis told a story about a man in Kosti who built an icon on his own and then suffered. "If you do something on your own, if you don't have a word from the boss, then you'll make a mess of things." Yavasis said that the konaki could never leave his house. If it did, it would be *their* decision, not the Saint's, and therefore it would be a bad decision.

After a long pause an officer of the Folklore Society asked if the festival would take place that year. Yavasis couldn't say for sure. "It always happens," said one Anastenarissa. "It has to happen." Another Anastenarissa agreed. Yavasis then offered everyone a drink of ouzo and a piece of hard candy. With wishes for "a good road" and calls for cooperation and unity the meeting drew to a close.

✛

In Kosti the leader of the Anastenarides was a poor man, so the rich people in the village didn't pay any attention to him. The day before the festival he was out in the fields working with his wife. He said to her, "Things will go well this year, but someone will be burned. Nikitas will be burned."

The next night Nikitas, one of the richest men in the village, went into the fire on his own. He was badly burned. His feet were all swollen up like drums, and they were covered with blood. That night he died.

✛

When People Speak Instead of the Icons

Late one night in the summer of 1975 Katina Pashali, the sister of Thanasis and Evripidis Petrakis, came alone by taxi from Thessaloniki to Ayia Eleni. When she arrived in the village square, she was barefoot, and her clothes and hair were in disarray. She woke people up with her screaming and shouting. Her nephew tried to restrain her, but she just pushed him away; she insisted on going to Yavasis' house. She had a wild expression on her face and was crying: "The icon is mine! The icon is not in its house!"

She broke open the door of the konaki, woke Yavasis up, and demanded that he give her the icon that belonged to her family—the icon that her grandmother had brought to Ayia Eleni from Kosti so many years before. She wanted to take the icon right then and there, but Yavasis said no, that was not the way to do things. He was afraid she would take it to Thessaloniki. By this time a crowd had gathered, and a neighbor had called the police. When Katina's relatives finally succeeded in calming her down, they found her a taxi and sent her back to Thessaloniki.

A few weeks later Katina and her two brothers, Thanasis and Evripidis, met with the Anastenarides in the konaki. Thanasis was a well-respected villager who had provided well for all six of his children. Evripidis, however, had left the village under difficult circumstances and moved to Thessaloniki twenty years earlier. He was generally disliked and was regarded with some suspicion by many people in Ayia Eleni. He was deeply involved with the Anastenaria but was always upsetting people and causing trouble. According to some people he wasn't an Anastenaris at all; he was just crazy, or else he drank too much.

Katina sat under the icon shelf and described in detail all the votive offerings and simadia that belonged to her family's icon—an icon, she said, she hadn't seen since childhood. Katina had suffered a great deal recently, and she claimed that her troubles had been caused by Saint Constantine. Therefore the icon had to be moved; only that would save her. Yavasis asked Thanasis if he would accept the icon in his house, and Thanasis said yes. After the Anastenarides danced briefly, they wrapped the icon in a white cloth and returned it to its proper place, accompanied by the music of the lira and the drum.

Some people thought that the Saint was punishing Katina; he forced her to act because he wanted to move. Other people felt that she had suffered a nervous breakdown or that she was "neurasthenic"; besides, her son had diabetes, and her husband didn't treat her well. Still others claimed that Evripidis was behind it all. He visited her in the clinic when she was sick and told her that the illness she had "was not for the doctors." He took advantage of a perfect opportunity to acquire more power and influence among the Anastenarides by gaining greater control over one of the icons. Some people were afraid he might even try to take the icon to Thessaloniki and set up his own konaki there.

In the fall of 1979 Yavasis called people to the konaki to tell them it was time for someone new to take over his responsibilities. His wife had died earlier in the year, and he was getting old. During the meeting Mihalis Kitsos was chosen to be the new leader of the Anastenarides.

At about the same time the Folklore Society built a new konaki near the site of the firewalk next to the ayiasma. Above the front door of the new konaki was a blue and white sign that read:

KONAKI OF THE ANASTENARIDES
FOLKLORE SOCIETY OF AYIA ELENI

The main room of the new konaki was much larger than the old konaki at Yavasis' house. In the corner opposite the door stood the icon shelf—bare and colorless except during the celebrations themselves, when it held the icons, the icon covers, and the large red simadia. Nearby was a small fireplace for the fire that was lit at the January festival of Saint Athanasios. Low benches and stools lined the walls. At one end of the room a door led to a small office where the executive committee of the Folklore Society met and where the political leaders of the village could often be found during festivals. On the walls of the office hung photographs of the Anastenaria, the village carnival, and some women from Ayia Eleni in traditional Thracian costumes. A back door led from the main room to a covered porch and a small kitchen where village women prepared the meals that were served to people who had come to see the Anastenaria.

Over the next few years the celebrations of the Anastenaria were marked by a great deal of conflict which could be attributed to a variety of factors. According to many villagers the real konaki was still at Yavasis' house. Many of these same villagers, including Yavasis, felt that Mihalis was only a temporary leader. No real successor to Yavasis had been found because *people* had chosen Mihalis, not the Saint. *People's* will, not God's will had been done. As Yavasis himself put it, "The sheep are without a shepherd. And without a good shepherd the sheep will be eaten by wolves, and the sheep dogs will fight among themselves."

According to other villagers Mihalis was just too young. How could an old Anastenarissa be expected to show the proper respect for a man young enough to be her son? Mihalis had only become leader of the

Anastenarides because one of the icons was in his father-in-law's house. The real power behind Mihalis was Evripidis. Villagers who supported Mihalis, however, argued that Yavasis "had not resigned well." He hadn't given Mihalis the two simadia that the leader of the Anastenarides always wore, nor had he given Mihalis enough advice and guidance the first few years. After all, everyone needs some help in the beginning.

THIS CONFLICT was all too apparent at the festival of Saints Constantine and Helen in 1981. Early on the evening of May 20 the only people at the new konaki were Mihalis, some officers of the Folklore Society, and a few older women. At the old konaki Yavasis, three influential Anastenarisses from Ayia Eleni, Keti, and several other young Anastenarides from other villages were sitting quietly. Yavasis' family icons now stood on the icon shelf next to the one remaining icon of Saints Constantine and Helen. On an icon shelf in another corner of the room stood a portrait of Yavasis' wife, painted by a young artist from a distant city, who had "come out" when he entered the fire for the first time two years earlier. He and Keti made dancing gestures with their arms, but they couldn't dance because there were no musicians present.

Several officers of the Folklore Society accompanied by Tasos Reklos, the doctor, arrived and tried to persuade Yavasis to come to the new konaki. They were upset with him for opening his konaki and for gathering his own "personnel" there. Yavasis replied that he couldn't just close up his house and leave. Finally, someone was sent to tell Mihalis to come to Yavasis' house and bring Yavasis' icon back to the new konaki. Yavasis would join them there.

At the new konaki more people had gathered, but the icon shelf was still empty. Only one young Anastenarissa was present. She started to dance, but there were no musicians here either. Abruptly Mihalis left the room. Ten minutes later he returned in his pickup truck with Papadakena, the oldest living Anastenarissa, the aunt of Thanasis Petrakis, Mihalis' father-in-law. Mihalis lit the incense burner and handed it to old Papadakena. As she began to dance, she shouted, "Come on! Let's go!"

When the small procession of Anastenarides made a wrong turn after leaving the new konaki, a young Anastenarissa told Mihalis to go the other way. After they reached the old konaki, Yavasis greeted them; he then criticized Mihalis for being late, but Tasos Reklos tried to prevent any further conflict. The procession then set off with Yavasis' icon and returned to the new konaki after picking up the other icon at the house of Thanasis Petrakis.

Mihalis placed the two icons on the shelf and carefully arranged all the simadia and icon covers. People seemed relieved that things were finally underway. Yavasis called for quiet.

"All the things we've done wrong are hanging over our heads," he said. "We have to correct our mistakes. Quarreling is hell. Don't argue; don't gossip; and don't judge other people! Just do things the way I did with the old women! Come do your job tomorrow, and come on your own! Don't be careless! Carelessness weighs us all down. We have to do *his* will. If we don't, we won't get our job done. If we do, it will be to the benefit of the whole world. I'm old, but I'll do what I can.

"Anyone with a complaint should speak up. We Anastenarides must be like sheep among wolves. Even if people gossip, we mustn't neglect our work. If we stop, we'll hurt ourselves and our ritual, which we inherited from our grandfathers. After we stopped performing our festival in secret, we made mistakes. One icon is in jail and no one can get it out. We should be good soldiers—without gossip, without drinking, with the power of Saint Constantine and all the saints. We must do what the grandfathers want, not what *we* want, because the things *we* want are things of this world. Do your job! Come and follow the lamb tomorrow! Now start the music! But first we'll incense for the whole world."

Over the next few days Yavasis watched over Mihalis closely. When Mihalis gave an icon to a young drama student from Athens wearing a flak jacket and running shoes, who was dancing for only the second year, Yavasis immediately took it back and gave it to a more experienced Anastenaris. Evripidis was also much in evidence. He played the lira and sang, occasionally improvising lyrics about the icon that was "in jail," which upset the other Anastenarides greatly. Evripidis often gave Mihalis advice. One evening Yavasis scolded Evripidis, telling him to mind his own business and stick to his lira. Tasos Reklos was constantly moving back and forth between Yavasis and Mihalis, checking on some detail with one or making a suggestion to the other. When the village president whispered something to Mihalis before the firewalk, Yavasis reprimanded him sharply, saying "We give the orders here, not you!"

In the evenings the Anastenarides from distant villages and towns, who in the past had spent the night at Yavasis' house, returned to their hotels in Serres. They could be heard commenting on the lack of warmth and hospitality that characterized the festival now and on the infighting and quarreling that gave the whole village a bad name.

The residents of Ayia Eleni echoed these sentiments. "Now people speak, not the icons," observed one Anastenarissa. "But the icons can still hear."

It was already growing dark when the Anastenarides finished their circuit of the village on May 23, 1981, the last day of the festival of Saints Constantine and Helen. Because it was so late, they went straight to the site of the fire without returning to the new konaki from which they had set out earlier in the day. Two rows of policemen opened a path through the large crowd that had already gathered. After dancing once around the huge pile of wood, they lit the fire and then went back to the konaki.

At about ten-thirty that night the Anastenarides were notified that the fire was ready. Following an initial flurry of activity when five or six Anastenarides crossed the fire, there were several long pauses during which no one was in the fire at all. Yavasis led two new Anastenarides in a circle around the fire; Keti danced up to the edge and stopped. Several Anastenarides had also stopped dancing and were standing at the edge of the fire exchanging angry words and glances.

Then the musicians seemed to regroup; they began playing again with a slower, more powerful rhythm. Two Anastenarisses with their arms around each other's shoulders crossed the fire. A few minutes later Soula Kara, who was usually the first Anastenarissa to enter the fire every year, shouted, "There's nothing the matter," and danced through the fire. After another long pause Soula's cousin, Matinio, danced up to Mihalis, who was standing off to the side holding an icon. She shook his arm in time to the music, but he just stood there, so she took the icon from him and danced into the fire with it herself. An officer of the Folklore Society shouted angrily at Matinio. Only three Anastenarides were still dancing. Then someone signaled the musicians to stop playing.

Soula tried to take the other icon out of the hands of the young artist, who had stopped dancing, but he wouldn't let go. They struggled for a moment until Mihalis came over and gave the icon to Soula. "*We* hold them!" she shouted defiantly and danced across the fire again. A moment later she danced over to Sotiria Fotiadi who was just dancing around the fire and shouted, "Either in the fire or in your house!" Now Soula and Matinio—two cousins, two women from Ayia Eleni—were the only dancers in the fire.

"What a disaster!" someone shouted. "What humiliation!"

"Enough!" cried Mihalis.

After a short dance around the fire led by Soula and Matinio, the Anastenarides returned to the konaki. While people in the crowd seemed not to have noticed anything wrong, the atmosphere in the konaki was anything but triumphant. People seemed quicker to put on their shoes than they had in other years. Soula and Matinio were the only Anastenarides who kept their shoes off throughout the meal that followed.

On the back porch Yavasis and Evripidis were arguing. Yavasis told Evripidis to leave Mihalis alone, to let him do his job by himself. He also told Evripidis that he shouldn't have taken the icon cover from Thodoros. When Evripidis defended himself by claiming that Thodoros didn't have an open road for the fire, Yavasis called Thodoros over. Thodoros was furious. He said that he wasn't welcome in Ayia Eleni and that he'd never come back again. Tasos led him away and tried to calm him down.

"You've hurt people," Yavasis told Evripidis. "You've ruined the festival."

Several days later Matinio talked about what had happened that night.

"Soula and I saved the day. We were victorious over the fire all by ourselves.

"Mihalis was just standing there with the icon, but the icon wanted to dance. 'Why did you stop?' I asked him. 'Have we finished the dance? I haven't finished.' He shouldn't have been standing off to the side while people were suffering and working hard in the fire. I was flying; I had great power. The icon wanted to come to me. I didn't take it on my own; I had a road to take it."

Matinio said that they'd made a big mistake by lighting the fire without first returning to the konaki. Even though it was late, they should have danced in the konaki first.

"The word for the fire must come from there," she said. "When people make mistakes, the responsibility is theirs. Every war, every

battle, has its casualties. Maybe there were some secret casualties that
night. Maybe the Saint gave people some little burns as signs."

Sotiria agreed.

"The Saint saw the mistake, so he didn't give people the power to
dance. The Saint has his konaki; the grandfather has his house. That's
where the word for the fire should come from. Yavasis took us right to
the fire and told us to light it himself, the Saint didn't give the word.
So our road was cut, and the firewalk didn't go well."

✣

THE ANASTENARIA:

A RELIGIOUS MYSTERY REDUCED TO

A TOURIST ATTRACTION

*The Folklore Society of Ayia Eleni in Serres . . . has literally castrated
the Anastenaria as it is celebrated there.*[1] *There are many villages in northern Greece where the Anastenaria comes alive each May 21, but the way
this happens is not everywhere the same. On the one hand, the Anastenaria
can be performed as a tourist attraction. . . . On the other, it can be performed traditionally and purely. Many people have not even noticed this
transformation of a traditional ritual into a tourist spectacle; some people
have actually sought it out. The Folklore Society of Ayia Eleni is responsible
for just such a transformation. . . .*

*The visitor no longer finds the konaki in the house of the hospitable old
man but contrary to all traditions in the building of the Folklore Society of
Ayia Eleni. There, in the building of the Folklore Society of Ayia Eleni,
with great savoir faire one is invited to come in and* SEE *and then to leave
so that others who follow can come in and* SEE *also. The environment is cold
and inhospitable. . . .*

*The Anastenarides, a small persecuted group, powerless and on the mar-
gins of public life, gave in silently. . . .*

*And in the village square the officers of the Folklore Society of Ayia Eleni
bask in their triumph, with their suits, their illuminated signs, their offices,
their little museum, their chairs, and their fluorescent lights. Their success
was not without significance. They succeeded in* SAVING *and* PRESERVING *a
ritual. . . .*

From now on the visitor is condemned by the Folklore Society of Ayia

[1] From a Greek newspaper article written by D. Miliadis in May 1984.

Eleni to remain a spectator and nothing but a spectator, for it has destroyed the conditions that created a sense of panhuman participation and coopera-tion in the performance of the rite. From now on the spectator is obliged to experience the entire ceremony from a distance, like a spectator who watches a magician or a charlatan performing on stage.

The Folklore Society has taken a ritual from the hands of its father. The initiate has been transformed into a guest, the high priest into a master of ceremonies, the believer into a spectator. Religious symbols have been trans-formed into exhibits; a miracle into a performance. The ritual has died.

✢

Scientists, Doctors, Students, and Artists

When I returned to Ayia Eleni in May 1986, ten years after my orig-inal stay there, I was impressed with the economic development the village had experienced and the increased prosperity the villagers en-joyed. The local agricultural cooperative now operated a general store and a gas station near the site of the firewalk. A bakery, a small saw-mill, and a butcher shop had also opened.

Village nightlife had been enhanced by conversion of a small restau-rant and coffeehouse into the CAFETERIA BLEU BIRD and the DISCO HIS-TERIA. The soccer field was surrounded by a new cinder block wall, garbage was collected weekly, and the village was now served by the urban bus lines of the city of Serres. Gone were many of the storks that had nested on the roofs of village houses—victims of the increased use of insecticides and the expanded cultivation of fallow land.

More villagers now owned cars and talked to each other on the tele-phone, and the patios, courtyards, and gardens that surrounded their houses were even more elaborate than I had remembered. The young people who had decided to stay in Ayia Eleni worked in the fields as their parents had, grew vegetables in hothouses, or repaired agricul-tural machinery. Those who had left had become high school teachers, factory technicians, bus drivers, and policemen. One of the wealthiest families in the village now lived in a four-story apartment building they had constructed for their two married daughters in Serres.

The first person I visited on my return was a woman who had lived across the street from us whose husband played the lira. She told me that she and her husband had been to Bulgaria, to Kosti, on several bus tours sponsored by the Thracian Hearth, the folklore society of Langadas. Her daughter, a nurse in a hospital in Athens, told me she had recently attended a seminar on Silva Mind Control and learned how to cure headaches with yoga, relaxation techniques, and the power of positive thinking. She had also read Claude Lévi-Strauss's *Tristes Tropiques*. The most surprising thing I learned that day, however, was that three years ago Tasos Reklos, the doctor, had become the new leader of the Anastenarides.

I remembered Tasos from 1976 as a tall, handsome young man with shaggy black hair and a thick black mustache. He had been a medical student at the University of Thessaloniki and planned to become a neurologist-psychiatrist. We were both students then, and the few times he came back to Ayia Eleni during my year of fieldwork there we talked about neuroses, psychosomatic illnesses, and the relationship between people's emotions and their health. He told me that the firewalk was a mystery, a kind of test. When people conquered their fear and entered the fire, they became Anastenarides and acquired the power that walking on fire gave them. "Faith conquers fear," he said. "It protects people from the fire in a way science has not yet been able to explain."

In 1976 Tasos played the drum at the festival of Saints Constantine and Helen. Villagers often spoke of how willing "Tasos, the doctor," always was to give them shots and take their blood pressure. According to one of his neighbors Tasos attended the Anastenaria so faithfully because some supernatural power drew him to the konaki. He was an Anastenaris even though he didn't dance. Five years later, in 1981, when I returned to Ayia Eleni with a group of students from Bates College, I only saw Tasos briefly. He had learned to play the lira and was showing some fellow medical students the old konaki at Yavasis' house.

In 1986 I heard many different accounts of why Tasos had initially become involved with the Anastenarides and how he had emerged more recently as their leader. Sotiria told me that as a young man Tasos spent much time with Yavasis and often asked him for advice. When Tasos' mother, a cousin of Sotiria's husband, confided in her how hard Tasos studied, and how much he worried about getting his degree, Sotiria would comfort her by telling her that some day he'd be number one in the village. Sotiria had *known* that he'd become leader of the Anastenarides, but she just told his mother that he'd be number one.

"The first year they danced in the new konaki," Sotiria continued, "Yavasis wouldn't give his icon to anyone to take to the new konaki.

He wouldn't take it off the icon shelf. He said, 'Whoever has the power to take it, should take it.' Then I did what I had to. I confronted the Saint. I said, 'Choose someone for a leader now and have him pick up the icon and take it to the new konaki!' I said to the Saint, 'You've chosen the young man, now send him up to the icon shelf!' And with those words Tasos stepped up and took down the icon."

Sotiria went on to tell me how Tasos had actually been chosen to be the leader of the Anastenarides. Several years earlier on the eve of the festival of Saints Constantine and Helen, Yavasis had gathered the Anastenarides at his house. After incensing around the room he told them that he had had a dream. He'd seen a young man whose head was covered with a scarf of white wool. Opposite the young man stood an army officer who said, "Stand up in front of me!" The young man was Tasos Reklos, the doctor.

Tasos described Yavasis' dream and what happened next somewhat differently.

"This was Yavasis' dream: 'I saw that I was walking around in the fields. I was upset; I realized I had grown old and couldn't do my job anymore. I was crying, and I begged the Saints to tell me what to do. Suddenly I found a snail. I bent down and took it in my hands; it was all closed up. Then I understood that this was the person who would succeed me. So I said, "Why are you afraid? Why are you all closed up? You know that this is a difficult road, but you also must know that the Saints have appointed you to take my place." '

"Yavasis continued talking like this to the Anastenarides: 'This snail comes from a good family, from a mother and father who are heirs of Saint Pandeleimon. That's why he became a doctor. You should respect him and honor him, and you should always respect the work that he does.'

"Then Yavasis put his simadi around my neck and kissed my hand. It was a moving ceremony. No one could object to what he had said. Kissing my hand was an actual demonstration of the recommendations he had given the Anastenarides."

Although some villagers were troubled by the fact that Tasos had never danced or entered the fire, most people were able to account for this one way or another. Tasos had "an open road to dance" but held back because he was a "scientist." He was an Anastenaris because he played the drum and the lira, even though he never danced. He was an Anastenaris because he knew what mistakes people made and what they must do to get well. One woman even claimed that Tasos had in fact danced when he first became leader of the Anastenarides.

On several occasions I was told that Tasos "wanted" to be the leader of the Anastenarides, or that Yavasis "had chosen" Tasos as his successor. When I said I thought that that was not something a person could "want" or "choose," the story changed. I was told that Tasos had had "problems" as a student, that he had been troubled and afraid, that he had shut himself in his house and talked nonsense.

The husband of one Anastenarissa said that Tasos wasn't an Anastenaris because he never shouted the way the other Anastenarides did. He was the leader, though; he was the person in charge. He did a good job maintaining order and keeping people in line. This was related to the fact that he was an educated man. The husband of another Anastenarissa said somewhat ambivalently, "The doctor's a good scientist, but he isn't God."

People who were less involved with the Anastenaria had a different view of Tasos' participation in the rite. They said he spent time with Yavasis when he was young because he wanted to learn how to fish with the old round nets that only Yavasis knew how to make. He learned to play the lira and the drum because he loved Greek folk music—he also knew how to play the bouzouki, the guitar, and the bagpipe. Some people said he had convinced Yavasis to appoint him leader because there wasn't anyone else who enjoyed enough respect to do the job right and put an end to all the infighting among the Anastenarides. More cynical people claimed that Tasos had pressured Yavasis to appoint him leader because he wanted to take over the rite or because he wanted to write a book about the Anastenaria.

WHEN I ARRIVED at the new konaki on the afternoon of May 20, 1986, several young men in their twenties, the new generation of officers of the Folklore Society, were outside talking to the police about traffic and parking problems. Inside Tasos was arranging the simadia and icon covers on the icon shelf. Next to him, in order, moving down the bench along the wall away from the icons, sat Mihalis Kitsos, Evripidis Petrakis, Sotiria Fotiadi, Maria Kondou, Keti, and others. In the middle of the room stood a small table covered with an embroidered tablecloth. On it lay a pair of scissors, a measuring tape, a piece of chalk, and a needle and thread.

Tasos incensed around the room and welcomed everyone to the konaki; then he gave Evripidis a bundle wrapped in a large red simadi Evripidis placed it on the table and unwrapped it. Inside lay an old pink icon cover with many votive offerings attached to it and two large pieces of shiny satin, one yellow and one purple. Tasos called Andreas Mylonas, who had once worked as a tailor, to the table and made the sign of the cross with the incense burner. Then Evripidis told Andreas to make a new icon cover exactly like the old one.

When Evripidis sat down in a different place from where he had previously been sitting, Tasos scolded him sharply: "You will *not* change your position!" A long period of tense silence followed, as people sat watching Andreas work. He measured the cloth, folded it, and made a mark. Then he remeasured it, but the material had slipped. He measured, folded, and marked again. More people entered, greeted the icons, and took their seats. Keti told someone that they were making a new cover for the icon of Saints Constantine and Helen that the Anastenarides of Mavrolefki had recently recovered from the Bishop of Drama. Someone else said that it was for the icon of Saints Constantine and Helen that belonged to the Petrakis family.

The tension in the room reached a peak when Andreas picked up his scissors, said, "To your health!" and cut the cloth. After Evripidis told him just where to attach a piece of embroidered cord, Andreas left with the bundle of material to return home to finish the job on his sewing machine.

People relaxed and waited for Andreas to return. I heard one woman say that an icon cover should be sewn by hand, not on a machine. "No!" said another. "That would take too long. The material's too fine." A third woman talked ominously about how many times Andreas had measured the cloth before he cut it. "He's sewn so many icon covers, but he still had trouble making this one. He had to measure it fifty times. This isn't a day for sewing; it's a day for dancing."

Tasos stood outside the konaki with some visitors from Athens. They were discussing Katerina Kakouri's book *Dionysiaka* and the various films that had been made about the Anastenaria. Tasos mentioned his own work with a professor of folklore from the University of Thessaloniki. Then a man carrying an expensive tape recorder gave Tasos an article about the songs and dances of the Anastenarides, which Tasos folded up and put in his back pocket.

Inside the konaki Keti was talking to some other people from Athens, a man who made silver jewelry and a woman who had translated the *Tao Te Ching* into Greek. They were discussing the differences between "initiation" and "self-initiation." According to Keti the Anastenaria involved "self-initiation." She thought that the state of ecstasy freed an inner power that prevented the Anastenarides from being burned. The silversmith talked about mysticism, spirit mediums, and the Sanskrit derivations of various religious words. In Brazil he'd seen a man put molten lead in his mouth and perform levitations.

Tasos, in the meantime, had come back into the konaki. He and the twelve-year-old grandson of an old lira player from Kosti who had recently died began playing the lira and singing. Huddled attentively around them were five or six photographers, folklorists, and musicologists. The Anastenarides and several other village women sat on the other side of the room by the icon shelf talking about dreams they had seen and the miraculous cures they had witnessed which testified to the great power of Saint Constantine. A little later a woman tried to pose for a photograph by standing in front of the icon shelf with an Anastenarissa. Tasos angrily told her that the konaki was not a museum. The next day when another woman asked him to explain some aspect of the rite to her, he told her to go talk to a reporter.

When Andreas entered the konaki with the new icon cover several hours later, an Anastenarissa began hissing and clapping. After putting in a few more stitches by hand Andreas placed the icon cover on the table and said, "Here it is! Use it with health!" Tasos, with two simadia draped around his neck, gave Andreas a small votive offering and told him to sew it on the new icon cover. When he finished, an Anastenarissa washed his hands.

Tasos signaled Evripidis to come up to the icon shelf. Evripidis incensed the shelf and the table where the new icon cover lay. Then he called for music. As the musicians began to play, Evripidis' head wobbled and shook, his hands trembled, and he cried out in pain. He held the new icon cover over his head and wept. Then he gave it to a cousin of his, the daughter of old Papadakena, to put on the Petrakis icon. Evripidis held his hands over his eyes mumbling to himself, "No. No. No." Finally Tasos placed the icon, now "wearing its new clothes," back on the shelf.

Over the next few days Evripidis complained several times that the icon cover was too small. He said that the Saint had confused Andreas and made him dizzy, as if he'd been sewing an icon cover for the first time. He measured one side and forgot the other; he picked up the scissors and put them down again. He couldn't go forward and he couldn't go back. A week later Evripidis and Mihalis went to Andreas' house and asked him to make a new icon cover.

THAT NIGHT several people danced whom I had never seen before. One was Dimitris, a young man well over six feet tall who had a degree in architecture from an American university. During the course of the festival he often stood for long periods of time in the middle of the konaki crying and sobbing with his hands over his face. None of the Anastenarides tried to comfort him. He just stood there in his blue T-shirt and sweat pants. Most of the photographers didn't pay any attention to him either; they were more interested in the old widows with the black kerchiefs and the lined faces. At last Dimitris approached the icon shelf, greeted the icons, and tenderly kissed the hands of the old village women seated on the bench along the wall. When someone referred to Dimitris as a ksenos, one Anastenarissa heard him reply, "I've been coming here all these years. I'm not a ksenos." She didn't say anything to him—she didn't want to hurt his feelings—but she thought to herself, "You sure are a ksenos. You just come and go."

I heard from some people that Dimitris was crazy, that he had been in a mental hospital, that he was schizophrenic. I also heard that he was the grandson of a priest. His parents had died, and his family icon had been sold. That's why he was suffering. He found the woman who'd bought the icon, but she wouldn't sell it back to him.

Dimitris told me about an epileptic girl who had come to see Yavasis the previous year. Dimitris thought she had a yin-yang imbalance and problems with her energy fields. He'd recommended acupuncture to her. When I asked Dimitris about his own experience with the Anastenaria, he criticized my interview style and said he thought anthropologists were only supposed to talk to "natives." I told him I thought we were all "natives." Then he commented sarcastically on my typically American clothes.

Kiriakos, a physics student at the University of Thessaloniki, was another person I'd never seen before. He had curly brown hair and spoke with a slight lisp. He was from Limnohori, Mihalis Kitsos' village. Last year he'd come to Ayia Eleni alone and danced for the first time. This year he brought his grandmother with him. She was an Anastenarissa.

When Kiriakos began dancing on the evening of May 20, he jerked

back and forth wildly and almost fell over backward. Tasos held him
for a few minutes and hugged him. Then he placed one of Kiriakos'
hands on Mihalis' back as Mihalis danced in place. With Mihalis leading Kiriakos by the hand, the two men danced across the room. When
Kiriakos' dance was done, his grandmother greeted him like a hero.
Dimitris came over and gave him a friendly pat on the cheek.

While Kiriakos knew that many people thought scientists desecrated
the sacredness of religious rituals with their attempts to explain everything, he welcomed the scientific study of the Anastenaria. His own
approach to it, however, was religious, in spite of the fact that he was
studying to be a physicist.

Kiriakos lived in a large student residence in Thessaloniki. It was
like a concentration camp, he said. He'd studied physics for two years
there, but then he stopped. For a whole year he didn't take any courses
or exams at all; he was passing through what he called "a crisis of transition." Then he changed the subject; he wanted to talk about Jack
Kerouac, Kent State, homeopathy, and health food.

Early the next day on the porch behind the konaki a folklorist from
Athens asked Tasos for the words to a particular song. Tasos dictated a
few verses for him but then took the folklorist's notebook and pen and
began writing himself. When Tasos realized there were several verses
he couldn't remember, he asked an old widow sitting near him if *she*
knew the song. As she recited the missing verses, Tasos jotted them
down in the folklorist's notebook.

The same folklorist was present later in the day when Evripidis
sang a song about the icon of Mavrolefki while the Anastenarides
danced.

Ο Κωσταντίνος ο μικρός, ο Μικροκωσταντίνος,
Μικρό ντον είχ' η μάννα ντου, μικρό ντ' αρραβωνιάζει,
Μικρό ντον επαράτησαν μέσα στη Μαυρολεύκη.
Δώδεκα χρόνια φυλακή τον έβαλε ο δεσπότης.
Κανείς δεν πήγε να το δει, τα δάκρυα να σκουπίσει.
Δε βρήκε σπίτι για να μπει, χωριό να πάει να μείνει.
Τα πάρει δίπλα τα βουνά, δίπλα τα κορφοβούνια.
Κοντά να πάει στη μάννα του . . .
Εμείς το λάθος κάναμε, κι άλλος θα το πληρώσει.
Μα τώρα μπήκε στο χορό . . .

Kostandinos the young, young Kostandinos,
His mother cared for him when he was young; he got engaged when
    he was young.
He was young when they abandoned him in Mavrolefki.
The bishop put him in jail for twelve years.
No one went to see him; no one went to dry his tears.
He couldn't find a house to live in or a village where he could stay.
He wandered through the mountains, through the high mountain
    peaks.
He wanted to be near his mother . . .
We made the mistake, and someone else will pay the price.
But now he has joined the dance . . .

When the Anastenarides had finished dancing, the folklorist asked
Evripidis to repeat the song, but Evripidis refused.

"We Anastenarides make mistakes," he said, "and others pay the
price. First we have to learn *his* language. Only then can we speak.
Otherwise everything we say is nonsense.

"I've talked with university professors," continued Evripidis.
"They say the rite can't be explained. I know things, but I don't talk;
it's not allowed. I talked to Tanagras when I was sixteen years old—
before I became an Anastenaris. Tanagras was the greatest psychologist
and theologian. He was a Theologian of Psychic Research. We asked
Tanagras what his conclusions were, what he thought it all meant. We
said, 'We're uneducated. We don't know anything.' And he said,
'From the very beginning until the moment you went into the fire I
was with you; I understood everything. But when you went into the
fire, I lost you; I was left behind.' So I said to Tanagras, 'Then you're
lower than the Anastenarides.'

"Believe and don't ask questions. That's what we say. Believe and
don't ask questions."

While the people who had come to study the Anastenaria were fascinated by ritual details, stories from the past, and the "secret" of firewalking, many Anastenarides were equally fascinated by the large reel-
to-reel tape recorders and long telephoto lenses that these outsiders
brought with them to record the rite. I remember Mihalis watching in
awe as a professional photographer quickly changed lenses and film as

if by reflex. In my case people were amazed by my writing. On my return visits to Ayia Eleni, I was often greeted with an incredulous, "Are you still writing?" or a mildly amused, "Keep writing. Just keep writing." People didn't understand how I could write while walking, without looking, in the dark. I said my hand just went by itself.

On the morning of May 23 I met Keti in the main square in downtown Serres where I'd spent the night. She invited me to join her for coffee, and I asked her about the rite. Keti felt that the Anastenaria involved a divine essence that took the form of a sacred flame; she quoted Pythagoras and Heraclitus. She said that for the Anastenarides Saint Constantine and the Orthodox Church provided the context for the expression of this divine essence, but that any other religion would work equally well. She talked about snake charmers, meditation, and metempsychosis; about reaching the "light of love" and experiencing communion with God.

Then Keti told me a little about her life in Athens. An exhibit of her paintings was opening soon in an art gallery in Athens, and in a few weeks she had to preside over an initiation at the Lodge of Free Masons where she was an officer. When I asked her what the initiation would involve, she hesitated for a moment and then asked me if I were a Mason. When I said no, she began talking very vaguely about some aspects of ancient Greek mystery religions that had much in common with the Anastenaria—passing over fire and blessing with water. She encouraged me to become a Mason; she said it was a good road.

Later in the morning I stopped at Yavasis' house and found him talking with Irini, a thin, fragile-looking young woman from Serres with pale white skin and long brown hair. She spoke softly with a shy, delicate voice, and when she danced her steps were small and timid, as if she were marching gingerly in place. Irini's mother and sister lived in Paris; her father was a busy lawyer in Serres. Irini herself lived alone in Thessaloniki, where she was studying architecture and working as a draftsman.

"Don't be afraid," Yavasis was telling her. "Some of the burden will leave you; you will be lighter tomorrow."

"But sometimes I'm afraid of myself," said Irini.

Yavasis asked her if her father could come to the festival sometime. Irini said that he was always really busy and wouldn't be able to. He knew that she came to Ayia Eleni and danced, but Irini was afraid of what might happen if he actually came himself. The night before she was watching television with him, and they saw some scenes of the Anastenaria on the news. Her father said something, and she lost her temper. He treated her like a child, so she got angry with him. Then he changed the subject. She hadn't slept all night.

"If he came here," said Yavasis, "I'd tell him not to worry, not to be upset. I'm like a father, too, an older father."

Irini began talking to Yavasis about her studies. She had one set of exams left to take, but whenever she was ready to take them, she seemed to have too much work to do in her office. She'd been working and studying like this for seven years; but other people had other dreams for her.

She asked Yavasis if she should go to Mavrolefki.

"Do you have a companion?" Yavasis asked.

Irini hesitated for a moment; she wasn't sure what he meant.

"Someone who's visible?" she asked.

Yavasis didn't answer.

"Did he say anything to you?"

"I can't talk about it now," replied Irini with embarrassment, glancing across the room in my direction.

Then Irini told Yavasis that the day before the festival she hadn't been able to stay in her apartment in Thessaloniki, so she set out for Ayia Eleni. But when she was halfway there, she stopped. She almost went back to Thessaloniki, but she couldn't. She couldn't go to her parents' house in Serres either. She had nowhere to go, no place to stay; so she came here, to Yavasis' house, the place she knew best. Maybe now she should go to Mavrolefki.

Yavasis said nothing. I decided it was time for me to leave.

That evening on my way to the new konaki I walked down the main street of the village—past vendors selling sandwiches, candy, soft drinks, and beer; past merry-go-rounds, swings, shooting galleries, and bumper cars; through a gauntlet of stands filled with stuffed animals, plastic toys, embroidered tablecloths, watches, cassettes, and pocket calculators. Under the icon shelf sat Tasos; next to him on the long bench sat Evripidis, Mihalis, Sotiria, Keti, and five or six other Anastenarisses. Dimitris and Kiriakos sat at their feet. Next to them, holding hands and sitting on the same small stool, were Irini and a heavy-boned young woman with weathered hands from a small village near Langadas. As the lira players started to tune their instruments, Tasos incensed around the room. He asked Evripidis and Mihalis to do the same. Then the dancing began.

Later in the evening, when the fire had been lit and the floor of the konaki was crowded with dancers, I was shocked to see Sofia Zora suddenly begin to dance. I had known her since 1976, and she had never danced before.

"It will all clear up," she shouted as she moved toward the front of the room. Her hands fluttered loosely in front of her; she was not dancing well at all. Her daughter Panayota, a dental technician who lived in Serres, was in tears. Sofia danced back to her husband and led him up to the front of the konaki. Panayota tried to stop her, but her father told her to leave her mother alone.

Sofia, dancing more forcefully now, cleared a path through the crowd in front of her with little shouts and waves. She danced toward her husband and gestured in front of his face as if waving something away from him. Panayota was still crying. Her young daughter was clinging to her, sobbing, as if she'd witnessed a terrible accident. She seemed about to faint.

A few minutes later Sofia was dancing wildly at the icon shelf. Tasos calmed her down and gave her a simadi. Then she danced back to her husband, kissed him on the cheek, took his hand, and continued to dance. Again Panayota tried to stop her, but Sofia cried, "Here!" and kept on dancing. Another Anastenarissa danced toward Panayota and clapped angrily, but Tasos pulled her gently away. Sofia danced in front of one of her husband's nieces, and then in front of one of his cousins, who called out to her, "Have patience! Hang on!" The Anastenarides were now ready to leave the konaki for the fire. Still dancing, Sofia joined them, followed by her husband, her daughter, and her granddaughter.

Sofia Zora and her husband Yannis were well respected by the people of Ayia Eleni. Yannis worked hard; his tractor was one of the oldest in the village, and he still lived in his parents' old mud-brick house, but all three of his children had continued their education past high school. Two or three years ago Sofia and Yannis had left Ayia Eleni and moved to Serres. More recently Yannis had had an operation on his stomach; he couldn't hold down any food. Sofia had been sick, too. People said she had heart trouble.

Yannis was the person who slaughtered the lamb every year on May 21. His mother had been an Anastenarissa. I talked with Yannis and Sofia about her several times in 1976. She had never danced in public or in the fire—her husband wouldn't let her—but she danced in the

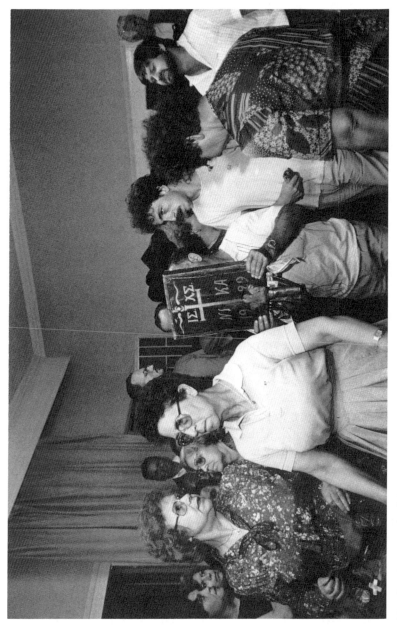

Dancing Anastenarides fill the new konaki (Photograph by John Demos/Apeiron)

house when the icons came or when someone in the family was sick. She'd tell Sofia to light some incense, and then she'd dance in front of the family icon shelf. When she was done, she'd assure everyone in the family that things would be all right. In 1976 I actually asked Yannis if he would let his wife or daughter dance. He said he would, but one of his daughters added, "I hope it never comes to that."

I knew that Yannis' mother used to serve a meal to the Anastenarides on May 22. Sofia had continued serving the meal after her mother-in-law's death but stopped when Panayota married an elementary school teacher. He was not from Ayia Eleni, nor was he a Kostilis. In 1976 he told me that while he was engaged to Panayota he'd told his in-laws not to serve the meal to the Anastenarides anymore. It was a stupid thing to do; the rite was nothing but a foolish superstition. They stopped without a word.

On May 22, 1986, however, the day before Sofia danced for the first time, Yannis and Sofia had served the meal again. I heard Yannis tell an Anastenarissa standing outside his house that he was afraid he'd made a mistake and that he wanted to ask the Anastenarides a question. She suggested he call the Anastenarides to his house some Saturday or Sunday; they would tell him what they knew. Yannis told her he'd been sick the previous year and hadn't been able to come to the village for the festival. That's why his house had been closed. After the meal Yannis, the nervous host, offered people raisins and chickpeas and called for love and peace for everyone in the world.

THE ANASTENARIDES passed through the crowd and circled the bed of glowing coals. Soula, Mihalis, and Maria crossed the fire first. With her shoes still on, Sofia danced back and forth at the edge of the fire. Her daughter and another village woman were holding her by the arms. Sofia told them to let her go, but they ignored her request. She danced over to Tasos, who was standing by the fire holding an icon. After she and her husband both kissed the icon, Sofia danced away shouting, "Let me go! Give me my freedom!" Her husband stood by the fire holding her pocketbook and her sweater.

Thodoros, Maria, Sotiria, and Mihalis were all dancing in the fire when suddenly a man with curly black hair and a thin beard burst from the crowd and ran across the fire. I had never seen him before; he was a complete stranger. Tasos went over to him, took him by the hand, and stood by the side of the fire with him. Then Tasos gestured to another villager to take his hand. A few minutes later Thodoros danced over to the new man and looked at him questioningly.

In twenty minutes or so a line of Anastenarides gradually began to form around the fire. Tasos led the dance, followed by Sofia, her husband, and her daughter. Sotiria, Thodoros, and Mihalis continued dancing across the coals. Now Sofia led the dance around the fire holding a simadi in her free right hand, followed by Tasos, her husband, her daughter, and other Anastenarides. After they all returned to the konaki, everyone crowded around Sofia. Her daughter was blowing on her face in a desperate attempt to cool her off. At the same time one of her nieces was holding out a glass of water for her to drink, but Sofia just continued to dance.

Then Marika, a widow with a stern, imposing manner who had always refused to talk to me about the Anastenaria, danced past me, holding out the icon for people to kiss. When she realized she had gone

Marika dances in front of an Anastenaris who gazes intently at Saints Constantine and Helen (Photograph by John Demos/Apeiron)

past me, she came back, called to me by name, and held the icon out for me to kiss. I leaned forward and bowed my head toward the icon without actually kissing it, in a compromise gesture I had worked out over the years.

After Sofia stopped dancing, she kissed the cheek and the hand of several Anastenarides and was kissed twice in return. Then she went into the back room with her husband. An Anastenarissa came up to her and said excitedly, "We were together. I knew it would happen. I was going to tell you, but I held back." "I thought it might happen too," Sofia replied. "But where will it lead?" Several Anastenarides wished her a good road and assured her that everything would be all right— there was nothing wrong with her; she was fine. Then Sofia and her husband returned to the konaki and sat down near the icon shelf in front of the row of Anastenarides.

I went outside and found the bearded stranger who had rushed out of the crowd into the fire. He was washing his feet at a faucet behind the konaki. He told me that he did restoration work on old churches and that he'd read an article about firewalking in the *National Geographic* but that this was the first time he'd actually seen the Anastenaria in person. All of a sudden he just wanted to go into the fire. He didn't believe in Saint Constantine or in any one religion in particular; he believed in all religions. No one had given him a simadi to dance with, but later in the konaki one of the Anastenarides told him to go up and kiss the icons so he wouldn't insult anyone. He insisted on showing me his feet. "Usually, even little sparks burn you," he said. "But this was a big fire with huge logs, and I wasn't burned at all."

The village men who were responsible for the treasury of the Anastenarides sat down on the floor of the konaki and began to count the money that had been collected over the course of the festival. Two old widows dressed in black sat beside them holding lighted candles. When the men had finished, Tasos announced how much money had been collected, how much had been spent, and how much had been left over from the previous year. There were now several hundred dollars in "the grandfather's chest," as the treasury of the Anastenarides was called.

Tasos asked what people wanted to do with the money. He suggested buying a refrigerator for the konaki. Sofia Zora said she thought they needed blankets and mattresses for people to sleep on when they came to see the Anastenaria from far away. Tasos mentioned the fact that the fireplace in the konaki needed repairs. Yannis repeated his wife's suggestion about blankets and mattresses.

"This money was given by people in the village and all over the world," said Tasos, "and it goes back to them. How shall we spend it? Speak up so I can hear you!"

Several people made other suggestions, but no consensus was reached.

"I say no one has spoken," concluded Tasos. "We will leave the money in the grandfather's chest, and later the people in charge of it can fix up the kitchen or do whatever they think is best and then give what's left to the Folklore Society."

When the final meal of the festival was served, Tasos incensed over the plates of cheese and olives, the loaves of bread, and the huge pot of rice and lamb that had been laid out on an embroidered cloth on the floor.

"Good evening to all," he said. "This meal is served by the grandfathers. It's for the whole world; it's a meal of love. Enjoy it!"

The musicians started to play and sing as plates of food were distributed and people began to eat. There was some joking about the fact that Mihalis was as tall standing up as Dimitris was sitting down. Yannis Zoras sat awkwardly on his low stool; his three-piece gray suit seemed out of place among the plainer clothes of the widows and the older village women.

After the meal and the distribution of raisins and chickpeas that followed, people prepared to leave. Dimitris, Kiriakos, and Irini were obviously moved as they said good-bye to the old Anastenarides and kissed their hands. Tasos distributed the icons and simadia, and the procession of Anastenarides formed for the last time. I stood there as people lined up to greet the procession and bid farewell to the Saints, the Anastenarides, and their fellow Kostilides. One by one people kissed the icons, the simadia, and the hands of the people who held them. I watched a man from Ayia Eleni kiss the simadi that belonged to his mother before she died. Then he kissed the hand of his younger brother who was holding it.

⁙

That night I dreamt I was greeting the procession of Anastenarides myself. After I kissed all the icons and all the simadia, I wanted to get in line again and greet the procession a second time. I asked Marika, the widow, if I could. She said yes and showed me exactly what to do—just what to kiss and who to give my money to.

✣

The morning after the festival I found Tasos at his parents' house near the village square. He had just returned from plowing his family's fields with his father's tractor. After his mother served us coffee in the yard, he talked about his schizophrenic life—his interest in folklore and the Anastenaria, on the one hand, and the research he was doing on multiple sclerosis for his doctoral dissertation, on the other. He emphasized how hard it was for him to leave his patients at the hospital and at the private clinic where he worked to come to Ayia Eleni for several days at a time. If he lived in the village, he would know more about local issues and be in a better position to resolve some of the conflicts that arose during the festival.

Tasos realized now that the founding of the Folklore Society and his early involvement with the Anastenaria had been misguided. It had been a disaster, but he'd been motivated by what he called a "chauvinistic" desire to protect the Anastenaria and the village of Ayia Eleni. More recently, he said, the relationship between the Anastenarides and the Folklore Society had improved greatly. Several years ago, for example, the government sponsored a program to teach handicrafts to poor village women, and the president of Ayia Eleni wanted to use the new konaki as a classroom. On the last day of the festival of Saint Athanasios, Tasos brought the issue up for discussion in front of everyone. One man said he thought it would be fine—poor women would learn a skill and earn some money—but someone else thought the Anastenaria would get a bad reputation if the konaki were used for such purposes. The officers of the Folklore Society, which actually owned the building, thought it was a good idea. Tasos had no objections either, but he insisted they ask the Anastenarides for their opinion. Several women began to dance and shout, "No! No! No!" In the end the classes were not held in the konaki.

Then Tasos and I talked about the events of the previous evening. Tasos said that Sofia Zora did not have heart trouble; her chest pain was a case of somatization associated with hysteria. He said he was speaking now as a psychiatrist and cited *DSM III*, the latest diagnostic and statistical manual of the American Psychiatric Association. Tasos thought that Sofia's daughter didn't want her to dance because of the strain it would put on her heart. I told him I thought it had more to do with the shame and the fear that people associated with becoming an Anastenaris.

Tasos was amazed at the elasticity of the symbolism of the rite, the way it could appeal to so many different kinds of people: women who were oppressed by their families and young people who had to remain subordinate to their parents for so long. He felt that a person like Dimitris might not be helped very much by the rite because he lived in a world that didn't readily accept religious phenomena like the Anastenaria.

When I told Tasos that some people claimed that he himself wasn't really an Anastenaris because he had never danced, he replied that although he never felt the need to dance, he *was* an Anastenaris because, like Yavasis, he had the ability to heal people. The Anastenarides accepted him as their leader because he was able to maintain order and harmony; they cooperated with him because he showed them the proper respect. During the festival the Anastenarides forgot he was a doctor and a scientist; they just saw him as a fellow villager.

I mentioned the bearded man who had run into the fire the night before. Tasos thought he'd been burned because when he took his hand, the man seemed relieved that he didn't have to go into the fire again. Tasos said he took his hand in order to give him a simadi, so the Anastenarides wouldn't be embarrassed. Another time a complete stranger entered the fire, Tasos tried to take the man's hand, but he pulled loose and ran back into the fire. Tasos felt that more experiments needed to be done before scientists could explain why the Anastenarides were not burned.

It was time for me to leave. As Tasos and I walked across his parents' yard to the street, I told him about my dream. "From a psychoanalytic point of view," he said, "the meaning is clear. You want to come back. You haven't had your fill."

VI

The Celebration of Community in a Changing World

❖

THE ANASTENARIA not only plays an important part in the personal lives of individual Anastenarides, it also plays a central role in the collective life of the village of Ayia Eleni and the community of Kostilides as a whole. The Anastenaria has been a powerful symbol for the shared identity of the Kostilides ever since their arrival as refugees in Greek Macedonia. It epitomizes all that it means to be a Kostilis in a society that is experiencing the homogenizing effects of mass media, a national educational system, and rapid modernization and urbanization. In addition, the festival of Saints Constantine and Helen has come to be the most important event of the year in the village of Ayia Eleni. Because of the Anastenaria, Ayia Eleni enjoys a nationwide reputation and a degree of power and influence in regional political affairs it would otherwise lack.

More specifically the Anastenaria employs a spirit idiom to make a symbolic statement about the community of Kostilides in Ayia Eleni and throughout northern Greece. Through the Anastenaria what it means to be a Kostilis is constantly being explored and negotiated. Saint Constantine personifies the community of Kostilides. His icon is a symbol of their unique identity; his will an expression of their collective moral power.

The illnesses treated by the Anastenaria can, therefore, be seen as an expression of some social failing. The ritual faults held responsible for people's suffering frequently involve an offence against important social values and norms. Conversely, service to Saint Constantine in the hope of regaining one's health constitutes service to the community of Kostilides as a whole, just as developing a positive relationship with the Saint constitutes achieving solidarity with and integration into this same community.

When Anastenarides are possessed by Saint Constantine, they come to personify the collective ideals and traditional values of their community; they come to embody the moral and social order of the Kostilides. In this way they acquire power—the power of Saint Constantine, the power of the community of Kostilides. Not only may this process be therapeutically effective for the individual, it may also have significant beneficial effects for the community as well. Just as individuals who participate in the Anastenaria are empowered and transformed as they are rhetorically moved from a position of illness to a position of health, so the entire community of Kostilides acquires a sense of identity and unity through the successful performance of the Anastenaria. The entire community is empowered, transformed, and healed as well.

"THE SAINTS WON'T LET US FORGET OUR KIN"

The Anastenaria is both a model *of* and a model *for* the community of Kostilides (Geertz 1973b:93). It constructs for them a sacred image of their community; it makes a religious statement about the way in which their social world is organized. Through the celebration of the Anastenaria the community of Kostilides defines itself and exerts a hold over the people who belong to it.

The icons of the Anastenarides themselves provide the most powerful example of the dialectical relationship that exists between the symbolic system of the Anastenaria and the social system of the Kostilides. The relationships believed to exist among these icons replicate precisely the relationships that exist among important social categories of the Kostilides. The icons of the Anastenarides, referred to collectively as *papoudes* (grandfathers, ancestors, or old men), are said to be related to one another through genealogical ties of kinship and to be descended from the oldest icon of them all, an icon that is linked metonymically with Saint Constantine himself. The oldest icon of Saints Constantine and Helen, known as "the old one from Kosti" (*Yerokotsianos*), which was brought from eastern Thrace to the village of Mavrolefki, is often referred to as the "father" of all the other icons. Some Anastenarides say that the linen cloth on the face of this icon was actually cut from a piece of Saint Constantine's clothing.

The other icons of the Anastenarides are called "children" of this icon. Hourmouziadis (1961:151) reports that when Anastenarides from Kosti traveled to neighboring villages, they said that the saint of one village was going to visit his "brother saint" in another village. As the husband of one Anastenaris told me when we were discussing the nature of the relationships between the various icons, "All the icons of Saints Constantine and Helen came from one, just as all men are descended from Adam. Icons have children and multiply just like men." According to most Kostilides, certain icons of a particular saint have more power than others, and the older an icon is the more powerful it is. When a new icon is made, it acquires power because some material substance from its "father" is incorporated into it.

This genealogical model of the relationships among the icons of the Anastenarides closely parallels the Kostilides' system of social classification. In this system categories of nationality, ethnicity, regional identity, and kinship are collapsed and expressed in a common idiom of *ratsa*, or race. As Herzfeld (1980b:290) has pointed out, "Ratsa is a segmentary or hierarchical term, and its use corresponds to a similarly organized discrimination between insiders (*diki*) and outsiders (*kseni*) at several levels." This concept of ratsa and the opposition between insiders and outsiders constitute what Herzfeld (291) has called a "semantic taxonomy of social groups" based on conceptual discriminations that express the moral superiority of insiders over outsiders.

People who are considered to be members of a particular ratsa at any level of the segmentary hierarchy are said to share certain traits or characteristics. They are residents (or descendants of residents) of the same geographical region, generally called a "fatherland" (*patrida*). They are also said to have the same "habits and customs" (*ithi ke ethima*), which include a traditional form of dress, a common accent or dialect, and a shared body of rituals and folklore. Another important aspect of the concept of ratsa is the biological metaphor that conflates common regional identity and shared cultural traits, on the one hand, with a notion of shared biological descent, on the other. This notion of descent is expressed in terms of a continuity of blood that is transmitted primarily in the male line. While mixed descent is recognized in some contexts, it is generally held that people belong to the ratsa of their father. As Kostilides say, "the ratsa depends on the father." A variety of physical characteristics are also attributed to people as a result of their identity as members of a certain ratsa.

At the level of national identity the Greek people as a whole are referred to as one ratsa as opposed to the Turkish ratsa or the Bulgarian ratsa. At the more restricted level of regional identity, the Thracian ratsa is distinguished from the Macedonian ratsa, while at a still more restricted level of the segmentary hierarchy the village is the relevant social group with respect to which ratsa is defined. In this sense "every village has its ratsa." This level of usage is of central importance in a discussion of the Anastenaria as a religious model of the community of Kostilides because it is at the village level that Kostilides define themselves as a ratsa.

For Kostilides living in Ayia Eleni in the 1970s, over fifty years after their arrival as refugees in Greek Macedonia, being Kostilides (being members of the ratsa of Kostilides) was still a crucial part of their identity. For example, a thirty-year-old man, born and raised in Ayia Eleni, whose father was from Kosti but whose mother was not, strongly asserted his identity as a Kostilis on the grounds that he had "blood of Kostilides" (*Kostilidiko ema*) flowing through his veins. For the Kostilides the village of Kosti continued to serve as the reference point with respect to which the categories of insider and outsider were defined. Kostilides from Ayia Eleni referred to Kostilides from Mavrolefki or Meliki as "insiders" (*diki*), or even as "fellow villagers" (*horiani*). Conversely they usually referred to residents of Ayia Eleni who were not Kostilides as "outsiders" (*kseni*). As more than one Kostilis told me, "Your ratsa is more important than where you live."[1]

At an even more restricted level ratsa is used interchangeably with soi to refer to a patrilineally defined surname group. For example, a man whose surname was Dragoulis would be referred to as a member of the Dragouleiki ratsa. When used in this sense, Kostilides say that a

---

[1] Other residents of Ayia Eleni resented the tendency of Kostilides to use Kosti as the reference point for categories of inclusion and exclusion rather than the village of Ayia Eleni where they now live. This emphasis on the past is consistent with the observation of De Vos and Romanucci-Ross (1975:363) that ethnic identity is "in essence a past-oriented form of identity."

man's ratsa depends on his "root" (*riza*), which is his paternal grand-father or ancestor (*papous*). When Kostilides want to emphasize the closeness and the unity of the ratsa of Kostilides, they use images from this more restricted domain of kinship. After greeting her fellow Kos-tilides in the konaki at a festival of Saints Constantine and Helen, one woman said "We are all fellow countrymen (*patriotes*). We're all one family (*ikoyenia*), one [paternal] line (*yenia*)."

The analogy between a soi and the community of Kostilides is sug-gested by the narrative account of the founding of Kosti which opens Chapter V. I heard this story from an elderly Kostilis who had been marginally involved with the Anastenaria earlier in his life; it was dis-missed by several other Kostilides as the meaningless ramblings of an eccentric old man. According to this account all Kostilides were ulti-mately descended from a common apical ancestor, "the old man Kostis" (*o papous o Kostis*), who was also the eponymous founder of the village of Kosti.[2] As a more widely accepted tradition has it, the village of Kosti was named after Saint Constantine, who is also referred to as papous.

It seems clear, then, that "the old man Kostis" and Saint Constantine are simply different personae of the same ancestor, founder, and unify-ing spiritual principle of the community of Kostilides. Thus there is a powerful and pervasive kinship metaphor involving descent from a common male ancestor that provides a key to understanding the rela-tionships among the icons of the Anastenarides, the conceptual orga-nization of the Anastenarides, and the ratsa of Kostilides. The icons of the Anastenarides are "descended" from "the old one from Kosti"; the Anastenarides are "children" of Saint Constantine, the papous; and the Kostilides are all descended from "the old man named Kostis."

This metaphor of genealogical descent also characterizes the rela-tionship between individual Kostilides and members of their soi, on the one hand, and their relationships with particular icons of the Anastenarides, on the other. In 1976 many Kostilides claimed that be-fore they left eastern Thrace the icons of the Anastenarides belonged to the entire community. They did so in spite of arguments to the contrary they had been forced to put forward in 1971 in order to regain posses-sion of their icons from officials of the Orthodox Church. Some Kos-

---

[2] The name Kostis, which is accented on the second syllable as is the name of the village Kosti, is one of several abbreviated forms of the name Kostandinos.

tilides, however, have more responsibility for an icon than others. In this sense an icon is "hereditary" (*klironomiko*); it belongs to the descendants of the person who originally discovered it or who was originally responsible for having it made.

According to this conception of ownership a special relationship exists between this group of people and a particular icon. These people are said to be *klironomi ap' afti tin ikona*, which can be translated "heirs to," "heirs of," or even "descendants of this icon." These people are heirs *to* the icon in the sense that they stand to inherit responsibility for its care and maintenance. Although all Kostilides are said to have a "share" in the icon, the klironomi have a larger share in it than others. With regard to inheritance of the icon preference is shown for a patrilineal heir—and more specifically for the youngest son of the previous heir—because in this way the icon stays in the soi and in the paternal house as well. Other klironomi may have a simadi from the icon indicating their special relationship to it, particularly if they are Anastenarides or if they have suffered an illness attributed to Saint Constantine.

These klironomi, however, are not just heirs *to* an icon; the icon is not simply a piece of property they may inherit. They are heirs *of* the icon as well; they are actually *descendants of* the icon. The icon is so powerfully identified with the saint from whom they are descended that their relationship with the icon of the saint is also conceptualized as one of descent. Just as all Kostilides are metaphorically descended from Saint Constantine, so at a more restricted level a group of klironomi, a segment of the ratsa of Kostilides, is metaphorically descended from a particular icon of Saint Constantine.

This metaphoric relationship of descent which links a group of Kostilides with a particular icon is expressed more explicitly in the use of the word *akrabas* (from the Turkish *akraba*), meaning relative, to refer to the klironomos of an icon. A Kostilis whose grandmother had brought an icon of Saints Constantine and Helen with her to Ayia Eleni from Kosti said that he and other members of his soi were *akrabades* of this icon; they belonged to the ratsa of this icon. Another phrase often used to express this relationship was *vastame ap' afti tin ikona* (we are descended from that icon, or we belong to that icon), which is exactly parallel to the phrase *vastame ap' afti ti ratsa* (we are descended from that ratsa, we belong to that ratsa).

This metaphoric expression of the segmentary pattern of the Kostilides' social organization through the icons of the Anastenaria recalls Herzfeld's (1984b) discussion of the segmentary properties of Greek iconography. Herzfeld, drawing on Evans-Pritchard (1956) and Campbell (1964), points out that Orthodox saints are "refracted" through the conceptual segments of Greek society. Each icon of a particular saint is a refraction of that saint which serves as an emblem of the social identity of a group at any level of the segmentary hierarchy. Each icon is a material representation of an "*aspect* of the saint's essence," which is associated with a particular region, village, or kinship group (Herzfeld 1984b:654). The existence of "patron saints" and "family icons" throughout Greece illustrates this fissioning process very well.

In the context of the Anastenaria Saint Constantine is a symbol of the community of Kostilides. Just as the ratsa of Kostilides is segmented conceptually into many soia, so Saint Constantine is refracted through his icons into many images, each a symbol for a particular soi. Thus the Saint and his icons are at once symbols of the common descent and unity of the social groups they personify and vehicles for the expression of opposition and conflict between groups at the same level of the segmentary hierarchy.

When Kostilides from throughout Greek Macedonia gather at the konaki of Ayia Eleni for the festival of Saints Constantine and Helen, they re-create both symbolically and literally the community of Kostilides that was so tragically uprooted after the Balkan Wars. Kostilides from one village who rarely see their relatives from another village eagerly look forward to the festival as an opportunity for an extended family reunion, a chance to renew relationships with distant kin. Contact among Kostilides in different villages is also maintained by visits Kostilides from one village make to the konaki of another village in fulfillment of a vow or in the hope of regaining their health.

Whenever Kostilides gather, the conversation invariably turns to the subject of how important it is to maintain ties with one's relatives and with other Kostilides. At the festival of Saints Constantine and Helen in May 1986 a woman who had grown up in Ayia Eleni and moved to Thessaloniki after her marriage sat in the konaki talking with some women from the village. "When you live in the city," she said, "you're among kseni all day. When you see a person from your own village, you get all excited. It's a shock. You think you're seeing your God." The segmentation of God and the analogy between the emotions evoked by the sight of a fellow villager and the sight of God are significant. On another occasion Yavasis, referring to an Anastenarissa who was the daughter of one of his wife's cousins, said, "If it weren't for the saints, she wouldn't even know me. She'd just say, 'I have an uncle somewhere.' People forget their kin, but they're always there. The saints won't let us forget them."

People who have a simadi from one of the icons of the Anastenarides because they are klironomi of that icon bring it to the konaki for the celebration of the two major festivals each year. During these festivals the simadia are kept on the icon shelf, held by Anastenarides when they dance, and carried in procession through the village. Because each simadi is identified with a specific icon, when all the simadia are placed on the icon shelf at the konaki of Ayia Eleni together with the two icons from Ayia Eleni, it is as if all the icons of the Anastenarides had been reunited, as if the icons from Mavrolefki, Meliki, Mesopotamo, Limnohori, Serres, Langadas, and Ayia Eleni were together again, as they had been in the konaki in Kosti a long time ago. Thus at festivals of the Anastenarides the original unity of the ratsa of Kostilides is recreated symbolically as well as socially in the konaki of Ayia Eleni.

During the procession of Anastenarides, each icon (and each simadi) should be carried by a klironomos of that icon (or of the icon the simadi represents). Therefore, the structure of the procession is a replication in miniature, almost a map or kinship diagram, of the social organization of the ratsa of Kostilides. In this procession the emblems of the various villages and kinship groups that constitute the ratsa of Kostilides, as well as actual members of the groups themselves, are arrayed in a public display of the power and unity of the community of Kostilides.

The procession is not the only part of the festival whose successful completion requires the participation of members of many of the different social groups that make up the ratsa of Kostilides. Virtually all the jobs associated with the Anastenaria must be performed by members of specific soia. If a man makes a vow to serve the Saint in a certain way, then one of his descendants should continue to do so after his death. These jobs, which are described as *klironomika*, include holding the candle and the censer at the head of the procession, cutting the throat of the lamb that is sacrificed, butchering the carcass, distributing the meat, lighting the fire, tending the fire, and serving meals to the Anastenarides during their circuit of the village.

The procession of Anastenarides makes its way through the streets of Ayia Eleni (Photograph by Loring M. Danforth)

The dancing of the Anastenarides is another expression of the social identity of the Kostilides. The Anastenarides communicate the unity and solidarity of the ratsa of Kostilides by dancing powerfully and joyfully together through the fire and by dancing hand in hand in a circle around the village square. Through dance, however, they also express the conflicts and tensions that often develop within the community, as when one Anastenaris knocks another down in the fire or strikes another on the head with an icon. When two Anastenarides from different villages who have not seen each other for a long time first meet at a festival, they often dance briefly before they greet each other with a warm embrace. Kostilides say that the saints of the different villages are greeting one another.

As Spencer (1985:35) has pointed out in his analysis of the social meaning of dance, through dancing people are "caught up in a very dynamic way in the powerful forces underlying community life." In the case of the Anastenaria the power that moves people to dance, the power that "catches people up," is the power of Saint Constantine, who personifies the ratsa of Kostilides and embodies their highest ideals.

As the Present Becomes the Past

The past is a crucial component of the social identity of the Kostilides. In many ways the Anastenaria is a celebration of this past, a celebration of the origins and the history of the community of Kostilides. It is a festival of remembrance in which the Kostilides continually re-create their past through powerful symbolic performances involving saints, icons, music, and dance. Like a memorial service for the dead, the Anastenaria resurrects the people and the places of a past that has been lost. It enables the Kostilides of the present to enter into a symbolic conversation with the Kostilides of the past. In this way Kostilides are able to assert a continuity with their ancestors and to define themselves in terms of their collective past.

The most obvious expression of this worship of the past is the use of the term *papoudes* to refer to the saints and the icons of the Anastenarides. In a variety of ways the saints, the spiritual ancestors of the Kostilides, are identified with the human ancestors of the Kostilides. Saint Constantine, the papous, was often identified with Yavasis, the leader of the Anastenarides, who was also referred to simply as the papous. I once heard a woman who had just placed a pair of socks on the icon shelf at the konaki say to Yavasis, "I brought these socks for Saint Constantine to wear first. Then you can wear them."

The close association between the saints of the Anastenarides and the ancestors of the Kostilides, whether alive or dead, is also suggested by the parallels that exist between icons and family photographs, an analogy also reported by Herzfeld (1984b:654). One Anastenarissa, for example, kept a family photograph on her icon shelf next to her family icons—a photograph of Yavasis, her uncle, dancing in the fire.

The way in which the Anastenaria is able to keep alive memories of the past is also illustrated by the following incident, which took place at the konaki of Ayia Eleni on the eve of the festival of Saints Constantine and Helen in 1981. A very old Anastenarissa went to kiss the hand of a much younger Anastenaris. He thought this was inappropriate because he was so much younger than she was, so he tried to pull his hand away. The old Anastenarissa insisted, explaining that she was not kissing *his* hand but the hand of his grandmother, who had died several years earlier and who had also been an Anastenarissa. The young man relented and let her kiss his hand. The fact that he was the klironomos of his grandmother, that he was an Anastenaris and danced, kept her memory alive, just as the common Greek practice of naming children after their grandparents ensures that the names of the grandparents will continue to be heard.[3]

Another aspect of the celebration of the Anastenaria bears a striking resemblance to memorial services held throughout Greece during which women visit the graves of the dead to light candles and oil lamps and to sing laments.[4] As they process through Ayia Eleni, the Anastenarides stop at the houses of Anastenarides who have died or who are too old and infirm to participate actively in the ritual. At these houses one Anastenaris usually "dances" the simadi that belongs to the Anastenaris of the house and is kept on the family icon shelf. In this way the memories of Anastenarides of the past are honored, their positions in the community preserved.

The Anastenaria, then, is a celebration of the past. In Greece, however, there is not just one past; there are many, each contributing in different ways and for different segments of society to a definition of

---

[3] The implications of rural Greek naming practices are analyzed by Herzfeld (1982b).

[4] These rituals are described in greater detail in Danforth (1982).

the present. One of these pasts which plays an important part in the Anastenaria is the early Christian and Byzantine past whose most powerful symbol is Constantinople, the city founded by Saint Constantine himself.

As suggested in Chapter IV, many of the traditions of the Anastenaria serve to set the history of the ritual and the community of Kostilides firmly in the wider context of the history of the Byzantine Empire. Saint Constantine, the father or grandfather of the Anastenarides (and by extension of all the Kostilides), is generally considered to be the founder and savior of all that is Greek and Christian. In many of the stories Kostilides tell, the origin of the Anastenaria and the founding of Kosti are identified with important events in Byzantine history. Their oldest icon was made from a piece of Saint Constantine's clothing; Saint Constantine performed the first firewalk when he had his miraculous vision; the church of Kosti, from whose burning remains the icons of the Anastenarides were rescued, was built by Saint Constantine. With these stories the Anastenarides, their icons, and the community of Kostilides acquire power and sanctity both because of their great age and because of their association with an important religious figure of the past.

Another past celebrated by the Anastenaria is the past symbolized by the village of Kosti in eastern Thrace, the lost homeland of the Kostilides. In 1976 most Kostilides over the age of thirty-five, and all who participated in the Anastenaria, had either been born in Kosti or were children of people who had been born there. For these people being a Kostilis was a very important part of their identity. For them the Anastenaria was the most powerful expression of this identity; it was their closest link to this aspect of their past.

The catastrophic events of 1922 marked the end of the past symbolized by Kosti as in a larger context it marked the end of an era in modern Greek history. Until 1922 Greek communities had existed for centuries scattered throughout eastern Thrace, Pontus, Cappadocia, and other parts of Asia Minor. With the disastrous defeat of the Greek army by the Turks in the Asia Minor campaign well over a million Greeks were forced to abandon their homes and flee to Greece. The tragic experiences of these refugees and the loss and destruction of their homelands are powerful themes in modern Greek culture.[5]

[5] On Greece's ill-fated venture in Asia Minor see Dobkin (1972) and Smith (1973).

To the people they encountered when they arrived in Greek Macedonia the Kostilides were simply "refugees." In Ayia Eleni in 1976 this was still the term most frequently used by non-Kostilides to refer to Kostilides. The negative connotations of being a refugee are suggested by the teasing wordplay some Kostilides encountered involving the words *prosfiyes* (refugees) and *prostihes* (low, cheap, vulgar) (Christodoulou 1978:16), as well as by the parallels that are often drawn between refugees and itinerant gypsies (Loizos 1981:121). As refugees the Kostilides had been separated from their homeland, a crucial component of their identity. They had not lost their icons, however, and it was with these icons (often the only personal possessions they were able to bring with them to Greek Macedonia) that the Kostilides could continue to perform the Anastenaria. It was with these icons that they could continue to be Kostilides.

In a sensitive analysis of the experiences of Greek Cypriot refugees after the Turkish invasion of Cyprus in 1974, Peter Loizos (1981) compares the situation of refugees to that of bereaved people mourning the death of a close relative. Greek Cypriot refugees, like Kostilides, were very concerned with keeping alive the memory of their lost homeland. They talked at length about specific places and particular pieces of property they had left behind, and they named stores and coffeehouses after their former villages. In this way they maintained the symbols of their old identity in new and often very different contexts.

Loizos points out, however, that, unlike the bereaved, refugees do not have any religious rituals or mourning ceremonies to help them deal therapeutically with their emotions and to provide them with support in time of need. I suggest that for Kostilides the Anastenaria fills this gap. It serves as a memorial service for their ancestors, for Kosti, and for all they have left behind. Processions, visual images, exchanges of food, and songs of loss and separation all suggest the many similarities that exist between the Anastenaria and rural Greek death rituals. Both are festivals of remembrance in which people define themselves as individuals and as a community in terms of their relationship with the past.

The Anastenaria has become, in a sense, a repository for the past. Aspects of the traditional culture of Kosti that were not specifically associated with the Anastenaria before have, with the passage of time,

On the exchange of populations between Balkan nations that followed World War I see Ladas (1932), Pentzopoulos (1962), and Petropoulos (1976).

become inextricably linked with it. In eastern Thrace, for example, all icons were traditionally encased in cloth coverings (Mihail-Dede 1983:207). Now in Ayia Eleni these coverings are a unique feature of the icons of the Anastenarides. Similarly, the large red kerchiefs known as simadia were once a standard part of formal male dress. Now they too are a unique feature of the Anastenaria. In addition, "old" words like konaki and akrabas, dialect forms, and traditional Thracian folksongs have all condensed around the Anastenaria so that virtually everything from Kosti, everything from the past, has come to be associated with it. The role played by the Anastenaria in keeping alive the past is conveyed by the greeting with which a Kostilis living in Serres welcomed his fellow Kostilides who had gathered there for the festival of the Virgin Mary on August 15, 1976. "Long live Kosti!" he shouted. "May Kosti never die!"

The continued importance of the Anastenaria in the lives of many Kostilides has led them to maintain contact with their homeland in eastern Thrace in an even more direct way. On several occasions the Thracian Hearth, the counterpart in Langadas to the Folklore Society of Ayia Eleni, has organized bus tours to Bulgaria for the Anastenarides and their families to visit Kosti and the surrounding villages. During these visits the Anastenarides tried to locate the churches and the ayiasmata they had heard so much about. On their pilgrimages to the sacred places of the past they also danced and occasionally performed a small firewalk.

These trips from Ayia Eleni and Langadas to Kosti replicate structurally parallel events in stories about the founding of Kosti and the original discovery of the icons of the Anastenarides. In those stories Saint Constantine forced people to visit the sites of the destroyed villages that predated Kosti: Tripori, Stavrohori, Kastania, Palioklisia. Often the people telling those stories recalled visiting these very sites as children. Through the Anastenaria, then, the Kostilides of one generation, one time, and one place, are led back to their ancestors, to the past, and to their lost homeland.

Since the 1950s observers have been predicting that the Anastenaria would not survive long in the face of the many social and cultural changes occurring in rural Greece.[6] They said that the Anastenaria would not withstand the persecution of the Orthodox Church, the in-

---

[6] See, for example, Furley (1981:235), Hadjipandazis (1972), and Kranidiotis (1956:277).

vestigations of scientists, or the curiosity of tourists; that the religious faith of the Anastenarides was out of place in a secular age; that young people would not become Anastenarides and continue the rite. Soon, they said, memories of Kosti will fade and the traditions of eastern Thrace will disappear. The Anastenaria will lose all meaning. The ritual will die.

However, as the celebration of the festival of Saints Constantine and Helen in Ayia Eleni in 1986 attests, this could not be further from the truth. The sewing of the new icon cover in fulfillment of a vow and the "coming out" of Sofia Zora testify to the continued power the Anastenaria has in the lives of the people of Ayia Eleni. The recent recovery of their icons by the Anastenarides in Mavrolefki, the establishment of a new konaki and firewalk in Thessaloniki, and the continued success of the celebration of the festivals of Langadas and Ayia Eleni clearly indicate that the Anastenaria remains a vital form of religious expression. It is obvious, though, that by 1986 the Anastenaria of Ayia Eleni had undergone many dramatic changes. A neurologist-psychiatrist had emerged as the new leader of the rite, and educated young people and bohemian artists from Athens had begun to participate in the rite in significant numbers.

These important developments in the Anastenaria must be understood in the context of the rapid urbanization and modernization that has been taking place in Greece over the past thirty years. The industrialization and economic development of postwar Greece has led to a remarkable concentration of the population in Athens, Thessaloniki, and other urban centers. This massive exodus of people from rural areas of Greece has been fueled by the promise of a higher standard of living, the security of wage labor in contrast to the uncertainties of farming, and the high status accorded an urban way of life.[7]

Unlike so many villages in more isolated and mountainous parts of Greece, Ayia Eleni has not suffered economically or demographically during this period because of the success of agricultural practices in the Serres basin made possible by large-scale mechanization and irrigation. Nevertheless, the Kostilides of Ayia Eleni have whenever possible taken advantage of the opportunities offered by an increasingly acces-

---

[7] For a more thorough treatment of these important changes in Greek society see Campbell and Sherrard (1968), Friedl (1962, 1976), McNeill (1978), Mouzelis (1978), Sutton (1983), and Vermeulen (1983).

sible educational system to provide their children entry into a skilled trade or profession. In this way their children are able to exchange the hardships of farming and village life for the comfort and prestige of urban living.

In their quest for upward social mobility, however, these young people leave behind the secure world of family and fellow villagers. The village of Ayia Eleni and the community of Kostilides come to play an increasingly less important part in their lives when they enter the very different worlds of the urban middle class or the university-based youth culture. As a result they often pay a high price in terms of difficult personal adjustments and experiences of isolation and alienation.

As students they confront the competitive pressures and the impersonal bureaucracy of an overcrowded system of higher education. They also have to deal with the difficult living conditions of student dormitories and student cafeterias. If they successfully complete their education and training, they face the prospect of being unable to find jobs commensurate with their skills in what is still in many ways an underdeveloped economy. Women in this situation, often under a great deal of pressure to marry at a relatively early age, face a difficult choice between a family and a career. These are the young people who had begun to participate in the Anastenaria when I returned to Ayia Eleni in 1986.

One young woman from the village who had recently begun to show signs of becoming an Anastenarissa was studying mathematics at the University of Thessaloniki. She was the niece of an Anastenarissa and had an interest in astrology. At the festival of Saint Athanasios the previous January she cried and trembled, but she didn't "come out." According to some people her parents didn't let her dance because she was still unmarried; they were afraid that if she became an Anastenarissa it would be hard to find her a husband.

Another young woman people thought would "come out" soon had left Ayia Eleni twelve years earlier at the age of twenty-three to live alone in Thessaloniki. She ran a small textile factory that employed six other women. Her parents were very worried about her because she had apparently decided not to get married. She refused to enter into an arranged marriage because she wouldn't know what kind of person her husband would turn out to be, but she also refused to go out and meet men herself because she was afraid people would gossip about her. So she just sat at home and watched television. For the past three years she'd been sick; she had fainting spells at work all the time, but the doctors couldn't find anything wrong with her.

While the Anastenarides accepted the participation of young Kostil-ides in the rite without hesitation, they expressed ambivalence, even skepticism, concerning the participation of people who were total strangers. This was especially true in the case of young men like Vasilis, whom I met at the festival of Saints Constantine and Helen in Ayia Eleni in 1981. Vasilis was from a wealthy Athenian family and had traveled extensively abroad. He was a vegetarian and wore his straight black hair pulled back in a long ponytail. Although he was enrolled as a student in law school in Athens, Vasilis was really interested in the folklore and culture of the Gypsies, the Vlachs, and the other ethnic minorities of Greece. More than anything else he wanted to learn Romany. Vasilis seemed strangely out of place in a world where most young men were interested in soccer and motorcycles. People who felt sympathy for him said he was "sensitive"; people who didn't accused him of having seduced a young woman from the village a few years earlier.

At times during the festival Vasilis sat in the konaki crying, hugging himself, and rocking back and forth; at times he took notes. He'd been coming to Ayia Eleni for several years. Some people said he actually danced in 1979, after his elderly father had been in a serious car accident and suffered a nervous breakdown. That's when Vasilis became close to Yavasis. He'd stay in Serres for a week or two after the festival and come talk to Yavasis every day. One morning during the festival of 1981 Vasilis asked Yavasis if it was time for him to go up to the new konaki. "I can't tell you what to do," said Yavasis. "The other one inside decides."

It is clear that the Anastenaria appeals to a generation of young people who have left behind the traditional rural culture of their parents' villages in order to make new lives for themselves in Athens and Thessaloniki. Cut off from their roots in this way they often experience a loss of identity, a sense of alienation and confusion. This predicament is poignantly illustrated by another young man who had been coming to see the Anastenaria for several years. He didn't dance or carry a tape recorder or notebook. He was just there year after year—watching. He'd left Greece after finishing high school to study in Germany; now he worked there as a computer scientist. When we exchanged addresses in Ayia Eleni in May 1986 after the festival, he gave me three: the village near Corinth where he had grown up, the address in Athens where his parents now lived, and his own address in Munich where he worked. Over the course of his life he had lived in three very different worlds. It would not be at all surprising if at times he felt like an outsider, a ksenos, in all of them.

Just as the symbolic system of the Anastenaria provides a religious idiom for the articulation and resolution of problems associated with isolation, alienation, and loss of identity for earlier generations of Kostilides, so it does for the troubled young people who have recently begun to participate in the rite. The structural parallels that exist between the psychological and social situations in which these young people find themselves and the symbolic language of the Anastenaria is particularly evident in the case of Irini, the young architect from Thessaloniki. As May 21 approached, she couldn't stay in her apartment in Thessaloniki; but when she set out for Ayia Eleni, something made her stop when she was only half way there. She couldn't go back to Thessaloniki, but she couldn't go to her father's house in Serres either. She had nowhere to go.

This feeling of paralysis or immobility, this sense of wandering around hopelessly lost, is perfectly captured in the song Evripidis sang about the icons of Saints Constantine and Helen that had been "imprisoned" by the Bishop of Drama. Like Irini, Kostandinos had nowhere to go and no one to take him in, so he just wandered alone through the mountains. When Irini finally reached the village of Ayia Eleni, she wanted Yavasis to tell her whether she should go to Mavrolefki, but only Saint Constantine could tell her that.

Participation in the Anastenaria, then, provides young people like Dimitris, Kiriakos, Vasilis, and Irini with an opportunity to reestablish ties with a rural community and with the traditions of the past. They acquire an extended family, ancestors—*papoudes*—and a village they can return to year after year. Through the Anastenaria they gain a sense of identity, a sense of belonging, a rootedness in a particular place, that they seem to have lost. It is as if the icons of the Anastenarides could take the place of their family icons—the icons whose loss, some said, was responsible for Dimitris' suffering in 1986; as if the village of Ayia Eleni, or an idealized vision of it, could substitute for "their villages," the villages they left behind a long time ago. Saint Constantine and Yavasis himself are powerful symbols through which these young people can explore their relationships to their own fathers and grand-

Two Anastenarides—one a university student, the other a village farmer—holding simadia for people to greet (Photograph by John Demos/Apeiron)

fathers. By participating in the Anastenaria they are adopted, in a way, into the community of Kostilides.

The appeal of the Anastenaria to this relatively small segment of Greek youth is part of a more general trend in Greek culture toward seeking out the folklore and the traditions of the rural past. This trend can be seen in the establishment of museums of folk art throughout Greece, the popularity of television programs devoted to Greek folk dancing, and the increase in travel by Greek tourists to places like Crete, Pelion, and Mani, which are known for their distinctive regional costumes, music, and architecture. The Anastenaria, however, represents more to these educated urban youth than a romantic return to their rural past. Somewhat paradoxically, it also appeals to them for many of the same reasons that aspects of the counterculture do. Like eastern mysticism, spiritualism, astrology, and parapsychology, which have recently become popular in Greece as they have in Western Europe and the United States, the Anastenaria is attractive to these young people because it holds out the promise of a powerful religious experience—direct contact with the supernatural—as well as membership in a close-knit and supportive community. Participation in the Anastenaria allows these young people to experience something that is both old and traditional, on the one hand, and new and exotic, on the other. Kiriakos, for example, can enter an altered state of consciousness for the first time surrounded by the symbols of the Orthodox Church he grew up with. He can be possessed by the same spirit that possessed his grandmother.

The Anastenaria still represents the past to these young people: not the past of Kosti and eastern Thrace but the past of Ayia Eleni and other Greek villages. The past of these educated urban youth is the present of their parents and grandparents. The grandchildren of refugees from Kosti are themselves refugees, refugees from villages like Ayia Eleni; for the distance from Ayia Eleni to student housing in Thessaloniki is as great as the distance from Kosti to Ayia Eleni.

THE NEGOTIATION OF SOCIAL BOUNDARIES

Because the Anastenaria embodies so much of what it means to be a Kostilis, an assertion of belief in the Anastenaria is often an assertion of identity as a Kostilis or as a resident of Ayia Eleni. For example, when I asked a woman from Ayia Eleni who had married into a nearby village if she believed in the Anastenaria, she replied, "I'm from Ayia Eleni, so I believe in the rite." On another occasion an elderly Kostilis referred to the Bulgarian-speaking residents of a village near Kosti by saying, "They had the Anastenaria, so they must have belonged to our ratsa." Belief in the Anastenaria, then, represents the epitome, the defining feature, of being a Kostilis. Similarly, becoming an Anastenaris is an assertion phrased in a religious idiom of becoming a member of the community of Kostilides. The question of who can become an Anastenaris is actually a question about the precise nature of the boundaries of the Kostilides as a social group.

Social groups such as these are most productively understood, following Barth (1969:10), as "categories of ascription and identification" that are employed by members of the groups themselves in their everyday social relations. Instead of focusing on a list of cultural characteristics that define these groups, it is much more valuable to examine the different ways in which the boundaries between them are defined and maintained despite what is often a constant flow of people across them. While ratsa and the social categories established by the distinction between "insiders" (*diki*) and "outsiders" (*kseni*) cannot be identified in any strict sense with specifically ethnic categories (Herzfeld 1980b), an analysis of the precise nature of the boundaries between these two categories as suggested by Barth still offers many important insights. In the case of the Kostilides the Anastenaria plays a central role in the ongoing process of negotiating the definition of the boundary of the community and regulating the flow of people across it.

The most fundamental principle governing membership in the Anastenarides is that only Saint Constantine has the power to make a person an Anastenaris. When a woman whose identity as a Kostilou cannot be questioned shows signs of becoming an Anastenarissa, the will of Saint Constantine is clear, and events usually proceed smoothly. Her suffering is attributed to the Saint, she is welcomed and comforted by the other Anastenarides, and she is given a simadi or icon cover to hold while she dances. If she behaves appropriately and does the will of the Saint as revealed to her by other Anastenarides, she will recover her health. If she enters the fire, she will not be burned.

But when a woman who is not a Kostilou (or whose identity as a Kostilou is open to question) shows signs of becoming an Anastenarissa, complications often arise, and conflict may ensue. Some people may claim that she is acting on her own and that she is not really an Anastenarissa. They may call her "crazy" and argue that she should not be given anything to hold while she dances. They may say that she will continue to suffer and that if she enters the fire, she will be burned. Whether or not a particular person in this situation—Sotiria, Keti, or Dimitris, for example—is accepted as an Anastenaris and thus symbolically incorporated into the community of Kostilides depends on a variety of factors, including the stance of the leader of the Anastenarides, the attitudes of any factions that may exist within the Anastenarides, and the specific identity of the person involved.

According to most Kostilides it is ultimately the ability to walk through fire without being burned that separates people who are really Anastenarides from people who are not. The spectacular firewalk that the Anastenarides perform twice a year seems to offer incontrovertible proof that they and they alone enjoy the divine protection of Saint Constantine. If you are not burned, you are accepted as an Anastenaris; you are healed. If you are burned, however, your status as an Anastenaris is denied; you are humiliated and rejected, and you continue to suffer.

Needless to say things are not always so simple and clear-cut. Occasionally Anastenarides are burned, and people who are not Anastenarides emerge from the fire unscathed. In fact, neither of these situations, both of which appear to contradict the ideology of the Anastenaria, presents a serious challenge to it. An Anastenaris might respond to the claim that a total stranger entered the fire and was not burned by saying that on May 21 Saint Constantine protects everyone who enters the fire or by arguing that even though he was not a Kostilis the stranger had great faith in Saint Constantine.

Conversely, many people told me that one Anastenaris was burned because he went to Ayia Eleni to perform the firewalk in spite of the fact that Saint Constantine had ordered him to go to Langadas. When he entered the fire at Ayia Eleni, people said, he was severely burned and was rushed off secretly to a doctor. On another occasion an Anastenaris crossed the fire once without incident, but when he entered the fire again to show off for the television cameras, he was burned because "his road was not open." Later, when a doctor came to examine his feet, he was hidden by the other Anastenarides.

These examples illustrate the flexibility of the interpretive system of the Anastenarides and show how it can be manipulated to account for what seems to be the obvious empirical fact that some people are burned when they walk on fire and others are not. I suggest, however, that whether a person is burned is most definitely *not* a question that has a straightforward, empirical answer—particularly in the context of the Anastenaria. On the contrary, it is a question that is answered through an often complex process of negotiation that only involves an examination of a person's feet if an official from outside the community, such as a doctor, policeman, or "scientist," wants to conduct one. Among the Kostilides statements about whether people were burned or not have nothing to do with the condition of their feet; they have to do with who they are and what kind of a relationship they have with the majority of Anastenarides. Accusing people of having been burned is a rhetorical strategy, a way of humiliating and excluding them from the community. It is a way of denying their status as Anastenarides endowed with the power of the Saint.

A burn, in other words, is a cultural construct. Whether a person was burned or not is defined by social consensus, not by medical examination. It is a decision made about a person, not about the skin on a person's feet. Frequently claims that an Anastenaris was burned are based solely on the fact that he entered the fire on May 21 and not on May 23 or that he danced one year but not the next. If a man is not a Kostilis or if he drinks too much, if a woman has been divorced or is not well-respected for some other reason, then he or she will be accused of having been burned. If the accusation is accepted by others, the person will be denied status as an Anastenaris.

Even when the condition of an Anastenaris' skin *is* taken into consideration, which is rarely the case, the definition of a burn remains problematic and open to interpretation. As Kostilides are aware, the effects of a burn may be slow to appear, and there are burns of various degrees. Furthermore, the diagnosis of a burn depends on the situation. A woman who touches a hot stove and later notices a small red spot on her finger would probably say that she got burned, but if the same small red spot appeared on the ball of her foot after she danced repeatedly through a bed of glowing coals, she would probably say that she did not get burned.

The ambiguity involved in defining exactly what constitutes a burn is illustrated by the account an Anastenarissa gave me of what happened to her nephew, also an Anastenaris, when he entered the fire at a recent festival. Someone, probably at the instigation of a priest or bishop, had thrown some incense into the fire; it had melted and stuck to her nephew's foot when he crossed the fire. "He went into the fire and got burned," she said. But then she immediately corrected herself: he felt the heat, so he left the fire; but he didn't have any wound, so he hadn't really been burned after all.

One year a "local," a Macedonian from Ayia Eleni, entered the fire while the Anastenarides were still dancing on the coals. According to most Kostilides he was badly burned and left the site of the firewalk immediately. One Kostilis told me that a policeman examined his feet right after he left the fire and said that he had not been burned. Several hours later, however, signs of burning appeared on his feet. He stayed at home for a month, too injured or embarrassed to leave his house. Another Kostilis said that he didn't know if the Macedonian had actually been burned but added that he definitely should have been.

Most Macedonians, including the man who entered the fire, told me that a doctor had examined his feet and concluded that he had not been burned. They said that when he entered the fire, the Anastenarides immediately withdrew and asked the police to remove him from the site of the firewalk. Later, according to some Macedonians, the police threatened him and warned him never to try to enter the fire again. Many Macedonians resented the fact that the Kostilides, with the help of the police, excluded them from participating in the rite because they belonged to a different ratsa and then claimed that it was Saint Constantine who didn't accept them. "We're not Turks," complained one Macedonian. "Don't we get baptized? Aren't we Christians too?"[8]

In the context of the Anastenaria, then, the claim that a person was not burned is a statement of acceptance and inclusion; the charge that a person was burned is a statement of rejection and exclusion. A decision as to whether a person was burned or not is based on social, not biomedical, criteria. It is a culturally constructed response to an act of firewalking, a symbolic statement about the social position of a person, not a simple description of the physiological condition of a person's feet.[9]

[8] The wide range of conclusions that can be drawn from any specific act of firewalking is suggested by several firewalks that were performed by a group of men in a village near Ayia Eleni (Tsarouhas 1974:94). These men danced through a fire holding wine bottles and women's underwear and singing obscene songs associated with carnival rites. They wanted to expose the Anastenaria—to prove that it has nothing to do with religion and that anyone can walk on fire. They claimed that they were not burned, or that if they sometimes were, it was because the fire they lit was so large. Kostilides, however, claimed that these men *were* burned, or that if they sometimes were *not*, it was because the fire they lit was so *small*.

[9] Herzfeld (1983b:171) makes a similar point in his discussion of rural Greek sexual

A burn, therefore, is comparable to an illness rather than a disease, because a burn is a symptom, a somatic symbol, which does not have an exclusively biological referent. This analogy between a burn and the symptom of an illness suggests a further analogy between not being burned after performing the firewalk and being healed after becoming an Anastenaris. Both processes involve the acquisition of supernatural power and the transformation of a negative condition characterized by low status, isolation, and vulnerability to a positive condition marked by high status, acceptance, and invincibility.

The ability to walk through fire without being burned, an ability all Anastenarides must possess, is also a powerful symbol for membership in the community of Kostilides. The most important criterion for being a Kostilis is being from Kosti or being descended (preferably in the male line) from someone who is from Kosti. Concern for the purity of the ratsa of Kostilides and for the integrity and inviolability of its boundaries is expressed clearly in the account of the founding of Kosti by "the old man Kostis" and the incestuous marriages of his children. This story provides Kostilides with one common ancestor from whom they are all descended and stresses the importance of endogamy with respect to the ratsa. Marriages with non-Kostilides were avoided from the beginning because of the threat foreign women posed to the unity and the continuity of the social group. [10]

The dilemma that old Kostis resolves so neatly by marrying off his children to one another is a very real one in communities like that of the Kostilides where residence is virilocal and membership in important social groups is inherited patrilineally. At the level of the ratsa of Kostilides endogamy often provided a satisfactory solution to this dilemma. However, at the level of the soi, the incorporation of women from outside the group was a necessity. Rogers' (1985:74) description of this dilemma, based on her study of a rural community in southern France, applies equally well to the Kostilides of Ayia Eleni: "Reproduction of the . . . [male] line obviously requires the recruitment of an in-marrying bride at each generation, but as an outsider to the . . . [male] line, she is perceived as potentially disruptive." In an analysis

---

morality when he suggests that "virginity is above all an ascriptive rather than a medical condition."

[10] In "Genesis as Myth" Leach (1969:22) argues in similar fashion that the ancient Israelites' claim to unambiguous descent from a common ancestor "is achieved only at the cost of the breach of the incest rule."

of patricentrism in Balkan societies, Denich (1974:251) states that "the basic dilemma of the agnatic group is to deal with the anomalous presence of those people who are in the group but not of it."

The threat posed by women who have crossed social boundaries by marrying into their husband's soi is vividly illustrated by two of the songs that are sung during ritual gatherings of the Anastenarides. In the "Mikrokostandinos" song Kostandinos killed his mother for interfering with his relationship with his wife, a relationship that is necessary to the continued existence of Kostandinos' soi. With divine assistance Kostandinos asserts the priority of the relationship between husband and wife over that between mother and son.

In "Daskala pou 'ne to pedi" Kostandinos' mother, by committing adultery and killing her son, does the exact opposite of assuring the continuity of her husband's soi: she destroys it. Kostandinos' father, who enjoys his son's complete loyalty and receives divine assistance as well, dramatically asserts the priority of the relationship between father and son over that between husband and wife by killing Kostandinos' mother. Together these two songs portray the conflicts that arise generation after generation between the men of a soi and the women who are brought into it from the outside in order to provide it with new generations of members. Over the course of a man's life his loyalties must shift from his mother to his wife to his son. The two former ties must ultimately be sacrificed in favor of the third to assure the continuity of the soi, a principle upheld in the songs both by Kostandinos himself and by supernatural forces.

The Anastenaria is associated with the problematic incorporation of outside women into a patrilineally defined social group in several other ways. As part of the traditional wedding ceremony of the Kostilides the mother of the bride sent ring-shaped biscuits (*koulouria*) to the Anastenarides of the community as a gesture of respect. The evening before the Sunday wedding service the bride also brought olive oil, a candle, and a kerchief or embroidered cloth to the konaki as an offering to Saints Constantine and Helen.[11]

In addition, Anastenarides sometimes danced at weddings of their close relatives. A woman who was not a Kostilou, but who had become an Anastenarissa after her marriage to a Kostilis, told me that the eve-

---

[11] Both of these rituals were performed during the weddings I observed in Ayia Eleni in 1975 and 1976.

ning before her wedding her future brother-in-law, an Anastenaris, had danced alone in front of his family icons. "He danced," she said, "because Saint Constantine was happy. The Saint knew that one day I'd become his slave and dance too." She interpreted her brother-in-law's dance as an indication that Saint Constantine had accepted her into her husband's soi and into the ratsa of Kostilides, an acceptance that was confirmed when she later became an Anastenarissa herself.

On another occasion the son of a man who had an icon of Saints Constantine and Helen in his house became engaged to a Macedonian woman. Three days later he suddenly broke off the engagement for no apparent reason, in spite of the vehement protests of the bride's family and the attempted mediation of a priest and a village president. When he confided in several members of his family that he had broken the engagement because he had been unable to have intercourse with his fiancée, they immediately interpreted his impotence as a sign that Saint Constantine did not want a kseni in the house. Later the young man was engaged to a Thracian woman whose parents were from a village near Kosti. He was no longer impotent, and they were married. This further strengthened his family's convictions that his first fiancée had been rejected by Saint Constantine. These examples of the involvement of the Anastenarides in wedding ceremonies and marriage negotiations reveal another aspect of the role played by Saint Constantine in defining and maintaining the boundaries of the community of Kostilides.

The nature of these boundaries has changed a great deal since the end of World War II and the Greek Civil War that followed, as more and more young Kostilides have married non-Kostilides and left the rural communities where their parents and grandparents settled in the 1920s. According to elderly Kostilides marriage in Kosti had been endogamous. After their arrival in Greek Macedonia the Kostilides of Ayia Eleni continued to practice endogamy with respect to the village of Ayia Eleni and the ratsa of Kostilides. Before 1950 approximately 90 percent of the marriages that took place followed this pattern. During this time one man even preferred to have his daughter marry a Kostilis who was a widower rather than a young man from another ratsa. Non-Kostilides of Ayia Eleni acknowledged this greater exclusivity on the part of Kostilides by saying that Kostilides were "more faithful to their ratsa." Frequently Kostilides attributed the continuation of the practice of endogamy to the need to keep the Anastenaria secret from all outsiders.

After 1950 the community of Kostilides became much more open. The Anastenaria began to be performed in public, and with the improvement of systems of transportation and communication the traditional pattern of endogamous marriages gradually changed. From 1950 through the early 1960s only half of the marriages of Kostilides were endogamous with respect to the village of Ayia Eleni and the ratsa of Kostilides. Another 25 percent were marriages with other Thracians from Ayia Eleni. Between the early 1960s and 1976 well over half the marriages that took place were exogamous with respect to both the village of Ayia Eleni and the ratsa of Kostilides.

I often heard elderly Kostilides express their opposition to this rapidly growing trend of marrying non-Kostilides. This opposition was usually based on a concern for the future of the Anastenaria. Marriage with other Kostilides was the surest guarantee of the continued performance of the rite, while marriage with outsiders presented a definite threat to the many traditions associated with it. The greatest danger was posed by bringing *ksenes nifes*—brides, sisters-in-law, and daughters-in-law who were not Kostilides—into families deeply involved with the Anastenaria. Because married sons continued to live with their parents and inherit their parents' house, these *ksenes nifes* were the women who inherited the ritual responsibilities and obligations of their mothers-in-law.

In several instances meals served to the Anastenarides were discontinued because young women who were not Kostilides were unwilling to continue the tradition observed by their mothers-in-law. There have also been cases in which the unwillingness of a woman in this position to perform the duties associated with having an icon of the Anastenarides in her house has led to the removal of the icon from the family's possession and its placement in the house of a family more willing to care for it. Conversely, when women from Ayia Eleni married non-Kostilides, there was always the possibility that should they show signs of becoming Anastenarides later in their lives their husbands would forbid them to participate. Finally, the migration of young Kostilides to the cities of Serres and Thessaloniki was also said to pose problems for the continued vitality of the rite. By 1986 a meal was no longer served to the Anastenarides on July 27, the festival of Saint Pandeleimon, because the woman who used to serve it had died and her only son no longer lived in the village. In this way, then, the Anastenaria is still invoked by elderly Kostilides as justification for continuing the

A meal for the Anastenarides is laid out on the floor (Photograph by John Demos/Apeiron)

practice of marrying within the community of Kostilides. At best, outsiders do not believe in the Anastenaria and ridicule the Kostilides for their participation in it. At worst, they actively oppose the rite and present a genuine threat to its continued existence.

As the community of Kostilides has changed and its boundaries have become more permeable, the definition of who can become an Anastenaris has changed as well. Traditionally most Kostilides maintained that participation in the Anastenaria was "hereditary" (*klironomiko*) and that only Kostilides could become Anastenarides. The only "real" Anastenarides were those who were *akrabades*, descendants of Anastenarides. According to this view the ability to become an Anastenaris was inherited "in the blood." As one Anastenarissa told me, "If you don't carry blood from an Anastenaris [in your veins] (*an den kratas ema apo Anastenari*), then you can't be a good Anastenaris."

The belief that Kostilides are uniquely privileged by virtue of their special relationship to Saint Constantine has contributed to the sense of superiority and exclusivity that many Kostilides feel toward non-Kostilides. That this belief was shared by many people of Ayia Eleni who were not Kostilides is an indication of the high status that Kostilides enjoyed within the village. For example, a Macedonian woman from Ayia Eleni told me that the power of Saint Constantine goes only to the Kostilides because they are all members of the same ratsa. "It's in their soi; it's in their veins. It goes from parent to child to grandchild. We can't dance in the fire because we're from another ratsa."

In the 1960s, however, several women from Ayia Eleni and surrounding villages who were not Kostilides but who had married Kostilides became involved in the Anastenaria. Kostilides who opposed their participation in the rite argued that being an Anastenaris was klironomiko, that only Kostilides could be Anastenarides, and that these women were not real Anastenarides. If these women did not enter the fire, it proved that they did not dance with the power of the Saint. If they did enter the fire and were not burned, the Saint only protected them to avoid humiliating the other Anastenarides.

Kostilides who favored their participation in the rite argued that they *could* become real Anastenarides because they had married Kostilides. According to this view the meanings of the words klironomiko (hereditary) and akrabas (descendant) were extended to include relationships by marriage. People who supported this view often cited the case of a woman who was not a Kostilis but who had married a Kostilis whose father had been an Anastenaris. When she began to dance at the konaki, these people said that she was a real Anastenarissa because she had "become one blood" (*eyine ena ema*) with her husband when she married him and gave birth to his children. She was "an akrabas from her father-in-law"; she even pounded the fire out with the palms of her hands, just the way he had. People who opposed her participation in the rite claimed that a daughter-in-law had "different blood" (*allo ema*) from her husband. Therefore this woman was not an akrabas and could not be a real Anastenarissa. The fact that she only slapped at the fire with her hands (and did not actually walk through it) proved that she was simply dancing because she wanted to and that she did not enjoy the protection of Saint Constantine.

Still other Kostilides claimed that it was not necessary for someone to be an akrabas or even a Kostilis in order to become an Anastenaris; anyone the Saint loved could become an Anastenaris. People who held this view criticized those who tried to exclude outsiders from participating in the rite, saying, "We human beings discriminate; God doesn't." In this way rather than being denied status as an Anastenarissa because she was not a Kostilou, a woman became a Kostilou because she was accepted as an Anastenarissa. When Keti danced for the first time in May 1976, several elderly Kostilides asked Yavasis who she was. Yavasis, who always treated Keti very warmly, replied: "She's a kseni, but the Saint took a liking to her and made her one of us (*diki mas*)." On another occasion Yavasis said, "She became a fellow villager (*horiani*). She became one of us—from the Saint."

When Kostilides argued for the acceptance of people like Keti as Anastenarides, they sometimes said that you could never be entirely certain what ratsa a person belonged to anyway. They pointed to a woman from Thessaloniki who only learned as an adult that she had been adopted and that her real parents had been Kostilides. Several years later she met some of her real relatives in Mavrolefki, and a few years after that she became an Anastenarissa.

Through the religious idiom of the Anastenaria Kostilides not only can argue against the incorporation of outsiders into their community, they can also argue against the movement of insiders away from their community. On many occasions the Anastenaria has served as a powerful force militating against the departure or withdrawal of Kostilides from their community. The emergence of Sofia Zora as an Anastenarissa in May 1986, while certainly related to her own poor health and that of her husband, was also related to their move several years earlier from their home in Ayia Eleni to an apartment in Serres. With their departure from the village their house was closed, and the simadi of Sofia's mother-in-law was "locked up." As a result of Sofia's involvement with the Anastenaria, she and her husband will in all likelihood continue to perform the ritual obligations to the Anastenaria they had resumed in 1986. In this way they can reaffirm their ties with the village of Ayia Eleni as well as their membership in the community of Kostilides.

The departure of Kostilides for more distant places has also been discouraged through the religious idiom of the Anastenaria. For example, Stelios, a young Anastenaris from Langadas, had made plans to go to Germany to work as a *gastarbeiter*. His only brother was already living abroad, and his parents, who were both Anastenarides, did not want him to go. Shortly before he was to leave, he had a dream. A priest came up to him and asked, "But where are you leaving me?" "What business is it of yours?" Stelios asked in turn. "You're my child," said the priest. "But you're not my father," replied Stelios. Only then did Stelios notice that he was in the cemetery of Langadas, the cemetery of Saint Constantine. Suddenly he understood the meaning of the dream: the priest was Saint Constantine, and Saint Constantine did not want him to leave. Stelios has remained in Langadas ever since.[12]

The Anastenaria exerts a kind of centripetal force on the Kostilides, drawing them in spatially toward the center of the community and back in time toward the past. It also provides powerful ideological justification for the exclusion of outsiders and the maintenance of a closed and unified community. The Anastenaria does much more, however. As the world of the Kostilides changes, the Anastenaria changes also. A new konaki is built, a new site for the firewalk is found, and a new generation of young people begins to dance. In this way the Anastenaria is able to deal with the new dilemmas and problems that constantly arise over the definition and maintenance of important social groups and social boundaries.

---

[12] Note that the priest's original question is identical to that of Kostandinos' wife in line 9 of the "Mikrokostandinos" song. Stelios is thus identified with both the powerful figure of Kostandinos about to abandon those who are dependent on him and the obedient son who must subordinate his will to that of the priest (Saint Constantine) and his parents.

Sacred Power in a Secular World

Unquestionably the Anastenarides acquire great power by virtue of the fact that when possessed by Saint Constantine they are able to diagnose and heal illnesses and walk on fire without being burned. It is not only Anastenarides as individuals who are empowered by the rite, however; the Anastenarides collectively, the village of Ayia Eleni, and the entire community of Kostilides are empowered by it as well. Just as individual Anastenarides acquire the power to deal more effectively with other people in their personal relationships, so the Anastenarides as a group and the Kostilides of Ayia Eleni as a whole acquire the power to deal more effectively with important institutions and forces in Greek society. Because of the Anastenaria relatively powerless village men and women can often assert themselves successfully in their struggles with political leaders at the village level and above, with officials of the Orthodox Church, and with scholars, scientists, doctors, and other members of the educated, urban elite.

The history of the Kostilides since their arrival in Greek Macedonia parallels, in a sense, the career of a person who becomes involved with the Anastenaria. A closed community of refugees too afraid of persecution and ridicule to celebrate the Anastenaria publicly has been transformed into a proud, assertive community whose rituals attract national and even international attention. It is as if the entire community of Kostilides has "come out" and now "dances with the power of the Saint" every year; as if the entire community has been healed of a sense of inferiority and alienation.[13]

The supernatural power of Saint Constantine, which the Anastenarides acquire when they are possessed and dance, is the source of the charismatic authority that the Anastenarides enjoy. According to Weber (1964:358) charisma refers to the personal qualities by virtue of which a person "is set apart from ordinary men and treated as endowed with supernatural, superhuman, or at least specifically exceptional powers or qualities." In religious contexts charismatic authority is based on some form of divine calling; it is legitimated, in other words, by direct experience of supernatural power or grace.[14]

[13] See Peter Loizos' discussion of the development of a powerful new sense of identity among Greek Cypriot refugees after the Turkish invasion of Cyprus in 1974 (1981:157–187 and 195–206).

[14] The Greek *charisma*, meaning "the gift of God's grace," is derived from *charis* or

In an analysis of the Catholic pentecostal movement, McGuire (1982:45) defines "charismatic empowerment" as "the result of a process by which the social power of the group is transformed into personal power." An individual, in other words, acquires power which according to a specific religious interpretation is supernatural, but which, following Durkheim (1965), can also be understood as the embodiment of the collective force of the community. Given its frequent association with enthusiastic or ecstatic religious experiences charismatic authority contrasts sharply with rational, institutional, or bureaucratic forms of authority based on political office and economic privilege. The opposition between these two forms of authority is often expressed in outright conflict between religious and political leaders or in conflict between charismatic religious leaders and other religious leaders who are part of hierarchical religious institutions. Such conflict often involves a struggle for the control of powerful religious objects, which as Tambiah (1984:335) points out, are "repositories of power" in which charisma has been "concretized" or "sedimented."[15]

The Anastenarides acquire their power from Saint Constantine, the personification of the community of Kostilides. In turn the villages of Ayia Eleni and Langadas, and the Kostilides in other parts of Greek Macedonia as well, acquire power from the Anastenaria. The ritual has become a resource for these communities, a real source of political and economic power, as many Kostilides are aware. The existence of the Anastenaria has always provoked the interest of outsiders, particularly local politicians, church officials, folklorists, and medical researchers. This was true in Kosti as well as in Macedonia when the rite was performed in secret. It has become increasingly true since World War II and the beginning of public celebrations of the Anastenaria.

By the 1970s the Anastenaria had become a major tourist attraction in Ayia Eleni and Langadas. The festival of Saints Constantine and Helen has been described in the *Blue Guide to Greece* (Rossiter 1977:557) and listed in calendars of cultural events that appear in foreign-language periodicals such as *The Athenian*. Books have been written and documentary films produced about the Anastenaria. Every year in May, newspaper articles and television newscasts announce "the re-

---

haris (demotic *hari*), meaning "grace" or "favor," which is the term regularly used by Kostilides to refer to Saint Constantine and the other saints of the Orthodox Church.

[15] Valuable works that explore the concept of charisma further are Bauman (1983), Fabian (1971), McGuire (1982), and Tambiah (1984).

vival of the ancient ritual of firewalking." As a result Yavasis and a few
other elderly Anastenarides have attracted the attention of the national
media.

Every year larger and larger crowds gather in Ayia Eleni and Langadas to witness the Anastenaria. The rite particularly appeals to Greek
tourists, who can combine a vacation with a religious pilgrimage, and
to the increasing number of foreign tourists who are interested in the
folklore and popular culture of modern Greece as well as the art and
archaeology of ancient Greece.[16] The newly formed Folklore Society of
Ayia Eleni has assumed responsibility for the elaborate arrangements
that the celebration of the Anastenaria now requires. With the financial
support of several government agencies major projects have been undertaken to improve the appearance of the village and assure as impressive and spectacular a festival as possible. The Anastenaria has become a significant source of income, public attention, and prestige for
the community. The Anastenaria, in short, has put Langadas and Ayia
Eleni on the map.

As a result of these developments many conflicts have arisen between
the Anastenarides and the Folklore Society of Ayia Eleni. The construction of the new konaki in 1979 and 1980 and the emergence of
Mihalis Kitsos as the leader of the Anastenarides only exacerbated the
situation. The authority of the Folklore Society was essentially political
and economic; its officers were drawn from the wealthiest and most
important families in the village. They were part of a local elite that
had always looked upon the Anastenaria with a certain degree of skepticism and embarrassment. The authority of the Anastenarides was religious, derived as it was from the power of Saint Constantine, while
the Anastenarides themselves were primarily old, female, and poor.
The Anastenarides and the Folklore Society found themselves compet-
ing for control over a ritual that had become a valuable community
resource. The Anastenarides now presented a challenge to local politicians because the Anastenaria had become relevant to the overall power
structure of the community.

The conflict between the charismatic sacred power of the Anastenarides and the secular power of village leaders was the subject of some
good-natured joking when the Anastenarides were being served a meal

[16] On the relationships between tourism, archaeology, and folklore see Loukatos
(1981:157–173).

at the house of the village president during the festival of Saint Athanasios on January 18, 1976. When people gathered in the room where
the family icons were kept, Yavasis sat down on the one low chair that
stood underneath the icon shelf. The village president, a tall large-
boned man in his forties, kneeled awkwardly on the floor. "You took
my chair," he said to Yavasis. "I'll have to put my name on it, so I can
use it next year." Yavasis, smiling mischievously, replied, "You can sit
in this chair every day of the year except today. Today it belongs to me."

By 1981 this conflict had become so pronounced, and the Anastenarides themselves so divided over the issues of Mihalis' leadership and
Evripidis Petrakis' disruptive influence, that the success of the firewalk
on the final day of the festival was seriously jeopardized. In spite of
many delays caused by the lack of strong leadership, village politicians
pressured the Anastenarides to begin the firewalk on time. As a result
the Anastenarides were rushed; they made mistakes; they may have entered the fire too soon. Because of the tension and conflict that existed
within the group, the Anastenarides argued among themselves over
who would hold the icons. Only a few Anastenarides entered the fire,
and they just danced for a short period of time. People said that their
road had not been open, that the power of Saint Constantine had not
been with them. There were even rumors that some of them had been
burned.

The interference of village politicians with the religious affairs of
the Anastenarides, plus internal disputes among the Anastenarides
themselves, had disrupted the spirit of unity, cooperation, and solidarity upon which the successful performance of the firewalk depends. In
their efforts to gain control over the Anastenaria the political leaders of
Ayia Eleni were running the risk of destroying the very phenomenon
they sought to control.

By 1986 when Tasos Reklos, the founder and first president of the
Folklore Society, had become the leader of the Anastenarides, a remarkable resolution of this conflict had been achieved—a resolution I
would have thought inconceivable five years earlier. Two diametrically
opposed forms of power had been consolidated in the hands of one
person. On the one hand, Tasos possessed the secular power of an educated member of a wealthy village family. One of his father's brothers
had been president of Ayia Eleni for many years; another had succeeded Tasos as president of the Folklore Society. On the other hand,

Tasos also possessed the sacred power of a charismatic healer who had been designated as Yavasis' successor by Saint Constantine himself.

Tasos had founded the Folklore Society to preserve and protect the Anastenaria, but he had chosen the wrong idiom to do so, a political idiom. As Tasos himself later realized, it had been a disaster. His efforts had not only failed; they had actually threatened the integrity of the rite. In his position as leader of the Anastenarides, however, Tasos appears to have succeeded in accomplishing the very same objectives by employing a *religious* idiom, the idiom of the Anastenarides themselves. In this way Tasos seems to have restored the Anastenaria to a central place in the community life of the Kostilides of Ayia Eleni.

For a long time the Anastenarides and their supporters have also been engaged in an often bitter struggle with the Orthodox Church, one of the most powerful institutions in Greek society. The opposition of the Orthodox Church to the Anastenaria is a specific instance of attempts made by hierarchical religious organizations throughout the world to suppress, or at least control, enthusiastic or ecstatic forms of religious worship based on direct personal experience of the divine. While the arguments of church officials against the Anastenaria have generally focused on what they claim are the ritual's pagan origins in the orgiastic worship of Dionysos, there are clearly important political and economic dimensions to the conflict as well. The Church and the Anastenarides have long been engaged in a struggle for control of the icons of the Anastenarides and the power that they possess.

According to one of the earliest accounts of the Anastenaria written in 1873 by Anastasios Hourmouziadis, a professor at a theological school in Constantinople, the Orthodox Church had at times unsuccessfully persecuted the Anastenaria "with axe, fire, and whip." Hourmouziadis suggested that with education, sermons, and counseling the Church might be more successful in suppressing the rite and in that way "attend to the enlightenment and spiritual salvation of its wretched children who have already been wandering for so long in the depths of darkness" (1961:158). A different perspective on the conflict between the Anastenaria and the Orthodox Church in eastern Thrace is conveyed by the following story which an elderly Kostilis told a Greek folklorist in 1938 and which I heard in a slightly different form in 1976.

Once the Bishop of Sozopolis [a city on the coast of the Black Sea] came to Kosti to try to prevent the Anastenaria from being celebrated. After putting on women's clothes and covering his head with a silk kerchief he sat at a window and watched the Anastenarides dance on the fire. Afterwards, when a leader of the village asked him for his impressions, the bishop replied, "What can I say? Do whatever you want. I can't tell you anything" (Deliyannis 1938-39:131).

In this story, strangely reminiscent of Euripides' account of Pentheus' dressing up as a woman to watch the maenads worship Dionysos, a high church official is rendered speechless by the firewalk. He is reduced to a position of passivity, impotence, and powerlessness after witnessing dramatic proof that the Anastenarides are protected by the supernatural power of Saint Constantine.

When the Anastenaria began to be performed in public in Greek Macedonia in the 1950s disputes between the Church of Greece and the Anastenaria centered on whether local priests would participate in the rite, whether the icons of the Anastenarides would be kept in the village church or the konaki, and whether the Church or the Anastenarides would receive the money people left as offerings to Saints Constantine and Helen. In the early 1970s the opposition of the Church of Greece to the Anastenaria intensified. Church officials seized possession of the icons of the Anastenarides in Ayia Eleni and Mavrolefki and applied pressure on the Anastenarides of Langadas to stop performing the rite.

The Church of Greece, however, did not succeed in suppressing the Anastenaria. The Anastenarides of Ayia Eleni regained possession of their icons within a year, and by 1986 the Anastenarides of Mavrolefki had as well. Now that the Anastenaria is being celebrated regularly in Thessaloniki, as well as in Ayia Eleni and Langadas (and on a smaller scale in several other villages in Greek Macedonia), the rite seems safe from further persecution.

The resolution of this conflict in favor of the Anastenarides is due in large part to the support the Anastenarides have received from civil authorities at all levels of government. Mayors and prefects have recognized the important economic benefits that celebrating the Anastenaria on a large scale has to offer. The National Tourist Organization of Greece and various ministries of the national government have supported the rite financially, while coverage of the Anastenaria in the press and on television has been quite sympathetic.

Such broad support for the Anastenaria cannot be attributed solely to the desire to promote tourism and economic development. The continued celebration of the Anastenaria is highly valued because of the important role traditional rituals and customs play in scholarly discourse about Greek national identity. The folklore of rural Greece is often cited as proof of the continuity between ancient and modern Greece, a continuity that is central to virtually all conceptions of modern Greek identity. Demonstration of this continuity has been a primary goal of folklore research in Greece. It is in this context that many modern Greek folklorists who have written about the Anastenaria have actively opposed the attempts of the Orthodox Church to suppress the rite.

In a series of newspaper articles published in the early 1950s, for example, Polidoros Papachristodoulou, a folklorist writing on behalf of the Society for Thracian Studies, defended the Anastenaria as a valuable expression of "Hellenic identity." In 1974 Katerina Kakouri, author of a book on the Anastenaria entitled *Dionysiaka*, made a plea for financial assistance that would enable scholars to ensure the continued performance of rituals such as the Anastenaria on the grounds that they were treasured heirlooms of Greek national identity (Kakouri 1975:77). Finally, Nestor Matsas, a well-known Greek folklorist, concluded a newspaper article he wrote shortly after the 1984 festival of Saints Constantine and Helen by saying, "We have an obligation to protect the Anastenarides in any way we can because they express . . . in its most genuine form the incomparable spirit of Greekness (*Romiosini*)." The continued strength and vitality of the Anastenaria, therefore, can be attributed to the fact that it serves not only as a system of religious healing but also as a powerful symbol of Greek national identity.[17]

Ultimately the most serious threat to the integrity of the Anastenaria may be posed not by local politicians trying to exert their control over the rite, nor by church officials trying to suppress it, but rather by scientists trying to explain it. Fundamental to the Anastenaria as a sys-

[17] For an analysis of the scholarly discourse on the Anastenaria see Danforth (1984). On the ideological context of the discipline of folklore more generally see Herzfeld (1982a).

tem of symbolic healing is a religious perspective or world view in which the supernatural power of Saint Constantine is accepted as the ultimate source of the Anastenarides' ability to walk on fire without being burned. A religious interpretation of the Anastenaria ("believing in the Anastenaria," as Kostilides would say) also involves believing that the Anastenarides both suffer from and are healed by Saint Constantine and that they dance and speak with his power.

Opposed to this religious perspective or world view is a scientific outlook committed to systematic investigation, logical analysis, and rational explanation. The scientific approach that has impinged most directly on the Anastenaria is that of the natural sciences. Over the years a wide range of medical researchers have investigated the Anastenaria with the goal of providing a scientific explanation of the ritual that would be consistent with the natural laws and scientific principles of physics, chemistry, and biology. A scientific explanation of the state of consciousness the Anastenarides enter when they dance and, even more importantly, a scientific explanation of their ability to walk on fire without being burned would constitute for many people "proof" that the Anastenarides are not protected by the power of Saint Constantine and that the firewalk is not a miracle.

The approach adopted by "scientists" (*epistimones*) to the Anastenaria is perceived by most Anastenarides as essentially hostile. As such it is identified with a larger tradition of skepticism, lack of belief, and disapproval that dates back to the time when the rite was still performed in eastern Thrace. Traditionally wealthier, more educated Kostilides—those who were upwardly mobile and had the greatest contact with people outside the community (such as merchants, teachers, doctors, and lawyers)—have either distanced themselves from the Anastenaria or actively opposed it. In their eyes the dancing of the Anastenarides, like the sexual explicitness of carnival rituals and the intense expression of grief in funeral laments, is an embarrassing indication of rural backwardness and superstition.

In the 1970s and early 1980s teams of medical researchers from Greece and Germany conducted a variety of scientific tests on the Anastenarides of Langadas in order to explain how they were able to walk on fire without being burned. These scientists recorded the temperature of the bed of burning coals and analyzed slow motion films of the Anastenarides to determine exactly how long their feet were in contact with the fire. They measured the flow of blood to the Anastenarides' feet and the thickness of their calluses; they even took samples of skin from their soles. In addition they attached wireless electroencephalographs to the Anastenarides' heads and used electrocardiographs and psychogalvanometers to study their physiological responses to the firewalk. From a scientific perspective it was clear that the Anastenarides' amazing ability to perform the firewalk safely could only be understood by studying the pattern of their brainwaves, the rate of their heartbeat, and the electrical resistance of their skin. There was no place in a scientific explanation of the rite for mystery, miracles, or the power of Saint Constantine.[18]

One group of German scientists, who conducted a particularly thorough study of the firewalk of the Anastenarides and who themselves performed several experimental firewalks under laboratory conditions, very straightforwardly and unambiguously concluded that it is possible "for ordinary people to walk barefoot on coals without any special preparation, altered state of consciousness, or walking technique." The authors claimed that their study finally "frees the rite of firewalking from the aura of mysticism connected with divinities and special states of consciousness" (Lesk et al. 1981, as abstracted by Engelsmann 1982:290-291).

A Greek writer, who also performed an experimental firewalk himself after witnessing the Anastenaria, arrived at the same conclusions: "The trial firewalk was completed successfully without ceremony, without icons, without faith, without ecstasy. Something natural, something well within the range of human possibilities has been wrapped up in mystery long enough" (Evangelou 1971:159). The force of these conclusions is to debunk the false claims of religion by exposing the Anastenaria to the hard, cold light of objective science.

In this struggle between a religious and a scientific interpretation of the Anastenaria newspaper accounts of the rite have generally failed to acknowledge the claims of scientists to have "explained" the firewalk as something ordinary and natural, something in fact that requires no "explanation" at all. In an account of the Anastenaria that appeared in the New York Times, for example, a neurologist at the Max Planck Institute in West Germany is quoted as saying, "If we could learn the

---

[18] These experiments are described in popular form by Gage (1980), Manus (1978), and Petrides (1982), and in more technical terms by Ballis et al. (1979), Lesk et al. (1981), and Tsantila and Hoogestraat (1983).

secret of their incredible psychomastery of pain, it could be of enormous significance. . . . Why are they not burned? . . . I don't know. . . . One thing I am sure of is that it is not a trick, and it's not paraphysical. There must be a neurophysical explanation" (Gage 1980). Reports of the Anastenaria that appear in Greek newspapers every May invariably refer to the firewalk as a "phenomenon which for decades has engaged the attention of scientists and specialists, with no logical answer ever having been given for why the feet of the Anastenarides are not burned" (Papagrigoriou 1986).

It is not surprising that Greek folklorists, who have often cast themselves as scholarly defenders of the Anastenaria against the charges of paganism and idolatry leveled at it by the Orthodox Church, also seem to be protecting it from the danger of being "explained away" by science. Mihail-Dede (1983:222) attributes people's fascination with the Anastenaria to the firewalk and to the trance state of the Anastenarides, a state, she says, which "still has not been defined by science." Makrakis (1982:56) refers to the Anastenarides' ability to walk on fire without being burned as a "strange, unusual, mysterious, and unexplained phenomenon" that still constitutes a "psycho-physiological enigma." Matsas (1984) also sides unambiguously with the Anastenarides and against the "scientists" by accepting a religious explanation for the Anastenarides' ability to walk on fire. "Is it only their faith and autosuggestion which protects them from the fire?" writes Matsas. "Science has not yet been able to give an answer, and perhaps it never will."

Many Anastenarides are aware of the incompatibility of a scientific and a religious interpretation of the firewalk. As one Kostilis put it, "Education doesn't leave any room for faith." Many Anastenarides are also aware of the threat a scientific explanation of the rite poses to their religious beliefs. They vigorously defend their beliefs against scientific attempts to explain them away, confident that the power they possess, the power of Saint Constantine, is greater than the power of science. They are convinced that any attempt to understand the rite rationally or scientifically is doomed to failure. Elderly Kostilides often concluded conversations with me about the Anastenaria by shaking their heads and saying, "You'll never get to the bottom of these things." The attitude of most Anastenarides toward the conflict between science and religion is summed up by the motto "Believe and don't ask questions" (*Pisteve ke min erevna*).

Anastenarides also expressed their conviction that the power of Saint Constantine is superior to the power of science whenever they discussed attempts by scholars and scientists to understand specific aspects of the rite. I was told, for example, that no one had ever been able to determine exactly how old the icons of the Anastenarides were—their incredible age defied scientific analysis. Similarly, Anastenarides said that Saint Constantine would temporarily blind a doctor who was about to examine the feet of an Anastenaris who for some reason had been burned. The Saint would also render scientific instruments useless, so that they could not be used to explain the rite.

The interaction that took place on May 22, 1986, between Evripidis Petrakis and the folklorist who wanted to record the song Evripidis had just improvised illustrates this confrontation between the power of religion and the power of science in a very revealing manner. Evripidis, an uneducated Greek villager, "knew things" because he was an Anastenaris, but Saint Constantine did not let him talk. University professors, on the other hand, could not explain the rite. The Anastenarides, although they were subordinate to Saint Constantine, were endowed by him with divine knowledge which was superior to that of even the most educated men.

On several occasions I heard Evripidis boast about all the advice he gave to doctors, psychiatrists, and foreign scientists. Sometimes he even asked them questions they couldn't answer. Once he overheard two scientists discussing the electrodes they had placed on the head of an Anastenaris. Someone inside Evripidis—Saint Constantine—told him to go up and speak to them. The Saint enlightened him, gave him wisdom, and told him what to say. He asked the scientists, "Who gave the inventor of the electrodes the ability to build such amazing machines?" "God," they replied. Evripidis then told them that it was that same God who protected the Anastenarides from the fire.

The story Evripidis told the folklorist about the investigations of Dr. Angelos Tanagras is a favorite of many Anastenarides. The great Tanagras admitted that when the Anastenarides stepped into the fire, he was defeated; he was brought to his knees. This proved that he was "lower than the Anastenarides." According to another story, when Tanagras first witnessed the firewalk, one Anastenarissa crossed the fire wearing nylon socks. The socks were not burned. Tanagras then tied an identical pair of socks to the end of a long pole and placed the pole down on the fire wherever the Anastenarissa had stepped. The socks burst into flames. Some people say those socks are now in a museum in Athens.

Evripidis' stories about his previous dealings with Tanagras and other "scientists" were thinly veiled commentaries on his relationship with the folklorist to whom he was telling the stories. Evripidis had been inspired by Saint Constantine to sing a song that the wealthy, educated folklorist wanted to record. Evripidis, therefore, had power over the folklorist because he had knowledge that the folklorist lacked. Evripidis did not repeat the song, and the folklorist went away frustrated, just as Tanagras and other university professors had before him. Once again the religious power of the Anastenarides prevailed over the persistent attempts of scientists to explain it away. Once again the integrity of the Anastenaria was preserved in what is in many ways an increasingly secular and scientific world.

With the emergence of Tasos Reklos, a physician, as the new leader of the Anastenarides and with the increasing involvement of educated young people in the rite, an impressive reconciliation of what had seemed to be opposed, even mutually exclusive, world views has taken place. The power and prestige of science has been enlisted in the service of religion. With the inability of medical researchers to explain the firewalk the forces of science had been defeated; but with a doctor as leader of the Anastenarides they have been won over. They have been converted, as it were, and incorporated into the ritual itself. A physician who heals with the secular power of science has become the leader of the Anastenarides who heal with the sacred power of Saint Constantine. A scientist searching for a cure for multiple sclerosis with the aid of computers has become a religious healer trying to cure people suffering from Saint Constantine with the help of holy water, incense, and icons.

While some Kostilides were skeptical of Tasos' motives for becoming involved with the Anastenaria, most Anastenarides interpreted his participation in the rite in a traditional religious idiom. He had suffered; Yavasis had seen a dream; Saint Constantine had called him. When I told one Anastenaris that I was surprised to see Tasos and other educated young people becoming involved with the rite, he smiled and said: "Saint Constantine didn't see much progress with uneducated

Anastenarides, so he decided to enlist the help of some more educated ones."

In contrast to the phrase "Believe and don't ask questions," which I had heard so often before, I was now told that it was good to study something carefully before believing in it. Kiriakos, the physics student who danced in the konaki in 1986, had quite a sympathetic attitude toward science. While his own approach to the Anastenaria was a religious one, he didn't feel threatened by scientific attempts to study it. On the contrary, he welcomed them.

The emergence of Tasos Reklos as leader of the Anastenarides represents not only the participation of a "scientist" in the rite but the participation of someone interested in folklore as well. The traditional stance of folklorists toward the Anastenaria has been a somewhat paternalistic, even condescending one, in which educated urban scholars maintained their distance from the Anastenarides while at the same time supporting them in their struggles against the persecution of the Orthodox Church. By 1986 people who had been drawn to the rite initially as spectators because they were interested in folklore had begun to participate actively in the rite themselves.

Tasos once described himself to me as "an amateur musician and a lover of Greek folk music." He knows many of the folklorists who have studied the Anastenaria and is familiar with their work. He too is a scholar; he is part of their world. Many of the other young people who had begun to participate in the rite were also very interested in folklore. They belonged to various organizations and clubs devoted to folk dancing and folk music. Old songs, traditional costumes, and village ways of life all held a powerful appeal for them.

In Tasos Reklos the Anastenarides of Ayia Eleni have a leader who is a doctor, an amateur folklorist, and the founder and first president of the Folklore Society. He personifies the worlds of science, scholarship, and village politics and derives power from all three of them. As leader of the Anastenarides, however, these worlds have been integrated into the religious world of the Anastenaria. The secular power Tasos derives from these other worlds has been subordinated to the sacred power of Saint Constantine.

Contrary to the expectations of many, the forces of science, tourism, economic development, and social change have not destroyed the Anastenaria. The traditions of the Kostilides have not been lost; the

Anastenaria is not dead. It still has an important role to play in many peoples' lives.

THE ANASTENARIA celebrates the community of Kostilides.[19] It is a sacred performance that symbolically re-creates this community every year. The Anastenaria provides Kostilides with a symbolic idiom with which to make important statements about who they are and what it means to be a member of their community. It also allows them to comment on and even change the many kinds of relationships that constitute their world. Through songs, dance, and firewalking, in a language of burns and illnesses, power and knowledge, icons and saints, Kostilides explore relationships between parents and children, men and women, insiders and outsiders, human beings and the divine.

In addition the Anastenaria keeps alive the past of the Kostilides. The lost homeland of Kosti is re-created symbolically on the icon shelf, in the konaki, and in the processions of the Anastenarides. Personal experiences of the present recall stories from the past, while events from the past are used to make sense of the present.

Above all else stands the figure of Saint Constantine. He personifies the community of Kostilides and plays a central role in defining and maintaining its social boundaries. It is in the spirit idiom of the Anastenaria that these boundaries are challenged, renegotiated, and redrawn each generation in order to accommodate ever-changing social circumstances. The Anastenaria, then, is a valuable resource that enables Kostilides to deal with new situations and to resolve new problems in creative ways. It empowers them both as individuals and as a community in their dealings with the wider world.

[19] In this conclusion I have drawn on Anna Caraveli's excellent essay "The Symbolic Village: Community Born in Performance" (1985).

VII

A Full Moon
Firedance in Maine

✤

AND EVEN AN AMERICAN . . . "ANASTENARIS"

An American "stole the show" at the firewalk that took place yesterday in Langadas.[1]

Together with the Anastenarides of the region an American crossed the glowing coals three times without suffering any burns at all.

The forty-year-old man from Maine said he had taken part in similar firewalks in other countries.

After receiving permission from the Anastenarides the American, whose name was Ken, passed quickly over the burning coals three times in his bare feet.

The third time the Anastenarides told him to remain on the coals with them longer, but he declined and left.

It should be noted that before he took part in the firewalk the American made the same movements around the fire as the Anastenarides did.

As always a huge crowd watched the Anastenaria in Langadas. Among them was an Italian who took part in the firewalk last year but suffered severe burns on his feet.

This year the Italian watched the Anastenaria from a safe distance.

✤

[1] From the newspaper *Thessaloniki*, May 22, 1985.

A First Meeting

On a warm June evening in the summer of 1985 Ken Cadigan visited me at my home in Lewiston, Maine. Ken was a tall, handsome man with a dark beard and a warm smile. I had invited him for dinner, but he was fasting now that he had returned to Portland from Europe where he'd led firewalking workshops in Germany and danced with the Anastenarides in Langadas. Ken said he'd found my name in the card catalog of the Berkeley library; he was sure it wasn't a coincidence that we lived so close to each other in Maine. Ken was eager to tell me about his experience firewalking with the Anastenarides.

When he arrived in Langadas on May 21, Ken showed the owner of a restaurant a photograph of himself walking on fire. The man took Ken right to Stamatis Liouros, the leader of the Anastenarides in Langadas. When Stamatis saw the photograph, he smiled and told Ken to come to the konaki that evening. He said Ken could participate in the firewalk but couldn't dance in the konaki.

That night at the konaki someone tried to discourage Ken from entering the fire. "It would be better if you didn't," he said. "Think twice about it. If Stamatis said it was all right, then it's all right, but I don't think you should." He warned Ken about the Italian who had been burned the previous year and said that no foreigner had ever gone into the fire before without getting burned.

Ken managed to make his way through the crowd to the site of the firewalk together with the Anastenarides. He danced around the fire with them for a few minutes. Then, after Stamatis crossed the fire, Ken went across too. He was dressed in white and held his arms up high over his head. "I didn't have the dance down right," he said. "I just went boogying across."

After Ken crossed the fire two or three times, he saw Stamatis motion to another Anastenaris to take Ken through the fire with him. The Anastenaris grabbed Ken by the arm, but Ken broke free. Ken went back into the fire again, and this time he stayed in for a long time; he really *danced* in the coals. Just then the Anastenaris grabbed his arm a second time, held him in the fire, and stepped on his foot. Ken hesitated to attribute any evil intentions to him, but he was sure the Anastenaris had tried to pull him down into the coals so he would get burned.

Ken broke free again and left the fire. When he sat down at the edge of the fire, he was surrounded by reporters who all wanted to know what had happened. Had he been burned? How had he done it? Could anyone do it? Some people in the crowd had seen what had happened and were booing. Ken said it was like a professional wrestling match between Gorgeous George and the Evil Anastenaris. After talking for a few minutes with a man from the Psychotronics Society of Poland Ken went to a coffeehouse nearby where he met the man who had sacrificed the bull that morning. He treated Ken like a hero, like some kind of supernatural being.

Ken told me that he had in fact been burned when the Anastenaris stepped on his foot.

"It was a burn deep under my skin, down to the nerve, but it didn't come out until the next day—just a little red spot. That was the only time I've ever been burned right to the nerve. It opened up the next night; the nerve was exposed. It was never very painful—about like the sting you feel when you clap your hands really hard."

Ken thought the Anastenaria had the atmosphere of a side show at a circus. "It was all ego and courage," he said, "and that took away from the spiritual side of it. But I got what I went for. I saw it with my own eyes; I saw it, and I tried it. It was great. I learned how to dance."

For Ken there was a big difference between a fire*walk* and a fire*dance*. A fire*walk* was a serious goal-oriented activity concerned with overcoming a specific barrier of fear; a fire*dance* was more celebratory. Ken said that there were probably sixty or seventy people in the United States who led firewalking workshops, including about twelve full-time professionals like himself. But he was the first person to bring firedancing to the United States, and he wanted to do it right. He wanted to help as many people as he could. His plan was to find someone like Stevie Wonder to cut a firedancing record that would make a lot of money. Then Ken could do his workshops for free. He had visions of hundreds of people dancing all day to live music, with six fires and a huge feast afterward—just like a big rock concert.

Ken showed me a Greek newspaper article about his firewalk at Langadas. When I translated it for him, he said that no one *told* him to remain on the coals; someone *forced* him to remain there. That's why he didn't stay on the fire longer; his background with firewalking didn't allow for that sort of intervention. He *chose* to stay off the coals after being forced on them by the Anastenaris. What's more, he danced *slowly*, not quickly, through the fire as the article claimed.

"I know the Anastenaris had to do it," Ken said later. "I didn't feel critical of him. I wanted to heal my relationships by not criticizing and by not judging. That was the healing experience I had in Greece; I learned not to criticize other people."

Later in the summer Ken was going to return to Europe to conduct more workshops and retreats. He had made plans to do motivational programs for some German businesses. He said he'd also received an invitation from the government of Poland to hold a firewalking workshop there.

"With all these workshops," Ken said, "sometimes I have to enter the fire even without guidance. I have to keep my word. That's made me more responsible in other areas of my life. It's helped me learn to fulfill my obligations."

Then Ken told me a little about his own views on firewalking. For him firewalking was a spiritual experience but not necessarily a religious one. He believed that a confident, positive attitude was able to change people's brain chemistry, which in turn changed their skin chemistry and prevented them from being burned. He took off his shoes and socks to show me the soles of his feet. A few small red spots and a little dead skin were the only indication that he had walked through more than a hundred fires over the past year. At a firewalk Ken led recently in Germany a psychiatrist complained about how late it was getting. His fear came out as anger and spoiled the whole evening. Several people were burned.

"Firewalking is a metaphor," said Ken. "We need to try to understand the element of fire in our lives; we need to bring the fire home. The fire within us is a fire of transformation. We're afraid we're going to change, so we sit separately in fear and doubt. We have to try to use the fire as a mirror for the fire within ourselves. It's an open door. You can walk through fire, and you can heal your relationships."

Toward the end of the evening Ken gave me a nicely mounted, autographed color photograph of himself striding confidently over a glowing bed of coals at a firewalk he had led near Portland. He invited me to be his guest at a firewalk he planned to hold sometime during the coming winter. Then he asked if I'd be willing to give a presentation on the Anastenaria there. Ken was interested in having me write about his workshops, but he hoped that I would participate in the firewalk myself so I could really understand it—so I wouldn't be a foreigner to the other people there.

Ken Cadigan walks through fire on a winter night near Portland, Maine (Photograph courtesy of Ken Cadigan)

FULL MOON FIREDANCE CELEBRATION!

A Very Special Event with Ken Cadigan

Special Guest: Loring M. Danforth Ph.D.
with a Slideshow on FIREDANCERS

Friday, December 27, 10 am - 10 pm

$100 ~ A Festive Feast is Included!

Box 279, Rt. 85, Raymond, Maine (Northern Pines)

THE FIREDANCE IS A PROLONGED COMMUNION WITH THE FIRE...A NATURAL EXTENSION OF THE FIREWALK EXPERIENCE. THE DAY WILL BE A JOYFUL CELEBRATION OF FREEDOM FROM FEARS & LIMITING BELIEFS.

For Reservations & Information: (207) 774-0263; For Directions (207) 655-7624

-SPONSORED BY THE HUNDREDTH MONKEY PROJECT-

KEN CADIGAN has been directly involved with the human potential movement since 1965. He has been presenting seminars and trainings in the area of natural healing for ten years and has studied with many prominent healers throughout the country. Ken currently teaches firedancing in the United States and Europe. The firedance is an extension of the firewalking technique which he learned from Tolly Burkan, originator of the firewalking workshop.

LORING M. DANFORTH, Ph.D. is a foremost Anthropologist on Firedancing, the Firedancing Process and Grecian Rituals, having lived for one year with the Anastanarians - the firedancers of Northern Greece.

✜

A DOORWAY OF POSSIBILITY

After driving for an hour on a cold snowy morning I turned down an icy dirt road that led to Northern Pines, a health resort on Crescent Lake in Raymond, Maine. Northern Pines was advertised as "the perfect place to undertake a program of personal rejuvenation." Guests could attend classes in stress management, participate in noncompetitive exercise programs, or fast; the staff offered "massage, facials, and various forms of body work."

I parked next to an old truck that was loaded with three-foot-long oak logs. It belonged to Tom Wells, a heavy man with a big beard, who was wearing a wool hat and thick woolen pants. He lived in the town of Litchfield and built Finnish masonry stoves. When I introduced myself to him, he said, "Oh, you're the anthropologist. You

studied firewalking in Greece. Did you firewalk when you were there?"
"No," I replied, "I only studied it."

Inside the main building at Northern Pines, in a store that sold incense, vitamins, and books on holistic health, Tom told me that he had
firewalked once before at the Healing Arts Festival in Kezar Falls,
Maine. Afterward he'd noticed a small red spot on the ball of his foot,
an area that corresponded to his lungs. "I smoke," he said, "so I probably have a weakness there." Then he explained to me some of the basic
principles of foot reflexology, a science that deals with anatomical cor-
respondences between parts of the foot and other organs of the body.

Tom described himself jokingly as a pyromaniac; he remembered
lighting little fires in back alleys when he was a child growing up in
Chicago. He told me about the stoves he built—double combustion
stoves that were pollution free and gave off high-temperature flue
gases. He said he was fascinated by fire—he called it the most basic of
all elements. He'd been burning wood for heat exclusively now for
fourteen years. Tom had brought the wood for Ken to use to build the
fire that night because he didn't have a hundred dollars to pay for the
workshop.

I found Ken in the building next door standing with several other
people around a big stone fireplace in a comfortable lounge. Mary Deacon, a thin athletic-looking woman with short blond hair who lived at
the Greely Corner Sauna Bath, worked as an instructor for Outward
Bound in the summer. We talked about the relationship between Outward Bound and firewalking, and she recommended I read a book entitled *The Conscious Use of Metaphor in Outward Bound*. I also met
David "Health" Richardson, a nutritionist and biofeedback therapist;
Sarah Jacobs, who was studying to be a minister in the Unity Church;
John Hawkins, who ran a vegetarian restaurant in Portland; and
Lynda Harrison, a therapist from California.

For the next hour or so I helped Tom and a man named Richard
load the wood from Tom's truck into Richard's four-wheel drive Su-
baru pick-up. We had to bring it up the unplowed road to the clearing
on top of the hill where the firewalk would take place. Richard, a
friendly man with a red beard, calloused hands, and a strong Maine
accent, had served in Vietnam and been through a drug rehabilitation
program. He worked now as a heavy equipment operator. Our conversation shifted easily from truck engines to wood stoves and finally
to healing.

Shortly after noon ten people gathered in a large room above the store. A thick purple carpet covered the floor, while posters of mandalas, goddess figures, and shamanic visions hung on the walls. The windows opened out onto the snow and the tall pines that surrounded the building. On a table by the door were release forms, which we all signed, stating that we had undertaken the firewalk voluntarily and that neither Ken Cadigan nor Northern Pines could be held responsible for any injuries we might suffer.

We sat cross-legged in a circle on the floor. In the center was a beachball globe, a square red candle, and a copy of my dissertation on the Anastenaria. Behind Ken stood an easel with a big pad of paper, on which Ken had written:

WELCOME TO THE FIREDANCE
A CELEBRATION OF INNOCENCE

Ken began by encouraging us to be open to the experience of healing.

"Be open to who you are," he said. "Step out of your head. Be open to the theater of possibilities. This process is concerned with overcoming fear and limiting beliefs in your life once and for all. You won't *eliminate* fear and limiting beliefs; you'll learn how to use them as guides, instead of letting them stop you."

Ken illustrated this with a story about Don Juan who stepped into his fear and put it on his shoulder. Fear was his ally and guide.

"Be careful," continued Ken. "Make sure you follow your guidance. After today you won't have any excuses for not following through on your heart of hearts' desires because of fear. You'll be able to handle it with love.

"Who feels fear now?" Ken asked. Most of us raised our hands.

"The fear of fire is programmed into our genes; it's reinforced generation after generation. The firedance is a rite that's thousands of years old too. It's the most primal rite of passage in the world. You won't be harmed by contact with the fire, you'll be healed. Life won't be the same for you tomorrow.

"All you need is the fact of who you are, the awareness of who you are. That will get you through any fire in your life. Who you are can never be burned because fire only consumes the *appearance* of who you are. Egos get burned. If you go into the fire to show off or to show how macho you are, then you'll get burned. You need to approach the fire with reverence.

"Today will help you come to a place that's more open, more innocent. Firewalking is a rite of passage of the heart; it's an empowering
act of healing. You'll be empowered at the level of the heart to go
through fire in everyday life with love. I don't know how it's possible,
and I've walked a hundred times all over the United States and Europe.
Scientists talk about the conductivity of coals and the dispersion of heat,
but I can stop and stand in the coals without moving for ten seconds
and still not get burned. I'm talking to the scientist in us. We know it's
impossible. But even if scientists do explain the firewalk someday, fire
will still be fire, and people will still be people.

"The fire tonight will be between fourteen hundred and two thousand degrees farenheit. Aluminum is poured at eleven hundred degrees. At that temperature protein turns to carbon in an instant."

Ken paused.

"But any fool can do the firewalk; it's not reserved for certain people.
If you're here just to prove you can do it, then you're in the wrong
place. If that's your attitude, when you're done you'll say 'So what?
What's for dinner?'

"What goes on in *here* is the real fire," said Ken gesturing to his
heart. "The real fire is going on in here all the time. The fire inside
consumes everything. This is the essence of ourselves; this is who we
really are.

"The firewalk itself is not ultimately satisfying. It's the icing on the
cake, the cherry on top of the ice cream, the last step of purification. I
present today as a gateway of possibility. I want you to think 'If I can
do this, what else in my life can I do that I've always been afraid of?'
You need to know who you actually are, beyond fear and limitations.
You should use the firewalk as a vehicle for the next step in your life."

Then Ken talked about the history of firewalking. After a brief discussion of recent scientific research on neuropeptides and endorphins,
Ken explained the two kinds of healing that firewalking can bring
about: physiological healing—cancer patients who go into remission
after a firewalk, for example—and psychological healing "in the area
of completion." Ken said that after a firewalk people complete things
they've never been able to finish because of fear and doubt. "After firewalking major healing can take place. Our goal today is the healing of
relationships."

At this point Ken mentioned his relationship with Mary. Some conflict or problem had ended their relationship, and they had separated;

but then a healing had occurred, and they had come together again. Now they were friends. Ken was able to forgive people now because of the healing that had taken place during all the firewalks he had done. "I've learned that it's more healing to be happy than to be right, whatever form coals have come to me in my life.

"Mary will be our fire tender today," continued Ken. "The fire will teach her. The wisdom that comes from the fire is the grandfather principle. This wisdom flows from the fire to the fire tender and to all of us. The teaching for Mary is to listen to the fire, to support it, not to manipulate it. It takes a special person to nurture the fire so it will be healing for all the rest of us." Ken held his palms together and bowed to Mary in a gesture of respect and thanks.

Ken contrasted the conscious act of firewalking with accidental contact with fire. One day when he was five years old, his father was burning leaves in the yard. Ken thought the fire was out and ran through it. Both his feet were badly burned, and he spent several days in the hospital recovering. Years later when he heard about firewalking workshops for the first time, he signed up for one right away. It was definitely a healing experience for him. He knew that if he could walk on fire consciously, then he'd be healed. According to the principles of homeopathy, if a lot can harm you, a little can heal you. At this point Tom, who had firewalked once before, said that after he crossed the fire the first time, he thought he'd been burned; he felt a moment of fear. But then the words "Fire heals" came to him, so he crossed the fire again. The painful spot became electric; it was energized. The burn came out and was healed.

Next Ken touched on what was for him the main theme of the evening in terms of his own personal growth. He talked about what the real fire was for him and how he wanted to be different tomorrow. He had decided not to charge money for his workshops anymore.

"I'm letting go. I'll only ask for donations from now on. This walk is on a donation basis—whatever it's worth to you to overcome fear and doubt for the rest of your life. This is your chance to stop the search. You can contribute now or later. It can be nothing or it can be a thousand dollars. This is all I do, and I'd like to be supported."

Ken mentioned a friend of his he hadn't seen in a long time who'd stopped by his house recently. He'd won twelve hundred dollars in the lottery and wanted to give Ken a thousand dollars to support his work.

"Give from your heart. There's a basket on the table by the door.

Charging money for this never felt right to me. For me this is a step into faith and trust. People have barriers when it comes to money. . . ."

Ken stopped. His face grew red, and he started to cry. He said money was a barrier for him; he worried about where lunch was coming from. He wanted to let go of that; he wanted to overcome his attachment to money and stop playing his little security game.

"The doorway of possibility for me is not charging money. The whole world says you can't do that, that it can't be done. I spent five hundred dollars on advertising for today's workshop. I closed out my bank account, but now I feel free."

Ken knew he was taking a big risk. He felt nervous, but at least this way he could do what he did for love. It removed the barriers for people who could benefit from his work but who couldn't afford it.

Then Ken told us about the Hundredth Monkey Project. It wasn't an organization; it was just the title of a book by Ken Keyes about avoiding nuclear war by raising people's consciousness. In the 1950s scientists in Japan were feeding some monkeys on a small island by dropping sweet potatoes to them from airplanes. One little monkey started to eat a sweet potato, but it was covered with dirt and sand, so he washed it in the sea. Other monkeys began to imitate him. At a certain point, when a hundred monkeys were doing it, other monkeys on other islands and on the mainland four hundred miles away suddenly started washing their sweet potatoes too. "There's an old Sufi saying: if 10 percent of humanity were to awaken to who they really are, then all of humanity would. Each of us makes a difference. We need to go ahead into the fact of life in spite of all our fears and doubts.

"Our project today is to go beyond our belief systems and dogmas to the way things really are. Healing the world of separation and ignorance and war is our goal. We don't have to blow ourselves up. There's no cure for nuclear war, just prevention. The button exists for fear and doubt. I invite you to use the firewalk to heal your relationships with others. I've been doing healing work and consciousness work for twenty years. It's the most meaningful thing anyone can do in life."

Ken asked if the people who had firewalked before had anything to say.

"I was a skeptic the first time," said Tom. "I had a lot of ego involved. I wondered if I could have stayed in longer or if I could have done it if the fire had been hotter. But I was left with strong empowerment afterwards; I felt closure."

Richard said that the firewalk had enabled him to do everyday things he hadn't been able to do before.

"Ever since my first firewalk I have all this energy to do things. I went as an observer, and then I became part of it. My intention in passing through the fire was to be less critical of people, and it's happened naturally. I've gone through real fire in my life. What I've gone through makes the firewalk here seem like a piece of cake. Now I'm more calm and accepting. I don't worry about money, and I can do things without fear. I've been able to stop smoking and go on a macrobiotic diet. The firewalk is a hell of a battery charger."

Ken smiled and said, "It's a giant maxibustion treatment—acupuncture without needles. We all have our own stories of walking through coals in our lives. Firewalking dissolves the barriers of a lifetime. The fire out there is a mirror of the fire inside. This fire tonight is nothing; the absolute fire is the self. The real work is with that fire.

"After the firewalk you'll feel several days of being up, several days of light and clearness. You will have eliminated a major tape—that fire burns. Tapes and programs limit you and get in your way; they're barriers. But over the next few weeks you'll experience a shift in your life at some level. Time will show you what was healed here tonight."

Ken outlined the program for the rest of the evening. He commented on the full moon, how beautiful it was, how meaningful it was for the women present. He said we would go up and build the fire, come back and see slides of the Anastenaria, and then share with others why we were here.

"You'll share what your intentions are. You'll look inside yourself and see what motivates you. You'll ask yourself 'How will I use this experience? What difference will it make to me?' Those are the things you should be thinking about."

Then Ken asked us to close our eyes and pray.

"Great divine mystery of life, creator of all that is. Thank you for giving us an opportunity to heal all areas of our lives. Only you know what needs to be healed. Guide each of us to partake of this experience in a manner most meaningful for us. Please allow us to take this experience to other people in our lives that we'll be touching, so it can heal them, even if they don't have the opportunity we have here tonight. Thank you for all you have given us: breath, bodies, hearts. Please allow us to use these gifts always in the service of love and truth. Thank you for that fire of the heart that consumes all hesitation and resistance forever. To the divine: thank you, thank you, thank you. So be it."

Ken took a small black cylindrical container out of his pocket and told us that it contained coals from other firewalks he had done: in California, in Germany, and in Greece. He would pour them into the fire we lit later in the evening. This was a symbol that all his firewalks were connected, a symbol of the common humanity of the firewalking movement. "This isn't the first firewalk or the last," he said. "It's part of a whole movement of powerful healing."

According to Ken there were four points of empowerment at any firewalk. The first was just showing up. The second was making the firewalk meaningful. The third was the intention-setting, and the fourth was the first step into the fire. We were now at the second point of empowerment. Ken gave us all a pencil, on which was printed "It's better to be happy," and an index card.

"Write down something that doesn't work for you, something you want to give up; an attitude, or cigarettes, for example. Take your past and offer it to the fire so you can be finished with it. Be specific. Put down something that you can actually see change, like 'What is not healed in me that makes me critical of others?' This is the first point of healing."

Ken told us to write "As of tonight I want to leave behind. . . . So be it," and then sign our names.

When I put down my pen and the small notebook I'd been writing in all afternoon, I suddenly realized how important they were to me, how naked and vulnerable I felt without them. They seemed to be the only things that separated me from the other people in the room. They made me an anthropologist. Here in Raymond, Maine, I was much more conscious than I had ever been in Greece of the fact that it was the act of writing that created such a distance between me and other people. In Ayia Eleni I'd been different in so many other ways. I wasn't Greek, I wasn't an Orthodox Christian, and I didn't believe in Saint Constantine. But here, if I put down my pen and my notebook and stopped writing, what would distinguish me from the people who had come to firewalk? Nothing! I was a part of their world; we belonged to the same generation, the same subculture. And yet I was not like them. I was an anthropologist.

I picked up the pencil Ken had given me and wrote: "As of tonight I want to leave behind my feeling that I need to control things."

"This is the second point of empowerment," said Ken. "It's not wrong to break the commitment. There shouldn't be any guilt. It's just a broken commitment, and we all know what that means. It creates contractions. We should just try to grow with it. Empowerment doesn't take place in the head; it takes place in the heart. Loving absolutely is empowering. This is the power of love, the transforming power of love." Ken said his favorite image for this was a red heart with a Popeyelike arm coming out of it flexing its muscles.

Now we would go out and light the fire in silence. Ken told us to look inside ourselves during this silence and ask for guidance. "Ask yourselves 'Is today the day for me to have this be a healing experience as the divine order would have it?' "

It was starting to grow dark as we walked up the hard snow-packed path through the pines to the clearing at the top of the hill. Tom carried a shovel and a rake; Richard a big can of kerosene. We had stacked the wood in a pile at the side of a small square clearing that had been shoveled in the snow. Following Ken's instructions carefully we built a square crib of logs five or six feet high. Then we placed logs vertically at the corners of the crib, both inside and out. Finally, we stuffed dead branches, scraps of wood, and crumpled sheets of newspaper in any open spaces we could find. It was an impressive pile of wood, and building it together in silence had created among us a definite sense of community.

We joined hands in a circle and began chanting a low, droning "Ohhhmmmm." I had never done this before, and I felt a little foolish. Ken poured the kerosene on the pile of wood and lit it with a match. Hot flames and smoke swirled up into the cold night air. As we stood there, Ken told us to bend our knees slightly, so we would feel closer to mother earth. One by one, starting with Ken, we stepped up to the fire, read our cards to ourselves, paused, and threw them into the fire. The heat was so intense that it was hard to get close enough to really throw the card into the fire. One person's card fluttered down and landed in the snow, charred and black around the edges. People later said their eyebrows and hair had been singed. It was frightening to think that in a few hours some of us would actually dance on this fire.

For several minutes we stood there chanting. The front half of my body was uncomfortably hot, the back uncomfortably cold. Just then there was a break in the clouds, and the bright light of the full moon shone through. People smiled knowingly, as if it were some kind of

Joining hands in a circle around the fire (Photograph by Brian Garland)

sign. We stood together watching the fire in silence for a moment more. Then with a bow to Mary, who would remain outside with the fire all evening, Ken led us back down the hill.

WHEN WE WERE all seated again on the thick purple rug, I began my slide presentation on the Anastenaria. I talked about icons, votive offerings, and Saint Constantine's ability to heal illnesses; about Yavasis, Mihalis, Maria, and Sotiria. I was acutely aware of how different this audience was from any I had ever spoken to before about the Anastenaria. I was addressing people who had their own language with which to talk about firewalking, people who were about to firewalk themselves. In the past I had been accustomed to talking about firewalking in one of two idioms—a spirit idiom or an anthropological idiom. In my previous work I had attempted to translate from a language of saints, punishment, and open roads into a language of guilt, somatization, and catharsis. Now I was confronted with a third language—a language of chakras and karma, empowerment and healing relationships, neuropeptides and endorphins. In spite of the fact that this language was both English and at times scientific, it sounded even more foreign and exotic to me than either of the other two languages I had used to talk about firewalking before.

I found that as I spoke about the Anastenaria to this group of American firewalkers, I made a conscious effort to translate from the two other languages I was familiar with into this new language. I tried to speak the language of my audience in order to reduce the distance between us, in order to sound less impersonal, less academic. In addition, I stressed the similarities between what the Anastenarides did and what American firewalkers were doing because I wanted to reduce the distance between them too. Ken also emphasized points that linked his firewalking workshops with the Anastenaria. As he often said, he wasn't doing anything new. People all over the world have been walking on fire for centuries.

When my presentation was over, Ken played a tape of the "Mikrokostandinos" song, a tape he had made from a record I'd bought in New York City. Ken asked me to demonstrate the dance steps and gestures of the Anastenarides. As I showed people the low sweep of the arm, the two hands moving back and forth holding a simadi between them, I felt extremely uncomfortable. I had never danced this way before. In fact, I hardly ever did any Greek folk dancing at all. I had always associated learning Greek folk dances with foreign tourists who wanted to experience "the real Greece" but who were only consuming a romantic stereotype of Zorba the Greek dancing on the beach. As I danced, I felt I was trespassing or doing something sacrilegious. I was pretending to be an Anastenaris, pretending to be possessed by Saint Constantine. I felt like a transvestite; I was impersonating Maria, Sotiria, or Marika.

Ken watched me dance and said, "Yeah. That's the way. That's how they do it." Tom came over and danced next to me, carefully imitating my steps and my gestures. After a while people stopped trying to dance like the Anastenarides and began dancing more familiar dances— square dances and contradances, moving around in circles swinging each other by the arm.

Then we sat down again in a circle on the floor. Ken reminded us that while the purpose of the firewalk for the Anastenarides was communion with Saint Constantine, the purpose of the firewalk for us was communion with the heart. Our goal was purification, healing, and openness. We had arrived at the third point of empowerment, intention-setting.

"Ask yourselves 'Why am I here? If I could get anything from being here tonight what would it be?' Don't say what you want or hope or expect; that's all in the future. Intention is not wanting something to be in a certain way. We want to be free of programs and tapes, but that's wanting. Intention is living in the moment.

"Visualize what you want. Take something you want and intend it; make it real in the present. Let's say you want to buy a new car, but fear and doubt get in the way. Say to yourself 'I know today is the day. Today is the day I'm getting it.' You close your eyes as you're riding the bus to the car dealer's, and you picture yourself in the seat of your brand new car. You picture yourself driving out of the showroom. That's intention! The essence of intention is not other than who you are. You don't get intention outside the self. When you get this intention thing, life looks a lot different."

Ken said we would take turns answering the question, "How do I want to change as a result of tonight?" He told us not to tell stories but to speak in the present tense and use the first person.

"There's no practice with life, and there's no practice with the fire. There's none here either. We create separation in our relationships. We need to eliminate that tonight. We need to overcome fear and doubt in our lives once and for all. That's the practical purpose of all this. The greatest fear in life is presenting yourself authentically in front of others. You'll overcome this major fear now, before the firewalk."

Each of us would speak in turn. We were not to let people stop talking until we felt they were "speaking from the heart." If people weren't being honest or if they were being vague and superficial, we should ask them to speak more concretely. When we were ready to accept people's statements, we should give them "twinkles" by holding both hands out in front of us and wiggling our fingers. They would receive our twinkles by looking at each of us in turn and responding with a smile or a nod. As we practiced giving twinkles to each other there was some nervous laughter at what seemed to be a silly, childlike gesture.

"This is a firewalk," said Ken seriously. "This will change your life. You should set your mind to get results now."

Ken was the first to speak.

"My name is Ken. My daily life is about leading groups. . . . My purpose here tonight. . . ."

There was a long silence.

"What's coming up for me is letting go . . . the donation thing . . . letting go of expectations, the way things should be. My purpose here tonight is to demonstrate that I am supported just because I am. My purpose is to dance on coals and not be burned. If I could have anything from being here tonight— . . . the money thing, . . . that I be supported more from donations than by charging money, . . . that I be financially secure. The resistance is . . . I'm only in it for money.

"It is my intention tonight to experience prosperity in my life, just because I am. I don't want to be fake. Did you receive me?"

Everyone immediately gave Ken twinkles. It was a friendly gesture of acceptance and approval.

Sarah spoke next. She was studying to be a minister in the Unity Church. In a few months she was scheduled to appear before a board of ministers who would evaluate her progress toward ordination. The first time she appeared before them she hadn't done well. She tried to say what she thought they wanted to hear; she tried to please them rather than be herself. Sarah said she intended the firewalk to give her confidence in herself so she would do well in her next appearance before the board. Her presentation was emotional and sincere, and she received twinkles right away.

David, the biofeedback therapist, began talking about his practice and the leaflets he would hand out later describing the workshops he offered. He spoke vaguely about a woman he really loved and wanted to treat better. When he finished, there was silence. No one gave him twinkles, so he continued talking. Ken interrupted him several times saying, "I'm not receiving you. Nothing is coming out," or "Your words are falling in your lap." David seemed to be groping for something to say. People finally gave him twinkles but without much enthusiasm.

Lynda spoke in very general terms about wanting to be more open in her communication with other people. She was extremely nervous and embarrassed. She interrupted herself frequently with comments like "Wow! This is hard!" or "Let me try again." Ken reassured her and told her to stand up, do some deep breathing, and speak with her whole body. Lynda relaxed slightly and spoke more specifically about her problems communicating with her mother. With more guidance from Ken Lynda finally received twinkles from everyone.

I took my turn next. I said I was a teacher; that I taught people about different cultures, different ways of life. I had come to share with them what I knew about firewalking in Greece and to learn more about firewalking in the United States. I said that my intention in being there that night was to deal with feelings of insecurity I had, to overcome fears I had that people wouldn't think I was smart enough, that they wouldn't think I was a good enough person. Everyone gave me twinkles right away. I felt relieved; I felt welcome; I felt accepted.

Then John spoke somewhat disjointedly about a psychological problem he had that he understood but that he couldn't put into words. It involved a death he'd experienced as a child that was still a barrier for him. Tom said he didn't have much use for this "verbal process stuff"; he was just there for the firewalk. Ken accepted his openness and gave him twinkles. The rest of us followed Ken's lead and gave him twinkles too. Richard talked about wanting to be more honest with people, and another woman said she wanted to be less possessive.

When the intention-setting was over, Ken described some of the barriers that confronted us in our lives and some of the preconceived ideas we had that prevented us from being the people we really were. He talked about all the tapes and programs that we believed in that weren't true and about the ease with which we were distracted from what was really important.

Ken put on a little skit to illustrate the way we maintained these barriers. He pretended that Richard was a good friend of his and placed a stool between the two of them.

"Richard, good buddy," he said, "It's great to see you! I'll come over and give you a big hug." He started walking toward Richard, but he tripped over the stool and stopped. "Whenever I want a hug, I run into my father. Boy! If my father had only hugged me, I'd be okay now. He's been dead for five years. I wish I'd been able to get through to him. If only. . . ." We blame other people for our problems; that's one way we maintain our blocks.

Ken stood the stool back up and started walking toward Richard again. "Richard, old buddy. . . ." He tripped on the stool a second time. "Wow! Look at my block! Isn't it a nice block? What a special block! I talk nonstop about my block. I tell everyone about it, but no one wants to listen." Fear causes us to talk constantly about our blocks; that's another way we maintain them.

"Richard, old buddy. . . ." Ken tripped over the stool again. "Me? A block? No way! I've got things together. I don't have any blocks. Won't it be great when everyone is together like me?" Ken walked around looking for his block, all the while holding the stool to the seat of his pants. Denial is the third way we maintain our blocks.

"Richard, good buddy. . . ." Ken tripped on the stool once more. "On my way over to hug Richard I bumped into my father, who's been dead for five years. How is this block put together? Oh! I see now. This piece is connected to that one over there by this screw. I'll get my tools. This is simple. All I have to do is unscrew this one screw. . . ." Ken pretended to take the stool apart. Then he placed it upside down on the floor in front of him, stepped over it, and gave Richard a big hug. "We need to get closer to our blocks, to understand them, in order to eliminate them from our lives."

At this point John said, "Fire is an illusion."

"Sure it's an illusion," replied Ken, "but you can get burned by it."

"Life's an illusion too," said Richard, "and you can really get burned by *it*."

To illustrate the "What if?" syndrome Ken told us a story about the first time he went skydiving during the Firewalking Instructor's Training Program he took with Tolly Burkan in California. Ken had been more afraid of skydiving than firewalking, but after six hours of lessons he put his life in the hands of his instructor and stepped onto the plane. All he could think about was "What if the parachute opens up three feet above the ground? What if they have to scrape me off the runway?" He was terrified. Then the instructor yelled at him to jump. A second later he was in ecstasy. "It's the 'What if?' syndrome that keeps us in place. That's the barrier that keeps us from growing and from experiencing empowerment and healing."

At this point Ken talked more specifically about the act of firewalking itself.

"There are two kinds of people—people who can walk on fire and people who can't. How do you know which kind of person you are? Can you take the first step? If you can, you're one of the people who can walk on fire. If you can take that first step, just keep on walking. If you can't, you'll ask, 'Where did my guidance go?' There will either be a response in you that says, 'I can do it,' or there won't. If you think you'll get burned, then you will—and *please* don't walk if you're going to get burned."

"How do you know if you're going to get burned?" someone asked.

"You'll know," Ken replied. "And if you do get burned, have that be okay. Sometimes it's more valuable to be burned than not to be burned. Make the burn a growth experience. It needs to be okay if you get burned, or else your resistance will get burned.

"Remember! It's a firewalk or a firedance. It's not a firerun or a firesprint or a firehop. If you run across the fire, it means you're afraid you'll get burned. You're thinking, 'If I go across quickly enough, then I won't get burned.' But you're never quick enough if you have that attitude. It's the fear that makes you burn.

"I've led over three thousand people through fire, and I've had two people in bed for a week with third-degree burns. Some people have actually died from firewalking. In Sri Lanka a monk slipped and fell in the fire. He died. In a town in Brazil one year twenty out of eighty people were badly burned, and one person died. It's not 'Let's pretend' fire."

Then Ken gave us some practical advice on how to firewalk. He suggested that we take off our socks and lace our boots loosely so we wouldn't fumble around in the cold trying to untie them at the last minute. He also suggested that we roll up our pants so they wouldn't get burned and that we scuff our feet or step in the snow if our feet felt hot after we crossed the fire.

"Start walking a few feet from the edge of the fire so you're already moving when you go in. Walk steadily and briskly. It will feel like a street on a hot summer day.

"Tonight I'll rake the fire into a circle, not a runway the way I usually do. We'll begin by going from west to east, into the rising sun."

"Why?" someone asked.

"That's the way they did it in the past, and that's the way they do it in Greece. It's also so we won't bump into each other, so there won't be any collisions. You don't want collisions in the fire."

Ken told us we could dance anyway we wanted to. He recommended a shouting breath and checked with me to confirm what I had said earlier—that the Anastenarides say they shout rather than sigh when they dance. He said we should cross the fire on an out breath, because it's harder to contract on an out breath. We could cross the fire more and more slowly, dancing longer on the fire each time. We would just stamp the fire out the way they did in Greece. Finally, he recommended that we bring a towel to stand on at the edge of the fire because the snowy ground would be cold.

"Have the fire accept you. Be open. Be with the fire and be with yourself. Develop a relationship with the fire. Say to yourself, 'My intention is to have a healing experience.' "

As the final step in our preparation for the firewalk Ken had us do a visualization.

"Close your eyes," he said, "and imagine yourself standing at the head of a path of fire ten feet wide with flames ten feet high on each side. The path is of infinite length. Now breathe in. Open yourself. Step out into the fire with gratitude, with acceptance, with a 'yes.' "

He told us it wouldn't be any different up at the site of the firewalk and reminded us to be silent from that point on. We danced one last time before setting out for the fire.

The night was beautifully cold and still. As we walked up the hill to the site of the fire, our shadows floated across the moonlit snow. The black trunks of the pines flanked us on either side. Mary was standing beside a big mound of red-hot coals. When we'd formed a circle around the fire and joined hands, Ken told us to do some deep breathing. Then he took a snow shovel and removed a few logs that had not burned down to coals and were still sending up flames. He put them in the snow bank at the edge of the clearing.

Ken asked us to say the one word that was foremost in our consciousness at that moment.

"Love."

"Fear."

"World."

"Whole."

"One."

"Peace."

"Let the coals invite you. Go in when you feel a big 'yes' in your heart."

With those words Ken raked out the coals into a smooth glowing red circle two or three yards in diameter.

I spread my towel over the snow a few feet from the edge of the fire and took off my boots, exposing my bare feet to the cold. I felt very vulnerable. "There's no way I'm going in that fire," I thought to myself. "I don't need to do this; I don't need to prove anything. I'm an anthropologist."

David, who had volunteered to cross the fire first, stood by the wood-pile to the west of the fire. The others stood with their hands folded in front of them or held out to the side, palms-up, in a gesture of supplication that reminded me of Yavasis standing before the icons of Saints Constantine and Helen.

"Take a deep breath," said Ken, "and enter the fire on the out breath. Walk first with a good pace. Your intention is to get off the coals. It should be a brisk walk, not a run. If you think you got burned, just jump in the snow. Now let's give David our intention and our love. Thank you, David, for showing us that it's possible."

David crossed the fire first, confidently, without hesitation, and with no apparent ill effects at all. When he reached the other side, he gave Ken a big hug. One by one everyone else entered the fire, taking three or four steps to get across. Ken asked me if I was ready; I said no, not yet. Then he told everyone to dance in a circle counterclockwise around the fire and to dance or walk through it whenever they were ready.

I was furious at myself. I didn't want to be the only person not to firewalk; I didn't want to miss an opportunity I might never have again. So I put my notebook and pen in the pocket of my down parka and walked around the fire a few more times. My feet were numb from the cold. I was more worried about getting frostbite than I was about getting burned. When I reached the point where David had entered the fire, I stopped and looked across the coals. The way was clear. I had an opportunity to enter the fire, but I was afraid. The moment passed.

I joined the circle and walked around the fire once more. When I came back to the side of the fire by the woodpile, I stopped again. Everyone else had walked through the fire unharmed, and they were just like me. They weren't Greek villagers; they weren't possessed by Saint Constantine.

I entered the fire the next chance I had. I felt no heat, only the rough coals giving way beneath my feet with a crunch. After I crossed the fire, I stood in the snow for a few seconds. I felt like I'd just rappelled down a cliff or run a marathon. I was ecstatic. Then I took out my notebook and my pen and began writing again.

The others danced through the fire more slowly and deliberately now. John and Tom were spinning and whirling and stamping the coals with their feet. Lynda and her twelve-year-old son Orion went across the fire together.

"Remember your intention as you go across," said Ken.

Only a few people were still in the fire. The firewalk was almost over.

"Does anyone want to go in again?" Ken asked. "Is everyone complete?"

At Ken's suggestion we celebrated our successful firewalk together with a cheer. We clasped hands and shouted, "Yeah! All right! Way to go!" as if we'd just won the World Series.

Then people began wiping off their feet, putting on their socks, and lacing up their boots. Richard picked up a coal in his hands and held it for a few seconds. I asked him how it felt. "Hot," he said, "but not burning hot. If it had been from a wood stove, though, I would have been burned." "Why?" I asked. "Faith," he replied.

When we were all back inside, several of us climbed into a bathtub together with our clothes on to wash off our feet. I kept looking at my feet, amazed that I hadn't been burned. After we gathered again in a circle on the purple rug, Ken told us that the firewalk made the extraordinary ordinary and the ordinary extraordinary. "You say 'I'm just an ordinary person.' But you're wrong. You walk on fire. You are extraordinary."

Ken held up a pencil.

"What's this?" he asked.

"A pencil," said one person.

"Wood," said another.

"What's wood?" asked Ken.

"Life."

"What's life?"

"Energy."

"And what's energy? . . . The mystery!"

"Allow yourself to be open to just this." Ken bent his arm at the elbow several times. "How can I do this? Scientists can't explain it. Open up to the mystery that is ever present but still a total mystery."

Ken told us that it was important for us to share our experience with other people in a positive way. We shouldn't boast about it; we should tell people in a way that would heal them. We should just tell the truth about an impossible experience.

Ken hugged Mary and asked us to thank her for the special fire. Then he asked if anyone had been burned. Everyone said no. Richard said he had one or two little red spots, which Ken referred to affectionately as "ouchies" or "kisses." By this time I too had begun to feel several tender places on one of my feet. Later I noticed three small red spots that disappeared in a few days, but I didn't have any blisters. I hadn't been burned.

As Ken handed out index cards and pencils again, he asked if any of us had begun to "negate the experience," to think that the fire hadn't been hot enough or that without the snow and the cold it would have been a *real* firewalk. No one had. On our cards Ken told us to write: "I walk (or dance) on fire. I can do anything I choose." He said to use the present tense, to underline "anything," and to put an exclamation point at the end. He suggested we put the card on our bathroom mirror and leave it there for three weeks.

Ken said he would have told anyone who had not walked to write. "I can always trust my inner guidance."

"People who don't walk often withdraw and feel isolated and rejected, but they shouldn't. It can often be more powerful not to walk than to walk. There's no right way, no failure. People who don't walk have to grow with it . . . if they choose to grow. If they don't choose to grow, that's their problem."

I put down my notebook and pen, took an index card and pencil, and filled out the card: "I walk on fire. I can do *anything* I choose!" Then I picked up my notebook and pen again and wrote in my notebook what I had just written on the index card. What I wrote on the card I wrote as a firewalker, as a participant in a workshop on overcoming fear and limiting beliefs. What I wrote in my notebook I wrote as an anthropologist, as a person doing ethnographic fieldwork. Writing on the card was, as Ken would say, an act of empowerment. Writing in my notebook, I sometimes think, was just the opposite. "When it comes to firewalking," Ken once told me, "you're either a participant or an observer."

As we prepared to go next door to eat, Ken reminded us that it was donation time. People left cash and checks on the table by the door. Later in the evening Ken announced that he owed the owner of Northern Pines a hundred and fifty dollars and that he needed to collect five more dollars from us in order to break even. Hearing this several people gave Ken a few dollars more.

The woman who cooked all the meals for Ken's workshops had prepared a big casserole, a salad, stuffed grape leaves, spinach pie, and Greek pastries. During the meal there was much warm conversation and friendly joking. People talked about taking the Enlightenment Intensive Ken was leading the next day; Richard joked about not wanting his "straight" friends at work to find out what he had done—they might think he was crazy; and when Mary referred to some job she had to do as impossible, John said, "That's right. It's impossible. You can do it."

After the meal we all said good-bye to each other with hugs and handshakes. While I sat warming up my car in the parking lot, Richard, who'd been cleaning the snow off his windshield, came over to me. I rolled down the window.

"Write good of us, okay?" he said.

As I drove home through the winter night, I glowed. I felt wonderful, the way I did after climbing a mountain or spending an evening with close friends in Greece. Everything was special. The ordinary *was* extraordinary—the full moon that night, my sleeping son, the bald eagle I saw the next day.

✣

TOLLY BURKAN'S
WORLD-FAMOUS FIREWALKING WORKSHOP
SATURDAY 7–11 PM

This seminar is not for everyone—it is only for those committed to extraordinary growth and mastery of excellence.[2] *The format is experiential and*

---

[2] From a publicity brochure distributed by *Sundoor Seminars.*

uses the latest accelerated learning techniques for greater ease in learning and longer-lasting results. It is jam-packed with practical demonstrations and applications of recent mind/body discoveries for peak performance and self-induced healing. You will be trained in skills developed by acclaimed scientists and medical doctors. As you absorb methods for controlling your state of mind and emotions, you will be overcoming fears and limitations that have prevented you from realizing your goals. You'll feel free and empowered with increased self-confidence and enjoyment whether you choose to participate in the firewalk or choose to observe. Either way, the evening is transformational because you'll be acquiring success strategies for both personal and professional power that virtually anyone can use. You'll get training, not teaching, receiving state of the art skills from Tolly Burkan himself. This seminar can have a dramatic impact on your life, your workplace and your community as well.

    GUARANTEED*! Your money will be refunded if you are not 100% satisfied.*

LOCATION: *S.F./Oakland Bay Bridge Holiday Inn*
DATE: *Saturday after first Friday of each month*
COST;   *$100 (Professional Firefighters admitted free with I.D.)*
    Pre-workshop Networking Party 2-4 PM/Holiday Inn.

✤

CONVERSATIONS

Tom Wells told me that he walked on fire for the first time at the Healing Arts Festival in Kezar Falls.

"They had everything there—meditation workshops, yoga workshops, massage workshops, attunements, workshops in psychic healing and developing your own psychic powers, group therapy sessions, chakra healings, sweat lodges—everything. It was a very gentle, loving, and supportive place. You came back from it and you couldn't help but be floating pretty high. It was at a lake, so there was water nearby, and that was a healing force too."

One woman was burned there, Tom said. She'd suffered a stroke, so she used a walker and dragged her feet when she walked. She went across the fire too slowly and got burned. According to Tom the secret was to go through the fire quickly. For that reason at Northern Pines he wanted to go through slowly. He wanted a hotter fire; he wanted to stand still in the fire and come away with nothing on his feet. He realized, though, that he couldn't stand in the fire; his feet got hot. In any event he'd taken enough steps in the fire so his feet shouldn't have looked as good as they did.

Tom thought that you needed the right attitude in order to avoid getting burned and that if you went into the fire you had the right attitude by definition—you weren't afraid.

"But in my case there were other forces operating. I was transcending my mind, and my body was transcending the heat of the fire. What I wanted to do was put myself in that space of being moment to moment. That's what I walked away with. I was really into those coals; that was the moment. My intention was to be in the here and now and not wander off into the future. Richard Alper, Baba Ram Dass, and all that."

I asked Tom if he had been empowered by the experience of firewalking.

"Yeah, I got empowerment from it. There was lots of group energy there. The empowerment comes from the group and the firewalk. That's the gain. You quiet yourself; you get some faith. The firewalk's a good thing to do; it rearranges your perspective."

Tom admitted that he had been bored with the "verbal trip" that preceded the firewalk. He just sat there and watched Ken's aura—the purple light at his finger tips, the halo of energy around his head. If there had been music at the fire, there would have been more of a group trance; the whole experience would have been more mystical.

Tom said that now sometimes he sits at home looking at the fire in his wood stove and thinks about firewalking. He wants to do it again on his own.

MARY DEACON described herself as "a gypsy, an itinerant, someone who refused to subject herself to the bottom line." She just lived at the Greely Corner Sauna and tended fires whenever she had the chance. Earlier in her life she had worked as a freelance writer; she wrote mostly about sailing and skiing. She had also done solo sailboat racing across the Atlantic.

I asked her what it was like being the fire tender.

"It was a holy experience, an experience of reverence. I felt like a pagan priestess being alone with the fire for four hours with the full moon coming up. It was a really powerful experience; I'm very gratified to have done it. When I was out there alone, I felt a tremendous connectedness to the fire. As Robert Bly said, 'There are a hundred ways to kneel down and kiss the earth.' It all harks back to the ancient sense of the earth mother and all that represents."

While Mary was tending the fire, she thought about things in her life that she wanted to change. She thought about affirmations, intentions, and relationships. She knew that after the firewalk she would feel lighter and clearer.

"I'll get on with things I've put off; I'll complete things; I'll attend to all the little things that have been nagging at me. The firewalk works for me that way. It's a symbol of going past self-imposed limitations. There are times with all my rationalizing and analyzing that I box myself in and paralyze myself. The firewalk helps me blast through all that. After the firewalk things start to go well again; I begin to run my life again. I feel more powerful, more in control. There's no more powerful metaphor than the firewalk. It thrills and empowers me. I just love it."

Then I asked her what relationship she saw between her work as an instructor for Outward Bound and her firewalking. She said they both involved the same kind of direct experience.

"The Outward Bound process is terrifying—the rock climbing, the ropes course—but the firewalk is on a different echelon; it's in a different realm. We've seen people do rock climbing, but we've never seen people walk on fire. Outward Bound is a long continuum of difficult experiences. The firewalk is a single episode of tremendous power."

Mary had already participated in three Enlightenment Intensives. "I'm an Intensives junkie," she said, adding that someone once described Enlightenment Intensives as "spiritual boot camps." She had also done workshops in Past Lives Regression Therapy that involved relaxation, guided imagery, and goddess work.

Finally, I asked Mary about the firewalk as a healing experience.

"We're all fragmented, we're all divorced from the sea and the earth and the sky that mean so much to us. This fragmentation and separation needs healing. That's the healing Ken's talking about." She mentioned the twin threats of pollution and nuclear war. "We'll destroy ourselves. We need healing, and healing means transcendence. We need a major transcendence of Western culture's understanding of who we are."

JOHN HAWKINS had what he called "an empowerment" in Haiti in 1976. He entered "an enlightenment state." It was more powerful than anything he'd ever experienced with drugs in California in the sixties when he'd been a "test pilot" in Los Angeles experimenting with different batches of LSD to see how much they needed to be diluted. "I'd come back after fourteen hours and say, 'You need to dilute that batch by ten.' Now I know I can go further without drugs.

"In Haiti I experienced meeting the oneness of the universe. It was a religious experience. Once you meet with God, what else can you do? When you come to one with one, to all with all, when you can really be there, who needs anything else? I was walking around four feet off the ground. I got empowerment from that, and I continued to go after other experiences that raised me up where I'd been."

After Haiti John lived in Boston, where he ran a recording studio and a television production company. He described himself as a "video artist." Then one day everything he owned—a hundred thousand dollars worth of equipment and merchandise—was destroyed in a fire in Jamaica Plain. That's when he decided to move to Maine.

"Fire has a great deal of meaning to me," he said. "For me, fire is associated with change."

"Isn't it associated with loss?" I asked.

"No, not loss. Change. That fire was the best thing that ever happened to me. I had too many irons in the fire; I was hyper. I was under a lot of stress. The fire was a sign that the great oneness wanted me to change, wanted me to be more mellow. Fire is a transformer; it takes wood and transforms it into light and heat. The firedance is just another point of transformation."

John said that while he was dancing on the fire he stepped on a hot ember. He thought, "I got myself a smartie." Later that night, when he washed his feet, he saw a blister on the ball of his foot the size of a dime, but it didn't hurt. It never hurt. And the next day it was gone.

"I've never seen a blister heal in one day before," he said.

I asked him how he explained it.

"It's the whole regeneration thing. I was cranked up by the whole experience. The healing process was in full gear."

Then John talked for a long time about his interests in neurolinguistic programming and therapeutic hypnosis. He said he could put himself into a kinaesthetic mode where he was able to switch consciously from one sensory system to another in order to block off pain. He associated this with his father's death, which occurred when he was ten years old. That's when he learned to block off painful emotions. Now he was trying to become a more feeling person.

John had gone to the firewalk "to exorcise an internal demon," the sense of loss that had caused him to shut off his emotions when he was a child. "It helped me open up. During the firewalk I felt a complete sense of freedom. I could have spread my wings and flown. I wasn't bound by gravity or by the normal constraints of life. I used the event as a release."

On his index card John had written "Let me wake up with joy in my heart." He called this "a kind of hypnotic suggestion" and said it had worked. The past few days he'd really felt happier.

When I asked John why people who firewalk don't get burned, he said that he knew all the scientific explanations. He knew the physics behind it: heat energy, conductivity, the rate of change, delta, and all that. He'd gone to MIT for a few years; he read *Scientific American*. But during the firewalk he'd been thinking about his feet. He'd really geared up his feet. Afterward he noticed that they were pinker than usual. They had better circulation and therefore better protection, better healing.

"A person has to be in the right state of mind or else he'll get burned. If I'd been in the wrong state of mind, I would have had blisters all over the place. But at the firewalk I had a proper spiritual sense. I was on a higher plane of experience; I was part of the sensation. I didn't feel any discomfort; I didn't feel any hot or cold.

"When I realized that, I got a hit of freedom. I didn't have to worry about anything. I had a total experience of freedom that's really rare. I felt the joy of sensation and the loss of care, and I captured that feeling. I bottled it, and I can recall it anytime. Once I've been there, I can go back whenever I want. I get the greatest return from the firewalk; it's a resource I can draw on anytime. I can relieve myself of the negativity of life in thirty seconds. I can exorcise the devil that makes me feel bad by bringing back the firedancing experience. I can be back where I was when I was dancing on the fire."

LYNDA HARRISON lived by herself in California now; she was an artist, a gardener, and a therapist. Before leaving Maine, she had been interested in orgone energy and had worked with Wilhelm Reich's daughter. She also worked with Tarot cards, crystals, and herbs in order to learn how to channel this universal energy to heal people.

In San Francisco Lynda was part of a group that met weekly to do energy therapy. She worked with people who had migraine headaches, cancer, or AIDS, as well as with people who had problems with relationships. When the group gathered, they would meditate, leave their bodies, and enter the sick person. They would visualize where the person's energy was blocked up. Then they would work to change the color and the feel of that part of the person's body in order to restore it to health again. They also did levitations and group past-lives regressions.

One day while Lynda was back in Maine visiting her parents and her son Orion at Christmas time, she saw Ken's poster about the firewalk at a natural food store in Portland. As she looked at the poster, she heard an inner voice—her unconscious—telling her she should go. She felt a physical shift in her body and just knew it was the right thing for her to do. The night before the firewalk she didn't sleep at all. She was terrified.

When I asked Lynda for her impressions of the firewalk, she said she really liked the full moon and the spiritual side of things. She made connections with people there; she felt that a universal consciousness was definitely present.

"The seminar Ken did was a loving way to do the firewalk. It was a chance to work on your fears and limitations. I have a problem with money, and I'm working to overcome it. I work with healing crystals: quartz, amethyst, topaz. Different stones have different affinities; they work on different parts of the self. Each stone is tied in with a chakra, an energy center in the body. You want to open the chakras in order to heal yourself. You want to align all the energy centers so the energy flows, so it's not stagnant. If the energy gets stopped up, you get sick.

"The lack of money is a limitation. The firewalk breaks through that limitation. It eliminates the stops you put on your energy flow. Money is a form of energy; it's an energy flow. You need to have energy to attract money and jobs. You put energy out, and it comes back to you in forms you can use, like money. Love is another form of energy. It can get stopped up too."

Lynda had no rational explanation for why she hadn't been burned when she walked through the fire.

"Fourteen million scientists could come up with a logical explanation, and that would still only be part of it. After we danced to the music, I was more centered. I felt spiritually and physically connected to the whole family there. It was like going back to the time when the first people were on earth.

"When I saw David go into the fire, I wasn't afraid anymore. The fire visibly changed for me then. At first it looked just like a fire, then it changed and looked like a carpet. I heard a female voice inside my head say 'Welcome!' Then I saw a pathway across the fire, and I saw an image of myself on the opposite side under the full moon. I was standing there waiting for myself; I was smiling. It meant I could do it. I had already done it. So I just walked to myself.

"Then the same voice said, 'I am Ayesha, the spirit keeper of the eternal flame. Welcome!' I felt a strong pull from below the navel area. Part of my brain told me I wouldn't be burned. My feet tingled, and I felt a huge rush of euphoria, as if something inside me had broken and the flood waters had come rushing out. I felt the energy flow from my head to my feet and back again."

At the time, Lynda said, she had never heard of Ayesha. Later, back in San Francisco, she met a black woman who told her that Ayesha was an African goddess associated with fire.

"While I was walking on the fire, I was in touch with the universal consciousness. I was able to tap into the information available to us all. It was like plugging into a switchboard or a library. While I was in that state, I bumped into that African consciousness.

"The fire felt like a friend to me, as if I was playing with someone when I was walking. Afterward I felt a blue light around my body. The palms of my hands and the soles of my feet had a lot of energy coming out of them—that was the tingling sensation. I washed them off, but it didn't stop. I do lots of psychic work, and I get the same feelings then. I heat up quickly, and then I can't cool down easily. So much energy was coming out of my palms and soles that it lasted two days. Sometimes it comes back at odd times, like when I'm driving along fading in and out of awareness. When I work at it consciously, I can bring the energy back."

Toward the end of our conversation I asked Lynda if the firewalk had been a healing experience for her. She said that before the firewalk she'd had several bad relationships with men but that the walk had opened her up to attracting more positive things in her life. It had given her a sense of direction as to what kind of relationships she wanted to get involved in. Since then she's felt more open to talking to people as a normal human being, more open to developing deeper relationships with people.

Lynda thought she would spend the summer in a tent in the wilderness up in the Sierra Nevada mountains. She didn't have enough money to keep her son in California with her all year, but she wanted to bring him out there in August because she missed him a lot.

✥

Fire Dancing ✳ *The Sacred Tradition*

A two-week, learn-by-doing framework allows each participant to engage fully in a profound process of healing and self-Transcendence. The Enlightenment Intensive is the foundation for this Work. As all alternatives and strategies to Living as the Heart ItSelf become obsolete, entering the Fire for as long as One chooses becomes joyously possible.

Live and original Fire Dancing music will be provided by *Prana*, a musical family from Wales.

Kenneth Cadigan has been directly involved with the human potential movement since 1965. Having learned firewalking from Tolly Burkan, the originator of the firewalking movement in the U.S., Ken learned the Fire Dance from the Anastenarians of Northern Greece. He is presently involved with leading Fire Dancing and Enlightenment Intensives throughout the world, using the Fire Dance as the Rite of Passage.

Price: $2000 U.S.
$500. non-refundable deposit by August 1

Include with your deposit a 500-word biography (commenting on your health); a statement of purpose for attending this event; and a recent photograph of yourself. Enrollment is limited.

For more information, contact:

O*ne Foundation*

United States: **28 Roundabout Lane**
Portland, Maine 04102
(207) 774-0263

Europe: **c/o Barbara Szepan**
Antonius Str. #2
D-4773 Möhnesee-Günne
West Germany

September 14-28, 1986 United States
October 19-November 2, 1986 West Germany

✥

PLANS FOR THE FUTURE

A week after the firewalk at Northern Pines I visited Ken at his parents' home in an attractive suburban neighborhood in Portland. We went upstairs to the master bedroom and sat down on a beautiful oriental rug that was covered with boxes full of articles and clippings on firewalking and piles of brochures and leaflets advertising Ken's workshops. Around the room were several bookcases filled with New Age books and tapes dealing with parapsychology, Eastern religions, and shamanism. On tables stood candles, incense burners, and prayer bundles; on the walls hung a map of the stars, a picture of Christ, and a photograph of Avatar Meher Baba.

We talked for a while about the firewalk at Northern Pines. Ken thought the biggest problem had been the lack of music at the fire; that was the one thing he would do differently next time. When I asked Ken about twinkles, he said, "That's to crack the veneer, the masking effect, that keeps people from being open. It's a way into intention-setting; it opens the door for people to reveal themselves."

Ken told me that before he'd ever heard about firewalking, he'd done *est*, Silva Mind Control, Relationships, Iridology, and the Dyad School of Enlightenment. He'd also done Rebirthing, which he called "the fastest-growing New Age process." Ken had been leading Enlightenment Intensives for a long time. Enlightenment Intensives were three-day workshops that provided people with an environment in which they could "go beyond their mental constructs and break through to the Absolute." More recently he'd been running a New Age growth center in Portland, which had a library, a bookstore, a classroom, and a networking office. Ken referred to himself with a smile as "Maine's Mr. New Age."

About a year ago Ken took a three-week-long Firewalking Instructor's Training Program from Tolly Burkan in northern California. It involved skydiving, spelunking, and firewalking all over California. Some people walked across the fire on their hands; other people actually swallowed the red-hot coals. Ken wanted to learn from Tolly's mistakes and support the community of people who teach firewalking. Since then Ken had led about eight firewalks in Maine and over forty in Europe, but he'd only done fire*dancing* since his trip to Langadas the previous May.

"I've stayed in the fire for five minutes. You can dance *in* the fire for as long as you can dance outside it. The only limitation is how long you can keep it up physically with the proper attitude. If you think you'll get burned, but go in anyway, then you'll get burned. But there are exceptions. Some people go in drunk and don't get burned; others go in with the right attitude and do get burned. Usually people get burned where they need to get burned—on whatever part of their body needs more energy. A burn can even be healing.

"A seventy-year-old woman who walked with me in Geneva suffered second-degree burns, but the burns helped her. Her way of being changed completely; she turned herself around. Getting burned was a healing experience for her. The doctors and nurses who took care of her in the hospital said that dealing with her had been a healing experience for them too."

At one firewalk Ken himself was burned when he was distracted by a group of reporters and television cameramen who were telling him what to do, where to stand, and when to walk. Sometimes Ken walked several times a week. That was draining—not healing—for him, and it increased his chances of getting burned. But that didn't matter because he didn't mind getting burned; the burns went away the next day anyhow. Ken explained the fact that people usually didn't get burned by saying that the coals didn't hold enough energy. People just weren't in contact with the fire long enough to get burned.

Then Ken talked more generally about his work.

"It consists of the essence of the major humanistic approaches to self-actualization that I've come across. My goal is to help people in the shortest period of time. Therapy is a process; it takes place gradually, consciously. The firewalk is beyond therapy because there's no process about it. It's all or nothing. 'What if?' syndromes can hold up longer in therapy than they can in the firewalk.

"The firewalk is an open door. People should use it to look at what creates suffering in their own lives. It's not a mental process, it's a spiritual process, a process of the spirit emerging because of our willingness to see how we are.

"The goal of all my work is to enable people to open the heart, to experience the heart, to live the heart—to let people do the impossible. Mind is only the awareness of something; the heart is the living of it. The key is dissolving fear and doubt. That's attitudinal healing. We need to live without the attitude 'I'm in control.' Tapes and programs are things we should get free from. We should get free from 'shoulds.' We should get free from thinking that there's a right and a wrong; we should get free from judging others. We should lose the sense of us and them, us and the Russians. The Russians aren't 'them.' My goal is to have people practically experience that there is no duality in truth.

"I believe in you and me and our innate power to do anything we choose. There's no power outside human beings. We are responsible for ourselves. We are God. That's all there is, but fear and doubt and cultural traditions keep us from realizing this. We're all looking for the Father, but no one can get it together except us. If we could get it together, we could solve all our problems, even the nuclear one."

Ken described an experience he once had with a friend after an Enlightenment Intensive he'd led in San Francisco. They went to a park by the Golden Gate Bridge and just sat there looking at flowers.

"Imagine the flowers we are if we can only get out of our own way," Ken said to me. "Flowers are gifts; they're here for our enjoyment. My satisfaction comes from getting out of my own way and helping others—in their own estimation—emerge to more wholeness. It's not my decision whether you're more whole or not; it's yours.

"I want to be a doorway, but not a doorway with a message on it."

As I was leaving, Ken drew my attention to the large picture of Christ I'd noticed earlier. It was a clear, detailed representation of Christ's face. Ken said it was a photograph of the Shroud of Turin. It came from a friend of a friend who told Ken that a team of scientists had gone to Italy and taken thousands of photographs of the shroud. This was the *only* one that had turned out so well. Ken explained this by saying, "It's as if He said 'I'll show you what I can do.' "

The last time I met with Ken was six months later, in July 1986, when I visited him again in Portland. He showed me a new book by Anthony Robbins called *Unlimited Power*. Ken said that Tony Robbins was probably the most famous of all the people leading firewalking workshops in the United States. He had done the firewalk first with Tolly Burkan, but he'd never taken Tolly's Instructor's Training Program. According to Ken, Tony Robbins' approach was more mental than his; it was concerned primarily with self-improvement. Tony had been a salesman for years, and his approach was geared toward business people. If Tony mentioned love, peace, or God, people would walk out on him. Ken put more emphasis on the spiritual side of things. He was more interested in the whole person, more concerned with helping people heal their relationships. In spite of these differences, however, Ken stressed the unity of the American Firewalking movement. He and Tolly and Tony all had the same goals, the same intention. They all wanted to empower people and help them live happier lives.

Then Ken talked about his plans for the future. He was organizing the One Foundation, a nonprofit, State of Maine corporation. He envisioned it as a "New Age United Way," a kind of umbrella organization that would receive contributions from people and support organizations like The Hunger Project, Green Peace, Save the Children, and Beyond War. The One Foundation would also support Ken; it would take care of all the organizational, promotional, and logistical work connected with what he did. This would let Ken concentrate on the part of his work that he found most fulfilling—actually leading firewalks and Enlightenment Intensives.

Ken hoped to go out to Hawaii soon to lead a firedance in the crater at Diamond Head, but he was devoting most of his time and energy now to setting up a two-week program in California in the fall. It would be the first Western Leadership Training in Firedancing and would be held at Campbell Hot Springs in the High Sierras. For the first ten days people would do "enlightenment work," which would include supportive activities such as conscious breathing, a medicine wheel, and a North American Indian sweat lodge. After that they would be ready for "a prolonged communion with the fire": four "celebration days" of music, dancing, and firedancing.

Ken told me he had recently been to Wales to make arrangements with the group Prana to provide live music for the firedance in California. He had commissioned them to write original firedancing music and would pay their way to the West Coast. Ken played me two of their songs that he planned to use on a firedancing cassette he was producing. He said the lyrics expressed his message really well.

High eerie voices chanted to the rhythm of cymbals and drums.

> "We are the power in everyone.
> We are the dance of the moon and the sun.
> We are the hope that will never hide.
> We are the turning of the tide."

> "Look into the fire.
> OM NAMAHA SHIVAYA.
> Let go of all desire.
> Love will get you higher.
> Learn to be a flier
> And fly higher and higher.
> OM NAMAHA SHIVAYA."

Before the firedance Ken was going to hold several preview evenings in Berkeley, Los Angeles, and Marin County. He said that over seventy thousand people had already firewalked in the Bay Area alone. Ken hoped to enroll two hundred people and have a staff of thirty-five assistants. It would be the biggest event of its kind ever. At this point the assistants were coming "for the growth of it," but if the program made a profit, Ken would divide it up evenly, "just like the Anastenarides did." Twenty people had signed up already, but he needed thirty-three people to break even. He had already spent sixty-five thousand dollars setting things up, but he really wanted people to see the value of his "heart-oriented" approach. Ken was amazed at himself. Here he was, a person with no college education and no business experience, organizing such an elaborate event. "My firewalk," he said, "is setting all this up."

Two years passed. Then late one summer night Ken called me on the phone from Hawaii. He was teaching at a healing center in the town of Haiku on Maui. The center's name was Hale Akua, which meant House of the Divine. Ken said that Maui was a very healing place; there were lots of body workers there and people who knew how to listen. He and his daughter, Sierra, were living in a geodesic dome in the middle of a garden filled with papaya and banana trees.

Ken told me that he'd just returned from Iceland, where he'd led a firedance at the foot of a glacier named Snaefellsjökull. The glacier was on a holy mountain—like Mt. Shasta in California. According to a legend Ken had heard, anyone who walked across the top of the glacier would receive the gift of prophecy. They held the dance during the only two hours of darkness they had each night. Three hundred people came, and only three didn't walk. One person got burned, but he was all right the next day. Ken said it was the first firewalk ever held on the island.

There was a possibility that Ken would go to New Zealand and Australia in the fall to lead a whole series of firewalks. He also wanted to take a side trip to Bali—just to see it. "But you never know," he said, "things might work out so I do some walks there too."

VIII

The American
Firewalking Movement

❖

New Age Healing and
Alternative Religious Movements

FIREWALKING is certainly one of the most dramatic activities that take place at the many classes, seminars, and workshops attended by the increasing number of Americans who hope to bring about a "New Age" of peace, unity, and higher consciousness through personal growth and spiritual transformation. By the 1980s a wide range of belief systems, social causes, and healing practices, whose origins lay in the counterculture of the 1960s, had come together under the general rubric of New Age phenomena. The women's movement, the environmental movement, and the peace movement; health food, renewable resources, and appropriate technology; parapsychology, astrology, and witchcraft have all found a place in the New Age movement. The incredible diversity and richness of this movement is nowhere more evident than in the field of alternative healing. The seemingly endless proliferation of therapeutic techniques and practices that constitutes New Age healing includes centering, channeling, astral projection, guided visualization, iridology, reflexology, chromotherapy, rebirthing, shiatsu, and healing with the power of pyramids and crystals.

Most of the groups active in New Age healing are concentrated on the East and West coasts; many first came into being in California in the San Francisco Bay Area. Participants in these groups typically enroll in evening classes at growth centers or attend more expensive weekend retreats at holistic health resorts. Many people participate in more than one program at a time or join one group for a short period only to leave it and join another in a restless search for something that will "make their lives work." Group leaders are usually people without formal academic training in psychotherapy who earn their living from the enrollment fees they charge for their programs, which are often effectively marketed and well-advertised in such New Age publications as *Omni, Meditation, Shaman's Drum, Futurist, Whole Life Times,* and *New Age Journal.*

Adherents of the New Age movement are generally white, well-educated, upper-middle-class, and urban. They are people who came of age in the 1960s, people who had been part of the counterculture but who are now well into their thirties and are trying to make their way as adults in the very different world of the 1980s. Many of them appear to suffer from a kind of existential uneasiness or malaise. They are searching for opportunities to interact with other people on an intense emotional level in a small group setting. They want to find more meaning in their lives; they want to solve some of their problems and heal their relationships with other people.

The world view of the New Age movement is often regarded as posing a threat to both the Judeo-Christian tradition and the ideology of secular humanism. Although it does have much in common with many of the alternative religious movements that have developed in the United States since the 1960s, people involved in the New Age movement prefer the term spiritual to the term religious because it lacks what are to them the negative connotations of mainstream American religions with their traditional institutions and values. Where the New Age movement does differ from other more clearly religious movements is the degree to which it draws on areas of American culture that would be considered not only secular but scientific as well. In characteristically eclectic fashion people involved in the New Age movement have made full use of recent scientific developments in the fields of psychology and biology. Paradoxically, then, although much New Age thinking is characterized by a lack of faith in science, it would not be an exaggeration to say that in the New Age science has become a sacred symbol, psychology a religion.

Much New Age healing is concerned with helping people escape the patterns and habits of everyday life and achieve some higher state of consciousness in which the world can be experienced more intuitively, more immediately, and more directly. This heightened sense of awareness, this deeper insight into the meaning of life is often described as "cosmic consciousness" or "enlightenment" and is brought about by a variety of psychospiritual techniques that involve "balancing polarities, manipulating energy, and ridding consciousness of the fragmenting effect of reason and the predefining limitations of belief" (Burrows 1986:18).

The ultimate goal of New Age healing is self-realization. In order to realize one's full potential one must come to know the true self that lies beyond the everyday self. This higher self, this real self, is equated with pure consciousness or awareness. A powerful experience of self-realization is often accompanied by a sense of euphoria and a mystical insight into the essential nature of the universe or the ultimate unity of God and self. In other words, an experience of the self becomes a transpersonal experience in which one goes beyond the self to a transcendent experience of God as a source of cosmic energy or a life force that unites all.

Essential to such a theory of personal growth is the belief that all human beings have an unexplored ability to gain control over a variety of inner psychological and physiological states. When people learn to control these inner states, they also acquire power over objects and people in the external world. In this way they are able to take charge of their own lives; they are no longer helpless victims of a society over which they have no control. Participants in the New Age movement, then, are seeking to enhance their sense of personal power and well-being, to reach a state of complete physical and mental health, and to be more successful in both their personal and professional lives. This view of self-transformation is often associated with a vaguely articulated belief that if enough people realize their full potential as individuals, then society as a whole will somehow be transformed as well, and a "New Age" will be at hand.[1]

Just as the American Firewalking movement must be understood in the context of the New Age movement, the New Age movement in turn

---

[1] On the New Age movement generally see Bordewich (1988), Burrows (1986), Ferguson (1980), Satin (1979), and Wasserman (1985). On New Age healing specifically see Levin and Coreil (1986).

must be understood in the context of even broader developments in American culture. Since the 1960s a wide variety of alternative religious movements have flourished in the United States, constituting what Glock and Bellah (1976) have called "the new religious consciousness." Of all the movements that have contributed to this new period in the history of American religion it was the Human Potential movement that was the most direct precursor of the New Age movement. Drawing widely from Asian religious traditions and popular developments in the fields of humanistic and social psychology, the Human Potential movement of the 1970s encompassed a wide range of spiritual and therapeutic programs all concerned with personal growth and self-realization through some kind of transcendent or mystical experience. Some of the most important approaches that came to be considered part of this movement were encounter groups, *est*, Rolfing, Psychosynthesis, Transactional Analysis, Primal Therapy, and Silva Mind Control (Stone 1976).

In addition to the Human Potential movement there were two other types of alternative religious movements that contributed to the development of a new religious consciousness in the United States in the 1970s. There were those whose roots lay in Indian and Asian religions, such as Transcendental Meditation and the International Society for Krishna Consciousness, and those that had their origins in mainstream Christianity, such as the Jesus movement, the Born Again Christians of various Protestant fundamentalist and evangelical movements, as well as Pentecostal Catholics and Catholic Charismatics.[2]

In *Getting Saved From the Sixties* (1982) Steven Tipton argues persuasively that alternative religious movements arose in the 1970s in response to the dramatic conflict that existed between mainstream American culture and the counterculture or youth culture that emerged in the 1960s. During that decade young people who were raised according to traditional ethical and moral values questioned them, found them wanting, and rejected them in favor of the values of the counterculture. In the long run, however, sixties youth found these countercultural values impossible to live by. Therefore they eventually turned

---

[2] An additional source of inspiration for people involved in some alternative religious movements has been the religious traditions of Native Americans and other tribal peoples. Shamanism, vision quests, and sweat lodges have become popular through books like *The Teachings of Don Juan: A Yaqui Way of Knowledge* (Castaneda 1968) and *The Way of the Shaman* (Harner 1982).

to alternative religious movements in an effort to integrate elements from these two very different, even opposing, world views in a way that would make sense of their lives and give them a coherent set of values with which to face the future.

According to Tipton there have been two important interpretations of reality that have contributed to traditional moral culture in America: biblical religion and utilitarian individualism. In the world view of American biblical religion to be good is to be obedient and faithful to God's will, while the ideal social order is one characterized by Christian charity and civic virtue (Tipton 1982:3-6). In a world view characterized by utilitarian individualism, however, human beings are agents seeking to satisfy their own wants who should act in such a way as to maximize their own self-interest. Right action is that which produces the greatest amount of good consequences, but precisely what consequences are good is never made explicit. Vague concepts such as pleasure, happiness, and success are simply assumed to provide satisfactory definitions of what is good. According to this world view people should be free to pursue their own ends; their behavior is judged not in and of itself but rather by its effectiveness in producing the desired results. Therefore, as Tipton points out, utilitarian individualism "is disposed inherently toward moral normlessness" (9). In general the conflict between these two moral traditions has been resolved in favor of utilitarian individualism, as biblical religion over the course of the twentieth century became ever more concerned with the rewards for virtue that accrued in this world rather than the next. In this way biblical religion was often corrupted to the point where it became little more than "a means for the maximization of self-interest with no effective link to virtue, charity, or community" (Bellah 1976:336).[3]

The counterculture of the 1960s was a powerful testament to the fact

[3] A particularly striking example of this subordination of biblical religion to utilitarian individualism is the message of Norman Vincent Peale, a minister and "master salesman" who in the 1950s was promoting a mixture of psychology and religion that is remarkably similar to the ideology of the New Age movement of the 1980s. In *You Can Win* (1938) Peale proclaimed that "God and You Are Unconquerable" and that "You Have It in You to Succeed." In *A Guide to Confident Living* (1948) he revealed "How to Get Rid of Your Inferiority Complex" and "How to Achieve a Calm Center to Your Life" (see Meyer 1980). Peale's "gospel of success" continues to be preached in the 1980s by "television evangelists" like Oral Roberts, Jimmy Swaggart, Jim Bakker, and Pat Robertson, whose "health and wealth theology" proclaims that Christianity "is not just a religious experience, but a life-style of success" (Hadden and Swann 1981:33).

that mainstream American culture, guided as it was by a morality of utilitarian individualism, had failed to provide a meaningful moral framework for a new generation of American youth. This "crisis of meaning" (Bellah 1976:339) was a reaction against the impersonal, bureaucratic, and technological nature of modern American society. It was an expression of the disillusionment and alienation that many young people felt when they realized that the "affluent society" created by the economic development that followed World War II could not provide emotional or spiritual fulfillment. The serious erosion of faith in the legitimacy of important American institutions such as big business, churches, the government, and the family led to the dramatic cultural and political upheaval of the 1960s. This disenchantment with the status quo was expressed in many ways—from the women's movement to civil rights demonstrations, from the environmental movement to student protests against the war in Vietnam. Watergate, a growing underclass of poor and unemployed, and the threat of nuclear war all contributed to the feeling of many people in the "sixties generation" that the institutions that dominated American life had failed.

As a result many young people rejected the utilitarian world view and the middle-class way of life of their parents' generation and began to search for radically different moral systems and alternative life styles that would restore a sense of meaning and purpose to their lives. One aspect of the traditional social order that was subjected to a particularly severe critique by the counterculture was the perceived irrelevance of expressive roles and relationships in public life. For this reason sixties youth placed great emphasis on direct experience and emotional fulfillment as central features of their lives.

The ethic of the counterculture was an expressive one that placed high value on sensitivity, impulsiveness, and living in the present. Individuals should be introspective and self-aware; communities should be small and egalitarian; affective relationships and charismatic leadership should replace the impersonal bureaucracy that seemed so pervasive in American life. For many members of the counterculture little emphasis was placed on the need for direct political action against the established social order. Social change, "the greening of America," would take place naturally as the new way of life "spread of its own loving momentum from the interstices of the old society to the whole of a new one in a process of transformation from the inside out" (Tipton 1982:313).

Although in many ways the counterculture of the 1960s constituted an explicit attack on the utilitarian individualism that dominated mainstream American culture, nevertheless it somewhat ironically retained important aspects of the very morality it was so eager to reject. For members of the counterculture acts were still considered to be good if they satisfied people's interests. These interests, however, were defined differently than they had been in traditional American culture. Money, power, and success were replaced by love, peace, and joy as the desirable ends that good acts brought about. According to Tipton, therefore, mainstream American culture and the counterculture are similar in that "good consequences determine right actions for both," yet "there is a crucial difference between them in answering the question of *what* consequences are good" (1982:15; emphasis in the original).

When the young people of the sixties became the middle-aged adults of the eighties, the relative freedom of adolescence was limited by the contraints of adulthood, and concerns for peace and social justice were replaced by concerns for employment and financial security. Although for most people the life styles and institutions of the counterculture proved unworkable in the long run, the underlying discontent with traditional American values and the search for alternatives it inspired continued. It was precisely this search that led to the development of alternative religious movements in general and the New Age movement in particular.

According to Tipton these alternative religious movements were "mediative successors" to the conflict between mainstream American culture and the counterculture of the 1960s (1982:315). They represented attempts to resolve the tension between traditional and countercultural values—attempts to reconcile what in the 1960s seemed to be the mutually exclusive goals of external achievement and material or worldly success, on the one hand, with those of inner happiness and personal fulfillment, on the other. By participating in these alternative religious movements people who came of age in the sixties were trying to preserve their countercultural values and at the same time deal with the realities of adult life. They were "seeking to synthesize the most valuable elements of the counterculture with the most functionally necessary conditions of modern society" (Tipton 1982:30).

The New Age movement, which is a direct continuation of the religious upheaval that accompanied the social and cultural changes of the 1960s, provides its followers with a world view through which they are able to integrate the apparently contradictory ideologies of mainstream American culture and the counterculture. They no longer have to make the difficult choice between being true to themselves and being successful, between dropping out and getting ahead. They can be themselves *and* succeed; in fact they learn that the key to success lies precisely in being themselves. In this way a materialistic concern for upward social mobility is given legitimacy in the context of the ideology of the counterculture; utilitarian individualism is given a new religious sanction. A practical result of this remarkable synthesis is that many alienated dropouts of the sixties have been reintegrated into society and have begun to follow conventional middle-class career paths (Bellah 1976:342-343).

Utilitarian individualism, then, which was forcefully rejected by the counterculture of the 1960s, has persisted in the New Age movement of the 1980s. People who were "exposed to the expressive values of the counterculture" in their adolescent years and who are now "faced with the instrumental demands of adult middle-class public life" are promised both "inner satisfaction as well as external success" (Tipton 1982:230-231). They are learning that they can maximize their well-being only by realizing their full potential. Material success has become the highest form of self-realization. Alternative religious movements like the New Age movement help sixties youth "adapt to adulthood in conventional society, but they also enable their alternative visions of that society to endure within it" (Tipton 1982:249).

Firewalking is but one of many ways, some more exotic than others, of trying to accomplish this most difficult task.[4]

HEALING EXPERIENCES

Tolly Burkan is "the founding father of American firewalking," the man "who introduced firewalking to the Western World." He has appeared on National Public Radio's *All Things Considered* and on the *Donahue Show*; he has given lectures at the University of Arizona Medical School and the Mandalla Growth Center in Oslo, Norway. Through Sundoor, Inc., an organization based in the Sierra Nevada

---

[4] Valuable essays on alternative religious movements in the United States are contained in Glock and Bellah (1976), Needleman and Baker (1978), and Zaretsky and Leone (1974). See also Wuthnow (1976) and Yankelovitch (1981).

Mountains east of San Francisco, Tolly Burkan and his wife Peggy Dylan Burkan market their books, cassettes, and films. In addition they offer evening seminars and weekend retreats on "Feminine Spirituality and Personal Power" and "Sexuality, Spirituality, and Tantra," as well as fasting programs and spiritual pilgrimages to places like "Mystical Peru."

In his autobiography *Dying to Live* (1984) Burkan recounts his transformation from "a person who wanted to kill himself into a person who is happy with life" (Galloway 1986). At age nineteen he staged his own death by drowning and ran away to California. Two months later, having been given up for dead, he came home to newspaper headlines that read: "Son Returns After His Wake." After attempting suicide twice in the early 1970s, Burkan experimented with LSD and traveled to India several times before moving into Ken Keyes' Living Love Center in Berkeley, where he became deeply involved in the Human Potential movement. In 1974 Burkan healed a tumor in his scrotum by using the power of his mind to rearrange the atoms in his body. When the surgeons operated on him, "the tumor that had clearly been observed in X-rays . . . was nowhere to be found" (Burkan 1984:110). From that time on he devoted himself to teaching and healing others.

Burkan learned to firewalk while he was living in a trailer in the mountains of northern California. One night a friend suddenly took off her shoes and socks and walked through the glowing embers of a dying camp fire. Burkan followed. "A part of me died that instant, and another part of me was born," Burkan wrote in his autobiography. "What died was a constricting belief system, and what was born was a sense of life's limitlessness" (137). After doing some research on the subject Burkan concluded that "firewalking was still a mystery, . . . another example of our not yet knowing all the laws of the Universe. What I was left with was my own experience of it—an experience that I knew, from the moment I had walked across the coals, would change my entire life" (138).

Several years later in 1977 Burkan incorporated firewalking into his workshops on self-awareness, spiritual transformation, and personal growth. Then in 1982 he and his wife developed a four-hour firewalking workshop designed to help people overcome their fears and limitations because they realized that "the firewalk was the perfect metaphor to encompass all aspects of life, the full spectrum: from anguish to

Tolly Burkan: "From anguish to bliss" (Photograph by Brian Garland)

bliss. It was the perfect catalyst to raise fears and doubts as well as to challenge people's concepts about physical reality, what is possible and impossible" (204).

In their promotional material the Burkans promise that their workshops and seminars will improve the quality of people's lives by showing them "how to integrate spirituality and prosperity" as well as how to create "friendships, knowledge and increased earning capacity."

Participants in the Burkans' Firewalk Instructor's Training learn "how to be spiritually open in a power-oriented world." They also develop "self-confidence, personal power, and the ability to project a professional image," while receiving information about "organizing workshops, advertising, dealing with the media, taking initiative, and building [their] career."

Anthony Robbins is the other nationally known leader of the American Firewalking movement. He has appeared on the *Merv Griffin Show* and been written up in *Life* magazine, the *Los Angeles Times*, and the *Washington Post*. According to his publicity brochures Robbins has become known as "the One-Stop Therapist" for his ability to eliminate lifelong "phobias and relationship difficulties" in a one- or two-hour session at a cost of a thousand dollars an hour. Robbins is also founder and president of the Robbins Research Institute, through which he has served as a consultant for Olympic athletes, prominent corporate executives, and the United States Army.

Robbins teaches people how to walk through fire in a seminar entitled "Fear into Power: The Firewalk Experience," the first of a three-part program called "The Mind Revolution: Three Steps to Personal Power." Robbins' seminars have the same basic goal as the Burkans' workshops—to use the experience of firewalking as a metaphor that will enable people to accomplish things they had always considered impossible. Because they are designed for a more traditional audience of business people and other professionals, however, they are more conservative in style and tone. While Burkan wears sandals, plays a folk guitar, and chants mantras, Robbins dresses in three-piece suits and plays theme songs from movies like *Rocky* and *Chariots of Fire*.

One of Robbins' most publicized seminars was held at Hilton Head, South Carolina, in September 1985, as part of the annual convention of Record Bar, Inc., the second largest retailer of records and tapes in the United States. The seminar, for which Robbins received seventy-five thousand dollars, was part of the company's "human systems" program for developing its workers' potential to the fullest. As the chairman of the board of Record Bar told a reporter, "If you can walk on hot coals, it's fairly easy to sell a record" (Handelman 1985).

The most complete statement of Robbins' message is contained in his book *Unlimited Power: The New Science of Personal Achievement* (1986). This "guidebook to superior performance in an age of success" claims to offer "practical tools" (not "mystical skills") that will heal

Anthony Robbins: "Fear into Power" (Photograph courtesy of Robbins Research International, Inc.)

people who are suffering from "any kind of illness—emotional, mental or physical." Under headings such as "The Ultimate Success Formula" and "The Five Keys to Wealth and Happiness" Robbins provides instruction in the fundamentals of neurolinguistic programming, a "scientific" approach to personal growth and achievement that enables people to "change their physiology," "unleash the magic within them," and accomplish whatever they want—"whether it's walking on fire, making a million dollars, or developing a perfect relationship" (182). Robbins' publicity material is full of testimonials of people whose lives have been transformed by his program: a lifelong fear of public speaking eliminated in one hour, twenty-five pounds lost in thirty days, two hundred and fifty thousand dollars earned in two weeks.

Firewalking workshops led by Tolly Burkan, Anthony Robbins, Ken Cadigan, and others are designed to provide people with "healing experiences." In the context of the American Firewalking movement healing is understood in a very broad sense and is virtually synonymous with what could be called personal development or spiritual growth. Healing involves learning how to "make your life work," learning how to "get what you want out of life." When people are healed, they realize their full potential, they function more effectively in society, and they live happier, more meaningful lives.

The Burkans emphasize the ability of firewalking to heal people of their fears. They encourage people to "form a working relationship with fear." This way the anxiety that people usually experience as paralyzing is transformed into a sense of exhilaration (Burkan and Burkan 1983:88). The Burkans use firewalking to help people "uplevel [their] experience from one of suffering to one of joy" (9, 15) and to teach them that they are "God-like beings" who have the potential to obtain whatever they desire.

Ken Cadigan stresses the religious and mystical aspects of the healing he seeks to bring about through his work. This emphasis is apparent in the content of his Enlightenment Intensives as well as in his recent shift from firewalking to firedancing, which Ken describes as "high play," "a celebration of joy and innocence," and "a prolonged communion with fire."[5]

A primary concern of Ken's is "healing relationships." At a firedance the fire should be a "healing fire" that will enable people to overcome fear and doubt in the context of their interpersonal relationships. Comments made by people during the "intention-setting" phase of his workshops offer additional insight into the kind of healing that Ken is

---

[5] The ability to offer a new and different product also has obvious advantages in what Berger (1965:37–38) has called "the private identity market" in which "a population of anxious consumers" is supplied with "a variety of services for the construction, maintenance, and repair of identities."

concerned with: "I want more harmony in my relationships"; "I want to be able to enter a room full of people and not suffer an attack of anxiety"; "I want to take the next step on a spiritual journey I started many lives ago"; "I want to fall in love again with my life partner."

Firewalking in the United States, then, generally attracts people who by most commonly accepted standards would not be considered "sick" at all. In Kleinman's terms these are people who are suffering from illnesses that consist of minor or chronic life problems—illnesses, that is, that often occur in the complete absence of disease.[6]

The healing discourse of the American Firewalking movement is dominated by several powerful rhetorical systems that are central to the therapeutic process: the rhetoric of empowerment and the rhetoric of transformation (Csordas 1983). The firewalk is above all an "empowering experience." By walking on fire people acquire power, and it is this power that is responsible for the healing they experience. The power of firewalking stems most immediately from the intense emotional response people have to the simple fact that they have just walked barefoot across a bed of red-hot coals without being burned. An initially somewhat skeptical reporter who participated in one of Robbins' seminars described his reaction to having completed the firewalk as follows: "The feeling of exhilaration and personal accomplishment was incredible. At that moment there was nothing I felt I couldn't do." He went on to say "Now whenever I think back to that moment . . . I re-experience that same feeling of power and confidence. And it's a good feeling" (Medoff 1984).

The power that lies at the heart of the healing experiences firewalking workshops provide is the power to transform people in such a way that they are more fulfilled in their personal lives *and* more successful in their professional lives. This rhetoric of transformation, therefore, encompasses both the expressive goals of the counterculture and the utilitarian goals of mainstream American culture. Firewalking is intended to give people the power to transform the impossible into the possible and to experience the world in a new and different way. In a successful firewalk fire is transformed from something dangerous into something benign; contact with fire is transformed from an experience

---

[6] At firewalking workshops references are occasionally made to work being done by Carl Simonton (1978) and Norman Cousins (1982 and 1983) with cancer patients which involves nontraditional, holistic therapeutic techniques. Simonton actually encourages his cancer patients to walk on fire.

that burns into one that heals. Even an unsuccessful firewalk has the potential of bringing about a transformation that is both positive and therapeutic. Burning itself can become a healing experience.

A common metaphor for this process of transformation is that of reprogramming. People are like computers that have been programmed with fear and doubt. By walking on fire they "can effectively reprogram unwanted conditioning" by experiencing firsthand that something they had always believed was true (that fire burns) is in fact false. Through the firewalk they learn that F.E.A.R. is nothing other than "False Evidence Appearing Real" (Burkan and Burkan 1983:33 and 86).

The source of the power that firewalking provides is ultimately the self. According to the Burkans (1983:3) firewalking enables people to discover "their hidden potential" by tapping "a reservoir of magic" they didn't even know existed within them. "Be all that you can be!" the Burkans urge. This self, often called an "inner voice" or "true guide," is an important source of wisdom, energy, and power that people must come in contact with and learn to use, because it is from this self that healing energy in the form of love or money ultimately flows. It is this self that, unlike the ego, cannot be burned.

Paradoxically, then, the search for self-realization is simultaneously a search for self-transformation, and central to this rhetoric of transformation is a set of metaphors of release, opening up, and letting go. For the Burkans the ultimate goal of firewalking is to release people from "a confining experience of life." Just before the firewalk they instruct participants in their workshop to chant "Release your mind and see what you find." In general they recommend the practice of deep breathing because it "opens up blocked channels of energy and makes reprogramming considerably easier" (1983:73). In a similar manner Ken Cadigan refers to the firewalk as an "open door," as a "doorway of possibility." Lynda Harrison told me that after the workshop at Northern Pines her energy centers were open so her energy was no longer stopped up; it was flowing freely. In that condition she would experience improvements in her physical condition, her personal relationships, and her financial situation, since health, love, and money were all just different forms of energy.

In most cases fear is the obstacle that prevents people from reaching this desired state of openness because fear is associated with contractions, tension, and limitations. When people take their first step into the fire, they break through "a membrane of fear"; they "dissolve barriers of a lifetime." These "barriers" or "blocks" are the limiting beliefs, the "tapes" and "programs," that dominate so many aspects of people's lives and prevent them from realizing their full potential. Paradoxically, it is only by letting go of the things we most truly want that we can ever hope to obtain them.

THE ANASTENARIA AND
THE AMERICAN FIREWALKING MOVEMENT

The Anastenaria and the American Firewalking movement exhibit many remarkable similarities. They both offer people who feel alienated and powerless the opportunity to enter an altered state of consciousness and walk on fire without being burned. They are both powerful systems of ritual therapy that are able to transform people's experience of themselves and their world. Finally, they both make use of complex sets of metaphors involving fire, burns, release from confinement, and removal of obstacles to move people from a negative state of illness to a positive state of health.

There are, of course, equally striking differences between the Anastenaria and the American Firewalking movement, differences that have to do with the widely contrasting social and cultural contexts in which they exist. A juxtaposition of the two therapeutic systems highlights the differences between them in a way that offers valuable insight into them both. While the Anastenaria and the American Firewalking movement both help people who are suffering from a wide range of social and psychological problems, in Greece the majority of these problems are expressed initially in a somatic idiom and then treated in a religious or spirit idiom. In the United States, however, these problems are both expressed and treated in a resolutely psychological idiom.

Somatization is by far the most common idiom for the expression of distress in rural Greece because no form of psychotherapy is readily available and because a psychological idiom of distress is heavily stigmatized. In the case of the Anastenaria social and psychological problems, such as family conflict or depression, are often somatized with the result that Kostilides generally turn to the Anastenaria complaining of headaches, chest pains, dizziness, or loss of appetite. Kostilides also turn to the Anastenaria when they are suffering from diseases such as cancer that physicians are unable to treat successfully.

Among the people who participate in the American Firewalking movement, however, the situation is very different. Psychological idioms for the expression of distress abound. Not only is there no stigma attached to them; they are elevated to the status of religions. As a result the ability and the willingness to express problems in a psychological idiom is highly valued. Americans involved in firewalking workshops not only deal with their social and psychological problems in a thoroughly psychological idiom. They also psychologize other more serious problems from very different domains of American culture ranging from diseases like cancer to political and economic problems like poverty and nuclear war.

The prominence of psychological idioms of distress in New Age healing practices represents the culmination of the "psychologizing process" that, according to Kleinman (1986:55), has increasingly characterized American culture since World War I. Kleinman argues that this psychologizing process is part of a "cultural transformation in which the self has been culturally constituted as the now dominant Western ethnopsychology." As Kleinman also points out, psychologization and somatization are both cultural constructions; they are both interpretations placed on a variety of social, psychological, and physiological processes. Furthermore, from a cross-cultural perspective it is not somatization, but psychologization, that is the more recent and more unusual phenomenon (Kleinman 1986:56, 63).

In the case of the Anastenaria problems that were initially expressed in a somatic idiom are translated into an explicitly religious idiom, and it is primarily in this idiom that the therapeutic process takes place. People suffer because they have insulted Saint Constantine or disobeyed his orders; they recover when they correct their mistakes and carry out the will of the Saint properly. In the Anastenaria social, psychological, and even somatic problems are treated in a religious idiom through the manipulation of saints, icons, and simadia, all of which are sacred symbols with social, psychological, and somatic referents. Through involvement with the Anastenaria people transform in a positive way their relationship with Saint Constantine and therefore with important family members and with the community of Kostilides as a whole. While people who "suffer from the Saint" are not held directly responsible for their suffering, they *are* held responsible for carrying out the will of the Saint and regaining their health in that way.

In the American Firewalking movement no such translation takes place. The therapeutic process is carried out in the same explicitly psychological idiom in which people's problems are initially expressed. Healing does not involve a search for some power outside the self; it involves a quest to reveal the unexplored inner power of the true self. It is one's relationship with the self that must be changed, not one's relationship with Saint Constantine. It is the self, not some spirit, saint, or god, that has the power to heal.

From the perspective of leaders of the American Firewalking movement the beliefs that constitute religious systems like the Anastenaria are limiting beliefs; they are the "programs" and "tapes" that keep us from further spiritual growth. No higher power is responsible for our suffering. We are responsible for ourselves. The highest good is not obedience to the will of some supernatural being but self-expression and direct experience. It isn't Saint Constantine who protects us from the fire; it's the fact of who we are. When we identify with who we really are, we don't get burned because who we are can never get burned.

A striking feature of what Tipton (1982:252) calls the "psychologized individualism" that has become so prevalent in American culture is the lack of any specific doctrinal or ideological content that is characteristic of firewalking and other forms of New Age healing. The relativistic view that all paths toward the goal of enlightenment are equally valid was expressed by Ken Cadigan when he said, "I want to be a doorway, but not a doorway with a message on it." Similarly, the promotional material for Ken's Enlightenment Intensives states that they teach "no belief system or particular view of life. . . . No one tells you what the truth is."

In the utilitarian individualism of the American Firewalking movement the self and direct personal experience are elevated to the position of highest moral authority; no specific course of action is right in and of itself. Furthermore the self that is discovered in the search for fulfillment is ultimately a very private self, one that is subject to very few external social controls. The result of such a mysticized and psychologized individualism is, as Tipton points out, a tendency toward moral normlessness. This contrasts markedly with the morality of a religious system such as the Anastenaria which is firmly grounded in a belief in the necessity of obedience to a divine being whose will is determined by the consensus of the community of believers.

The differences between the psychological idiom of the American Firewalking movement with its search for a true inner self, on the one hand, and the spirit idiom of the Anastenaria with its worship of Saint Constantine, on the other, can only be understood in terms of the very different social contexts in which they exist. The rapid rate of social and cultural change that Greece has recently experienced notwithstanding, the village of Ayia Eleni and the community of Kostilides are still quite stable social worlds when compared with the very fluid and mobile society of the people involved in the New Age movement. The Anastenarides of Ayia Eleni form a permanent, localized therapeutic community, something that is generally lacking in the American Firewalking movement. In the case of the Anastenaria, although a new konaki might be built, a new icon painted, or a new leader emerge, the same people gather in the same places on the same religious holidays year after year. When a woman becomes an Anastenarissa, she aquires a new and usually permanent identity by becoming a member of a new social group. She enters into a long-term therapeutic relationship with the leader of the Anastenarides, with other Anastenarides, and with the entire community of Kostilides as well, a process that is expressed metaphorically by her new relationship with Saint Constantine. Her new personal identity is a social one, firmly grounded in the community she has just joined. Thus healing in the Anastenaria is not simply a psychological process; it is a social one as well, and the highly structured social context in which it takes place is central to its effectiveness.

The vast majority of participants in the American Firewalking movement, however, do not become part of any permanent or localized therapeutic community, in spite of the fact that small "mountain communities," "healing centers," and "families of teachers" do exist. Because people like Tolly Burkan, Anthony Robbins, and Ken Cadigan are constantly traveling around the world leading workshops in new and different places people who attend these workshops do not acquire a new social identity as a result of their firewalking experience, nor do they establish any long-term therapeutic relationships with anyone. Responding to criticism from more traditional psychotherapists that his seminars might evoke emotional responses that some people were unable to handle, Robbins admitted that his "follow-up" had been poor and promised to train "surrogates" who would provide people with help after he had moved on (Griffin 1985).

In addition, the level of commitment required for participation in firewalking workshops is quite low since most people who attend these programs do so only once or twice. Firewalking in the United States is, as Ken Cadigan himself once put it, "a quick fix, a shot in the arm," although some people do say that they can recall the sense of power they felt during the firewalk at a later time. The healing that takes place in the American Firewalking movement, then, is fundamentally a psychological process; it lacks a significant social dimension. Furthermore, the sense of personal empowerment and transformation that is the goal of the therapeutic process is probably not long lasting in the American case because a new sense of identity can only be maintained in the specific context of membership in a new social or religious group.[7]

The contrast between the permanent therapeutic community personified by Saint Constantine which is provided by the Anastenaria and the focus on the true self which is central to the "one-stop therapy" of the American Firewalking movement must also be understood in light of the different conceptions of the relationship between the individual and society that prevail in rural Greece and in the United States. In a modern industrial society like the United States in which social relationships are fluid and atomistic and social mobility high, an important goal of any therapeutic system must inevitably be to foster self-reliance and individual autonomy. In the New Age movement this individualism is emphasized to such a degree that the self is no longer "fixed by social institutions"; it can "look to no authority beyond itself for confirmation" (Tipton 1982:251).

The goal of therapeutic systems like the Anastenaria, which exist in less fluid, less mobile societies, is quite different. It is to transform people's social identities and social relationships by enabling them to develop a new relationship with a powerful spirit other who personifies the very community into which they are being integrated, the very community from which their identities are derived. This spirit other is the moral authority that makes people's lives meaningful; it is the power through which people are healed.

---

[7] As Berger and Luckmann have pointed out, "Saul may have become Paul in the aloneness of religious ectasy, but he could *remain* Paul only in the context of a Christian community that recognized him as such" (1967:158; emphasis in the original).

In rural Greece people are defined to a great extent in terms of their relationships with other people and their membership in social groups. The ritual therapy of the Anastenaria reorders these social relationships and reintegrates people into society. In this way the Anastenaria provides people with a sense of community and a sense of social solidarity. It offers them the security and comfort, the moral certainty, of knowing that all will be well if they obey the will of Saint Constantine. At the same time the world of the Anastenarides is a very limiting world, a hierarchical world that stresses conformity and obedience to authority; a world in which people are most fully themselves when they are most fully integrated into their community.

Conversely, people involved in the New Age movement are defined as autonomous individuals. The ritual therapy of the American Firewalking movement asserts the power of the self, a self that is free from the limits and constraints imposed by social responsibilities and moral obligations. Firewalking offers people a liberating experience of self-realization and self-transcendence in a world where great value is placed on individual freedom of expression and self-determination, a world in which people must be able to be themselves even when the only community of which they are a part is a temporary one expressed in fleeting gestures of intimacy and alluded to in a vague rhetoric of peace and love.

This personal freedom and independence, however desirable it may be, is achieved at a high cost. The utilitarianism, psychologism, and mysticism that make such freedom and independence possible can lead very easily to a situation in which isolated and alienated private selves wander aimlessly in a world that has been emptied of any specific moral content. This is the "moral predicament" of the New Age (Tipton 1982:24).

"I GOT BURNED, AND SO WHAT? IT BECAME A POSITIVE EXPERIENCE"

The Anastenarides interpret their ability to walk on fire without being burned as a religious miracle, proof that they are protected by the supernatural power of Saint Constantine. In the United States firewalking is taken as proof that human beings have hidden deep within them the ability to accomplish anything they want if only they are able to realize their full potential. Leaders of the American Firewalking movement use the firewalk as a catalyst for the process of personal growth that is the ultimate goal of the New Age movement. They state explicitly that firewalking is a symbol or metaphor for the experiences of empowerment, transformation, and healing that they offer people who participate in their programs. According to the Burkans, firewalking is "a symbol which reminds us that being a mere human is not so 'mere' " (1983:3). Similarly Robbins says that "the firewalk is only a metaphor for what we think we cannot do. And once you've walked on fire, a lot of impossibilities become possible" (Griffin 1985:48). For Ken Cadigan the firewalk is a key that can unlock the door to our true selves. "If only we could be who we really are," he said, "then we wouldn't need to walk through fire."

Because the people who teach firewalking in the United States are explicitly aware that the literal firewalk which people perform when they walk through a bed of burning coals is a symbol or metaphor for the process of personal growth, they often downplay the significance of the actual firewalk itself; it is "*only* a metaphor," "*just* a symbol," or "*simply* a tool." As Ken Cadigan said at Northern Pines, "Any fool can do the firewalk. . . . The absolute fire is the self; the real work is with that fire."

But the fire people actually walk through is not just a metaphor for the self; it is a metaphor for the lives people lead and more specifically for the problems and challenges they encounter in living their lives. Ken compared the fire to life when he said there is no rehearsing, no practicing, with life or with the fire either. As Ken was fond of saying, coals come to us in many different forms. The fire we walk through is a symbol of the barriers and obstacles that we face in our daily lives that prevent us from being happy and successful.

If fire represents the lives people lead, then the act of firewalking represents the living of these lives and, more specifically, the struggle people are constantly engaged in to transcend their limits through personal growth. In the preface to their book *Guiding Yourself into a Spiritual Reality* the Burkans say that "life itself can often be a 'firewalk,' " and promise that their book "will assist you in crossing *that* fire without getting burned" (1983:3; emphasis in the original). The goal of firewalking workshops is to teach people to apply the lesson they learn from the act of walking through fire to other challenging situations in their lives, situations that present them with obstacles that seem to be insurmountable but in fact are not.

In the American Firewalking movement fire is also a powerful symbol of change and transformation, as it is in the Anastenaria. The firewalk is a rite of passage in which people consign some negative aspect of their past to the flames and state their intention to have a new and positive future. Fire, therefore, is a positive force that has the ability to eliminate all the fears and doubts that prevent people from growing and realizing their full potential.

Ideally Americans who walk on fire and are not burned "develop a new relationship with fire," just as Anastenarides develop a new relationship with Saint Constantine. The "essential ambiguity" of fire as a symbol, noted by Bachelard (1964), is resolved in favor of a set of positive meanings. Fire is no longer something that burns or causes harm; it is not something to be feared. Fire heals; its light can, in Ken's words, "disperse the shadows of fear and doubt." The firewalk is designed to eliminate the "tape" or "program" that fire burns. People learn experientially that this is just one of many limiting beliefs that have prevented them from getting the most out of their lives.

It is not only fire, however, that acquires a new meaning for those who attend firewalking workshops. Because fire is a symbol for the self and for the lives people lead, the firewalk also enables people to experience themselves and their lives in a new way. They acquire a new sense of identity, a more powerful self that cannot be burned, unlike the ego or "the appearance of who they are" which is all they had in the past and which can easily be burned. The American Firewalking movement, therefore, provides people with an opportunity to experience fire as a symbol of transformation and healing and in this way develop a more positive self-image and a greater sense of self-confidence.

According to American firewalk instructors the ability to walk through fire without being burned is a miraculous example of the power of positive thinking. Burkan (1984:204) says it is "a perfect example of mind over matter." Because people's subjective experience of the world determines their reality, it is their state of mind as they enter the fire that determines the outcome of the firewalk for them. If they are afraid, they will be burned; but if they have a positive mental attitude, they will not be burned. Robbins, for example, admitted that he once suffered third-degree burns when his concentration was broken in the middle of a firewalk by the distracting comments of a television announcer. On another occasion he was burned when he returned to his usual state of consciousness with some hot coals stuck between his toes (Krier 1984).

More specifically Burkan, Robbins, and others claim that positive mental attitudes have the ability to alter physiological processes in such a way that people are able to walk on fire without being burned. In his workshops and in his writing Burkan discusses recent developments in neurophysiology involving neuropeptides, endorphins, the pituitary and the pineal glands. "The simple act of stepping onto glowing coals demonstrates *the mind's knowledge that we will not be harmed*, and this positive thought alters the entire body chemistry in a way that permits the body to protect itself" (Burkan 1984:205; emphasis in the original). According to Burkan people can generate in their own bodies "any drug in a pharmacy;" he simply teaches them how to make use of this hidden potential in order to "create the perfect body chemistry" so they won't be burned.

Robbins argues in similar fashion that people can "change their physiology" by changing their beliefs. Adopting a new belief system creates a new "neurophysiological state." Robbins is convinced that "thought can create biochemical-electrical processes in the body that affect the way flesh molecules react to extreme heat, as well as to the destructiveness of disease and injury" (Worthington 1984). In this way the claim that a positive attitude or an extraordinary state of consciousness can protect a person's feet from burning is extended to include other types of physiological processes as well. Andrew Weil, M.D., author of *The Natural Mind* (1972) and *Health and Healing* (1983), is quoted in some of Burkan's publicity material as saying, "If you don't have to get pain, redness, and blisters on exposure to a certain range and type of heat, then you don't have to get infections on exposure to germs, allergies on exposure to allergens, cancer on exposure to carcinogens."

The attitude toward science adopted by people involved in the American Firewalking movement is fundamentally ambivalent. On the one hand, like the Anastenarides, they view scientific attempts to explain the ability of people to walk on fire without being burned as a threat, as an attempt to explain away the miraculous phenomenon of firewalking. On the other hand, however, these same people, unlike the Anastenarides, turn to science as a powerful source of legitimacy and support for the therapeutic programs they offer.

Popular journalistic accounts of firewalking in the United States often report that there is no generally accepted scientific explanation for the fact that people are not burned when they walk through fire. An article in *Life* magazine claims that "scientists cannot agree on how it is done without injury" (Griffin 1985:42). Another account of one of Robbins' seminars states that "scientists who have tried to debunk firewalking have been unable to come up with a plausible, purely physical explanation for why so many people are not getting burned" (Medoff 1984). The Burkans repeatedly claim that firewalking defies the laws of physics and that there is no "bottom-line explanation" for why firewalking is possible; it remains a "mystery" (1983:3).

For people involved in the American Firewalking movement (as for the Anastenarides) the claim that science is unable to explain firewalking is an assertion that firewalking is a miracle, that it transcends natural laws and surpasses rational understanding. This makes the experience of firewalking an even more powerful one. It also gives the leaders of the movement greater status and prestige because they can provide people with access to a power that science cannot.

This sense of superiority which the leaders of the firewalking movement feel toward scientists is expressed in the condescending way scientists are portrayed in the popular literature on firewalking. Burkan tells people who are about to walk on fire that "science says . . . your feet should be charred immediately to a black carbon residue." "The fact is," he continues, "we *won't* be burned when we walk on hot coals, and nothing terrible will happen if we do all the other things we refuse to do because our mind tells us not to" (Galloway 1986; emphasis in the original). In his autobiography (1984:205) Burkan quotes a doctor on the faculty of Stanford University Medical School who is the director of a burn unit in a local hospital as saying that there is no logical explanation for why people who firewalk do not suffer third-degree burns on their feet. The total defeat of science by the firewalking movement is signaled by the comment of a UCLA psychologist in a publicity brochure for Robbins' firewalking seminars: "I'm a University Professor with a Ph.D. in psychology. Robbins is the Master psychologist."

In spite of what seems to be utter contempt for science, firewalk instructors do not reject science completely. In their own attempts to explain people's ability to walk on fire they turn to science to enhance their credibility in the eyes of an American public for whom science enjoys great prestige and influence as an explanatory framework for the interpretation and validation of experience. For many people involved in the New Age movement "science" has become "a magical term redolent of the sacred" (Glock and Bellah 1976:75).

The science that firewalk instructors turn to as a source of legitimation, however, is not the same as the science that threatens to debunk firewalking. It is a new science, a science that confirms their own explanation of people's ability to walk on fire. By drawing on this new science firewalk instructors are able to avoid the charges of simplemindedness and triviality that the phrases "mind over matter" and "the power of positive thinking" would leave them open to. In this way they are also able to acquire a mantle of scientific respectability. Robbins (1986:267), for example, has grounded his approach to firewalking in neurolinguistic programming (known as NLP), "the new science of personal achievement," which consists of "a six-step reframing process for changing any undesirable behavior you may have into desirable behavior." Burkan has drawn on "a new science named psychoneuroimmunology (or PNI)," "the new medicine of mind and body," which offers a scientific explanation for the mysterious ways in which our minds influence our health.[8] Ken Cadigan's eagerness to involve me in his firewalking workshops was motivated at least in part, I suspect, by a similar desire to enhance his work with a certain academic and scientific, if not medical, credibility.

In addition to contempt for the traditional science they regard as a threat and respect for the new science they regard as a source of legitimation, leaders of the American Firewalking movement adopt still another stance with regard to scientific explanations of firewalking: indifference. According to this view, which is consistent with the anti-intellectualism of the New Age movement generally, rational scientific explanations of why people are able to walk on fire without being burned are irrelevant and uninteresting because direct experience is far more important than logic and reason. As Ken Cadigan said, "the scientist in us" knows that firewalking is impossible, but our experience proves just the opposite. "Even if scientists do explain the firewalk

---

[8] On neurolinguistic programming see Bandler and Grinder (1979); on psychoneuroimmunology see Locke and Colligan (1986).

someday," he added, "fire will still be fire, and people will still be people."

In the context of the Anastenaria people who do not enter the fire year after year are usually not accepted as Anastenarides, while people who are burned have demonstrated unambiguously that they do not enjoy the supernatural power and protection of Saint Constantine. In the Anastenaria people who are burned are excluded and rejected. They suffer; they most certainly are not healed.

In the context of the American Firewalking movement the situation is again very different. While people who do not enter the fire often experience a sense of failure, workshop leaders argue sincerely, but often unconvincingly, that not walking can be an even more empowering experience than walking. According to this argument people who do not walk demonstrate that they have learned to trust their inner guidance. A person who did not enter the fire at one of Ken Cadigan's workshops said afterward, "It was my choice not to. There are no 'shoulds' or 'ought tos.' I felt empowered by other people's joy." Many people who do not perform the firewalk, however, do react negatively and withdraw because they feel they have somehow failed.

An even more revealing difference between the Anastenaria and the American Firewalking movement is the fact that in the United States even burning becomes a healing experience. Getting burned is simply another opportunity to learn and grow. A man who was seriously burned when he walked through the fire at one workshop later said that "the five weeks he spent in the hospital was the best time he'd ever spent" (Remick 1984). The president of Record Bar, who suffered second-degree burns at the seminar he hired Robbins to lead at his company's annual convention, admitted that he had been burned and added, "I decided, 'Hey, get over it; I got burned, and so what?' It became a positive experience" (Handelman 1985).

The different interpretations placed on being burned by the Anastenarides and by leaders of the American Firewalking movement are closely related to the different social contexts in which the two therapeutic systems exist. The ideology of the Anastenaria, according to which firewalking without being burned signifies empowerment and healing, while being burned signifies exclusion, rejection, and suffering, is essential to the formation of a permanent therapeutic community in which insiders and outsiders are sharply distinguished. This ideology is also central to the role played by the Anastenaria in defining and maintaining the boundaries of the community of Kostilides, a community that has in the past been a very exclusive one.

The American Firewalking movement, in which both being burned and not being burned signify empowerment and healing, involves no such permanent therapeutic community or exclusive social group. The goal of firewalking in the United States is, on the contrary, to remove all boundaries, to include everyone, to demonstrate that we all are one. The firewalk, as Ken Cadigan put it, is "not reserved for certain people." This illustrates clearly the way in which the ideology of the American Firewalking movement is "emptied of specific content" through utilitarianism, psychologism, and mysticism in order to survive in a social context where flexibility and relativism are highly valued (Tipton 1982:24).

The different ideologies of the Anastenaria and the American Firewalking movement came into direct conflict when Ken Cadigan entered the fire with the Anastenarides of Langadas on May 21, 1985. The different accounts of Ken's firewalk, the different outcomes it had in these various accounts, and the different interpretations placed on these outcomes can all be understood in terms of these two contrasting ideologies. The newspaper account that opens Chapter VII is somewhat ambivalent. On the one hand, it acknowledges that an American "stole the show" by performing the firewalk "without suffering any burns at all." This would appear to refute the Anastenarides' claim that only they can walk through fire without being burned because only they enjoy the protection of Saint Constantine. On the other hand, the article states that Ken passed "quickly" over the burning coals and suggests that he was unable to remain on the fire as long as the Anastenarides. The reference to the Italian who was severely burned the previous year also suggests that only Anastenarides, and not outsiders or foreigners (*kseni*), can enter the fire without being burned. Finally, this ambivalence is indicated by the quotation marks placed around the word "Anastenaris" in the title of the article: AND EVEN AN AMERICAN . . . "ANASTENARIS." Ken became an "Anastenaris" because he walked on fire without being burned. He did not become an *Anastenaris*, however, because he was not Greek and because he was not a member of the community of Anastenarides.

I am quite confident that the Anastenarides of Langadas would say (and in fact have said) that Ken *was* burned—just like the Italian the year before and just like all the other *kseni* who have burst from the crowd and entered the fire in the past. The Anastenarides would support this claim by pointing out that Ken did not remain in the fire as long as they did, that he left the fire before the firewalk was over, and that he did not return the next evening to enter the fire again. They would interpret the fact that he was burned to mean that they and they alone are protected by the supernatural power of Saint Constantine.

According to Ken Cadigan's own account of his experience in Langadas, he was the popular hero of a melodramatic, almost farcical, struggle between good and evil. He demonstrated that he could dance on fire just as well as the Anastenarides. He insisted that he had danced as "slowly" as they had, that he was their equal in all respects. Ken readily admitted, however, that when an Anastenaris stepped on his foot he was in fact burned—contrary to the Greek newspaper account. What is more, Ken interpreted his firewalk in Langadas, a firewalk in which he was burned, as a "healing experience"; he learned not to criticize or judge other people.

THE AMERICAN FIREWALKING MOVEMENT: A CULTURAL CRITIQUE

Media coverage of the American Firewalking movement has generally been quite negative. While some writers treat it sensationally or try to expose it as fraudulent, most adopt a very skeptical and cynical attitude toward it or simply mock it outright. Participants in firewalking workshops are ridiculed for their naiveté, their materialism, and their desire for quick, easy personal growth. In newspaper articles with titles like "Hot Feat" and "Save Your Soles," the American Firewalking movement is described as just another "self-improvement scam" (Galloway 1986) or "the hottest new theosophy among those with upwardly mobile consciousnesses," (Krakauer 1984). Tolly Burkan is described as "the grand pooh-bah and founding guru of American firewalking" (Krakauer 1984) and as "just another in a long line of human-potential hucksters cashing in on the enormous gullibility of baby boomers" (Galloway 1986), while Anthony Robbins is referred to as a "Beverly Hills-based whiz-kid" (Medoff 1984). A man who had just completed a successful firewalk is quoted as saying, "I am convinced that if you had your shit together and really put your mind to it, you could survive a direct nuclear blast" (Krakauer 1984).

Observers of the American Firewalking movement invariably single out for particularly harsh criticism what they regard as the exorbitant cost of firewalking programs and the high incomes and sudden wealth of the movement's leaders. The cost of evening workshops ranges from fifty to a hundred and twenty-five dollars. Robbins' four-day Mind Revolution Seminar costs four hundred and seventy dollars, while the Burkans charge four thousand five hundred dollars for their Firewalking Instructor's Training, a price that includes the rights to use their copyrighted seminar on "Overcoming Fear and Limiting Beliefs" (Medoff 1984). Burkan is reported to earn two hundred thousand dollars a year (Dennett 1985), and references are frequently made to the fact that Robbins is already a millionaire (Pooley 1985).

These sums of money seem inappropriately, even outrageously, high to many people because of their apparently incongruous association with an activity as "nontraditional" as firewalking. However, it is just such a paradoxical synthesis of the ideology of the counterculture with its opposition to materialism and utilitarianism, on the one hand, and the economic realities of adult life in conventional society, on the other, that characterizes the New Age movement specifically and other alternative religious movements more generally. Robbins sums up his view of the relationship between countercultural and traditional values this way: "A lot of people on the planet think you can either have all those great feelings and be sensitive and spiritual or you can have money. I think you can have both" (Stewart 1984).

A career as a firewalking instructor, which the Burkans' promotional literature promises will "support both you and your planetary vision," is a wonderful expression of this synthesis, a perfect example of someone who is "successful *in* this world without being *of* this world" (Stone 1976:110; emphasis in the original). In the person of a successful firewalking instructor the old economic myth of the self-made man is perfectly reconciled with what Tipton (1982:217) calls "the new consciousness myth of the self-made self."

Tolly Burkan and Anthony Robbins seem to embody the complete integration of these two myths. They have achieved a significant degree of material success while remaining faithful to and actually promoting the values of the counterculture. For people like Ken Cadigan, however, the struggle to bring together these two worlds by earning a living as a firewalking instructor has been more difficult.

It was precisely this central theme of the New Age movement—the challenge of resolving the conflict between the values of the counter-culture and those of traditional American culture—that was troubling Ken so deeply at the firewalking workshop he led at Northern Pines in December 1985. On the one hand, Ken felt that it was improper for him to charge money for his workshops; he wanted to do what he did for love. On the other hand, he had to support himself; he wanted to be financially secure.

Ken tried to resolve this dilemma with the plan he adopted at Northern Pines. After much soul searching, he decided not to charge people a specific amount of money for his workshop, just to ask them for donations. In this way he hoped to free himself from his attachment to money. He realized he was taking a big risk, but, as he said, that was his fire. Ken's plans for the One Foundation represent another effort on his part to resolve the basic moral dilemma of the New Age movement by assuring his financial security while at the same time freeing himself from the need to be concerned with that very security.[9]

While the American Firewalking movement, like other forms of New Age healing, is above all concerned with personal growth and fulfillment at the individual level, it also purports to address certain social problems such as racism, poverty, the destruction of the environment, and the threat of nuclear war. This critique of American culture and of the international political and economic order is couched, not surprisingly, in the same psychological idiom that characterizes other aspects of the New Age movement as well.

In *Guiding Yourself into a Spiritual Reality*, a book dedicated to "The Transformation of the Planet," the Burkans state that the fourth and final stage of growth is networking, which involves developing relationships with "kindred souls with whom we can vibrate in harmony." This will lead to the formation of a "New Age Network . . . a leaderless society which may ultimately replace the existing forms of government . . . [a] universal network of enlightened humanity [that] might eventually inherit the earth" (1983:80). In a promotional brochure the Burkans describe Sundoor as "a community dedicated to spiritual

---

[9] A pamphlet Ken distributed at Northern Pines entitled "The Question of Payment" pointed out that "even an advanced therapist has some earthly needs." It went on to argue, however, that "only an unhealed healer would try to heal for money." The conclusion seemed to be that with "God's healers" those who gave would in turn be given. For a time Tolly Burkan asked people to pay for his workshops by making donations to their favorite charities (Burkan 1984:124, 147).

growth and planetary service" whose concerns are "abundance for all, nuclear sanity, ecological awareness, and effective human relationships."

This New Age approach to social and political change is set out in Ken Keyes' book *The Hundredth Monkey* (1982), which has had a strong influence on the teachings of Burkan, Robbins, and Ken Cadigan. Keyes uses the image of the hundredth monkey as a metaphor for the process of social and political change that must be set in motion in order to prevent the outbreak of nuclear war. "Your awareness is needed in saving the world from nuclear war," writes Keyes. "You may be the 'Hundredth Monkey.' . . . You may furnish the added consciousness energy to create the shared awareness of the urgent necessity to rapidly achieve a nuclear-free world" (19). According to Keyes all that is required to save the world from a nuclear holocaust is increased awareness and raised consciousness on the part of a large enough number of people. In Keyes' view, "The bomb is not the real problem— it's only an effect of our attitudes" (98). If we are to continue to exist as a species, we must change the way we as individuals think and feel; we must "replace the illusions of separateness with the emotional experiences of acceptance, cooperation and togetherness" (126).

This approach to social and political change is reductionistic in the extreme and is characterized by the mysticized and psychologized individualism that so dominates all aspects of the New Age movement. According to this New Age ideology, because society is nothing more than a collection of individuals, social and political problems are reduced to psychological problems. Social change is therefore equated with personal growth and self-transformation. American society, the human species, and the entire planet, which are all "ill," will be "healed" spontaneously when a critical mass of individuals becomes sufficiently aware of the problems besetting them.

Given this naive view of social change it is not surprising that leaders of the New Age movement rarely advocate any concrete programs for social or political change. They simply assume that people live in a social vacuum and ignore the fact that social problems are often structural in nature and have their origin in specific economic, legal, and political institutions and policies. In their exclusive focus on the individual, people involved in New Age healing completely dismiss the realities of social structure and class. They fail to realize that it requires more than personal growth and self-transformation to change long-standing public policies and powerful social institutions, nor do they realize that their idealistic and utopian visions for social change are doomed because they fail to take into account the oppressive aspects of the social, political, and economic order that are ultimately responsible for the problems of so many people. The liberation that is the goal of the New Age movement is exclusively psychological; it has no social or political dimension to it. As Edwin Schur concludes in his critique of New Age healing, "Belief in self-help as the major path to social change is an illusion. . . . there can be no real self-awareness without social awareness. . . . Whenever we begin to consider how to ameliorate specific problems of people in our society, the superficiality and emptiness of awareness thinking quickly becomes apparent" (1976:193-194).[10]

The American Firewalking movement has also come under sharp criticism from scholars and scientists who reject the fundamental claim of its leaders that people are able to walk through fire without being burned because of special mental powers that are able to alter or suspend normal scientific laws and physical processes. These are the scholars and scientists that leaders of the movement feel are trying to expose them as charlatans and frauds.

One of the most recent and most convincing statements of this scientific critique of the American Firewalking movement was published in 1985 in *The Skeptical Inquirer*, the Journal of the Committee for the Scientific Investigation of Claims of the Paranormal. Here Bernard J. Leikind, a UCLA physicist, and William J. McCarthy, a psychologist also at UCLA, offer a straightforward scientific explanation for the ability of people to walk on fire without getting burned.[11] This explanation depends on "the ordinary physics of heat and materials" and does not involve any appeal to religious beliefs, brain chemistry, or positive mental attitudes. Instead it relies on the distinction between temperature, on the one hand, and heat or thermal energy, on the other. It is this distinction that accounts for the obvious fact that we are *not* burned if we touch the hot air inside an oven, while we *are* burned if we touch an aluminum pan inside the same oven. Even though the air and the metal pan are at the same temperature, "the air has a low heat capacity

---

[10] This superficiality and emptiness is nowhere more apparent than in Robbins' comment about how to deal with poverty. "The best way I can help the poor," he said, "is not to become one of them" (Stewart 1984).

[11] A shorter version of the same article was also published in *Psychology Today* (McCarthy and Leikind 1986).

and a poor thermal conductivity, while the aluminum has a high heat capacity and a high thermal conductivity." Therefore, "when we put our hands in the hot oven air, . . . [the air] cools much more than our hands warm." When we touch the metal pan, however, "the metal does not drop in temperature very much . . . while our hands quickly warm" (Leikind and McCarthy 1985:23-34). That is why a hot metal pan will burn us, while air at the same temperature will not.

The ability of people to perform the firewalk without being burned can be explained according to these same basic principles. The coals on which people walk are quite light and fluffy. "Although they may be at a fairly high temperature (1,000° to 1,200°F), they do not contain as much energy as we might expect from our common sense notions of incandescent objects. Thus, so long as we do not spend too much time on the embers our feet will probably not get hot enough to burn" (Leikind and McCarthy 1985:30). Leikind and McCarthy go on to point out that some people who firewalk are in fact burned because of the many factors that vary from one person to another and from one moment to the next during a single firewalk. These factors include how long people stay on the embers, how many steps they take, how tough the soles of their feet are, and precisely where in the fire they step.[12]

This rational or scientific explanation of the firewalk is no more compatible with the world view of New Age healers than it is with that of the Anastenarides. In their "scientific assessment" of the American Firewalking movement Leikind and McCarthy advise people to "stay away" from firewalking workshops and seminars because they are "misleading," "deceptive," and "dangerous" (1985:34). Leikind, the UCLA physics department, and a group known as the Southern California Skeptics have held several free "lecture demonstrations" on "The Physics of Firewalking" in order to present a "common-sense" alternative to what another physicist has called "the superstitious non-

---

[12] This argument was put forth as early as 1939 in a *Scientific American* article based on research carried out by the University of London Council for Psychical Investigation. After many experimental firewalks the investigators determined that a "specially induced mental state" was not a prerequisite for a successful firewalk and that "the very low thermal conductivity of smouldering wood prevents damage to normal skin" if the time of contact and the number of contacts with the coals are not too great. The investigators concluded that "facts of a purely physical nature—namely, brief contact, few contacts and a poor conductor of heat—seem sufficient to account for the ability to do firewalking" (Ingalls 1939:177-178).

sense" taught by firewalk instructors like Burkan and Robbins (Ahn 1988, Seckel 1985, and Taylor forthcoming). The seriousness of the threat that this type of scientific explanation of the firewalk poses to the American Firewalking movement was readily apparent when Anthony Robbins "got cold feet" and "postponed" his first Australian tour because of a vigorous publicity campaign mounted by the Australian branch of the Committee for the Scientific Investigation of the Paranormal, a campaign inspired by an article written by Leikind and McCarthy (*The Skeptical Inquirer* 10 [1985]:9-10).

I personally accept the scientific explanation of firewalking offered by Leikind and McCarthy, and like them I am somewhat skeptical of many of the more grandiose claims made by leaders of the American Firewalking movement. I doubt, for example, that firewalking can instantly cure lifelong phobias, send malignant tumors into remission, or help people earn a million dollars. I also wonder how long the psychological benefits provided by an evening of firewalking can last, how permanent the changes it brings about can be.

However, I do not agree with Leikind and McCarthy's conclusion that people should necessarily "stay away" from firewalking workshops because they are "deceptive." As a form of symbolic healing, as a vehicle for promoting personal and spiritual growth, firewalking workshops in the United States cannot be evaluated according to the scientific accuracy of the principles on which they are based, anymore than the therapeutic effectiveness of the Anastenaria can be judged according to whether Saint Constantine actually exists or not. As leaders of the American Firewalking movement point out, scientific explanations of firewalking are irrelevant when it comes to evaluating the therapeutic effectiveness of firewalking workshops; they have no bearing on the emotional impact the experience of firewalking has on most people. Even Leikind and McCarthy, as skeptical as they are, acknowledge the "powerful persuasive effect" firewalking has on many people (1985:33).

In the context of the American Firewalking movement walking on fire is a metaphor for performing miracles and accomplishing the impossible, a metaphor that can be a very powerful one even for people who do not accept the explanation for the phenomenon offered by leaders of the movement. People who participate in firewalking workshops and seminars in the United States, like people who participate in the Anastenaria, are rhetorically moved from their present state, negatively defined as one of illness, to a new state, positively defined as one of health. Through firewalking they are empowered; their lives are transformed. They gain an enhanced sense of self-confidence and self-esteem and are able to function more effectively in the world in which they live.

IX

Contemporary Anthropology in a Postmodern World

❖

SELF AND OTHER: BLURRED BOUNDARIES

WHEN I LEFT the United States for Greece in August 1974 to begin my research on the Anastenaria, I had a fairly traditional idea of what ethnographic fieldwork would be like. I was an American, a graduate student in anthropology, and I had been brought up as a member of a liberal Protestant church in a white, upper-middle-class suburb of Boston. I was going to live in a Greek village, a warm emotional place where people ate exotic food outdoors late at night and men embraced each other in public—a place where people lived lives that were somehow more real, more genuine, than mine. Greek villagers were farmers, they lived in extended families, and they died in their homes. Greek churches were filled with candles, incense, bearded priests dressed in splendid robes, and icons depicting saints with names like Athanasios, Paraskevi, and Pandeleimon. I was going to study the Anastenaria, a ritual involving trance, spirit possession, and firewalking.

I thought—somewhat naively I now realize—that the Anastenarides and I were irreducibly different, that we inhabited totally separate, totally foreign worlds. The distance between us—the ethnographic distance between "anthropologist" and "native," between "self" and "other"—was sustained by a cultural relativism that led me to think it was possible "to study alien and disturbing behavior from a 'scientific' distance," untouched by the challenges it posed for my own view of the world (Fabian 1979:9). I took it for granted that my culture and that of the Anastenarides were distinct, self-contained entities and that it was impossible for me as an outsider to judge the truth or morality of any aspect of their culture. As a result, both during my fieldwork and for many years thereafter, I just bracketed the crucial question of the validity of the claims made by the Anastenarides. As an anthropologist I simply did not allow myself to ask: "Does Saint Constantine really exist? Can he actually cause or cure sickness? How are the Anastenarides able to walk on fire without being burned?"[1]

Somewhat paradoxically, however, on a more personal level I was fully committed to an anthropological interpretation of religious healing and to a scientific explanation of firewalking. I did not believe in Saint Constantine; I believed in anthropology and physics. Yet I felt that there was absolutely no context in which these beliefs of mine could be appropriately discussed. As an anthropologist I found them irrelevant and somewhat embarrassing, so I simply bracketed them.

When I began studying the American Firewalking movement in 1985, the situation became more complex. I could no longer claim to be the disinterested foreign ethnographer studying a totally alien and isolated culture. The sharp boundary between self and other, between subject and object, became blurred. The ethnographic distance that separated me from people who walk on fire was bridged.

The American Firewalking movement occupied an anomalous middle ground between my world and that of the Anastenaria. Ken Cadigan stood almost tricksterlike in a doorway that opened between Yavasis and me. Yavasis was a Greek shaman, a believer, a charismatic healer who inhabited a traditional religious world which fascinated me but which I ultimately rejected. I, on the other hand, was an American scholar, a nonbeliever, a scientist (in a way) whose secular humanism contrasted sharply with Yavasis' sacred world view and posed a definite threat to it. And Ken Cadigan? Ken Cadigan was an American shaman, a believer in an eclectic mix of religion and science, a New Age healer who inhabited a postmodern world that drew freely on sacred and secular traditions from many different cultures. While I had gone to

[1] On "the bracketing of truth" in American cultural anthropology see Rabinow (1983). For examples of such bracketing see Berger (1965:31-32) and McGuire (1982:50).

Greece to observe the Anastenaria and to interpret the religious healing I saw there from an anthropological perspective, Ken Cadigan had gone to Greece to participate in the Anastenaria, to learn to firedance. He wanted to add something new to his repertoire of shamanistic techniques. When I did fieldwork and walked on fire at Northern Pines in Raymond, Maine, Yavasis, Ken Cadigan, and I became inextricably linked in a complex set of overlapping relationships that are all too characteristic of the postmodern world of the 1980s.

It is clear to me, however, that Ken Cadigan is a member of my culture in a way that Yavasis is not, in spite of all the difficulties inherent in defining precisely what "my culture" is in this context. Ken is an American, he speaks English, he is even a member of my generation. Yet in many ways Ken and the American Firewalking movement seem just as foreign and exotic to me as the Anastenaria, and this cannot be attributed solely to the distancing effect produced by subjecting Ken's world to an anthropological gaze. Ken actually believes; he actually walks on fire. I am an anthropologist. I do not believe; I do not walk on fire. I only study people who walked on fire. But I *did* walk on fire. I did so as an anthropologist, though, not the way Ken and the others did. I was taking notes, I was writing, I did not believe.

Why do I feel the need to distance myself so strongly from the world of Ken Cadigan and the American Firewalking movement? Perhaps because it is so much more troubling, so much more threatening to me than the Anastenaria is. It strikes too close to home. It forces me to abandon the safety and comfort that my relativism has provided. I can no longer bracket the crucial questions I have always refused to address. My work with the American Firewalking movement has made the Anastenaria seem much less distant and foreign, but it has also estranged me even more from my own culture, a culture I thought I knew.

What I saw at the festival of Saints Constantine and Helen in Ayia Eleni in May 1986 made me realize that the situation was even more complex than I had realized. The distance separating me from the Anastenarides, which had been bridged by my involvement with the American Firewalking movement, had disappeared completely. The boundary that had been blurred was now completely gone. I could no longer even cling to the idea that there were *three* separate worlds, the worlds of anthropology, the Anastenaria, and the American Firewalking movement. Even this was an oversimplification. None of these worlds were discrete units, irreducibly distant and different from one another. They were all interdependent, constantly changing and being changed as a result of the interaction among them.

Tasos Reklos, the new leader of the Anastenarides, was a Greek, a shaman *and* a scientist, a religious healer who was also a physician. Tasos had been born into Yavasis' world, but now he seemed to inhabit mine. He and I appeared to share a secular, psychologically oriented world view. We talked about somatization and symbolism; we read the same articles in Greek folklore journals. Tasos' position with respect to the Anastenaria paralleled my position with respect to the American Firewalking movement. Tasos stood both inside and outside the world of the Anastenaria, as I stood both inside and outside the world of the American Firewalking movement. We had both acquired a scientific idiom with which to try to understand certain aspects of our lives, a scholarly "second language" into which we could translate our own experiences. In many ways, then, Tasos Reklos is more a member of "my culture" than Ken Cadigan because Ken, like Yavasis, stands fully within the healing tradition of which he is a part. Tasos and I, however, have both become alienated from our own experiences, marginal to our own traditions.[2]

In the postmodern world of the late twentieth century Ken Cadigan, Tasos Reklos, and I live simultaneously within and between cultures. We are displaced, condemned to what James Clifford has called "a pervasive condition of off-centeredness" (1988:9). After studying the Anastenaria and the American Firewalking movement I have come to realize that no one can "occupy, unambiguously, a bounded cultural world from which to journey out and analyze other cultures. Human ways of life increasingly influence, dominate, parody, translate, and subvert one another. . . . Now ethnography encounters others in relation to itself while seeing itself as other" (Clifford 1986:22-23).

It is as a result of these insights into the problems confronting contemporary anthropologists working in a postmodern world that the comparison between the Anastenaria and the American Firewalking movement presented in the previous chapter cannot ultimately be sustained. Although this comparison is valuable in and of itself, revealing

[2] Perhaps the final irony in this complex set of relationships is that Tasos Reklos, the leader of the Anastenarides, has never walked on fire, while I, the American anthropologist, have.

as it does the significant similarities and differences that characterize the paradoxical relationship between these two systems of ritual healing, in the last analysis it relies on an overly reductionistic division of human reality into distinct cultures. It depends on an artificial separation of traditional rural Greek culture from New Age culture in America, a separation that can only be maintained by ignoring the changes that the Anastenaria has undergone over the past ten years.

In drawing this comparison between the Anastenaria and the American Firewalking movement I suppressed the new generation of young people who have recently emerged as participants in the Anastenaria; I did not take into account the bohemian artists and intellectuals from Athens who sat beside elderly Kostilides on the benches of the konaki in Ayia Eleni. These new "Anastenarides" were not part of the rural community of Kostilides. For most of them participation in the Anastenaria did not lead to long-term involvement in a permanent therapeutic community; it was "a quick fix, a shot in the arm." They came to Ayia Eleni only once a year. Like Dimitris they were still *kseni*; they just came and went.

Many of the new Anastenarides I came to know in 1986 like Keti, Dimitris, Irini, and Kiriakos seemed to live in a world that was closer to the American Firewalking movement than to the Anastenaria. Their lives had been deeply influenced by recent developments in American popular culture. They were interested in Eastern mysticism and homeopathy; they talked about levitations, energy fields, and health food. Like people involved in the American Firewalking movement they were alienated and uprooted, part of a mobile, urban, middle class actively exploring new identities and alternative lifestyles quite different from any they had known earlier in their lives. They reminded me of troubled young anthropology students I had taught in the United States who were fascinated with the writings of Carlos Castaneda. In fact someone like Dimitris might have felt less like a *ksenos* at one of Ken Cadigan's firewalking workshops than at a celebration of the Anastenaria.

The emergence of this new group of Anastenarides undermines my comparison of the Anastenaria and the American Firewalking movement for another reason. Many of these new Anastenarides made use of a psychological rather than a religious or somatic idiom for the expression of distress. In this respect also they had more in common with people who firewalk in the United States than they did with an earlier generation of Anastenarides. Keti, for example, talked about an inner power that was freed by the ecstatic dance of the Anastenarides. Dimitris spoke of yin-yang imbalances, Irini of fear and family problems, Kiriakos of "a crisis of transition." The idiom Tasos Reklos used to discuss the Anastenaria—when talking with me at least—was a psychological one as well, but it was a scientific or scholarly idiom, not a popular New Age one. With his talk of neuroses, psychosomatic illnesses, and *DSM III*, Tasos sounded more like a psychological anthropologist than a leader of the American Firewalking movement.

This suggests that having subjected one aspect of "my culture" to the anthropological gaze, it would be valuable to subject the discipline of anthropology to this gaze as well. The juxtaposition of anthropology next to the Anastenaria and the American Firewalking movement makes it clear that anthropology can be seen as a third language or idiom with which to express experiences comparable to those of Anastenarides and people who firewalk in the United States. Anthropologists employ the idiom of the social sciences to communicate what most Anastenarides communicate in a religious idiom and what participants in the American Firewalking movement communicate in the eclectic but primarily psychological idiom of New Age healing. What Anastenarides attribute to the supernatural power of Saint Constantine and what American firewalkers attribute to the untapped power of the human mind anthropologists attribute to cultural, social, and psychological factors, to forces and processes that transcend the individual but are not defined as supernatural or divine.

The goal of my analysis of the Anastenaria has always been to translate in a sensitive and nonreductionistic manner from a religious or spirit idiom into an anthropological one. This translation, while difficult to do well, is a relatively straightforward process since it involves two idioms or languages that are different in fundamental ways. In the case of my analysis of the American Firewalking movement the situation is again much more complex because the two languages involved are so similar. It is not clear in fact whether the language of the American Firewalking movement and the language of anthropology constitute two separate languages or not, sharing as they do a common vocabulary and a common background. Like anthropologists, participants in the American Firewalking movement speak of the firewalk as a metaphor or a symbol for powerful psychological experiences. In addition, the discipline of anthropology (particularly the field of psychological anthropology) is a product of the same "psychologizing process" (Kleinman 1986:55) that has reached an extreme in the resolutely psychological idiom of the New Age movement.

Anthropological analyses of religious healing like those discussed in Chapter II are remarkably similar to interpretations offered by leaders of the American Firewalking movement for people's ability to walk on fire without being burned. Daniel Moerman, for example, advocates "a unitary conceptualization of the human organism" (1979:66) in a manner that is reminiscent of the holistic approach adopted by people involved in New Age healing. Moerman is interested in "the relationship between mind and body" and asks "What kind of control might thoughts have over physiological processes?" (61). Part of his answer to this question draws on biofeedback research which indicates "more extensive conscious control of physiological states than had been previously recognized" (61). He goes on to discuss the psychological and social factors that influence immunological resistance, as well as recent developments in neurophysiology involving the hypothalamus, the pituitary gland, neurotransmitters, and internal opiates.

Thus the theoretical foundation of my anthropological study of religious healing is an important part of the explanatory framework of the American Firewalking movement, which is itself an object of my study. Moerman's language is virtually identical to that of firewalk instructors in the United States. In fact, Moerman's argument, which I accept, could even be cited as support for their explanation of why people can walk on fire without being burned, which I reject. Needless to say, this troubles me. Just as the boundary between self and other became blurred when I did fieldwork and walked on fire at Ken Cadigan's workshop in Raymond, Maine, here the boundary between the scholarly discipline I am committed to and a New Age healing ideology I oppose has become blurred as well. Once again I struggle to keep the boundaries sharp and clear, but it grows increasingly difficult.

ANTHROPOLOGY AND THE QUEST FOR MEANING

Anthropology is not simply a third language or idiom into which the experiences of Anastenarides and American firewalkers can be translated. Anthropology—or more properly ethnographic fieldwork—is itself an experience which is analogous to that of the Anastenarides and to an even greater extent to that of American firewalkers. When the Anastenarides are possessed by Saint Constantine, they experience a powerful encounter with a spirit other. American firewalkers are also engaged in a search or quest for an other—not the spirit other of the Anastenarides but the other within ourselves, the true self. In both the Anastenaria and the American Firewalking movement this encounter with the other culminates in a dramatic act of firewalking.

An encounter with the other is also the defining characteristic of anthropology. Anthropologists come to know ethnographic others through fieldwork—an experience for which firewalking is certainly an apt metaphor. One could even say that many anthropologists are possessed by these ethnographic others, so intense is their desire to know and experience them fully. As James Clifford has pointed out, "the journey into otherness leads to a forbidden area of the self, the self which must possess" (1985:237). This is particularly true in the study of spirit possession and other exotic phenomena that, like the fetishes they are, have the disconcerting power to fascinate us, "to remind us of our own lack of self-possession" (Clifford 1985:244). One could say, then, that anthropologists are possessed by ethnographic others no less forcefully than these others are possessed by spirits, saints, demons, or even selves.[3]

A more general analogy exists between the discipline of anthropology and the religious movements anthropologists often study. An anthropological perspective or world view, no less than a religious one, is a "mode of seeing, . . . a particular manner of construing the world" (Geertz 1973b:110). The commitment of anthropologists to the social and cultural theories with which they interpret religious phenomena and their willingness to translate from the religious idioms they study into an anthropological one suggest that they themselves generally adopt a quasi-religious stance toward the material they study. It is in this sense that one can speak of secular humanism, cultural relativity, or anthropology itself as a religion.[4]

Anthropology, in the last analysis, involves a quest for meaning, a search for cultural and often personal identity through the practice of ethnography. It is ultimately concerned with "the comprehension of

[3] On the fascination of Europeans and Americans with spirit possession and the possibility of our own possession see Crapanzano (1977 and 1980).

[4] Robert Bellah develops this argument further in two essays entitled "Between Religion and Social Science" (1970) and "Religious Studies as the New Religion" (1978).

the self through the detour of the comprehension of the other" (Rabinow 1977:5; quoting Paul Ricoeur). In this light the analogy between anthropology and religious movements like the American Firewalking movement becomes clearer. Both anthropology and the religious movements it studies are "communal endeavors to make sense of intellectual situations which can no longer be interpreted within the limits of narrow, established traditions" (Fabian 1979:9).

In the 1960s American anthropology entered a period of what Clifford Geertz has called "postmodern self-doubt" (1985:624), a period characterized by widespread malaise, uneasiness, and uncertainty. A crisis arose in the professional paradigms that governed the way anthropologists thought and wrote about other cultures. During this "crisis of representation" (Marcus and Fischer 1986:7), which had both political and epistemological dimensions, the uncritical empiricism and positivism that had dominated much earlier anthropology were rejected. In addition, the genre conventions of traditional realist ethnography were challenged by an increasing number of experimental ethnographies that were self-consciously concerned with exploring the relationship between self and other.

It is precisely this same period of crisis and experimentation during which the counterculture emerged, and it is in response to this "crisis in meaning" (Bellah 1976:339), this "crisis in consciousness" (Glock 1976:356), that the New Age movement and other alternative religious movements developed. Therefore, both the reflexive and critical anthropological paradigms that have guided me in writing this book and the world view or ideology of the American Firewalking movement, the subject of at least a part of this book, have their origins in the same critique of American culture that was generated by what could be called at the most general level the "crisis in modernity." It is not surprising, then, given their common origins, that both the American Firewalking movement and experimental ethnographic writing exhibit many similarities. Both are characterized by "eclecticism, the play of ideas free of authoritative paradigms, critical and reflexive views of subject matter, openness to diverse influences embracing whatever seems to work in practice, and tolerance of uncertainty . . . and of incompleteness in some of [their] projects" (Marcus and Fischer 1986:x).

In a frequently cited passage Clifford Geertz writes: "The essential vocation of interpretive anthropology is not to answer our deepest questions, but to make available to us answers that others, guarding other sheep in other valleys, have given, and thus to include them in the consultable record of what man has said" (1973a:30). For many anthropologists, however, particularly those who were influenced by the developments of the 1960s both within anthropology and in American society as a whole, the practice of ethnography and the pursuit of anthropology as a career has involved a quest for meaning. For these anthropologists—and I include myself here—the essential vocation of a reflexive and critical interpretive anthropology most certainly *is* to answer our deepest questions. In this sense anthropology has a great deal in common with alternative religious movements, especially those that have been influenced by the social sciences or by non-Western religious traditions. The people involved in these movements, like many anthropologists, are clearly engaged in a serious search for meaningful alternatives in a world that seems to offer only disillusionment and alienation.

Unlike the participants in many of these alternative religious movements, however, anthropologists do not attempt to answer these "deepest questions" directly through introspection, through an encounter with the true self, the other within ourselves. They try to answer them through a detour, through an encounter with the ethnographic other. They try to answer them by consulting the answers given by other people in other places, but they try to answer them nonetheless.

If, as I have argued, the healing of illness is an essentially interpretive or hermeneutic process, if it involves the construction and transformation of systems of meaning with which to interpret experience, then anthropology itself can be seen as a form of therapy. The practice of anthropology, like participation in the American Firewalking movement or any other alternative religious movement, involves a search for meaning and identity that is ultimately therapeutic in nature. The metaphor of anthropology as therapy suggests that anthropologists suffer from some illness which ethnographic fieldwork and ethnographic writing are able to heal. The specific "difficulties in living," the particular "life problems" (Kleinman 1986:51 and 173) that anthropologists often confront revolve around the alienation and marginality that have so often been attributed to them. Marcus and Fischer, for example, associate the long tradition of cultural criticism in anthropology to the "qualified marginality of its practitioners" (1986:131). Tzvetan Todorov refers to "the modern exile" as a person "who has lost his country without acquiring another, who lives in a double exteriority," and as a person "for whom the whole world is a foreign country" (1984:249-250). This is a most apt description of anthropologists, moving constantly as they do across the increasingly blurred boundaries between the world's cultures.

Perhaps some anthropologists, like the young educated Greeks who have recently become involved with the Anastenaria, are also experiencing what Fischer (1986) has called "ethnic anxiety," the fear of losing or having already lost any sense of community or collective identity. The search for a sense of ethnic identity, which Fischer describes in terms that suggest spirit possession, is remarkably similar to many anthropologists' quest for meaning through encounters with ethnographic others. Fischer, in fact, explicitly compares the emergence of ethnographic knowledge with the creation of ethnic identity (1986:208). It is as if some anthropologists by conducting fieldwork in foreign cultures seek to adopt the ethnic identity of the ethnographic others they are studying. In this way anthropologists are able to discover or invent a new identity for themselves, an identity which they somehow felt they lacked.

In *Reflections on Fieldwork in Morocco* Paul Rabinow presents a revealing account of ethnographic fieldwork that offers an excellent illustration of anthropology as a therapeutic quest for identity and meaning undertaken by someone who feels deeply alienated from his own culture. Rabinow describes his departure for the field this way (1977:1):

> I left Chicago two days after the assassination of Robert Kennedy. . . . I had been mildly anxious about leaving, but the news of the murder had buried those feelings under a wave of revulsion and disgust. I left America with a sense of giddy release. I was sick of being a student, tired of the city, and felt politically impotent. I was going to Morocco to become an anthropologist.

Several months after his arrival in Morocco, when he learned of the Soviet invasion of Czechoslovakia, Rabinow felt "a horrified distance" from his own civilization (19). During the early part of his fieldwork Rabinow felt obliged "to become a sort of non-person, or more accurately a total persona" (46). He felt powerless and weak; he found it difficult to assert himself. Finally, toward the end of his fieldwork, after entering into a genuine dialogue with a Moroccan friend and being confronted most directly by their "fundamental Otherness" (162), Rabinow had "a strong sense of being American." He knew it was time to leave. But when he returned to the United States, "the maze of slightly blurred nuance, that feeling of barely grasped meanings" which he had experienced repeatedly in Morocco overtook him once again. But now he was home (148).

Rabinow's experiences resonate tellingly with my own. I left the United States for Greece five days after Richard Nixon resigned as a result of investigations into the Watergate scandal. The Vietnam War was slowly drawing to a close, and I felt as if I had spent the past five years dealing with my draft board over my application for Conscientious Objector status. I was disillusioned; I felt alienated from the world I was leaving behind. I seemed to lack any ethnic or cultural identity I could be proud of. I was ready to become a different person and begin a new life.

When I returned to the United States after more than two years in Greece, I immediately began searching out Greeks and Greek-Americans so I could continue speaking Greek. Whenever I did, I would refer to myself as a *ksenos* even though we were in the United States and I was the American. Once in Washington, D.C., I found myself gazing up at the American flag that stood on top of the white marble dome of the Capitol building; I was whistling the Greek national anthem.

For Rabinow, for me, and I am sure for many other anthropologists as well, the encounter with ethnographic others is at one level at least a therapeutic quest for meaning, a search for identity that can be considered a form of healing in the broadest sense. This therapeutic encounter is not confined to the practice of ethnographic fieldwork; it includes the process of ethnographic writing as well. Clifford Geertz, for example, suggests that the present "crisis in ethnographic writing" is characterized by "anxiety," "malaise," "estrangement," "epistemological hypochondria," and "a pervasive nervousness" that calls forth reflexivity, dialogue, rhetorical self-consciousness, and first-person narrative "as forms of cure" (1988:71-72, 97, 130-131, 138).

The experiences of anthropologists can thus be seen as analogous to the experiences of people involved in alternative religious movements in the United States and to a lesser extent perhaps to those of young Anastenarides. The same dramatic cultural changes that began in the 1960s, the same sense of alienation and disillusionment that led many young people in America to join alternative religious movements, also led me and others of the same generation to become anthropologists. Anthropology has provided me with the opportunity to integrate successfully the apparently contradictory values of the counterculture and those of mainstream American culture. It has enabled me to earn a living in a well-respected profession while continuing to explore my interests in shamanism, spirit possession, and firewalking. This is precisely the opportunity that alternative religious movements provide people with; this is precisely what people like Tolly Burkan, Anthony Robbins, and Ken Cadigan hope to accomplish through their work as firewalk instructors.

In addition, my experiences as an anthropologist in Greece generally and in Ayia Eleni in particular have done for me what the Anastenaria has done for people like Dimitris, Irini, and Kiriakos. They have provided me with a new identity, a new sense of rootedness in a specific place and a specific past. Ayia Eleni has become "my village," not in the sense in which anthropologists usually use the phrase (the village belongs to me), but in the sense in which Greeks use it (I belong to the village). After all, like the young computer scientist with whom I exchanged addresses at the festival of Saints Constantine and Helen in 1986, I too once had three addresses: the village of Ayia Eleni where I was doing fieldwork, Athens where I had taught for two years, and Boston where my parents lived. Although our careers had led us in opposite directions—his from a Greek village to a large European city, mine from a large American city to a Greek village—we were both drawn to the Anastenaria because it offered us a moving encounter with Saint Constantine, a powerful spirit other who personifies community, tradition, and the past in a postmodern world of mobility, change, and alienation.

Like the religious movements it studies, anthropology also holds out the possibility of such elusive and seemingly spiritual goals as transcendence and liberation. Richard Shweder (1986) in an essay on "the contemporary crisis of faith in the writing of ethnographies" argues that "good ethnography is an intellectual exorcism in which, forced to take the perspective of the other, we are wrenched out of our self. We transcend ourselves, and for a brief moment we wonder who we are, . . . whether it would be better if the other were us, or better if we were the other." Discussing a dialogical approach to ethnographic writing, Tzvetan Todorov suggests (quoting Levinas) that this new perspective on the other is defined by a concern for "transcendence of self which calls for epiphany of the Other" (1984:250). This use of the term "transcendence" in describing the goals of the ethnographic encounter is reminiscent of the language employed by people involved in New Age healing to refer to the heightened sense of awareness associated with the attainment of "enlightenment" or "cosmic consciousness." In the case of New Age healing, however, the other we encounter is not an ethnographic other but the other within ourselves.

In the context of the New Age movement liberation too is an exclusively individual goal. It is a psychological process in which people are liberated from the "fears and limiting beliefs" that prevent them from realizing their full potential. This sense of personal liberation is certainly an important part of the experience many anthropologists have when they encounter another culture for the first time. Miles Richardson, for example, reflecting back on his motives for becoming an anthropologist, writes: "I wanted freedom. To me, anthropology was liberation" (1975:518). Richardson goes on to say that anthropology offered him a "way out," an escape from the narrow confines of a life that had been dominated by a Southern Baptist church in a small Texas town. He concludes by suggesting that "the anthropologist may find his own salvation" by writing about the struggles of other peoples (530). Ethnographic writing may have a similar impact on other people as well. Richard Shweder (1986) describes the liberating effect Margaret Mead's *Coming of Age in Samoa* had on a whole generation of Americans.

While I feel that the analogies suggested here between the personal experiences of anthropologists and those of people involved in alternative religious movements are valid and must be taken seriously, I am well aware of the danger of reducing anthropology to just another approach in the vast array of "spiritual disciplines" that make up the New Age movement. This is precisely what has happened on what I would call the fringes of anthropology where healing the self has replaced understanding the other as the anthropologist's primary concern. In such a mysticized and psychologized "New Age anthropology" the anthropologist becomes a shaman or myth teller, while anthropology itself is reduced to a popular form of psychotherapy. Stan Wilk, for example, refers to "the culture theorist as a neoshamanic sensemaker" (1986:50) and calls for a "therapeutic anthropology" whose goal ("the attainment of culture-consciousness") can only be achieved by "embracing the mystery of experience and thus the mystery of the self" (1977:16-17). In a similar vein Stephen Tyler calls for a postmodern ethnography that is "an occult document," "a meditative vehicle" that can serve "a therapeutic purpose" (1986:128 and 140). Tyler describes the "new kind of holism" that will characterize this postmodern ethnography in terms of an "ever present, never present simultaneity of reality and fantasy . . . floating, like the Lord Brahmā, motionless in the surfaceless void, all potentiality suspended within us in perfect realization . . . (134).[5]

A truly critical or reflexive anthropology, however, must also be concerned with liberation of a different kind. It must be concerned with liberation of the other, not just the self, and with liberation in a sociopolitical, not just a psychological sense. It is the political dimension of liberation that Johannes Fabian has in mind when he challenges anthropologists "to go beyond uninvolved accounts of exotic cultures 'in their own terms,' " and join with leaders of religious movements "in the common task of interpretation as liberation" (1979:34-35). Bob Scholte has also stressed the importance for anthropology of a commitment to the social and political liberation of the other, a commitment that is totally lacking in much of the New Age movement. For Scholte critical anthropology is both liberating and emancipatory. Anthropological knowledge is "knowledge for the sake of freedom" (1974:446), and it must always be simultaneously knowledge of the self and knowledge of the other, for the two forms of knowledge are inextricably linked. Only through a firm commitment to understanding others and to the political and social liberation of others can anthropology escape the emptiness and superficiality, the eclecticism and the self-absorption that characterize the ideologies of many New Age religious and therapeutic movements.

It is essential that we as anthropologists see ourselves in the others of the New Age movement because we are struggling with many of the same questions, because we are engaged in such a similar quest for meaning. It is equally important, however, that we maintain a distance from these others, that we see precisely how anthropology differs from New Age healing. "Exile is fruitful," writes Tzvetan Todorov, "if one

---

[5] See also Castaneda (1968), Harner (1982), and Richardson (1975 and 1980).

belongs to both cultures at once, without identifying oneself with either; but if a whole society consists of exiles, the dialogue of cultures ceases: it is replaced by eclecticism and comparatism, by the capacity to love everything a little, of flaccidly sympathizing with each option without ever embracing any" (1984:251).

❖

PENTHEUS *Tell me about these mysteries of yours.*
DIONYSOS *I couldn't tell you. You're not one of us.*
PENTHEUS *What does this ritual do—I mean*
for those who join it?
DIONYSOS *We keep that knowledge to ourselves.*
But it's worth having.
PENTHEUS *You tell me nothing with so much cunning*
it makes me ache to hear more.
DIONYSOS *The wild dances of this god punish disbelievers.*
PENTHEUS *You've seen the god up close—what is he like?*
DIONYSOS *That's not for me to say. He can look like—*
anyone. . . .
. . . Would you like to see maenads
sitting together, up there on the mountain?
PENTHEUS *I would give all the gold I have to see that. . . .*
. . . Tell me again how I must dress.
DIONYSOS *I'll find you some elegant long hair.*
PENTHEUS *And then? You're changing me—how far will this go?*
DIONYSOS *I'll bind your hair and drop skirts to your feet.*
PENTHEUS *Is that all? Anything else?*
DIONYSOS   *I'll give you*
a green wand to hold and a fawn to wear.
PENTHEUS *That's what your women wear! Not me. I can't do it.*
DIONYSOS *People will die if you battle the maenads.*
PENTHEUS *That's right. Maybe we should reconnoiter first.*
DIONYSOS *It makes more sense than to kill and be killed.*
PENTHEUS *How shall I walk through Thebes without being seen?*
DIONYSOS *I'll see that we travel through deserted streets.*
PENTHEUS *That's a relief. The maenads must not laugh at me.*
I'm going indoors now to think things through.
DIONYSOS *I'm ready for whatever you decide.*

PENTHEUS *When I come out, I'll either be fighting, or I'll
put myself in your hands.*[6]

✛

The image of Pentheus has haunted me for years. Pentheus—the non-believer, the voyeur, at once so terrified and so fascinated by the total otherness of Dionysos. On the one hand, Pentheus saw Dionysos as a threat to reason and order. He tried to suppress his worship and in doing so denied the other in himself. On the other hand, Pentheus was possessed by Dionysos. He wanted to experience for himself the power and the joy that Dionysos had to offer those who worshipped him. He wanted to participate in the sacred mysteries and watch the maenads dance; he wanted to see water pour forth from rocks at their touch and fire burn harmlessly in their hair.

In the end, unable to resolve his ambivalence toward Dionysos, the terrible god, Pentheus was destroyed. His encounter with the other led tragically to madness and death. When *we* confront Dionysos, must we choose, as Pentheus thought, between fighting and surrender, between resistance and conversion? I believe not. As Charles Segal (1982) suggests, Euripides' response to *his* confrontation with Dionysos clearly demonstrates that a third alternative is possible. Euripides' encounter with Dionysos inspired him to write the *Bacchae* at about the time he was leaving Athens for a life of exile in Macedonia. The *Bacchae* represents a creative response to the encounter with the other, a response that leads to self-knowledge rather than self-destruction. More importantly, however, the *Bacchae* also contributes to knowledge of the other and to an understanding of what constitutes a positive relationship with that other. Such a response initiates a dialogue between self and other which promises to be a liberating experience for them both.

Anthropologists too respond to their encounter with the other by writing. It is my hope that this book will contribute to a genuine dialogue of cultures, that it will challenge us to reflect further on the nature of our relationships to the others who inhabit our world.

[6] From *The Bakkhai* by Euripides, translated by Robert Bagg, lines 645-55, 1095-97, and 1115-32, © 1978 by the University of Massachusetts Press. Permission to quote this passage is gratefully acknowledged.

Bibliography

Ahn, Eugene
1988   Physicists Take to Firewalking. *UCLA Daily Bruin.* May 23, p. 3.

Akadimia Athinon
1962   *Ellinika Dimotika Tragoudia (Ekloyi).* Vol. 1. Dimosievmata tou Laografikou Arhiou. No. 7. Athens.

Alexiou, Margaret
1974   *The Ritual Lament in Greek Tradition.* Cambridge: At the University Press.

Armstrong, Lucile
1970   Fire-Walking at San Pecho Manrique. *Folklore* 81:198–214.

Arnaudoff, M.
1917   Novi Svedenia za Nestenarite. *Spisanie na Bulgarskata Akademia na Naukite* 14, no. 8:43–102. (Cited in Greek translation in Megas 1961:493–503.)

Bachelard, Gaston
1964   *The Psychoanalysis of Fire.* Boston, Mass.: Beacon Press.

Ballis, Th.; A. Beaumanoir; and H. Xenakis
1979   Anastenaria. *Hellenic Armed Forces Medical Review* 13:245.

Bandler, Richard, and John Grinder
1979   *Frogs into Princes: Neuro Linguistic Programming.* Moab, Utah: Real People.

Barnes, Timothy
1984   *Constantine and Eusebius.* Cambridge, Mass.: Harvard University Press.

Barth, Fredrik
1969   Introduction. In *Ethnic Groups and Ethnic Boundaries: The Social Organization of Cultural Difference*, pp. 9–38. London: George Allen and Unwin/Bergen, Oslo: Universitetsforlaget.

Basso, Keith H., and Henry A. Selby, eds.
1976   *Meaning in Anthropology.* Albuquerque: University of New Mexico Press.

Bauman, Richard
  1983   *Let Your Words Be Few: Symbolism of Speaking and Silence among Seventeenth-Century Quakers.* Cambridge: At the University Press.
Beaton, Roderick
  1980   *Folk Poetry of Modern Greece.* Cambridge: At the University Press.
Bellah, Robert N.
  1970   Between Religion and Social Science. In *Beyond Belief*, pp. 237–259. New York: Harper and Row.
  1976   New Religious Consciousness and the Crisis in Modernity. In *The New Religious Consciousness*, ed. Charles Y. Glock and Robert N. Bellah, pp. 333–352. Berkeley: University of California Press.
  1978   Religious Studies as the New Religion. In *Understanding the New Religions*, ed. Jacob Needleman and George Baker, pp. 106–112. New York: Seabury Press.
Berger, Peter L.
  1965   Towards a Sociological Understanding of Psychoanalysis. *Social Research* 32, no. 1:26–41.
—, and Thomas Luckmann
  1967   *The Social Construction of Reality.* New York: Anchor Books.
Blum, Richard, and Eva Blum
  1965   *Health and Healing in Rural Greece.* Stanford, Calif.: Stanford University Press.
  1970   *The Dangerous Hour: The Lore of Crisis and Mystery in Rural Greece.* New York: Charles Scribner's Sons.
Bordewich, Fergus M.
  1988   Colorado's Thriving Cults. *New York Times Magazine.* May 1, pp. 36–44.
Bourguignon, Erika
  1968   World Distribution and Patterns of Possession States. In *Trance and Possession States*, ed. R. Prince. Montreal: R. M. Bucke Memorial Society.
  1976a   The Effectiveness of Religious Healing Movements: A Review of Recent Literature. *Transcultural Psychiatric Research Review* 13:5–21.
  1976b   *Possession.* San Francisco, Calif.: Chandler and Sharp.
—, ed.
  1973   *Religion, Altered States of Consciousness, and Social Change.* Columbus: Ohio State University Press.

Brewster, Paul
  1977   The Strange Practice of Firewalking. *Expedition* 19, no. 3:43–47.
Broch, Harald Beyer
  1985   "Crazy Women are Performing in Sombali": A Possession-Trance Ritual on Bonerate, Indonesia. *Ethos* 13:262–282.
Burkan, Tolly
  1984   *Dying to Live*. Twain Harte, Calif.: Reunion Press.
—, and Peggy Dylan Burkan
  1983   *Guiding Yourself into a Spiritual Reality*. Twain Harte, Calif.: Reunion Press.
Burrows, R.J.L.
  1986   Americans Get Religion in the New Age. *Christianity Today* 30 (May 16):17–23.
Campbell, John K.
  1964   *Honour, Family and Patronage*. Oxford: Clarendon Press.
—, and Phillip Sherrard
  1968   *Modern Greece*. London: Benn.
Caraveli, Anna
  1985   The Symbolic Village: Community Born in Performance. *Journal of American Folklore* 98, no. 389:259–286.
  1986   The Bitter Wounding: The Lament as Social Protest. In *Gender and Power in Rural Greece*, ed. Jill Dubisch, pp. 169–194. Princeton, N.J.: Princeton University Press.
Carmen, E., N. Russo, and J. Miller
  1981   Inequality and Women's Mental Health: An Overview. *American Journal of Psychiatry* 138, no. 10:1319–1330.
Castaneda, Carlos
  1968   *The Teachings of Don Juan: A Yaqui Way of Knowledge*. Berkeley: University of California Press.
Christodoulou, Stavroula P.
  1978   Continuity and Change among the Anastenaria, A Firewalking Cult in Northern Greece. Ph.D. dissertation, State University of New York at Stony Brook. Ann Arbor, Mich.: University Microfilms.
Clifford, James
  1981   On Ethnographic Surrealism. *Comparative Studies in Society and History* 23, no. 4:539–564.
  1983   On Ethnographic Authority. *Representations* 1:118–146.
  1985   Objects and Selves—An Afterward. In *Objects and Others: Essays on Museums and Material Culture*, ed. George W. Stocking, pp.

236–246. History of Anthropology. Vol. 3. Madison: University of Wisconsin Press.

1986   Introduction: Partial Truths. In *Writing Culture*, ed. James Clifford and George E. Marcus, pp. 1–26. Berkeley: University of California Press.

1988   *The Predicament of Culture: Twentieth-Century Ethnography, Literature, and Art.* Cambridge, Mass.: Harvard University Press.

—, and George E. Marcus, eds.

1986   *Writing Culture: The Poetics and Politics of Ethnography.* Berkeley: University of California Press.

Cousins, Norman

1982   *Healing and Belief.* Cincinnati, Ohio: Mosaic Press.

1983   *The Healing Heart: Antidotes to Panic and Helplessness.* New York: W.W. Norton & Company.

Crapanzano, Vincent

1973   *The Hamadsha: A Study in Moroccan Ethnopsychiatry.* Berkeley: University of California Press.

1977   Introduction. In *Case Studies in Spirit Possession*, ed. Vincent Crapanzano and Vivian Garrison, pp. 1–40. New York: John Wiley and Sons.

1980   *Tuhami: Portrait of a Moroccan.* Chicago, Ill.: University of Chicago Press.

—, and Vivian Garrison, eds.

1977   *Case Studies in Spirit Possession.* New York: John Wiley and Sons.

Crick, Malcolm

1976   *Explorations in Language and Meaning: Towards a Semantic Anthropology.* London: Malaby Press.

Csordas, T. J.

1983   The Rhetoric of Transformation in Ritual Healing. *Culture, Medicine and Society* 7, no. 4:333–375.

Dakin, Douglas

1966   *The Greek Struggle in Macedonia, 1897–1913.* Thessaloniki: Institute for Balkan Studies.

Danforth, Loring

1978   The Anastenaria: A Study in Greek Ritual Therapy. Ph.D. dissertation, Princeton University. Ann Arbor, Mich.: University Microfilms.

1979   The Role of Dance in the Ritual Therapy of the Anastenaria. *Byzantine and Modern Greek Studies* 5:141–163.

1982   *The Death Rituals of Rural Greece.* Princeton, N.J.: Princeton University Press.

1983   Power through Submission in the Anastenaria. *Journal of Modern Greek Studies* 1, no. 1:203–223.

1984   The Ideological Context of the Search for Continuities in Greek Culture. *Journal of Modern Greek Studies* 2:53–85.

Deliyannis, V. N.

1938–39 Ta Anastenaria Sto Horio Kosti Tis Periferias Agathoupoleos An. Thrakis. *Arhion tou Thrakikou Laografikou ke Glossikou Thisavrou* 5:129–132.

Denich, Bette

1974   Sex and Power in the Balkans. In *Woman, Culture, and Society*, ed. M. Rosaldo and L. Lamphere, pp. 243–262. Stanford, Calif.: Stanford University Press.

Dennett, Michael R.

1985   Firewalking: Reality or Illusion. *The Skeptical Inquirer* 10, no. 1:36–40.

De Vos, George, and Lola Romanucci-Ross, eds.

1975   *Ethnic Identity: Cultural Communities and Change*. Palo Alto, Calif.: Mayfield Publishing Company.

Dobkin, Marjorie Housepian

1972   *Smyrna 1922: The Destruction of a City*. London: Faber.

Douglas, Mary

1975   *Implicit Meanings*. Boston, Mass.: Routledge and Kegan Paul.

Doumanis, Mariella

1983   *Mothering in Greece: From Collectivism to Individualism*. London: Academic Press.

Dubisch, Jill

1986   *Gender and Power in Rural Greece*. Princeton, N.J.: Princeton University Press.

du Boulay, Juliet

1974   *Portrait of a Greek Mountain Village*. Oxford: Clarendon Press.

1986   Women—Images of Their Nature and Destiny in Rural Greece. In *Gender and Power in Rural Greece*, ed. Jill Dubisch, pp. 139–168. Princeton, N.J.: Princeton University Press.

Dumont, Jean-Paul

1978   *The Headman and I*. Austin: University of Texas Press.

Dunk, Pamela

1985   Greek Women and Broken Nerves in Montreal. Paper delivered at the 85th Annual Meetings of the American Anthropological Association. Washington, D. C.

Durkheim, Emile

1965   *The Elementary Forms of the Religious Life*. New York: The Free Press. (1st French ed. 1912.)

Dwyer, Kevin
  1982   *Moroccan Dialogues: Anthropology in Question.* Baltimore, Md.: The Johns Hopkins University Press.
Engelsmann, F.
  1982   Abstract of "Auf's Feuer Gehen." *Transcultural Psychiatric Research Review* 19, no. 4:289–291.
Euripides
  1978   *The Bakkhai.* Translated by Robert Bagg. Amherst: University of Massachusetts Press.
Evangelou, Iason
  1971   *I Goitia Tou Mistiriou.* Athens: Dodoni.
Evans-Pritchard, E. E.
  1956   *Nuer Religion.* Oxford: Clarendon Press.
Fabian, Johannes
  1971   *Jamaa: A Charismatic Movement in Katanga.* Evanston, Ill.: Northwestern University Press.
  1979   The Anthropology of Religious Movements: From Explanation to Interpretation. *Social Research* 46:4–35.
Favret-Saada, J.
  1980   *Deadly Words: Witchcraft in the Bocage.* Cambridge: At the University Press.
Ferguson, Marilyn
  1980   *The Aquarian Conspiracy: Personal and Social Transformation in the 1980s.* Los Angeles, Calif.: J. P. Tarcher.
Fernandez, James W.
  1971   Persuasions and Performances: Of the Beast in Every Body . . . And the Metaphors of Everyman. In *Myth, Symbol, and Culture*, ed. C. Geertz, pp. 39–60. New York: W. W. Norton & Company.
  1974   The Mission of Metaphor in Expressive Culture. *Current Anthropology* 15, no. 2:119–145.
  1977   The Performance of Ritual Metaphors. In *The Social Use of Metaphor: Essays on the Anthropology of Rhetoric*, ed. J. David Sapir and J. Christopher Crocker, pp. 100–131. Philadelphia: University of Pennsylvania Press.
Fischer, Michael M. J.
  1986   Ethnicity and the Post-Modern Arts of Memory. In *Writing Culture*, ed. James Clifford and George E. Marcus, pp. 194–233. Berkeley: University of California Press.
Frank, Jerome
  1961   *Persuasion and Healing: A Comparative Study of Psychotherapy.* Baltimore, Md.: The Johns Hopkins University Press.

Freed, Stanley A., and Ruth S. Freed

1964   Spirit Possession as Illness in a North Indian Village. *Ethnology* 3:152–171.

Friedl, Ernestine

1962   *Vasilika: A Village in Modern Greece.* New York: Holt, Rinehart and Winston.

1967   The Position of Women: Appearance and Reality. *Anthropological Quarterly* 40, no. 3:97–108.

1976   Kinship, Class and Selective Migration. In *Mediterranean Family Structure*, ed. John G. Peristiany, pp. 363–387. Cambridge: At the University Press.

Furley, William D.

1981   *Studies in the Use of Fire in Ancient Greek Religion.* New York: Arno Press.

Gage, Nicholas

1980   Greek Ritualists Invoking Saints Walk on Coals. *New York Times.* June 1, p. 11.

Galloway, Paul

1986   Hot Feat. *Chicago Tribune.* December 1, sec. 5, p. 1.

Geertz, Clifford

1973a   *The Interpretation of Cultures.* New York: Basic Books.

1973b   Religion as a Cultural System. In *The Interpretation of Cultures.* New York: Basic Books.

1983   *Local Knowledge.* New York: Basic Books.

1985   Waddling In. *Times Literary Supplement* 288, no. 4 (June 7):623–624.

1988   *Works and Lives: The Anthropologist as Author.* Stanford, Calif.: Stanford University Press.

Giorgakas, Dimitrios I.

1945–46 Etimoloyika Ke Simasioloyika. *Arhion tou Thrakikou Laografikou ke Glossikou Thisavrou* 12:40–46.

Glock, Charles Y.

1976   Consciousness among Contemporary Youth: An Interpretation. In *The New Religious Consciousness*, ed. Charles Y. Glock and Robert N. Bellah, pp. 353–366. Berkeley: University of California Press.

—, and Robert N. Bellah

1976   *The New Religious Consciousness.* Berkeley: University of California Press.

Good, Byron J., and Mary-Jo Delvecchio Good

1981   The Meaning of Symptoms: A Cultural Hermeneutic Model for Clinical Practice. In *The Relevance of Social Science for Medicine,* ed. Leon Eisenberg and Arthur Kleinman. Dordrecht, Holland: D. Reidel.

1982   Toward a Meaning-Centered Analysis of Popular Illness Categories: "Fright Illness" and "Heart Distress" in Iran. In *Cultural Conceptions of Mental Health and Therapy*, ed. A. J. Marsella and G. White. Dordrecht, Holland: D. Reidel.

Griffin, Nancy

1985   The Charismatic Kid; Tony Robbins, 25, Gets Rich Peddling a Hot Self-Help Program. *Life* 8 (March):41–48.

Hadden, Jeffrey K., and Charles E. Swann

1981   *Prime Time Preachers: The Rising Power of Televangelism.* Reading, Mass.: Addison Wesley.

Hadjipandazis, Theodore

1972   *To Paniyiri tis Ayias Elenis (The Firewalkers of Ayia Eleni).* A film script in Greek and English. The University of Thessaloniki.

Handelman, David

1985   Tiptoe through the Embers. *Rolling Stone.* November 21, p. 26.

Hanna, Judith Lynne

1978   African Dance: Some Implications for Dance Therapy. *American Journal of Dance Therapy* 2:3–15.

1979   *To Dance is Human: A Theory of Nonverbal Communication.* Austin: Texas University Press.

Haramis, P. C., and K. Kakouri

1969   *The Anastenaria.* A film.

Harner, Michael

1982   *The Way of the Shaman.* New York: Bantam Books.

Herzfeld, Michael

1979   Exploring a Metaphor of Exposure. *Journal of American Folklore* 92:285–301.

1980a   Honour and Shame: Problems in the Comparative Analysis of Moral Systems. *Man* (n.s.) 15:339–351.

1980b   On the Ethnography of "Prejudice" in an Exclusive Community. *Ethnic Groups* 2:283–305.

1981a   Meaning and Morality: A Semiotic Approach to Evil Eye Accusations in a Greek Village. *American Ethnologist* 8, no. 3:560–574.

1981b   Performative Categories and Symbols of Passage in Rural Greece. *Journal of American Folklore* 94:44–57.

1982a   *Ours Once More: Folklore, Ideology, and the Making of Modern Greece.* Austin: University of Texas Press.

1982b   When Exceptions Define the Rules: Greek Baptismal Names and the Negotiation of Identity. *Journal of Anthropological Research* 38, no. 3:288–302.

1983a   Interpreting Kinship Terminology: The Problem of Patriliny in Rural Greece. *Anthropological Quarterly* 56, no. 4:157–166.

1983b   Semantic Slippage and Moral Fall: The Rhetoric of Chastity in Rural Greek Society. *Journal of Modern Greek Studies* 1:161–172.

1984a   The Horns of the Mediterraneanist Dilemma. *American Ethnologist* 11:439–454.

1984b   The Significance of the Insignificant: Blasphemy as Ideology. *Man* (n.s.) 19:653–664.

1985   *The Poetics of Manhood: Contest and Identity in a Cretan Mountain Village*. Princeton, N.J.: Princeton University Press.

1986   Closure as Cure: Tropes in the Exploration of Bodily and Social Disorder. *Current Anthropology* 27, no. 2:107–120.

1987   "As In Your Own House": Hospitality, Ethnography, and the Stereotype of Mediterranean Society. In *Honor and Shame and the Unity of the Mediterranean*, ed. David D. Gilmore, pp. 75–89. American Anthropological Association Special Publications, No. 22. Washington, D.C.

Hirschon, Renée

1978   Open Body/Closed Space: The Transformation of Female Sexuality. In *Defining Females*, ed. Shirley Ardener, pp. 66–88. New York: John Wiley and Sons.

1981   Essential Objects and the Sacred: Interior and Exterior Space in an Urban Greek Locality. In *Woman and Space*, ed. Shirley Ardener, pp. 72–88. New York: St. Martin's Press.

1983   Women, the Aged and Religious Activity: Oppositions and Complementarity in an Urban Locality. *Journal of Modern Greek Studies* 1, no. 1:113–130.

Hopkins, E. Washburn

1913   Fire-Walking. In *The Encyclopaedia of Religion and Ethics*, ed. James Hastings. Vol. 6, pp. 30–31.

Hourmouziadis, Anastasios

1961   Peri Ton Anastenarion. *Arhion tou Thrakikou Laografikou ke Glossikou Thisavrou* 26:144–161. (Originally published in 1873 in Constantinople by Tipos Anatolikou Asteros.)

Ingalls, Albert G.

1939   Fire-Walking. *Scientific American* 160:135–138, 173–178.

Ioannou, Giorgos

1970   *To Dimotiko Tragoudi: Paraloges*. Athens: Ermis.

1975   *Paramithia tou Laou Mas*. Athens: Ermis.

Jackson, Michael
   1986   *Barawa and the Ways Birds Fly in the Sky: An Ethnographic Novel*. Washington, D.C.: Smithsonian.
Jameson, Frederick
   1983   Postmodernism and Consumer Society. In *The Anti-Aesthetic Essays on Postmodern Culture*, ed. Hal Foster, pp. 111–125. Port Townsend, Wash.: Bay Press.
   1984   Postmodernism, or The Cultural Logic of Late Capitalism. *New Left Review* 146:53–92.
Kakouri, Katerina
   1963   *Dionysiaka: Ek tis simerinis laikis latrias ton Thrakon*. Athens.
   1965   *Dionysiaka: Aspects of the Popular Thracian Worship of Today*. Athens: G.C. Eleftheroudakis.
   1975   Thrakomakedonika Dromena. In *A' Symposion Laografias tou Vorioelladikou Horou*, pp. 71–77. Thessaloniki: Idrima Meleton Hersonisou tou Emou.
Kaloyeropoulou, Eleni
   1973   *Stihia Laografias Ke Laikis Tehnis*. Athens: Ellinikos Organismos Tourismou.
Kane, Stephen
   1982   Holiness Ritual Fire Handling: Ethnographic and Psychological Considerations. *Ethos* 10, no. 4:369–384.
Kapferer, Bruce
   1979   Entertaining Demons: Comedy, Interaction and Meaning in a Sinhalese Healing Ritual. *Social Analysis* 1:108–152.
Katz, Richard
   1982   *Boiling Energy*. Cambridge, Mass.: Harvard University Press.
Kavakopoulos, Pandelis
   1956   I Triti Imera Ton Anastenarion Stin Ayia Eleni Serron. *Arhion tou Thrakikou Laografikou ke Glossikou Thisavrou* 21:282–299.
Kennedy, John G.
   1967   Nubian Zar Ceremonies as Psychotherapy. *Human Organization* 26:185–194.
Kennedy, Robinette
   1986   Women's Friendships on Crete: A Psychological Perspective. In *Gender and Power in Rural Greece*, ed. Jill Dubisch, pp. 121–138. Princeton, N.J.: Princeton University Press.
Keyes, Ken, Jr.
   1982   *The Hundredth Monkey*. St. Mary, Ky.: Vision Books.
Kiev, Ari
   1972   *Transcultural Psychiatry*. New York: The Free Press.

Kleinman, Arthur

1978   Concepts and a Model for the Comparison of Medical Systems as Cultural Systems. *Social Science and Medicine* 12, no. 213:85–94.

1980   *Patients and Healers in the Context of Culture: An Exploration of the Borderland between Anthropology, Medicine, and Psychiatry.* Berkeley: University of California Press.

1982   Neurasthenia and Depression: A Study of Somatization and Culture in China. *Culture, Medicine and Psychiatry* 6, no. 2:117–189.

1986   *Social Origins of Distress and Disease: Depression, Neurasthenia, and Pain in Modern China.* New Haven, Conn.: Yale University Press.

Kofos, Evangelos

1964   *Nationalism and Communism in Macedonia.* Thessaloniki: Institute for Balkan Studies.

Krakauer, Jon

1984   Get It While It's Hot. *Rolling Stone.* August 30, p. 22.

Kranidiotis, Pandelis

1956   Ta Anastenaria os Psyhosomatikon Fenomenon. *Arhion tou Thrakikou Laografikou ke Glossikou Thisavrou* 21:249–278.

Krier, Beth Ann

1984   The Curious Hotfoot It to a New Fad. *Los Angeles Times.* April 11, pt. 1, p. 1.

Ladas, Stephen

1932   *The Exchange of Minorities; Bulgaria, Greece and Turkey.* New York: MacMillan Company.

Leach, Edmund

1969   Genesis as Myth. In *Genesis as Myth*, pp. 7–23. London: Jonathan Cape.

Leikind, Bernard J., and William J. McCarthy

1985   An Investigation of Firewalking. *The Skeptical Inquirer* 10, no. 1:23–34.

Lesk, Michael, et al.

1981   Auf's Feuer Gehen. Feuerlauf in Grieschenland und Selbstversuche. *Curare* 4:169–192.

Levin, Jeffrey S., and Jeannine Coreil

1986   "New Age" Healing in the U. S. *Social Science and Medicine* 23, no. 9:889–897.

Lévi-Strauss, Claude

1967   The Effectiveness of Symbols. In *Structural Anthropology*, pp. 181–201. New York: Anchor Books.

Levy, Robert I.
 1984   Emotion, Knowing, and Culture. In *Culture Theory: Essays in Mind, Self, and Emotion*, ed. Richard A. Shweder and Robert A. LeVine, pp. 214–237. Cambridge: At the University Press.
Lewis, I. M.
 1966   Spirit Possession and Deprivation Cults. *Man* (n.s.) 1:307–329.
 1971   *Ecstatic Religion: An Anthropological Study of Spirit Possession.* Baltimore, Md.: Penguin Books.
Locke, Steven, and Douglas Colligan
 1986   *The Healer Within.* New York: E. P. Dutton.
Loizos, Peter
 1981   *The Heart Grown Bitter.* Cambridge: At the University Press.
Loukatos, Dimitris
 1981   *Ta Kalokerina.* Athens: Filippotis.
Lyotard, Jean-François
 1984   *The Postmodern Condition: A Report on Knowledge.* Minneapolis: University of Minnesota Press.
McCarthy, William J., and Bernard J. Leikind
 1986   Walking on Fire: Feat of Mind? *Psychology Today.* February, p. 10.
McGuire, Meredith B.
 1982   *Pentecostal Catholics: Power, Charisma, and Order in a Religious Movement.* Philadelphia, Pa.: Temple University Press.
McNeill, William H.
 1978   *The Metamorphosis of Greece since World War II.* Chicago, Ill.: University of Chicago Press.
Macrakis, A. Lily, and Peter S. Allen
 1983   *Women and Men in Greece: A Society in Transition. Journal of Modern Greek Studies* 1, no. 1.
Makrakis, Basil
 1982   *Fire Dances in Greece.* Greece: Privately published.
Manus, Willard
 1978   The Fire Dancers. *The Athenian.* May, pp. 22–25.
Marcus, George E.
 1986   Contemporary Problems of Ethnography in the Modern World System. In *Writing Culture*, ed. James Clifford and George E. Marcus, pp. 165–193. Berkeley: University of California Press.
—, and Dick Cushman
 1982   Ethnographies as Texts. *Annual Review of Anthropology* 11:25–69.

—, and Michael M. J. Fischer

1986   *Anthropology as Cultural Critique: An Experimental Moment in the Human Sciences*. Chicago, Ill.: University of Chicago Press.

Matsas, Nestor

1984   Pos Horevo sti Fotia. *Ethnikos Kiriks*. June 2–3, p. 2.

Mead, Margaret

1964   *Continuities in Cultural Evolution*. New Haven, Conn.: Yale University Press.

Medoff, Marc

1984   Walking on Fire Can Conquer Your Fears. *Whole Life Times*. October/November, p. 9.

Megas, George

1961   Anastenaria Ke Ethima Tis Tirinis Defteras. *Laografia* 19:475–534.

1963   *Greek Calendar Customs*. Athens: B. and M. Rhodis.

Messing, Simon D.

1959   Group Therapy and Social Status in the Zar Cult of Ethiopia. In *Culture and Mental Health*, ed. M. K. Opler. New York: MacMillan Company.

Meyer, Donald

1980   *The Positive Thinkers*. New York: Pantheon.

Michaelson, Evalyn J., and Walter Goldschmidt

1971   Female Roles and Male Dominance among Peasants. *Southwestern Journal of Anthropology* 27:330–352.

Mihail-Dede, Maria

1972–73 To Anastenari. *Thrakika* 46:23–178.

1978   Ta Tragoudia ke i Hori ton Anastenaridon. *Thrakika* 48:75–129.

1983   Skepsis ya to Anastenari apo Erevna stin Anatoliki Roumelia. In *D' Symposio Laografias tou Vorioelladikou Horou*, pp. 205–223. Thessaloniki: Idrima Meleton Hersonisou tou Emou.

Miliadis, D.

1984   Anastenaria: Mia Mistagoyia pou Katandise "Attraksion." *Eleftherotipia* (Athens).

Mischel, Walter, and Frances Mischel

1958   Psychological Aspects of Spirit Possession. *American Anthropologist* 60:249–260.

Moerman, Daniel E.

1979   Anthropology of Symbolic Healing. *Current Anthropology* 20, no. 1:59–80.

Mouzelis, Nicos P.
   1978   *Modern Greece: Facets of Underdevelopment*. New York: Holmes
           & Meier.
Needleman, Jacob, and George Baker
   1978   *Understanding the New Religious Movements*. New York: Seabury
           Press.
Nichter, Mark
   1981a   Idioms of Distress: Alternatives in the Expression of Psychoso-
           cial Distress: A Case Study from South India. *Culture, Medicine
           and Psychiatry* 5:379–408.
   1981b   Negotiation of the Illness Experience: Ayurvedic Therapy and
           the Psychosocial Dimension of Illness. *Culture, Medicine and
           Psychiatry* 5:5–24.
Obeyesekere, Gananath
   1978   The Fire-walkers of Kataragama: The Rise of *Bhakti* Religiosity
           in Buddhist Sri Lanka. *Journal of Asian Studies* 37, no. 3:457–
           476.
   1981   *Medusa's Hair: An Essay on Personal Symbols and Religious Ex-
           perience*. Chicago, Ill.: University of Chicago Press.
Papachristodoulou, Polidoros
   1934–61 A series of articles in *Arhion tou Thrakikou Laografikou ke Glos-
           sikou Thisavrou*.
Papagrigoriou, Dimitris
   1986   Ksipoliti Anastenarides Horepsan Pali Sti Fotia. *Makedonia*.
           May 22, p. 1.
Parkin, David, ed.
   1982   *Semantic Anthropology*. London: Academic Press.
Pavlides, Eleftherios, and Jana Hesser
   1986   Women's Roles and House Form and Decoration in Eressos,
           Greece. In *Power and Gender in Rural Greece*, ed. Jill Dubisch,
           pp. 68–96. Princeton, N.J.: Princeton University Press.
Pazinis, Goustavos
   n.d.   *O Alanthastos Onirokritis*. New York: Atlantis.
Peale, Norman Vincent
   1938   *You Can Win*. New York: Abingdon Press.
   1948   *A Guide to Confident Living*. New York: Prentice-Hall.
Pentzopoulos, Dimitri
   1962   *The Balkan Exchange of Minorities and its Impact upon Greece*.
           Paris: Mouton.
Peters, Larry G.
   1982   Trance, Initiation, and Psychotherapy in Tamang Shamanism.
           American Ethnologist 9, no. 1:21–46.

Petrides, Ted
    1982   The Anastenaria. *The Athenian.* May, pp. 21–22.

Petropoulos, Dimitris
    1938–39 Laografika Skopou Anatolikis Thrakis. *Arhion tou Thrakikou Laografikou ke Glossikou Thisavrou* 5:145–269.
    1958,
    1959   *Ellinika Dimotika Tragoudia.* 2 vols. Athens: Zaharopoulos.

Petropoulos, John A.
    1976   The Compulsory Exchange of Populations: Greek-Turkish Peacemaking, 1922–1930. *Byzantine and Modern Greek Studies* 2:135–160.

Politis, N. G.
    1920   *Laografika Simmikta.* Vol. 1. Athens: Tipografio Paraskeva Leoni.
    1978   *Ekloge Apo Ta Tragoudia Tou Ellinikou Laou.* Athens: Vayonakis.

Pooley, Eric
    1985   The Hottest Seminar in Town. *New York.* March 11, p. 29.

Price, Richard
    1983   *First-Time: Historical Vision of an Afro-American People.* Baltimore, Md.: The Johns Hopkins University Press.

Prince, Raymond
    1968   Therapeutic Process in Cross-Cultural Perspective: A Symposium. *American Journal of Psychiatry* 124:56–69.
    1974   The Problem of "Spirit Possession" as a Treatment for Psychiatric Disorders. *Ethos* 2, no. 4:315–333.

Rabinow, Paul
    1977   *Reflections on Fieldwork in Morocco.* Berkeley: University of California Press.
    1983   Humanism as Nihilism: The Bracketing of Truth and Seriousness in American Cultural Anthropology. In *Social Science as Moral Inquiry*, ed. Norma Haan and Robert N. Bellah, pp. 52–75. New York: Columbia University Press.

—, and William M. Sullivan, eds.
    1979   *Interpretive Social Science: A Reader.* Berkeley: University of California Press.

Remick, David
    1984   Going for the Coals: The Saga of a Tenderfoot at Firewalking Camp. *Washington Post.* December 18, p. B1.

Richardson, Miles
    1975   Anthropologist—The Myth Teller. *American Ethnologist* 2:517–533.

1980   The Anthropologist as Word Shaman. *Anthropology and Humanism Quarterly* 5, no. 4:2.

Robbins, Anthony

1986   *Unlimited Power: The New Science of Personal Achievement.* New York: Simon and Schuster.

Rogers, Susan Carol

1975   Female Forms of Power and the Myth of Male Dominance: A Model of Female/Male Interaction in Peasant Society. *American Ethnologist* 2:727–756.

1985   Gender in Southwestern France: The Myth of Male Dominance Revisited. *Anthropology* 9:65–86.

Romaios, Kostas

1944–45 Laikes Latries tis Thrakis. *Arhion tou Thrakikou Laografikou ke Glossikou Thisavrou* 11:1–131.

Rosaldo, Michelle, and Louise Lamphere, eds.

1974   *Woman, Culture, and Society.* Stanford, Calif.: Stanford University Press.

Rossiter, Stuart

1977   *Greece.* 3d ed. London: Ernest Benn Limited. (The Blue Guides.)

Royce, Anya Peterson

1977   *The Anthropology of Dance.* Bloomington: Indiana University Press.

Rushton, Lucy

1983   Doves and Magpies: Village Women in the Greek Orthodox Church. In *Women's Religious Experience*, ed. Pat Holder, pp. 57–70. London: Croom Helm.

Safilios-Rothschild, Constantina

1968   Deviance and Mental Illness in the Greek Family. *Family Process* 7:100–117.

Satin, Mark

1979   *New Age Politics: Healing Self and Society.* New York: Delta.

Scholte, Bob

1974   Toward a Reflexive and Critical Anthropology. In *Reinventing Anthropology*, ed. Dell Hymes, pp. 430–457. New York: Vintage Books.

Schortsanitis, T., and L. Haritos

1959   Paradosis Athamniou Artis. *Laografia* 18:535–538.

Schur, Edwin

1976   *The Awareness Trap: Self-Absorption Instead of Social Change.* New York: Quadrangle.

Shweder, Richard
    1986   Storytelling among the Anthropologists. *New York Times Book Review*. September 21, p. 1.

Seckel, Al
    1985   Southern California Skeptics: Fast-Rising Star in LA. *The Skeptical Inquirer* 10, no. 1:8–9.

Segal, Charles
    1982   *Dionysiac Poetics and Euripides' Bacchae*. Princeton, N.J.: Princeton University Press.

Simić, Andrei
    1983   Machismo and Cryptomatriarchy: Power, Affect, and Authority in the Contemporary Yugoslav Family. *Ethos* 11:66–86.

Simonton, Carl
    1978   *Getting Well Again: A Step-by-Step Self-Help Guide to Overcoming Cancer for Patients and Their Families*. Los Angeles, Calif.: J. P. Tarcher.

Smith, Michael Llewellyn
    1973   *Ionian Vision: Greece in Asia Minor, 1919–1922*. London: Allen Lane.

Spencer, Paul
    1985   *Society and Dance*. Cambridge: At the University Press.

Stewart, Richard H.
    1984   Neurolinguistics is a Hot Topic. *Boston Globe*. September 14, pp. 32–33.

Stone, Donald
    1976   The Human Potential Movement. In *The New Religious Consciousness*, ed. Charles Y. Glock and Robert N. Bellah, pp. 93–115. Berkeley: University of California Press.

Sutton, Susan Buck
    1983   Rural-Urban Migration in Greece. In *Urban Life in Mediterranean Europe*, ed. M. Kenny and D. Kertzer, pp. 225–249. Urbana: University of Illinois Press.

Tambiah, Stanley J.
    1984   *The Buddhist Saints of the Forest and the Cult of Amulets: A Study in Charisma, Hagiography, Sectarianism, and Millenial Buddhism*. Cambridge: At the University Press.

Taylor, John R.
    forth-
    coming   Firewalking: A Lesson in Physics. *The Physics Teacher*.

Thomas, E. S.
    1934   The Fire Walk. *Proceedings of the Society for Psychical Research* 42:292–309.

Thriskeftiki ke Ithiki Egkiklopedia
 1962–68 Athens: A. Martinos.
Tipton, Steven M.
 1982 *Getting Saved from the Sixties: Moral Meaning in Conversion and Cultural Change*. Berkeley: University of California Press.
Todorov, Tzvetan
 1984 *The Conquest of America: The Question of the Other*. New York: Harper and Row.
Tsantila, Maria, and Rol D. Hoogestraat
 1983 Anastenaria. *Spectramed*. December 1, pp. 15–29.
Tsarouhas, Kostas
 1974 Horos S' Anammena Karvouna. *Epikera*. June 14–20, p. 94.
Turner, Victor
 1967 *Forest of Symbols*. Ithaca, N.Y.: Cornell University Press.
Tyler, Stephen A.
 1986 Post-Modern Ethnography: From Document of the Occult to Occult Document. In *Writing Culture*, ed. James Clifford and George E. Marcus, pp. 122–140. Berkeley: University of California Press.
Vermeulen, Hans
 1983 Urban Research in Greece. In *Urban Life in Mediterranean Europe*, ed. M. Kenny and D. Kertzer, pp. 109–132. Urbana: University of Illinois Press.
Wallerstein, Immanuel
 1974 *The Modern World System: Capitalist Agriculture and the Origins of the European World-Economy in the Sixteenth Century*. New York: Academic Press.
Ware, Timothy
 1963 *The Orthodox Church*. Harmondsworth, Middlesex: Penguin Books.
Wasserman, Harvey
 1985 The Politics of Transcendence. *The Nation* 241, no. 5 (August):145–148.
Weber, Max
 1964 *The Theory of Social and Economic Organization*. New York: The Free Press.
Weil, Andrew
 1972 *The Natural Mind: A New Way of Looking at Drugs and the Higher Consciousness*. Boston, Mass.: Houghton Mifflin.
 1983 *Health and Healing: Understanding Conventional and Alternative Medicine*. Boston, Mass.: Houghton Mifflin.

Wilk, Stan

1977　Therapeutic Anthropology and Culture Consciousness. *Anthropology and Humanism Quarterly* 2:12–18.

1986　The Meaning of "Religion as a Cultural System." *Anthropology and Humanism Quarterly* 11:50–55.

Wilson, Peter J.

1967　Status Ambiguity and Spirit Possession. *Man* (n.s.) 2:366–378.

Worsley, Peter

1982　Non-Western Medical Systems. *Annual Review of Anthropology* 11:315–348.

Worthington, Rogers

1984　Strolling on Coals Cools Their Fears. *Detroit Free Press*. May 4, p. 1A.

Wuthnow, Robert

1976　*The Consciousness Reformation*. Berkeley: University of California Press.

Yankelovitch, Daniel

1981　*New Rules in American Life: Self-Fulfillment in a World Turned Upside Down*. New York: Random House.

Young, Allen

1982　The Anthropologies of Illness and Sickness. *Annual Review of Anthropology* 11:257–285.

Zaretsky, Irving I., and Mark P. Leone

1974　*Religious Movements in Contemporary America*. Princeton, N.J.: Princeton University Press.

Zotiadis, George

1954　*The Macedonian Controversy*. Thessaloniki: Society of Macedonian Studies.

Index